WOUNDED COUNTRY

QUENTIN BERESFORD has had a diverse career in academia, the public service and journalism. For many years he was Professor of Politics at Edith Cowan University in Perth. He is the author of numerous books on Australian politics and history, and has won several literary awards for his work. His most recent books are the *Rise and Fall of Gunns Ltd*, which won the Tasmanian Premier's Literary Prize, and *Adani and the War Over Coal*. Both are published by NewSouth. He is currently adjunct Professor of Politics at the University of the Sunshine Coast.

'*Wounded Country* is one of the most important books
to emerge in recent decades concerning both Australia's
dangerous environmental mismanagement and the indivisible
plunder of Indigenous society. The tragedy of this sorry story
is not just that it concerns Australia's, and one of the world's,
great river systems – the Murray Darling Basin – but also that
the attitudinal, legislative and political drivers behind this
ongoing despoliation remain both largely hidden and in place.

Based on forensic research, Beresford has written the definitive
work on this complex and contested riverine system: what
constitutes a shameful tragedian story. Particularly revealed is
a deadly mix of shambolic management, greed-driven graft
and political corruption that favours Big Cotton and Big
Irrigation at the expense of Indigenous people, other farmers
and graziers and the environment.

Wounded Country deserves to be placed alongside the classics
in this genre and with such writers as Francis Ratcliffe, Jock
Marshall, Bill Gammage and Bruce Pascoe.'

**Charles Massy, leading authority on regenerative farming
and author of *Call of the Reed Warbler***

WOUNDED COUNTRY

THE MURRAY-DARLING BASIN
A CONTESTED HISTORY

QUENTIN BERESFORD

NEWSOUTH

A NewSouth book

Published by
NewSouth Publishing
University of New South Wales Press Ltd
University of New South Wales
Sydney NSW 2052
AUSTRALIA
newsouthpublishing.com

A catalogue record for this
book is available from the
NATIONAL
LIBRARY   National Library of Australia
OF AUSTRALIA

ISBN   9781742236780 (paperback)
        9781742249988 (ebook)
        9781742239132 (ePDF)

Cover design Philip Campbell Design
Cover image River red gum at Chowilla Floodplain, South Australia, the largest
    remaining natural river red gum forest. Photo by Gary Sauer-Thompson
Internal design Josephine Pajor-Markus
Printer Griffin Press, part of Ovato

UNSW
SYDNEY

CONTENTS

Warning

Aboriginal and Torres Strait Islander people should be aware that this book contains words and descriptions written by non-Indigenous people in the past that may be confronting and would be considered inappropriate today. It also contains the names of deceased Indigenous people and graphic descriptions of historical events that may be disturbing to some readers.

The Murray–Darling Basin

INTRODUCTION

Australia's Murray–Darling Basin is under threat. This vast geographical region, covering one million square kilometres and spanning four states and the Australian Capital Territory, has been over-exploited for nearly 200 years. It is an engine of national economic wealth creation through its vast river system comprising 20 main rivers and 77 000 kilometres of waterways and extensive grazing lands. Its delicate ecosystems have, for decades, been in decline. Waves of settlers plundered the region's potential, with little consideration for the consequences. An economy cannot be sustained forever on a degrading environment.

Agriculture has been conducted on a grand scale in the Murray–Darling Basin. Pastoralism, wheat production and irrigated crops today generate agricultural production exceeding $10 billion each year; other industries, such as tourism and mining, lift the region's contribution to the Australian economy to an estimated $75 billion annually.[1]

In recognition of the deteriorating state of the Basin's ecology, and the economic consequences arising from it, the largest environment program in the nation's history was unveiled in 2012 in an attempt to find a balance between the need to restore the Basin's ecosystems and the demands of agriculture. But it is widely thought to be failing to stem the ongoing environmental decline. At stake is the future of Australia's premier food bowl and the two million people who depend on agricultural industries for their livelihoods, and the iconic status the Murray–Darling has for Australians, both Indigenous and non-Indigenous.

St George in south-western Queensland is as good a place as any to contemplate the start of the Murray–Darling River system that acts as the main artery through the Basin. This picturesque, isolated town, nearly 600 kilometres west of Brisbane, is reached along a gun-barrel straight highway that shimmers in the summer haze. When I visited in November 2020, the Balonne River was a magnificent sight, with water flowing majestically through stands of river red gums.

One branch of the Balonne flows into the narrow, winding Culgoa River and then on a 3000-kilometre journey through the Darling and the Murray, eventually flowing into Lake Alexandrina and the Coorong wetlands on the South Australian coast. It takes eight months for the water to meander from its source to its final destination. Along the way it traverses varied and unique ecosystems: internationally renowned wetlands, important for their abundant wildlife; arid, flat plains that challenged the perseverance of explorers Charles Sturt and Thomas Mitchell and where all manner of marsupials and native birds co-exist; alpine regions providing melting snows to re-charge the Murray; and the verdant grasslands of western Victoria. Each is a quintessential Australian landscape. But for two centuries European Australians failed to appreciate the delicate balance that had sustained these ecosystems for thousands of years.

This book sets out to be an environmental history of the Murray–Darling Basin. It seeks to explore Europeans' relationship to the landscape, from the epic story of its 'discovery' by explorers Sturt and Mitchell, through the invasion into Aboriginal traditional lands and the rapid dispossession of the Indigenous population, and on to the succeeding waves of settlement infused by grand ideas of nation-building. Both profiteers and the poor worked to fulfil the dreams of the nation-builders. But from the earliest years of white settlement, the exploitation of the Basin revealed Australians' destructive relationship with the environment. Generations have been driven to tame this wilderness. Many bent it to their will and made fortunes; many others were broken by its harsh realities.

Through the lens of history, the Basin presents Australians with an uncomfortable reality. The dreams that drove the development of the region were founded on the intersection of two forms of violence – initially, against the Aboriginal owners; afterwards, against nature. This book uncovers and explains the historical attitudes that drove this development-at-all-costs mentality.

The environmental degradation that has shadowed the region's European development has, at times, been shocking. Soil erosion, sand drifts, dust storms, salinity, algal blooms, the extinction or near extinction of native flora and fauna, the drying out of wetlands and steadily worsening droughts – all these are among the environmental catastrophes that have brought the ecosystem of large parts of the Basin almost to its knees.

As this book explains, the increasing frequency of such catastrophes is caused by a set of cultural attitudes that prioritised development at all costs with an indifference to environmental destruction. Australians have had a ready excuse to overlook the consequences of excessive development by falling back on the home-grown narrative of a 'sunburnt country' dictated by the naturally occurring rhythms of floods and droughts. But the devastation wrought upon the Basin exceeds the natural cycles of the climate; it has been man-made.

In St George, locals are familiar with this cycle. On my visit, it was as hot as Hades by midday. Rain threatened late one afternoon, but it was nothing more than a phantom storm; the swirling dark clouds scudded by quickly, leaving only the trace of a few precious drops on dusty surfaces. Good years are fleeting; locals have to work hard to make the most of them.

Cotton is king in south-eastern Queensland and northern New South Wales. In St George, locals pay homage to the industry with a large mural in the centre of the town. Appearing decades old, it seems to take its inspiration from Soviet-era socialist-realist art: happy workers and productive machinery producing wealth for all. But tension exists over the industry – what is a thirsty crop doing in an arid landscape? The answer lies in the floods that are harvested, a practice with catastrophic flow-on effects for the environment and for Aboriginal people's cultural rights to water.

Floods come with the periodic storms that roll in from southern and central Queensland. Huge volumes of floodwater spread out over the floodplains feeding the entire river system. It's a naturally variable system working to its own mysterious rhythms. Reminders of the devastation these floods can cause are found along St George's river walk. A red steel pole marks the height of the most recent ones. At the top of the pole is the marker for 2012 when the river peaked at 14 metres, inundating much of the town.

Droughts often follow the floods. And several times in recent years the Balonne at St George has run dry. Locals say that before the most recent drought broke in February/March 2020, the river bed near the town's main street was baked so hard by the sun that a game of cricket could be played on its surface. The image of dry river beds in the Murray–Darling Basin has been replicated many times in recent years as crippling droughts gripped the public consciousness. Towns have come close to running out of water.

The European record stands in stark contrast to the system of land management Aboriginal people practised over millennia. At the time of European settlement, 40 Aboriginal nations occupied the Basin; their descendants continue to live there. Whatever the severity of the floods and droughts, Aboriginal people adapted to them. Both Sturt and Mitchell were grudging admirers of Aboriginal people's knowledge of their country and their will to survive, but neither could transcend the racist assumptions of the age. And herein lies the central focus of this book.

The first European Australians decimated and dispossessed the Aboriginal people of this vast region, sidelining their intimate knowledge of the Basin's ecosystems. The economic model of extractive agriculture that sought to replace the system of Aboriginal land ownership was developed with a wilful disregard for the region's ecosystems. The soils, grasslands and water have been seen by Europeans as inexhaustible resources for profit and have been exploited to the full. The imposition of this model of agriculture had devastating effects on Aboriginal people in the Basin for generations, right through to the present day. While I have tried to capture some of these impacts, I have not set out to write a history of First Nations peoples in the Basin and their ongoing struggle for their rights.

The European struggle over the Basin's resources, which Aboriginal people husbanded for 60 000 years, has been a source of continual political drama and conflict. Since Mitchell and Sturt first set eyes on the region, the Murray–Darling has played a key role in nation-building, for the Empire and then for a federated Australian nation. The Murray–Darling Basin was seen as the gateway to the nation's success. But these grand dreams masked deeper tensions over who should have access to the riches of the Basin: powerful vested interests or hard-working ordinary Australians? The 19th-century battle over squatters and selectors was merely a forerunner of the modern-day struggle between agribusiness and family farmers. These battles highlight how vexed water is as a political issue.

But there were always doubters questioning the scale and impact of the dreams held for the Basin. Critics of the development-at-all-costs approach increasingly raised their voices during the second half of the 19th century when evidence of environmental destruction started to mount. They were a diverse and fragmented group – scientists working in government resource agencies, community-based naturalists and ordinary Australians observing what was happening around them. They called out the vandalism being conducted in the name of progress. They used a variety of terminology, but the word 'vandalism' speaks to their collective concern about the disappearance of the natural world. Until the 1970s, theirs was a persistent but marginalised voice; the exploiters have been the continual shapers of the landscape. One of the themes explored in the book is how warnings from experts about the consequences of excessive development were persistently set aside. History shows that environmental denialism has deep roots in Australia.

Glimpses of this tension between development and the environment emerged during my visit to St George. The town was on water restrictions … with the river in full flow. Asking why doesn't get you too far in St George. I asked one feisty local whether it had anything to do with the big irrigators whose huge earthworks can be seen not far out of town. The question invited a blank stare and a curt response: 'They keep the town going'. As if to anticipate my next question, she volunteered, 'Don't believe all you hear about Cubbie Station'. The station, located 100 kilometres down the road, contains huge, shallow dams, the full size of which can only be seen from the air, and which symbolise, for many, the mismanagement of the Basin's water system. The cotton industry of northern New South Wales and southern Queensland gets the first take of the floodwaters essential to the health of the Murray–Darling River system.

And what of the attempts to repair this damage so that a more sustainable system of agriculture can be established? Ever since pastoralists swept up the land in the 1830s and 1840s, powerful vested interests have dominated the politics of the Basin. They have reinforced a deep narrative of nation-building. The clash between development and the environment in the Basin has some enduring lessons as the country slides ever more gravely towards a future determined by climate change.

When I started this project, I had the ambition to travel the river system during 2020 from my home in southern Queensland to Adelaide to refresh and extend my experience of the Basin, parts of which I have visited many times over the decades. However, with the borders closed for the better part of the year under COVID-19 restrictions, the ambition collided with the determination of state premiers to closely follow health advice.

That advice has kept the nation safer than almost anywhere in the world. However, the contrast between the way political leaders have handled the scientific advice on health and that on water management couldn't be more striking. Unlike health science, environmental science is seen as discretionary; climate science even more so.

Australians got a rude reminder of the failure of the nation's political leaders to take environmental science seriously when, in January 2019, news of an ecological disaster in the upper Darling River sent shock waves through state and federal politics, consuming the media for weeks afterwards. Like many Australians, I looked on with horror as images of a million dead fish swamped the media and consumed the news cycle. I resolved to dig deeper.

1

ANATOMY OF AN ECOLOGICAL DISASTER

On the morning of 8 January 2019, 20-year-old Kate McBride was about to be thrust into the national spotlight over governments' handling of the Murray–Darling Basin. Accompanied by her father, Rob, and his friend, Dick Arnold, she made the short trek to the Darling River near the family's historic 2000-hectare sheep property, Tolarno, south of the small town of Menindee and more than 1000 kilometres north-west of Sydney, to inspect the quality of the water. The whole of south-eastern Australia was in the grip of a crippling drought, described by the Bureau of Meteorology as the worst in its 120 years of records.[1]

In fact, the river had stopped flowing. McBride could ride her motorbike through parts of the caked river bed. This was a dire situation because the Darling is the lifeblood of the region's stations, irrigated farmland and small towns. Equally dire was the suffocating presence of blue-green algae in the remaining stretches of water.

In heading out to the river, the McBrides and Arnold had feared that the toxic invader might have damaged native fish stocks. But what they encountered when they reached the river bank was little short of a carnage – a scene reminiscent of the Old Testament's 'bloody Nile fish kill'.[2] Dead fish blanketed the surface, displacing the green sludge. Rotting in the 40-degree heat were an estimated one million mostly native fish species. It was rated by fishing experts as a 'world-scale mass fish kill'.[3]

Kate pulled out her phone and filmed the outraged reaction of her father and Arnold. The footage showed two grown men holding back tears as they cradled two massive, dead Murray cod, estimated to be more than 50 years old. The species is the largest freshwater fish in Australia and listed as endangered, and it is central to Aboriginal people's Creation stories.

Looking straight at the camera, Rob McBride said: 'This is bloody disgraceful, this is the most disgusting thing I've seen in my life. This has nothing to do with drought, this is a man-made disaster brought to you by the New South Wales Government and the Federal Government.'

'It's Australia, we're not a bloody fourth-world, fifth-world country for Christ sake,' Arnold added. 'It makes me feel like crying.'

Kate took the video back to Tolarno and uploaded it to the station's Facebook page. They had been trying to get the word out about the devastation wreaking havoc on their region, without much success, but the reaction to their video exceeded their wildest expectations. Australians woke the next morning to saturated coverage of Kate's video and its distressing content. It went viral, and the international mainstream media took it up. The nation was shocked. Professor Mike Young from Adelaide University's Centre for Global Food and Resources described the event as 'an extreme ecological crisis'.[4]

The visual impact of the video was guaranteed to attract media coverage and distress the public – the sight of so many dead fish combined with the raw emotion of two weather-beaten outback farmers, people more commonly associated with stoicism. A correspondent for the *New York Times* wrote that the two had 'an authenticity that no amount of scientific evidence or talking heads can project'.[5]

Within days two million people had seen the video; the number rising to six million within a few months. Kate McBride became the public face of the drought, a position she used to argue that governments were mismanaging the Basin's precious water supplies.[6]

The Menindee fish kill was only the latest in a long history of ecological crises in the Murray–Darling Basin, but none had ever elicited such public outrage. The Murray–Darling rivers are etched into the consciousness of Australians; their history and beauty have attracted writers, artists and photographers over the nearly 200 years since their discovery and settlement by Europeans. Yet, if the river is so loved, why have Europeans let them degrade to the point of environmental crisis? And what had killed so many fish at Menindee? Who was to blame?

Answering these questions sparked weeks of rancorous debate across the media. In fact, the issue was rarely out of the public eye between the release of Kate's video in early January, and late February when the report of a scientific panel set up to investigate the fish kill was released. In the intervening two-month period the veil was lifted on the labyrinthine world of Murray–Darling Basin politics. The Murray–Darling Basin Authority (MDBA) – created in 2008 – shares power with state and federal governments according to a plan that purports to balance the competing interests of small farmers, big irrigators, townspeople across the region, environmentalists and Aboriginal people. The Menindee fish kill broke open the long-simmering disagreements between these disparate groups. Who was actually in charge of the Murray–Darling Basin and whose interests were being served? And was the fish kill a one-off tragedy, or a symptom of a far greater crisis in the Basin that planners had been trying their best to downplay?

The debate over the fish kill was messy. The various groups held sharply differing views on its causes and the state of the Basin generally. Resolving those views was impossible in the heat of the debate; the values separating the groups were too wide. Aboriginal people grieve over the demise of their Country in the Basin; small farmers curse the rapid rise in water prices; big irrigators deny they are greedy exploiters; and environmentalists warn that the future of the Basin is in jeopardy.

The debate heats up

Explaining how the fish died was relatively straightforward. The historic low water levels, combined with the long run of high temperatures, were ideal conditions for the growth of blue-green algae (cyanobacteria), and it bloomed out of control. A cold front hit the region. When the water temperature in the river dropped, the algal bloom died off, releasing bacteria into the water that then sucked out the oxygen, leaving the fish to die of asphyxiation, belly-up in the water.

But why had an expansive, blue-green algae taken hold in the river? Political leaders at the state and federal levels, along with leaders at the Murray–Darling Basin Authority, all pointed their collective finger at the drought, claiming that in dry spells fish kills from blue-green algae were 'normal'.

Such an explanation had deep cultural resonance as well as political convenience. Australia's natural climate variability had long been turned into folklore through the imagery of the 'sunburnt country' full of 'droughts and flooding rains' evoked in Dorothea Mackellar's poem, 'My Country', which has been read and loved by generations of Australians. Such folklore was a useful means for conservative politicians to avoid asking the deeper questions about the impact of climate change or, indeed, the mismanagement of the Basin's environment. But what constituted 'normal' no longer applied. This was pointed out by a fisherman in the wake of the disaster at Menindee: 'As someone who has been a passionate fisherman of the western rivers, including the Darling for over 70 years, I can attest that the ... claim that such fish kills are "normal" is a lie. Some of the large Murray Cod pictured are 50 plus years old and have survived many droughts'.[7] But what was becoming 'normal' on the river were 'cease to flow' events – 15 since 2001.[8]

In the following days, political leaders from New South Wales and the Commonwealth ducked for cover as if hiding from an inconvenient truth. The New South Wales Premier, Gladys Berejiklian, the state Water Resources Minister, Niall Blair, along with the federal Agriculture and Water Resources Minister, David Littleproud, all tried to avoid close questioning by the press over the causes of the fish kill. All repeated the mantra that governments couldn't control the weather, therefore they had no hand in the disaster. They had been practised at such obfuscation for the past decade over climate change.

None of the political leaders was prepared to meet Menindee locals in the days immediately following the mass kill. Niall Blair was the first to decline the opportunity. The day after the release of the video he was due to meet a group of 150 Menindee residents on the river bank but, just prior to arriving, he invoked security concerns. Following the release of the video, Blair claimed to have received death threats via social media.

A spokeswoman for Blair explained: 'There were threats made to the minister's safety on social media which meant that the location where he was meeting locals had to be changed to allow police to attend. But he still met and spoke with locals later'.[9] However, the closest the assembled group of residents got to him was seeing his speed boat whooshing up the lake in front of them. He later appeared on television, verbally floundering 'worse than a dying fish'.[10] Blair resigned his portfolio shortly afterwards.

Berejiklian didn't fare much better in terms of accountability to the folk at Menindee. She defended her decision to visit Wentworth on the Murray but not to tour Menindee saying she was 'on the ground in close proximity', despite the 240 kilometres that separate the two towns.[11]

And Prime Minister Scott Morrison was nowhere to be seen, as Kate McBride later explained. Invited onto Channel Seven's news show, *The Latest*, she was asked if Scott Morrison had been out to look at the river. She told a newspaper reporter later:

'When I said he hadn't, the bloke interviewing me was in disbelief that after the fish kills, this ecological disaster, the Prime Minister had not even been out.

'They're just going around to all these marginal electorates instead of going to where it really matters.'

Kate said she had invited the PM to visit the Darling some time ago.

'Scott Morrison still hasn't replied.'[12]

At least Phillip Glyde, a long-time resources bureaucrat and the head of the Murray–Darling Basin Authority, faced the media over the fish kill. However, his response was curious to say the least. Initially, he tried to deflect the seriousness of the event, sticking to the official script that such fish kills were a regular occurrence on the Darling River. But under questioning about the size of the Menindee disaster, he was forced to concede that it was 'unprecedented'. But as if to divert attention away from the performance of his own agency, Glyde offered the following observation: 'This is a river that has been overused for the last 100 years'.[13] In fact, Glyde's observation was more prescient than his bland acknowledgment suggested. As Richard Kingsford, Director of the Centre for Ecosystem Science at the University of New South Wales, has pointed out, historically 'the waters of the Murray–Darling were notoriously over allocated by overzealous government water agencies'.[14] The history behind how the various state governments, pursuing their own development agendas, created a series of rolling environmental crises forms a connecting thread to this book. But what has been learned from the crises?

A full month after the devastating incident, Nationals leader and Deputy Prime Minister Michael McCormack visited Menindee. It was an awkward occasion. McCormack, a political non-entity before he assumed the leadership of the Nationals from a scandal-tainted Barnaby Joyce in February 2018, had to fend off questions from the press about the role he and his party had played in creating the conditions that led to the fish kill. His mild-mannered demeanour hid hardline views on the Murray–Darling, the interests of which he represented in federal Parliament as the Member for Riverina, based around Wagga Wagga. On the day he visited Menindee he was in no mood for contrition; he had nothing to apologise for, he explained.

Nevertheless, sections of the press used the visit to recount how McCormack had 'form' on the issues now swirling around the debate over the fish kill: his attempts to limit the water returned to the environment in the design of Murray–Darling Basin Plan, calling it an 'assault on regional Australia'; his peddling of standard anti-global warming tropes such as 'the climate has been changing since year dot'; and his recent explanation for the mass fish deaths as being because 'it just hasn't rained'.[15] For a party that purports to defend the interests of farmers, the Nationals have had a shocking record over the decades in hiding from the threats posed by the over-exploitation of the Murray–Darling Basin.

The reluctance of leaders and officials to confront the causes of the fish kill was not surprising. Not only were there powerful vested interests to placate, it was hard to avoid questioning the apparent failure of government policy: how was it possible to spend billions in taxpayers' money recovering water for the environment only to have a million fish die of asphyxiation? Political leaders from Canberra and New South Wales stuck to a tight script as if any concession risked opening up a can of worms: where had the money gone and was there a need to review the 2012 Murray–Darling Basin Plan? Hailed as a major reform when signed by the Gillard Labor government, in reality it had pleased few stakeholders.

If the plan itself was flawed, its implementation was no less contentious.

Why did the lakes run dry?

Management of the Murray–Darling Basin and especially its valuable water resources has bedevilled Australian governments since the mid-19th century. The consequences have been disastrous. Menindee was just another example of the failure of federalism to manage the region's water resources. Mismanagement was the central claim made by the McBrides in their viral video: this was a man-made disaster. They highlighted an indisputable fact. Following good rains in 2016, the Menindee Lakes were full and set to provide water for several years.

The Lakes – there are four main ones – were originally a series of large natural depressions that were part of a chain of wetlands that filled during floods. This is the traditional land of the Paakantyi/Barkindji people, and artefacts and burial sites in the area date back at least 40 000 years. When good rains fell in the upper catchment and flowed into the Lakes, their combined capacity was the equivalent to three and a half Sydney Harbours. As the flow receded, the water in the depressions drained back into the Darling River, forming a natural cycle of flood and replenishment. In the 1960s, the New South Wales government reconstructed these shallow formations for the purposes of water storage for irrigation and for the general economic development of western New South Wales.[16]

Since their modification, nearly half the annual overflow into the Menindee Lakes had been used for irrigation.[17] In the years leading up to the fish kill, authorities pretty much emptied the Lakes twice – in late 2016 and in 2017. Who actually took these decisions, and why, is about as clear as staring into the western New South Wales horizon in the heat of the day. This is because the management of Menindee Lakes is a microcosm of the confusing, layered authority of the Basin in general. To explain that they are managed jointly by the New South Wales government and the MDBA seems straightforward enough. However, the New South Wales government takes over when the water drops below a certain level and, when it rises again, decision-making reverts to the MDBA. But this arrangement says little about what goes on behind closed doors, and it has left Aboriginal people marginalised from decision-making.

In the convoluted management structure of the Basin, the MDBA coordinates the management of the Lakes but does not control the flow of water. In fact, states can direct the management of the Lakes via the Ministerial Council and the Basin Officials Committee.[18] But because these decisions are not made public,[19] it is not entirely clear how the chain of decision-making to drain ('release') the Lakes occurred. The claim that draining the Lakes would have environmental benefits was challenged at the time by Kate McBride, who told the media that 'release is unnecessary and will damage river-reliant industries and create long term problems for the environment'.[20] Communities in far western New South Wales were 'at boiling point' over the release of water.[21]

Whatever the reasoning behind the draining of the Lakes, the decision reflected a shared bureaucratic philosophy about the management of the water, described by Phillip Glyde as 'use it or lose it'. Such an all-or-nothing approach was justified on the basis that, as the Lakes are a wide but shallow body of water, 30 per cent of the water is naturally lost to evaporation if not used.[22] The explanation reveals a culture among the bureaucratic managers of saving water for 'productive' uses rather 'wasting' it on the environment.[23] It's a sentiment that could have come from a 19th-century colonial politician or bureaucrat.

The draining operation was like rolling the dice on the future because of the region's uncertain rainfall. Critics of the MDBA and the New South Wales Government alleged as much. As Maryanne Slattery, a water accountant and former MDBA senior official, wrote in response to the Menindee fish kill: '[C]ausing an ecological disaster to avoid evaporation can hardly be described as good environmental management … There is nothing in the laws and regulations guiding the management of the Basin that directs its managers to prioritise evaporation efficiency over environmental and community outcomes'.[24]

And it wasn't just fish populations under threat. The Menindee Lakes are an integral breeding ground for the hundreds of bird, fish, mammal, reptile and macroinvertebrate species in the Murray–Darling Basin, one of the richest ecologies in the country. The lack of water in the Lakes from the drought and the draining caused bird numbers to plummet. The Lakes are home to around 60 species of birds, half of which are threatened. A number of species, like red-necked stints, use the Lakes to fatten up on their improbably long flight to Siberia.[25] Australia has international treaty obligations to protect such birds.

Many bird species had stopped breeding. In fact, the region was in the grip of a crisis of species loss, which will be examined later in the book. However, this broader ecological crisis went unexamined by the mainstream media at the time of the fish kill. Species that were simply no longer present lacked the compelling visuals essential for television.

However, in draining the Lakes, the idea that the MDBA was unwittingly making bad decisions is, in itself, open to question. Claims about its independence are disputed. Critics allege that it is too close to government and, in turn, too close to the big agricultural interests that back the National Party – in power with its Liberal coalition partners in both New South Wales and Canberra before and after the fish kill. The questions surrounding its independence will be taken up in chapter 12.

The credibility of the agency took a battering when – in the middle of the debate about its role in the Menindee fish kill – a South Australian Royal Commission into the Murray–Darling Basin released its report. The establishment of the Commission revealed the deep political tensions over the management of the Basin. South Australia went it alone to get answers as to the continued over-use of water in the system. However, the federal government under Prime

Minister Malcolm Turnbull refused to cooperate with the inquiry. As I will discuss in chapter 12, the inquiry collected valuable evidence and compiled important findings regarding the maladministration of the MDBA. Turnbull, who liked to spruik his own credentials on water reform, effectively ordered the federal government into hiding on the issue.

The media jumped all over the findings of the South Australian Royal Commission and helped keep national attention on the Murray–Darling. A few weeks after the Commission's report was released in January 2019, Phillip Glyde appeared before a Senate Estimates Committee where he faced some tough questioning relating to the Royal Commission's findings. According to one observer, Glyde's strategy was to 'deny, deny, deny'.[26] Calls were made for the Board of the MDBA to step down,[27] but the federal government didn't even bother to respond to the Commission's findings.

The National Party undermines the Basin Plan

The MDBA's lack of independence was exemplified by another of the organisation's failings – to properly monitor the impact of climate change on the Basin. For years, this had been 'a sleeper issue' for locals worried about declining rainfall and rising temperatures. How any government could properly manage the Basin's water needs while blithely ignoring climate change was highlighted by the South Australian Royal Commission. The Menindee fish kill gave added urgency to the issue.

The absence of climate change as an issue for the MDBA was symptomatic of the wider culture wars, which, almost by stealth, had enveloped the politics of the Murray–Darling Basin. Who gets to use water and in what quantities became not just an increasingly critical economic question, but also a political one. In this sense, the Menindee fish kill arose out of a political culture in which the interests of big irrigators were prioritised over the needs of the environment and townspeople. 'We predicted this fish kill would happen because the plan allows too much water to be extracted by irrigators,' according to Quentin Grafton, Professor of Water Economics at the Australian National University, and long-time researcher of the Basin. 'It is a nonsense to suggest the current Basin plan will work.'[28]

Those claiming that the management of the Murray–Darling Basin has been politicised point the finger at the role played by the National Party and especially its former federal leader and Water Minister, Barnaby Joyce. Joyce and the Nationals were never at ease with the Murray–Darling Basin Plan and its goal of balancing the needs of agriculture and the environment. The Menindee fish kill aired this claim. Critics had a compelling piece of evidence on which to base their claims. In July 2017 a recording emerged of Joyce skiting about his role in undermining the Murray–Darling Basin Plan. In a talk to irrigators in a Shepparton pub, with typical bravado, Joyce said: 'We have taken water, put it back into agriculture, so we could look after you and make sure we don't have the greenies running the show basically sending you out the back door, and that was a hard ask'.[29] Such action doesn't constitute 'mismanagement', but an undermining of the proper processes of government.

The Menindee fish kill came in the wake of a scandal exposed in a 2017 investigation by ABC TV's *Four Corners* program, concerning large-scale water theft by big irrigators. It was subsequently revealed that the MDBA knew about allegations of substantial water theft as early as July 2016 but took no serious action until an ABC investigation.[30] At the time, the NSW Ombudsman released a devastating report accusing the government water authority, WaterNSW, of turning a blind eye to the practice of water theft in the Basin and lying about its level of monitoring the issue.[31] I show in this book that turning a blind eye to the environmental consequences of development became established political practice from the time the Basin was opened to pastoralists in the early 19th century.

The draining of the Menindee Lakes – and the subsequent fish kill – have to be seen in this broader political, cultural and historical context. As revealed in the revelations in the *Four Corners* program, in the unwitting testimony of Barnaby Joyce, and in the findings of the South Australian Royal Commission, the management of the Basin had been captured by an 'insider' model of decision-making in which corporate and political interests had been covertly dressed up as the national interest. This model has been at the heart of numerous recent political scandals in Australia's resources sector such as the timber and coal-mining industries.[32]

The Menindee fish kill contributed to a loss of public confidence in both the MDBA and the Murray–Darling Basin Plan. However, at the time of the disaster, not all experts agreed on a way forward. Was the Murray–Darling Basin Plan in danger of collapse or did it remain the best available option? No one seemed to have clear answers. However, a persistent allegation hovered over the debate – that, in devising the Plan, politics mattered more than science.

Big irrigators versus the rest

For their part, the big irrigators denied that their business model led to the Menindee fish kill. The New South Wales Irrigators' Council chief executive, Luke Simpkins, and Cotton Australia general manager, Michael Murray, both defended their respective organisations' water use, while lamenting the fact the Menindee disaster occurred. Both blamed drought for the fish kill. Simpkins provided the defence:

> What has happened is as a result of the drought and no water flowing into the rivers … Without inflows, blue-green algae events will continue to kill fish … It should be remembered that irrigation farmers on the Upper Darling have not been allocated any water from the system for 18 months because of the drought.[33]

However, there were holes in Simpkins' explanation. Governments didn't keep data on on-farm water storage, making it impossible to verify the amount of water the industry had access to outside of the allocated system. Irrigators have constructed vast earthworks to funnel floodwater into enormous dams without a licence or the need to measure how much water has been taken. Known as 'floodplain harvesting', it was water free for the taking. However, critics have argued that this practice has denied crucial inflows into the Darling and, therefore, was a contributory cause of the Menindee fish kill.[34]

Not surprisingly, Simpkins sidestepped the murky politics involved in the operation of irrigation in the northern Basin. The absence of government monitoring of this free water says much about the power and influence of the cotton industry and the National and New South Wales Irrigators' Councils.

Yet photographs couldn't lie. On 19 January 2019, Senator Rex Patrick from the Centre Alliance Party took a light plane flight over southern Queensland near Goondiwindi. His published photographs showed cotton farms holding thousands of megalitres of water, while across the border in New South Wales, the Barwon and Darling rivers were a series of muddy pools.[35] On the surface, it appeared to be a case of the National Party in New South Wales 'giving away free water to their big irrigator mates' and in a manner calculated to undermine the Murray–Darling Basin Plan.[36]

Given the lack of regulation, it's not surprising that the big irrigators were a fault line in the disagreements about water management in the Murray–Darling Basin. For years, one property, in particular, had stood out. The Chinese-owned Cubbie Station, the largest irrigated property in the southern hemisphere at 96 000 hectares, was frequently depicted as the 'Great Satan', causing waterways to deteriorate. It certainly qualifies as a monster hoarder of water with its 28 continuous kilometres of shallowly constructed dams, the full impact of which has to be seen from the air. Defenders of irrigation in the Basin decried that Cubbie was a 'scapegoat'.[37]

Scapegoat or villain, the cotton industry found itself at the centre of an escalating 'water war' in the wake of the Menindee fish kill. It became the target of the fears and frustrations of just about every other group in the Basin. Why was a thirsty crop like cotton being grown on a large scale in a dry continent like Australia? It was a question to which many struggled to find a satisfactory answer. Few Australians realised how big the industry had become. By 2013, Australia was ranked as the world's fourth largest cotton exporter, and the industry was dominated by corporate and foreign-owned players.[38] In the wake of the Menindee disaster, calls to ban the industry were being raised in Canberra by the Greens and the Centre Alliance. I examine big cotton's impact on the Basin in chapter 10.

Menindee town in the spotlight

Meanwhile, the 500 residents of Menindee found that, in the wake of the disaster, their plight was finally receiving national attention. Surrounded by the Lakes, the town is a natural oasis in the vast red sand and saltbush country of western New South Wales. However, life in the town had been slowly atrophying as the water dried up through drought, followed by the draining of the Lakes.

Only six months prior to the fish kill disaster, a journalist from a national media organisation made a rare visit to the remote area and found a scene of quiet desperation. As Jed Smith, writing for News. com.au commented, his visit occurred 'months before the putrid state of the river produced a million dead fish, but the writing was already on the wall'. The once bustling agricultural and tourist hub was 'full of dilapidated houses, boarded up businesses and rotting vineyards'. With lives and businesses rendered worthless by the crippling drought and the draining of the Lakes, the locals 'feel like they've been abandoned'.

Smith found emus and kangaroos dropping dead of thirst and a mysterious parasite. The blue-green algae had taken hold in large sections of the Darling River. The Menindee Lakes were already bone dry and the town's water supply was in dire straits. Smith was dismayed to discover that water was being pumped out of the 'carcass-riddled dregs of the lake system'; it was 'brown, stank of death, and sometimes caused locals to break out in rashes'. The once thriving town was being turned into a 'dust bowl'.[39] The 'dust bowl' epithet harked back to the 1930s and 1940s when, after decades of dust storms, the entire Basin was at risk of 'being swept away by the wind'.[40] But that history had largely faded from the public memory.

Menindee residents felt dejected that the mainstream media had shown so little interest in the creeping disaster that had now engulfed their community.[41] At both the town's two pubs, water policy dominated the conversation; locals scoffing indignantly at the Murray–Darling Basin Plan, saying it was 'not worth the paper it's written on'.[42]

Then, with the mass fish kill, came the stench. In the days that followed, the putrid smell from the rotting carcasses and algae enveloped the town, permeating homes and outside areas. Residents were unable to use air conditioners or evaporative coolers because the stink was so bad.[43] The stench was too overwhelming for visiting Greens (soon to be independent) New South Wales MP, Jeremy Buckingham, who, soon after the mass kill, conducted a media interview on the lake shore. Addressing the camera, he said, 'This is what you get when you leave the National Party in charge of water in Australia — dead fish; a massive stink'. But he was suddenly overcome by nausea and apologised before starting to retch. He walked off-camera to vomit, later describing the experience as 'one of the most disgusting experiences of my life'; the smell was 'grotesque'.[44]

ABC journalist Paige Cockburn visited the town at the end of January 2019, two weeks after the disaster. She saw frail kangaroos lining the main road into town – 'so weak they can barely look up at passing cars'. Temperatures reached 47 degrees. The Bureau of Meteorology's thermometer at the local post office broke under the intense heat. She discovered an underlying fear that 'now the fish are dead, people here fear their town could be next'. She spoke to Richard Unsworth, who remembered when Menindee used to 'hum'. He had managed a large table grape farm, but the water was gone: 'Now, all that's left are hundreds of rusting trellises'. Cockburn also interviewed Sharon Bonselaar, a fourth-generation farmer in the area, who urged the Murray–Darling Basin Authority to actually come out to talk to local farmers and Aboriginal people: 'They might learn what happens here'.[45]

Of particular concern to the Aboriginal people of Menindee, who make up more than one-third of the population, is the trauma associated with the continual disturbance to ancestral burial sites from the ongoing draining of the Lakes and construction works carried out around them. This desecration, they feel, falls on deaf ears in government.[46]

Clearly this was a small town facing an existential crisis: could it survive? How much of the vast Basin could survive?

Kate McBride seized on the publicity she generated over the fish kill to turn the nation's attention to the social consequences of the mismanagement of the river. She blitzed the airwaves with interviews on the major news outlets and on Channel Ten's *The Project* and ABC's *Australian Story*. In both programs she highlighted the plight of the 'dying' towns along the banks of the Darling River, dying because the Lakes had dried up and rainwater tanks had been emptied by drought. Those who came into contact with the pools of remaining toxic river water risked serious health issues, including motor neurone disease, which has suspected links to blue-green algae. She repeated calls for a national inquiry into water management across the Murray–Darling Basin.[47] The impression from her interviews was as unmistakable as it was disturbing: towns like Menindee resembled those in developing nations with similar toxic and insecure water supplies.

At the time, Menindee was only one of several outback New South Wales towns that faced running out of water. The media soon circled over that story as well. How big was this disaster in the northern Basin going to get?

Indigenous groups lash out

If McBride was doing all she could to draw attention to the plight of the Darling River, so too was another group who felt equally marginalised – the Indigenous people of the region, the Barkindji. Evidence of their ancient links to Menindee have been found in the sand dunes around the Lakes – a virtual treasure-trove of fossils and marked stones comprising among the earliest remnants of humans on the planet.[48]

For 70-year-old Barkindji artist, educator and elder William 'Badger' Bates, the Menindee fish kill was the worst he'd ever seen.[49] He was brought up mostly by his grandmother, who had retained strong links to Barkindji language and culture, and she took Badger travelling with her, avoiding authorities and protecting him from becoming one of the stolen generations. Often living beside the river in tents, humpies and tin huts, he became familiar with

> every bend in the river, and everything about the river, billabongs, creeks and lakes, the plants and the animals. In those days the river was always fresh to drink and we could always get a feed of fish or yabbies, duck or turtle or something … there were birds everywhere along the river.[50]

Speaking to a journalist straight after the Menindee fish kill, Bates explained that the Barka, as the Barkindji called the Darling River, 'never ever went dry in my time'. For the last five to eight years, however, his people 'say the Barka's buka. That means the Darling River's dead'.[51]

In 2015 the Barkindji were awarded their native title rights to a 128 000 square hectare area of western New South Wales, including land on both sides of the Barka, but this conferred no rights to the waters of the river, upon which a large part of their culture rests. Consequently, authorities continued to ignore their voice.

The Barkindji are one of 40 Aboriginal nations whose traditional lands encompassed the Murray–Darling Basin before European settlement and who today number 75 000 people from across the various nations. They are represented by a number of different peak bodies, including the Northern Basin Aboriginal Nations, the Murray Lower Darling Rivers Indigenous Nations, Ngarrindjeri Regional Authority, and the Barkindji Native Title Prescribed Body Corporate. All have been highly vocal about the 'broken' system of management of the Basin because water was, in the words of Rene Woods, chair of the Murray Lower Darling Rivers Indigenous Nations organisation, 'being sucked up and turned into profits for a cabal of wealthy agribusinesses'.[52]

But protestations from Aboriginal groups that they should be partners in the management of the Basin continued to fall largely on deaf ears. A week after the Menindee fish kill, a meeting was convened in Canberra between fish scientists, relevant state representatives, water holders and the Murray–Darling Basin Authority to discuss the likelihood of more mass fish kills and the appropriate future management of the Basin's river system. Bates was not even informed of the meeting. 'This is what happens all the time,' he complained. 'They should be taking a bit more notice of us. My people have the Native Title.'[53] Nor was any other representative Aboriginal group invited. Northern Basin Aboriginal Nation's Director, Cheryl Buchanan, said in response to the Canberra meeting: 'when it comes to water … we must be there at the table … because the conversation is being driven by profit'.[54]

Bates summed up for all the Aboriginal groups of the region what the demise of the Darling meant to them. Surveying the disaster of the Menindee fish kill with a British journalist covering the event, Bates picked up a dead fish and tossed it into a pool of toxic, green water and said: 'You take this river from me and my people [and] we're not even black any more. We've got no culture, we've got nothing'.[55]

Most policy experts agreed with concerned farmers, townspeople and Aboriginal groups about the causes and extent of the ecological crisis facing much of the Basin. An Australian Academy of Science panel, formed to investigate the causes of the mass deaths of fish at the Menindee Lakes, brought down its findings at the end of February 2019. The panel rejected the drought as the cause of the fish kill and declared that unless urgent steps are taken to restore flows in the Darling, 'The Darling will die'.[56]

The Menindee fish kill was a significant event not just in the history of the Murray–Darling Basin but in national politics generally. It shocked the community into realising that the Basin – Australia's largest food bowl – faced an ecological challenge and possible long-term decline. Set against the wider challenge of climate change threatening the Basin's long-term future, what was witnessed on the Darling in early January 2019 was not just a tragedy of dead fish but a 'canary in the coal mine' moment for the ailing river system and the wider Murray–Darling Basin.

Yet, as the debate petered out, no lasting change had resulted. The vested interests won a temporary reprieve. The Commonwealth and New South Wales governments had together stared down calls for a federal Royal Commission into the Basin. Sticking to their well-rehearsed lines, and avoiding direct confrontation with the media and Menindee locals, governments rode out the political storm created by the mass fish deaths. And with a federal election looming, other issues soon took precedence.

We must now turn to examine the long journey to reach the point at which the Murray–Darling was widely seen in 2019 to be in a state of crisis. Only by examining the history of European settlement can we fully understand how the Basin's present state of degradation came about.

2

MEN OF EMPIRE

In the 1820s, European settlers knew nothing about the geography of inland Australia; it was a blank canvas onto which fevered colonial imaginations drew vivid pictures. The favourite theory was the possible existence of a vast inland sea, fed by westwards-flowing rivers, and expansive new grazing lands; the speculation 'took possession of the public mind'.[1] But there were doubters as well. Some early colonists were convinced that the interior offered no suitable land for settlement, that it might be a vast desert.[2] Solving this riddle drove the explorations of John Oxley, Hamilton Hume, Charles Sturt and Thomas Mitchell – the pantheon of explorers whose names are writ large in a country otherwise devoid of great heroes. The contribution they made to opening up the Murray–Darling Basin was of immense significance to the economic development of Australia. Among them, Sturt (expeditions in 1828–29 and 1829–30) and Mitchell (1831, 1835 and 1836), separately ventured farthest and for longer periods into these ancient lands.

Firmly in the minds of all the explorers was a vision of a land to exploit for the benefit of the colony and the British Empire. In fact, the Colonial Office required explorers to provide a 'circumstantial account of such articles, if any, as might be advantageously imported into Britain'.[3] Sturt was particularly seized with the prospect of being covered in glory by coming 'upon Mediterranean sea much nearer than has been imagined'.[4]

In their vision of extractive economics and nation-building, Sturt and Mitchell assumed that Aboriginal people, who had lived there for 60 000 years, would be displaced, and the environment, which they had husbanded for thousands of years, would be radically transformed into a Western economic model. It was a transformation based on an indifference, bordering on contempt, for nature. These views were as natural to an 18th-century mindset as a belief in the Almighty, from which many of the ideas were derived.

Sturt's and Mitchell's expeditions were followed closely in the colony, and their journals were widely read in both New South Wales and England. These two men, steeped in the traditions of Empire, slogged their way through a vast and strange landscape peopled by an ancient culture with deep spiritual ties to lands they intended to conquer. How would these two worlds collide?

The courage and commitment of both Sturt and Mitchell in undertaking such arduous journeys cannot be denied; such epic treks would test the qualities of any leader. The logistics of their expeditions involved military-style feats of organisation: provisions for up to five months; the transport of delicate surveyor's equipment; the inclusion of a whale-boat and small dingy – all loaded into heavy drays pulled by bullocks. For months on end, they trudged on with the assistance of convicts and Aboriginal guides. When heat exhaustion, fatigue, thirst and fear overcame their parties, Sturt and Mitchell had to find a way to keep moving. But theirs were journeys with a clear mission – to please their imperial masters by discovering productive new lands.

Both Sturt and Mitchell were conscious of the need to remain vigilant against what they perceived would likely be attacks by Aboriginal groups. Such dangers were merely one part of the steep challenges all the explorers faced in the remote wilderness of the Australian continent. Both men were fortunate in coming from a military background that included service in the Duke of Wellington's army in Spain. The British army under Wellington – the 'Iron Duke' – was famed for an officer training regime that fostered discipline and courage.[5] Such training proved crucial to survival against hunger, fatigue and the sheer isolation of Australia's vast interior.

The silence of the land heightened explorers' unease. Animal noises played on their minds. 'The native dogs', Sturt wrote, 'wandered about, though they had scarcely strength to avoid us' and their 'melancholy howl, breaking in upon the ear at the dead of the night, only served to impress more fully on the mind the absolute loneliness of the desert'.[6] Survival was sometimes a brutal struggle for Europeans traversing this region. Before turning for home on his 1829 expedition, Sturt described his men as 'haggard', 'emaciated' with their spirits 'wholly sunk'.[7]

Even though the original quest for the inland sea disappeared like a mirage, the discovery by both Sturt and Mitchell of one of the world's great river systems and areas suitable for grazing, facilitated the rapid development of the pastoral industry – the nation's first large-scale export industry. Hence, they have 'walked tall' in the pages of Australian history ever since.[8]

Yet only in recent decades has this heroic narrative been challenged as the dominant version of the nation's history. The violent dispossession of the Aboriginal people of the Murray–Darling – and, indeed, across the nation – is now accepted as a parallel version of this history and one that has overturned the myth that Australia was peacefully settled. More recently, the environmental consequences of European occupation have come into focus. But rather than being separate strands of the Basin's history, the economic dynamism of pastoralism, the dispossession of the Aboriginal population and the indifference to environmental destruction form a seamless thread in the European settlement of the Murray–Darling Basin. All of these elements coalesced in the thinking of Sturt and Mitchell and, more broadly, the colonial society that cheered them on.

Both expeditioners cast their eyes upon the alien landscape of the interior, and its ancient Indigenous culture, with the ingrained cultural assumptions of their age. Both men had been born in the United

Kingdom, arriving in the colony in 1826 and 1828 respectively. They were unfamiliar with the Australian outback and had little affinity with its rugged and often unforgiving landscape. In setting out on their expeditions, they didn't reckon on being able to survive off the land, other than shooting the occasional kangaroo and catching the odd fish.

In their willingness to brave such hardships, it's important to realise that both Mitchell and Sturt were products of their social position in the colony. Both were 'government men', eager to serve the British colonial power and to execute its aims of exploration; annexation was crucial to the nature of the expeditions.[9] In Britain, there was a readiness to believe that the Australian inland would constitute an ideal site for expansion of Empire.[10] And 18th-century English legal opinion maintained that all 'settled' lands automatically became Crown lands in cases like Australia, where it was perceived that such lands were 'unoccupied and without settled inhabitants'.[11]

But like all grand visions, reality often intruded during Sturt's and Mitchell's journeys. Both embraced the aim of finding land not only to develop for settlement but to plant the seeds of British civilisation and its cultural idea of turning 'waste lands' into 'cultivated' landscapes. However, they had to set aside the uncomfortable reality of the relationship Aboriginal people had with the land. They leaned heavily on socially derived stereotypes of Aboriginal people as 'savages' and the land as 'unoccupied', yet they made clear in their journals that they encountered permanent settlements and sophisticated methods of both agriculture and aquaculture.

International pressures for development

Propelling the search for new grazing land was a combination of local and international forces. In the fledgling colony of New South Wales, the story of Captain John Macarthur's entrepreneurial instinct for the potential of the fine wool industry in Australia has been told many times. Charles Sturt was aware that his trips into the interior came on the back of Macarthur's success. 'The colony are indebted to Mr. M'Arthur', he wrote, 'for the possession of an exportable commodity which has contributed very materially to its present wealth and importance'.[12]

But Macarthur's exploits have tended to gloss over the greed that gripped the colony as a consequence of wool becoming an export commodity. The rush for exploration was on in earnest by 1819, with the Sydney Gazette reporting stories of exploration of rich and promising lands. Colonists themselves were described as 'impatient landgrabbers' and the powerful elite class – known as 'exclusives' – like Macarthur and the Reverend John Marsden, had 'an insatiable thirst for more and better land'.[13]

By the time Sturt and Mitchell arrived in the colony, the land problem was growing increasingly acute. The rising population of native-born colonials considered a grant of land a 'natural inheritance' and the growing number of immigrants also sought to 'find a place in this new land'.[14] The population of the colony more than doubled, from 13 000 to 30 000, between 1815 and 1821.[15]

Up until 1831, successive governors had sought to develop the colony through a policy of land grants embodying the prevailing assumption that land was the basis of all wealth. Large grants were doled out to the colonial elites: military officers, government officials and immigrants of means. As the potential of the wool industry became apparent, the 'exclusives' grabbed the opportunities of pastoralism for gaining wealth and continued political influence. The Cumberland Plain, west of Sydney, became their fiefdom. Smaller grants were handed out to ex-convicts and poorer immigrants, and these folk concentrated on agriculture to feed the convict population.[16]

Far away from the fledging colony, the international political economy was undergoing transformational change. Australia was settled as the Industrial Revolution in Britain had begun to spread to other parts of the world, shaping patterns of land use, including those in Australia. New South Wales became linked to this emerging economic system whereby the colonies provided the 'mother country' with raw materials in exchange for the manufactured products of the new industrial powerhouse of Great Britain. The Australian Agricultural Company was formed in London in 1824 to take advantage of the new opportunities presented by the rise of a capitalist economy. It was created with the goal of cultivating and improving the 'waste lands' in the colony of New South Wales.[17]

But as the number of sheep (and cattle) grew, the allure of obtaining a flock or herd gripped the colony. By 1825–26, as prominent colonial clergyman John Dunmore Lang later wrote in his history of New South Wales, a *sheep and cattle mania* (Dunmore's italics) had descended on the colony.[18] Naturalist Charles Darwin noted a similar preoccupation when he landed in Sydney in March 1836. 'The whole population poor & rich', he wrote disparagingly, 'are bent on acquiring wealth; the subject of wool and sheep grazing amongst the higher orders is of preponderant interest'.[19]

Sturt was well appraised of these developments and the opportunities they presented. As he explained to readers of his journal, the traditional sources for British wool in Spain and Germany could be supplanted by growers in New South Wales because the latter source was increasingly competitive: 'The great improvements in modern navigation are such, that the expense of sending the fleece to market from New South Wales is less than from any part of Europe'.[20]

Both Sturt and Mitchell were also steeped in the military tradition of the British Empire. Both had served in the Duke of Wellington's rout of Napoleon's forces in Spain. They had experienced the glory of victory in war. Sturt was a product of the Empire, his father having served as a judge in India before losing the family's fortune. Both his father and mother hailed from 'country families of standing', and Charles carried the bearing of his class; he has been described as an English tory gentleman.[21] Tall and handsome, he had a 'striking singleness of purpose' to complement his noted ability to lead men.

Mitchell was similarly self-motivated, although he was a far more complex and curmudgeonly character than Sturt with whom he maintained a jealous rivalry. He had risen from an inauspicious family background with a profound belief in the virtues of European civilisation. Joining the British army offered him a ladder of opportunity, but his participation in Wellington's heroic and bloody campaign against the forces of Napoleon in Spain and Portugal seemed to have left a permanent mark. Firstly, it is where he honed his skills as a surveyor, later deployed on his expeditions. Secondly, Mitchell's service on the Iberian Peninsula developed his capacity for physical endurance: 'he could go for three days without food, wet through the whole time, in a bitterly cold wind'.[22] Lastly, he appears to have been psychologically affected by the protracted conflict. According to his first biographer, JHL Cumpston, he joined Wellington's forces at a 'most impressionable age' and 'could not have escaped the influence of such an environment'. It left him 'with a firm conviction that he was one of a special order of mankind'. This imperial mentality forged his ideas of leadership, responsibility and public service.[23]

Multilingual and widely read, Mitchell had arrived in the colony as an experienced surveyor. Becoming Surveyor-General after John Oxley died, he developed a reputation as hard-working and talented, and as a fiery character easily given to flashes of bad temper, disobeying orders and quarrelling with colleagues. He was one of the last people in Australia to fight in a duel.

Mitchell's military background influenced his dealings with the Aboriginal nations of the Murray–Darling Basin. He tended to view Aboriginal people as a natural enemy as if he were engaged in an undeclared war. Consequently, he was often contemplating military tactics in his dealings with them. On one occasion, he organised a surprise ambush against a particular group that resulted in a massacre. It's reasonably clear that Mitchell learned such tactics in Spain because Wellington was famous for deploying them.[24] And Mitchell carried with him the pride of Empire. Wellington's victory was one of the great campaigns in British military history because he was so outnumbered by the French.

As testimony to this lasting impact, Mitchell gave place names to honour his Spanish experience. As he wrote on one occasion, he named a 'little river', the Stokes, 'in memory of a brother officer, who fell at Bajadoz'. There are other, similar examples, which raise a troubling question: Was this a man still dealing with the trauma of war? Without stating as much, Mitchell's most recent biographer, William Foster,[25] raises the possibility of war-induced trauma when he writes: 'on lonely surveys in enemy territory he had hid at night in caves, and half slept with rifle always cocked, and at times rose sharply at the snapping of a twig. He had lived dangerously for three years'. And, as Wellington's forces marched through Spain, Foster writes that Mitchell had 'taken part in some of the bloodiest conflicts of the War' and had seen 'so much destruction and ravage'.

Such destruction only served to heighten Mitchell's inner conviction about the superiority of the British Empire, which gave him a sense of mission about spreading civilisation in Australia. Setting out on one of his expeditions he was overcome with the youthful memories of Empire, writing that 'war and victory, with all their glory' spread 'the light of civilization'. He was thrilled at the thought of discovering regions 'teeming with useful vegetation' and the chance to improve 'the natural beauty of the soil'.[26]

Sturt was even more mindful that he was on a mission to benefit the British Empire. He drew a connection between the 'evils' of Britain's surplus population, which he reckoned was about two million people, occasioning a huge financial burden to the British government, which could be redeemed by emigration to New South Wales. He saw the economic benefits to Britain. British settlers would increase demand for, and consumption of, 'every species of British manufacture'.[27]

Doubtless there was a degree of self-promotion behind each

of these men of Empire. Their journals were designed to be widely read, forming part of the popular genre of early 19th-century travel writing. But the pursuit of fame and glory combined with the belief in Empire were critical elements behind their success. The combination of motivations helped them frame up their expeditions as conquest. Mitchell once described his party as 'civilized intruders', and on another occasion as 'rather unceremonious invaders of their country'.[28] Mitchell relished his role as a harbinger of change. He believed that he was spreading 'the light of civilisation on a portion of the globe yet unknown', and a process in which 'almost by divine intervention that intelligent white man should inherit the land'.[29]

Of course, the land they sought to claim had been inhabited for tens of thousands of years by Aboriginal people. Sturt and Mitchell were the first to see and record Aboriginal life in inland Australia. With the potential for vast new lands up for grabs, their views on Aboriginal people had the potential to influence public opinion.[30] Their frequent encounters with Aboriginal nations spilled out into the pages of Mitchell's and Sturt's journals and were used by them to convey the racist stereotypes common to the age. While each had sharply different approaches to interacting with Aboriginal people, both regularly depicted them as savages and treacherous. Yet, beneath these common tropes, Sturt and Mitchell struggled with the realities of the Aboriginal life they witnessed.

The age of exploration of inland Australia commenced against a darkening climate on race. Two conflicting and irreconcilable undercurrents had seeped into official opinion. In the 1820s and 1830s, the campaign to abolish slavery in the British Empire was in full swing, highlighting growing humanitarian thinking that extended into parliamentary concern for the exploitation of indigenous peoples in the Empire.[31] Yet this unfolding of humanitarian ideas sat uneasily alongside the continuation of the age-old racist thinking of such peoples as 'savages' who had 'unrestrained passions'.[32] Australia had its humanitarians concerned about the fate of Aboriginal people, but their voices were outweighed by growing calls for what young Sydney barrister William Charles Wentworth termed 'an exterminating war' against Aboriginal people.[33] Some British officials, too, held uncompromising views. In 1838, James Stephen, Permanent Under Secretary in the Colonial Office, wrote that he did not think it possible 'to discover any method by which ... the extermination of the Black race can be long avoided'.[34]

Such hardening of attitudes followed violent acts of resistance by Aboriginal people towards British settlers. Resistance was met with military force. In 1816, Governor Lachlan Macquarie ordered a reprisal raid to bring to an end the war that had erupted on the Cumberland Plain when the local Dharawal nation resisted white settlers taking up land. In what became known as the Appin massacre, in the early hours of the morning of 17 April 1816, at least 14 Aboriginal men, women and children were killed when soldiers under the command of Captain James Wallis shot at and drove a group of Aboriginal women, children and old men over the gorge of the Cataract River.[35]

In 1824 Governor Brisbane had imposed martial law in the Bathurst region, home to the Wiradjuri people, just nine years after Macquarie founded the town on the eastern edge of the Murray–Darling Basin. Troops fanned out from Bathurst with a licence to conduct an 'exterminating war', which decimated the Wiradjuri people and their campsites. Historian Peter Read has described Brisbane's actions as 'the largest official military force ever to set out against the blacks to placate the settlers'.[36]

Given this history of resistance and repression, it is not surprising that Sturt felt that it was unsafe to travel into the interior with less than 15 men. As military and combat-trained expedition leaders, neither he nor Mitchell liked putting himself in a position where Aboriginal people had the tactical advantage. Steeped in the discipline, training and courage expected of military officers in Wellington's army,[37] they were conditioned to see 'the other' as responsible for any aggression.

They were spooked by Aboriginal behaviour radically different from their own: the 'war songs', dancing, jumping, throwing dust, the din created by hitting spears on shields. Such outwardly aggressive behaviour put them on edge, confirming notions of Aboriginal savagery.[38] When they thought there was no other form of control, both Sturt and Mitchell resorted to threats or violence.[39]

Nonetheless, Mitchell and Sturt had the expertise of Aboriginal people, who, in a variety of roles, were instrumental to the success of their expeditions. They acted as guides, interpreters, cooks and servants. Some became minor celebrities in their own right, while the contributions of others faded into obscurity.[40] Mitchell developed a close relationship with two of his Aboriginal companions. He described John Piper as 'the most accomplished man in the camp', and Yuanigh as his 'guide, companion, councillor and friend'.[41]

Yet neither explorer allowed such personal relationships to colour his overall views of Aboriginal people or the goal of conquest. Neither was trained in anthropology; indeed, the comparative study of human kind as a separate discipline is usually dated to 1859 when the Société d'Anthropologie de Paris was founded. Although the two explorers produced the first observations of Aboriginal society and culture in Australia's interior, neither Sturt nor Mitchell 'succeeded in interpreting the subtleties of the interlocking social system of the tribes'.[42]

It is almost certain that members of the various Aboriginal nations grasped the grand aim of European conquest as the explorers' parties trudged through their lands and rowed down their waters. A Victorian magistrate, T McCombie, who claimed a long acquaintance with Aboriginal people, believed this to be the case. Giving evidence to a Victorian parliamentary inquiry into the decimation of the Aboriginal population just over a decade after Mitchell's last trip down the Murray, he said: [T]hey [Aboriginal people] saw Sir Thomas with horses, and mules, and men and all armed. Ignorant and low as they [Aboriginal people] are ... they know well enough when their land is going to be taken away from them'.[43]

Friends and enemies

Despite the inevitable tensions that arose between the explorers and members of Murray–Darling Aboriginal nations, both Sturt and Mitchell had complex and contradictory attitudes towards Aboriginal people.

As the first of the explorers to venture farthest along the Darling and then the Murray rivers, Sturt brought with him a distinctive temperament that governed his dealings with the local Aboriginal people. Outwardly his manner was calm, gentlemanly, English; inwardly he was prepared to use violence against Aboriginal people at a moment's notice if he thought it necessary.

However, Sturt's insistence on avoiding conflict did defuse the most threatening situations. As he explained:

> The great point is not to alarm their timidity, to exercise patience
> in your intercourse with them; to treat them kindly and to watch
> them with suspicion even at night. Never permit your men to steal
> away from camp … and at every station so arrange your drays and
> provisions that they may serve as a defence in case of your being
> attacked.[44]

Sturt prided himself on his ability to avoid outright confrontation. During his 1829 journey in a boat down the Murrumbidgee River, he and his party came across a 'large body of natives' on the river bank. The situation immediately became tense for, as Sturt quickly realised, the group of Aboriginal people was intent on resisting the intruders. 'They showed every disposition for combat', Sturt later wrote in his published journal of the incident. With spears in hand, 'the Aborigines ran along the river bank waiting for an opportunity to throw them at us'.

Sturt thought he had the measure of the situation when, suddenly, he noticed another party had gathered on the opposing bank. Racing through his mind was the realisation that the stretch of river through which they were passing was not sufficiently wide to avoid danger should both groups attack simultaneously. As luck would have it, Sturt's party avoided direct confrontation when one of the groups swam across the river to join the other, allowing Sturt and his men to float past. Nonetheless, when formed into one larger party, the traditional owners followed the boat, continuing their fierce display of displeasure. According to Sturt, they were bent on 'intimidation' such was their 'dreadful shouting' and 'beating [of] their spears and shields together'.[45]

Out of immediate danger, and aware that his men were fatigued from the day's exertions, Sturt landed his craft and instructed his men to pitch the tents for the evening while he and a crew member walked back up the river to make contact with the group that had been following them. It's not clear why Sturt thought this was a good idea; the men remaining with the boat understandably thought it an entirely risky action. But Sturt possessed supreme confidence in his ability to engage with Aboriginal people and to defuse potentially troublesome situations. And he had formed the view that the 'natives' were, at heart, mostly docile; that, by treating them with respect, their overt display of aggression would give way to conciliation. Sturt was proud of the fact that no Aboriginal people had been killed by his party during his two lengthy expeditions.

For the last part of his voyage down the Murray, Sturt's party was followed by members of the Ngarrindjeri nation. Sturt was on guard as the Ngarrindjeri kept a watchful eye on his party while he was in their country. They neither 'welcome[d] him with open arms, but neither did they molest him', despite possessing lethal weapons – spears made from hardwood, which, when hurled from a spear thrower, constituted 'a deadly missile'.[46]

We don't know why the Ngarrindjeri held their fire. They lived in a rich and sophisticated culture, steeped in spiritualism and ancient customary law, which conditioned them, according to George Taplin, the pioneer anthropologist, to be 'a most law-abiding people'.[47] Moreover, the Ngarrindjeri lacked a tradition of blood-thirsty battles; fighting between the affiliated tribes ceased 'after one or two people were badly injured'.[48] How these cultural traditions played out along the banks of the Murray River will forever be lost, but, for whatever reason, Sturt was given a free passage. He was able to write gushingly about the beauty of the country he had 'discovered' and its potential. It was land that the Ngarrindjeri would soon be dispossessed from.

Sturt may have thought that his approach to the Ngarrindjeri and to the other nations he encountered was noble, but it amounted to little more than an attempt at conquest by conciliation, because in his journals Sturt makes it plain that he was able to take advantage of Aboriginal people by adopting friendly relationships with them. 'I doubt very much', he acknowledged, 'whether we should ever have pushed so far down the river, had we not been assisted by the natives themselves'.[49] And, behind the outward show of conciliation, Sturt was prepared to resort to violent means if thwarted. As he wrote, he was prepared to confront Aboriginal people 'with a power they had little dreamt of'.[50] On another occasion, he wrote that he 'took up my gun, therefore, and cocking it, had already brought it down to a level. A few seconds more would have closed the life of the nearest of the savages'.[51]

Despite the pride he took in not killing any Aboriginal people, violence was still justified in Sturt's mind because of the overall imperial aims of his expedition and because he saw Aboriginal people as 'at the very bottom of the scale of humanity'.[52] And, according to one of Sturt's early biographers, 'he did not question the principle of invasion'.[53] In fact, during his 1829 expedition when he realised he had discovered the Darling River, Sturt ordered the Union Jack to be hoisted, whereupon the crew stood up in the boat and gave three cheers.[54]

While Mitchell shared the same overall objectives as Sturt, his sharply different temperament made him much more prone to use violence against the Aboriginal nations he encountered. Always at the forefront of his mind were his experiences of war. 'I remember exactly on that morning', he wrote as he set out on his third expedition, '24 years before, I marched down the Glasis of Elvas [a Portuguese garrison] … Now without any of the pride, pomp, and circumstances of glorious war I was preceding on a service not very likely to be peaceful'.[55] Not surprisingly given his background, Mitchell was forever on edge about the 'hostile intentions' of Aboriginal people, referring to one group as 'our old enemies' and, on another occasion as simply 'the barbarians'.[56]

Combined with these fixed views was Mitchell's 'ungovernable temper', as Governor Darling noted of his Surveyor General.

Yet Mitchell's journeys into Aboriginal Country also challenged his racist stereotypes. His naturally curious mind took a keen interest in Indigenous culture, and he once described watching a corroboree better than any ballet he had seen at Covent Garden.[57] He also marvelled at Aboriginal hunting, fishing and tracking skills. On one difficult day on the Murray River during his third expedition, Mitchell allowed his very British view of the world to temporarily fall aside, conceding that Aboriginal people were the more skilled race: 'the intelligence and skill of our sable friends made the "white-fellows" appear rather stupid. They could read traces on the earth, climb trees, or dive into the water, better than the ablest of us'.[58]

On one occasion he expressed a hint of regret at disturbing their 'contentment and happiness within the precincts of their native woods', knowing that this 'seemed to derive so directly from nature'.[59]

Mitchell could proffer such an observation because he had seen the crippling effect of dispossession on Aboriginal people. Early on in his 1831 expedition he came upon the remnants of one group and wrote sympathetically about their plight. 'These unfortunate creatures', he wrote, had lost access to their traditional hunting grounds and were hemmed in by 'the power of the white population', and had been forced into seeking 'a precarious shelter'.[60]

Any positive experiences with Aboriginal people or their culture quickly gave way to threats of violence if Aboriginal people became aggressive. Mitchell wrote about a number of instances when he was roused to anger:

> I never saw such unfavourable species of the Aborigine as these children of the smoke, they were so barbarously and implacably hostile and shamelessly dishonest … it is probable they might ere long force upon us the painful necessity of making them acquainted with the superiority of our arms.[61]

On his first expedition, Mitchell's characteristic 'parade-ground formality'[62] jumped into gear when, journeying down the Bogan River into Wiradjuri Country, he suddenly became alarmed at the unheralded appearance of one of their camps. Mitchell ordered the bugle to be sounded but to little effect; the Wiradjuri did not appear to be unusually intimidated by 'this martial flourish'. By his own account he was besieged by friendly people along the Bogan. However, his relationships with Aboriginal people deteriorated, especially along the Darling and among the Barkindji. He was involved in two episodes involving the murder of Barkindji people.

On his second expedition in 1835, Mitchell's party had been camped for a few days near the Darling River. On one afternoon when Mitchell was in the camp, shots were heard coming from near the river where a few of his men were watering the bullocks. Two or three Aboriginal people were shot. Claim and counter claim surrounds what happened, and the only direct evidence comes from Mitchell's men at the scene. However, it's almost certain that the cause of the deaths was not a result of an unprovoked attack, as claimed by Mitchell's men, but as a consequence of a quarrel centred around the refusal of one of the men to hand over to an Aboriginal woman a kettle promised in return for sexual favours.[63] Interestingly, Sturt had avoided such situations, by never letting his men wander off from camp.

The second episode of murder occurred a year later on Mitchell's third expedition and was orchestrated by him. In setting out on this expedition Mitchell prepared his team as if they were a military force. He 'armed the men' and distributed uniforms which gave the men 'a military appearance ... This was the army with which I was to traverse unexplored regions'.[64]

And by this time, he had fixed, stereotypical views about Aboriginal aggression, even though he had had a variety of encounters with groups – exhibiting at times curiosity, timidity or conciliatory behaviour; aggression on other occasions. But Mitchell couldn't see either the nuance of their responses or the likelihood that his presence excited their anger. He now saw everywhere proof of Aboriginal aggression in a binary mentality that dictated that his party were invaders and Aboriginal people were the enemy. In a revealing gesture at the termination of the third expedition, he gave Piper a brass plate inscribed with 'Conqueror of the Interior'.[65]

The details of the massacre on his 1836 expedition are disputed. Historian Don Baker argues that Mitchell believed the group to be the same as the one involved in skirmishes the previous year, and feared that they were about to attack him.[66] Other accounts maintain that Mitchell came across a large group of Aboriginal people preparing for a celebration and mistook their actions as a sign that they were about to attack.[67] Whatever the actual circumstances, Mitchell decided on a pre-emptive strike, setting up an ambush in a military-style operation and putting into practice some of the techniques he'd witnessed in the campaign against the French. Over several days Mitchell's party attacked the Aboriginal group, killing at least 12.

Back in Sydney, Governor Bourke ordered an investigation into the atrocity. In his account to Bourke, Mitchell defended his actions as if he was giving his account from a war zone: 'Their system of warfare', he wrote, 'was to follow us, being ready to pick up any stragglers, and to gather in our rear as we went on, the whole savage population along the banks of the rivers'.[68]

Although later acquitted of any wrongdoing by the official inquiry, the incident strained Mitchell's relationship with the Colonial Office, which, while commending him on his feats of exploration and his leadership, was disturbed by the massacre and, consequently, declined to grant him a knighthood until 1839. But Mitchell's actions also need to be seen in a wider context. They revealed the universal dark side of humanity; how racial antipathy combined with territorial ambitions, and a propensity to use violence in settings free of legal and moral constraints, could foment atrocities. In other words, here was a colonial version of a phenomenon known throughout history: ordinary people becoming killers. Mitchell, of course, was merely part of the wider pattern of frontier violence, but his actions foreshadowed the onslaught of destruction that would dispossess Aboriginal people throughout the Basin.

Although both men saw their expeditions as foreshadowing the removal of Aboriginal people from this vast area, neither was clear on how this would be executed. Mitchell penned contradictory opinions. On one occasion he foresaw the dispossession of Aboriginal traditional lands because 'the advent of such a powerful race' as the Europeans made such 'expiration' inevitable.[69] He even glimpsed the genocide that, in a few years' time, would be unleashed on the Basin's Aboriginal population. Australia, he said, could 'never be explored with safety except by very powerful parties'.[70] Yet, reflecting a decade later, Mitchell wrote that it was the responsibility of the conqueror to consider the fate of the conquered: 'Surely it behoves a nation, so active in the suppression of slavery, to consider betimes, in taking up new countries, how the Aboriginal races can be preserved'.[71]

The striking contradiction in these men's thinking was the disconnect between their culturally shaped worldview of Aboriginal people and what, as explorers, they discovered about the culture of the people they encountered. In their journals, both Sturt and Mitchell penned richly documented observations on the deep ties Aboriginal people had to the land. These observations made clear to both officials and the broader public that these were not simply nomads.

Sturt found evidence of 'permanent habitation', paths 'like well-trodden roads', villages of 70 huts that held up to 15 people each, and 'beautifully made' fishing nets.[72]

Mitchell was likewise struck by the challenge to his pre-existing views about the nomadic nature of the traditional owners. In the Darling River region, he saw several large villages with circular or semi-circular huts with conical roofs. Some of the huts could accommodate up to 15 people, the substantial nature of the buildings forcing him to admit that '[t]hese permanent huts seemed also to indicate a race of more peaceful and settled habits'.[73] Mitchell was also taken by the elaborately constructed fishing nets as if they 'had been the work of a carpenter'.[74]

The significance of such revealing comments is obvious – they called for a major rethinking of the cultural stereotype constructed by the British about Aboriginal people's nomadism, one of the principal justifications for appropriating Aboriginal land. This task of reinterpreting the Aboriginal nomadic lifestyle – of Aboriginal people actively farming their land and developing permanent habitations – has been taken up by two recent historians, Bill Gammage and Bruce Pascoe.[75]

The point here is that both Sturt and Mitchell continually referred to the Murray–Darling country as 'uninhabited' and 'uncultivated' at the very same time they witnessed the opposite. In one striking sentence in his journal, Mitchell, who had several times commented on the impressive construction of Aboriginal people's 'permanent' houses, wrote: 'It may be difficult for those unused to the habits of Australian natives, to understand … that these people hav[e] no fixed domicile'.[76] How is this disconnect explained? Perhaps their racism was just too embedded. But, as we have seen in their journals, racist thinking wasn't the only justification for the conquest of the Murray–Darling lands and the dispossession of its 'nomadic' Aboriginal population. The explorers – and their colonial backers – wanted the land for economic and cultural reasons. As Mitchell triumphantly wrote at the conclusion to his third expedition: 'It would be an everlasting monument to the beneficial influence of British power and colonisation … [to establish] a new and flourishing state on a region now so desolate and unproductive'.[77] And clearly, the 'permanent' markers of Aboriginal civilisation they observed would not, in their minds, have equated with the virtues of British civilisation.

The 'waste' lands of the Murray–Darling

If the concept of race was deeply embedded in 19th-century thinking, so too were views on the environment. Sturt and Mitchell were both products of the long-standing Western tradition that conceived of humans as separate from nature and naturally inclined to dominate it. These ideas found expression in the Christian story of Creation.[78] From this came the parallel ideas that only land that was settled and cultivated could be valued; that which wasn't was 'waste'. As Mitchell stated several times in his journals, he found all but the most striking landscapes 'a naked wilderness' and 'a melancholy waste'.[79]

Mitchell famously named the region of the Western District of Victoria as Australia Felix ('fortunate Australia') so delighted was he to have fulfilled his mission to report on finding such a large area of productive land. The name was chosen 'to better distinguish it from the parched deserts of the interior country where we had wandered so unprofitably for so long'. The vast region, he wrote, had the appearance of a well-kept park, and 'the rich black earth produced in greater luxuriance than I had ever seen in Australia'. Mitchell didn't understand that this cultivated landscape was the product of Aboriginal land and water management practices. Even if he had understood this reality it wouldn't have made a skerrick of difference because this man of Empire felt that he had truly fulfilled his mission:

As I stood, the first intruder on the sublime solitudes of these
verdant plains, as yet untouched by flocks and herds, I felt
conscious of being the harbinger of mighty changes there, for our
steps would soon be followed by the men and the animals, for
which it seemed to have been prepared.[80]

To the 18th-century British mind, 'wilderness' was a derogatory term.
In an age in which wealth was measured by land ownership and by
the individual's right to own and improve property – an approach
developed from philosopher John Locke's ideas – the existence
of 'waste' in the form of undeveloped wilderness was anathema.
Britain exported these ideas to parts of their Empire. As the French
philosopher Alexis de Tocqueville noted on his tour of the American
colonies, settlers 'could only see their wilderness as an obstacle to
progress'.[81]

Conversely, Sturt became dispirited when he was travelling
through harsh country of the sort with which he was entirely
unfamiliar. For Sturt, this type of landscape wasn't just unproductive
country, it was country without intrinsic worth. In this way both
Sturt and Mitchell reflected and amplified the corrosive feeling of
alienation that permeated early British colonisers' attitudes towards
the Australian landscape: 'the fearful absence from the landscape of
any natural or cultural elements with which they could identify'.[82]

It's not that Mitchell and Sturt couldn't occasionally be moved by
some of the beauty of the wild landscapes they saw, they just placed
these observations into the wider context of their cultural mental
maps about the suitability of the land for colonisation. Often the
Australian landscape is seen as 'ready made for the occupation of a
European power and its agriculture'.[83] It was ripe for exploitation.

A land of drought and floods

Both Sturt and Mitchell undertook their respective expeditions in the midst of severe droughts. In fact, two prolonged dry spells afflicted much of the south-east of the continent during the two decades of exploration of the Murray–Darling, between 1824 and 1830, and 1835 and 1843. Both explorers saw the effects of drought on the landscape: dry creeks and waterholes and a parched landscape. Both explorers wrote vividly about these effects. Sturt wrote that the drought he experienced felt like 'the vegetable kingdom was almost annihilated'[84] and that 'the earth may literally be said to have gasped for moisture', while Mitchell saw how the 'summer heat had parched the earth'.[85]

For Europeans living in the 1830s and 1840s, the study of climate was still in a primitive phase, of trying to formulate patterns by direct observation. Neither Sturt nor Mitchell was present in the Murray–Darling Basin long enough to record such patterns. But their observations form the first recorded descriptions of the ecology of the Basin.

Despite the all-pervasive effects of drought, both men were able to observe evidence of regular flooding. As Mitchell wrote of his 1835 expedition along the Darling: 'The banks everywhere displayed one peculiar feature, namely, the effect of floods in parallel lines, marking on the smooth sloping earth, the various heights to which the waters had in different floods arisen'.[86] Given the variability of these markings, Mitchell deduced that flooding was cyclical. Interestingly, the prospect of alternating floods and droughts did not dent his enthusiasm for the overall mission; that this was 'a fine country for colonisation'.[87]

What about the condition of the Darling during severe drought? Sturt and Mitchell had different experiences of the river as a potential lifeblood to the settlers they imagined streaming into the Basin. Sturt wrote that he 'found and left the Darling in a complete state of exhaustion. As a river it had ceased to flow'.[88] Mitchell found the reverse. The Darling River never ran dry, for which he was eternally grateful.

The rivers were the lifeblood for the dream of Empire-building that drove the extraordinary feats of both Sturt and Mitchell. Yet buried in Sturt's voluminous journal was a warning about the threat that drought posed to this dream. In two separate passages he wrote the most serious disadvantage under which the colony of New South Wales laboured was drought, 'to which it is periodically subject'. He acknowledged that differences of opinion existed as to whether the climate was 'too dry' or 'one of the most delightful under heaven'. Sturt speculated that dry seasons occurred every ten or twelve years. However, he realised, too, that it was difficult to 'judge a country on a partial and hurried survey'.[89]

Sturt and Mitchell had an incalculable influence in shaping the European history of the Murray–Darling Basin. They laid down the ideas upon which its development proceeded: annexation of the land, systematic dispossession of Aboriginal people, an extractive model of agriculture and an implied indifference to the environment. Moreover, they surveyed, mapped and gave place names throughout the region, which, in their minds, legitimised the legal ownership of the Basin by the British.

More broadly, they promoted the Basin as an appeal to nation-building: the region could service the needs of the colony and the Empire. As Australia developed its version of a British identity, Sturt and Mitchell were lionised for their contribution. On the centenary of Sturt's first expedition, the explorer was immortalised as a true 'Empire builder'. The *Daily Mercury* sounded a triumphalist note when it wrote that Sturt had paved the way 'for the expansion of a great outpost of the white race'.[90] And on Empire Day, the same year, the *Riverina Gazette* wrote that Sturt had 'blazed the track. His work was real Empire building'.[91]

Yet, the consequence of these imperialist ideas was first raised at the very time Mitchell and Sturt were promoting large-scale occupation of the Basin. It came in the form of a warning about unregulated human activity on the environment.

In 1833 the British economist William Forster Lloyd coined the phrase 'the tragedy of the commons' as a label for problems involving managing natural resources not held under emerging Western ideas of individual property ownership. At the time, 'the commons' was a time-honoured tradition in which pasture was set aside for anyone to use and especially the poor, who could graze cattle on it to supplement their income. What Lloyd noticed, however, was the tendency for each person to use the resource to the full, leading to some areas becoming bare earth with no one taking responsibility for the damage. Out of this observation, Lloyd developed his general theory that resources held 'in common' by the public, including pasture, forests, rivers, the oceans, the atmosphere, wildlife and fish, would likely be misused and overused with detrimental consequences for everyone unless they were carefully managed through collective agreement.

Lloyd wrote a short pamphlet detailing this concept, but it was mostly unknown until 1968, when environmentalist Garrett Hardin wrote an article in *Science* magazine that popularised Lloyd's work at a time when the modern environmental movement was taking shape. In the long term, the Murray–Darling Basin has become a test case of Forster's and Hardin's theory of the tragedy of the commons. The rush to take advantage of the opening up of the Basin was an early demonstration of the risks of putting short-term economic greed over long-term environmental sustainability.

3

THE GREAT WHITE LAND GRAB

In 1932, several country newspapers in the Murray–Darling Basin published an article headed 'Old Queensland Memories' written by an anonymous 'Old Timer' who had a shocking tale to tell about the murderous exploits in the late 1830s of Thomas Crampton, an ex-convict-turned-stockman who had a share on a squatter's property. The papers were most likely reprinting the memories of William John Best Gray, the oldest white inhabitant of the Darling Downs, who was in a position to recall the earliest days of white settlement. Written in a derring-do style of 'brave white man taking on the cattle-stealing savages', the republication of such early squatting experiences revived the history of frontier violence that, by the 1930s, had mostly succumbed to white historical amnesia. The writer wanted to explain why Aboriginal people in that part of the country had 'a rather bad name'. Reports of the spearing and killing of whites, he wrote, were almost a daily occurrence in the 1830s. Word began to pass from station to station and 'reprisals were discussed and ... foregatherings to carry them out'.

Enter Crampton. The Bigambul people were 'really frightened of him', according to Old Timer. He always carried a rifle and 'a brace of pistols', which he fired at will, 'shooting the blacks as he came upon them'. On one occasion in the late 1830s, he left his hut to take his daily ride through the herd and noticed some cattle missing. He rode to the nearest Bigambul camp where, he surmised, Aboriginal people were waiting for the cattle to come to the nearby lagoon to drink.

Dismounting from his horse, Crampton let fly a volley of bullets killing everyone in the camp – 20 people in all.[1] This was not the only incident involving Crampton and the local Bigambul people; he executed a reign of terror over them. In fact, Old Timer acknowledged that Crampton was 'regarded with especial terror by the blacks'.

The atrocities committed against the Bigambul were but a small episode of the frontier violence in the Murray–Darling Basin, which witnessed some of the bloodiest massacres in the nation's history. In fact, the Basin was the site of a determined war over land – a struggle between Aboriginal people to resist the invasion of whites and, conversely, the savage response from settlers to enforce the conquest of land for the pastoral industry that Sturt and Mitchell had so enthusiastically promoted.

The sheer scale of the adoption of pastoralism across the Basin – an area the size of Germany and France combined – has few parallels anywhere in the world. It was certainly greater than in any other British colony.[2]

Pastoralism – linked inextricably to British capitalism – shaped the speed with which Aboriginal people were dispossessed. The industry demanded vast areas for the burgeoning numbers of sheep bred to supply wool to the textile mills of Britain. As a consequence, write historians Beinart and Hughes, there were few other places in the British Empire where the Indigenous population was so systematically dispossessed and displaced.[3] By the late 1840s, whites had control of most of the Basin, a decade later in the Queensland part of the Basin; Sturt's first expedition had taken place only in 1829.

This process of dispossession occurred at such a rapid pace and over such a vast area because of the interplay of four critical developments: the sweep of smallpox (and other introduced diseases) down the Murray–Darling river system between the mid-1820s and late 1830s; the loss of Aboriginal access to traditional food supplies once the settlers moved in; the resort to mass violence by settlers, backed by the state, to enforce the seizure of land; and, lastly, the economic lure of the growing demand for wool from Britain which attracted unprecedented numbers of immigrants from Britain seeking their fortunes. The combination of these developments overwhelmed Aboriginal resistance, particularly as they faced technological disadvantages against European guns.

In the very same decades as the decimation of the Aboriginal population occurred, the pastoral industry fanned out across the Basin with flocks spreading over all available grasslands. The settlers, called by the colonial and British governments 'squatters' because they illegally occupied Crown land, blazed trails into the large areas of the Basin that neither Sturt nor Mitchell had been able to traverse. In their incessant search for more grasslands, they completed the opening up of the Basin.[4]

The smallpox epidemic

In early 1829, during his first expedition into western New South Wales, Sturt reached the Darling River, near the present town of Bourke, where he came across a group of 70 Aboriginal huts that looked to him to be permanently occupied. As he was assessing the scene, he was approached by an elderly Aboriginal man, an 'old chief', he later explained, who 'threw a melancholy glance upon them'. The reason for his distress soon became apparent; a great sickness had befallen the clan and it 'weighed heavily' on the old chief. Smallpox is an easily recognisable disease because of the permanent scaring to the skin of survivors. Yet Sturt himself had had no direct experience of smallpox and, therefore, he described what he saw in a non-specific way – an outbreak of 'a violent cutaneous [i.e. skin] disease'. It was likely, therefore, to have been smallpox, especially because its catastrophic effects were all too apparent. Sturt described the disease as having 'raged throughout the tribe … sweeping them off in great numbers'. Sturt thought that the few left were in a state of mourning.[5]

It is now well understood that smallpox and other introduced European diseases had a 'lethal history in Aboriginal Australia'.[6] Less well understood are its links to the rapid occupation of the Murray–Darling Basin.

The susceptibility of First Nations peoples to smallpox was witnessed within months of settlement in 1788. In April 1789, the Judge-Advocate and Secretary of the Colony, David Collins, wrote of its devastating toll. Anyone sailing around Sydney harbour 'reported, that they found … the bodies of many of the wretched natives of this country'. In the coves and bays there was not an Aboriginal person to be seen. It seemed as if, 'flying from the contagion, they had left the dead to bury the dead'.[7]

It is not surprising that Aboriginal people, with no immunity to smallpox, would be swept away in the numbers indicated by Collins. The disease – one of the most infectious known to humans – had wrought havoc among populations in the West Indies, Mexico and North and South America since European explorers carried it to the New World during the 16th century. Death rates of between 25 and 50 per cent were common.[8] Some claim the that figures for both the New World and Australia were likely much higher.[9]

Attempts to find out how Australia's Aboriginal population came to be infected have been dogged by debate and disagreement. In the early 1980s, economic historian Noel Butlin argued that the British released the disease deliberately in an act of extermination. Yet Butlin had little but conjecture for such a claim and later researchers, notably Judy Campbell, advanced the alternative theory: that Aboriginal contact with Indonesian fishermen along the far north coast of Australia introduced the disease to the continent and that it spread southwards in chains of Indigenous contacts.[10] However, others find this theory unconvincing because of the enormous distances involved and the thinly spread Aboriginal population.[11]

Whatever the epidemic's origins, Sturt's report of the likelihood of the disease in 1829 indicates that it was spreading in advance of the frontier.

On his return upstream, Sturt came across another large group of Aboriginal people, many of whom had the same 'violent cutaneous eruptions' all over their bodies. He noticed on this occasion, too, that they appeared few in number in comparison to their dwellings and concluded that the population had been thinned.[12]

Mitchell also witnessed the ravages of smallpox on his second expedition in 1835. He returned with alarming reports about the depopulation of the Darling Aboriginal nations. He found solid evidence of the destructiveness of the disease. Near Lake Poopelloe, out towards Wilcannia, Mitchell came across 'three large tombs of the natives'. These burial grounds were nearly two metres high, piled up with withered branches. Clearly moved by what he saw, Mitchell wrote that 'I could scarcely doubt, that these tombs covered the remains of that portion of the tribe, swept off by the fell disease, which had left such marks on those who survived'. He concluded that 'the population of the Darling seemed to have been much reduced by smallpox'.[13]

The first settlers in the Murray–Darling lands – the squatters, magistrates and the ministers of religion – picked up the story about the ravages of smallpox. In 1845, a number gave evidence to the New South Wales Legislative Council Select Committee on the Condition of the Aborigines. As two magistrates from Dungog explained to the Committee: 'About ten years ago an epidemic of a variolous nature [i.e. smallpox] carried off about half their number'.[14] From Scone, a Justice of the Peace reported that 'About ten or twelve years ago a great number were carried off by a disease resembling smallpox'.[15] In Bungonia, another JP reported that 'There are no aborigines permanently in this district; the tribe, a pretty numerous one ... has nearly disappeared'.[16] The Mulwarree nation had diminished by a third over the first ten years, according to information provided to the Committee.[17] At the same time, artist and naturalist George French Angas visited South Australia and reported that the epidemic had depopulated the banks of the Murray 'for more than a thousand miles'.[18]

Although smallpox spread more quickly along the river system, the epidemic also advanced inland. In South Australia, for example, it is known that the disease spread westwards from the Murray River to the nations of the Adelaide Plains, mid-north, and Yorke and Eyre Peninsulas. In New South Wales it spread eastwards to Dungog and northwards to the Darling Downs. To the early settlers of these regions, the pockmarked faces of survivors were the telling evidence of its visitation. In Dungog, for example, a Dr Mackinlay had visited the region in 1840, a few years after the disease raged through the district, and passed on his observations, which then became part of the knowledge of local settlers. He claimed smallpox so reduced Aboriginal numbers 'that the tribe was never afterwards able to recover'. According to Mackinlay, they had died 'in such heaps' that survivors left the dead unburied 'hoping to escape from the plague'.[19] Such a catastrophic fall in population must have had tragic consequences for the Basin's Aboriginal nations. It likely threw their communities into chaos. Permanent village sites were abandoned.

The loss of family and community, and the social, cultural and economic disruption, very likely resulted in what today would be termed a collective trauma for nations throughout the Murray–Darling. The mournful reaction of the elder Sturt encountered hints at this trauma, as does the insight of William Thomas, a local guardian of Aboriginal people in Victoria, who, in evidence to a Victorian parliamentary inquiry in 1858, acknowledged the trauma associated with colonisation:

> Their hunting grounds have been taken up by whites; their presence in large bodies is incompatible with the occupation of their country by whites; [and] they have usually only the lowest classes of the white to associate with.[20]

Such a sudden loss of population had another, often overlooked, impact. It placed Aboriginal people at a distinct disadvantage in resisting the European invaders. As David Dunlap, a Justice of the Peace from Wollombi, told the 1845 New South Wales Select Committee, 'They [Aboriginal people] are a peaceable people now, and too few in number to have fights on a grand scale'. And, it was easy to see why they were so powerless when he outlined the decimation of Aboriginal nations in his district on the Macdonald River. They comprised only twelve men, three women, and two boys when, in the early days of settlement 'this latter tribe ... exceeded three hundred'.

Lack of access to traditional foods

Exacerbating the effects of smallpox was the impact of pastoralism on reducing Aboriginal people's access to their traditional foods. This had been a source of conflict since the arrival of the British, but the changes wrought by pastoralism greatly worsened the problem. By 1840, squatters had established themselves in a continuous belt from Port Phillip in the south of the Murray–Darling Basin to the Darling Downs in the north.[21] Vast areas were claimed in this rush to grab land. One squatter, Edward Ogilvie, claimed 'a minor kingdom' of several hundred square kilometres with 90 kilometres of river frontage on the Upper Clarence River on which he erected a 40-room castle, lived like an English squire and founded a pastoral dynasty.[22] The number of sheep in the Basin ballooned as a consequence of the land grab by the likes of Ogilvie; by 1850 there were more than 12 million grazing in south-eastern Australia.[23]

The lack of access to traditional foods had a diabolical impact on Aboriginal people, and knowledge about this dribbled out in evidence to the 1845 New South Wales Legislative Select Committee on the Condition of the Aborigines. The Reverend William Schmidt explained what had happened. Aboriginal access to traditional foods, he said 'has diminished amongst these tribes in the immediate neighbourhood of whites; for instance the kangaroos, opossums, and birds have diminished, and also the roots upon which they partly subsisted.' Of the latter, he further explained, 'the stock spreading over districts, not only destroyed the roots, but prevented the natives from frequenting many places where the roots are growing'.[24]

Joseph Docker, a Justice of the Peace from Scone, noted the same problem in his district: he had observed a decline in the number of kangaroos because of 'the prevalence of stock feeding'.[25] This, he thought, forced Aboriginal people to become dependent on the supplies handed out to them by whites. In the New England district, observers noticed the same problem: Aboriginal people's 'ordinary means of subsistence must have diminished by a considerable extent [with] the introduction of five hundred thousand sheep into the original hunting grounds of the district'.[26]

In some instances, access to water was cut off by pastoralists. In other cases, drought dried out much of the landscape, threatening the survival of many Aboriginal people. Yet rivers were 'drained to the bottom by flocks of sheep and herds of cattle'.[27]

Dispossession also affected Aboriginal aquaculture – an important source of food made available through a series of fish traps that were built and operated along the rivers and tributaries of the Murray–Darling. These traps are examples of elaborate Aboriginal technology and are thought to be among humankind's earliest constructions.[28] Fish were so plentiful that it is thought that they fed thousands of people in various parts of the Basin. However, the fish traps – along with other Aboriginal fishing techniques – fell into disuse once the pastoral invasion drove Aboriginal people from their land.[29]

The restrictions on Aboriginal access to traditional foods were among the earliest signs of the environmental changes brought on by the rapid uptake of pastoralism, and discussed in more detail in chapter 5. As Aboriginal people survived by living in a sustainable way, any alteration to the ecosystem was going to heavily affect them.

GA Robinson, the Chief Protector of Aborigines in the Port Phillip District, told the 1845 New South Wales inquiry that white settlers were indifferent to the environmental damage they were causing, noting that Aboriginal means of subsistence had 'diminished greatly' since European occupation because of the settlers' 'wanton destruction of forest animals' and the grazing of stock which had 'rendered edible roots exceedingly scarce'.[30]

Robinson was the first person to be appointed in the role to protect Aboriginal people from further depredations by whites following a recommendation by the British government. But protection didn't equate to defending the rights of Aboriginal people. In fact, Robinson had had a problematic relationship as the self-appointed 'saviour' of the last of Tasmania's full-blood Aboriginal people. He oversaw their tragic passing away in exile on Flinders Island.[31] Thus, he likely had a troubled conscience when he was harshly critical that Aboriginal people 'were being shut out of their own lands' and, consequently, their traditional sources of food had become 'precarious'.[32]

Adverse environmental changes associated with pastoralism were noted a few years later in the course of a 1858–59 Victorian parliamentary inquiry into the Condition of Aborigines. Witnesses observed that whites had affected the health of the Murray River: 'the fish have been disturbed by steamers, and the snag boat in particular has removed many old logs which were favourite spots with the fish … Wild fowl are more shy since guns have been used. Snakes and reptiles are much scarcer … Neither kangaroo nor emu is to be seen within many miles'.[33] Another noted that the lack of access to traditional foods had forced many Aboriginal people into living a 'gipsy-like life, moving in small parties from station to station [because of the] … chances of obtaining food from settlers'.[34]

The declining birth rate was another issue. The diseases mentioned above affected the young more than the elderly, causing a decline in the number of people of childbearing age. Scattered references to this fact emerged in the course of the 1845 New South Wales Select Committee where it was reported in cold language, that the steep decline in population was exacerbated by the fact that 'there are very few children born to supply the waste'. Victorian Aboriginal people were quoted as stating that there was no point having children as the Europeans had taken all the land,[35] an observation supported by William Thomas. In evidence to the 1845 New South Wales Select Committee he reported that Aboriginal people of the 'Yarra and Western Port Tribes' had an 'indifference to prolong their races', on the ground, as they state, 'Of having no country they can call their own'.[36]

The war of resistance

For the best part of a decade, Aboriginal people across the Murray–Darling Basin waged a war of survival. They did so along a moving frontier that was a complicated and confounding place, at once anarchic and lawless, but where a few squatters and Aboriginal people could find ways to accommodate each other.

In some parts of the Basin, groups of Aboriginal warriors inflicted real damage to pastoral operations. Jacob Lowe, a squatter who came to the Macintyre River in southern Queensland, told an 1861 Queensland Legislative Assembly inquiry that, in the mid-1840s, settlers in the region 'were all driven away by force from their stations, and when I came up … I was only taking up runs from which the settlers had been driven by the natives, and which had been abandoned'.[37]

This was not an isolated example of the disruption to squatters' operations by Aboriginal raids. Alexander Patterson, the first Commissioner of Crown Lands for the Liverpool Plains, explained that settlers were deserting their runs and cattle due to the 'daring' and overwhelming number of raids by Aboriginal people.[38]

And in the lower Murray region, attacks 'of a very serious character' were carried out on newly established sheep stations. Francis Flanagan JP told the 1845 New South Wales Select Committee that several squatters in his district had to flee in fear of their lives and lost substantial numbers of sheep and cattle from Aboriginal attack; the attackers, said Flanagan, were 'in a state of great excitement'.[39]

In a number of cases the size of squatters' stock and property losses from Aboriginal raids could exceed $1 million in today's money. These losses were all the more damaging because most pastoralists had all their capital tied up in their stock.[40]

Members of the Barkindji nation succeeded in severely disrupting overlanders – drovers who moved herds of cattle and sheep from Sydney to Adelaide in the newly established colony of South Australia. Using Mitchell's detailed maps, the route became so well travelled that it compacted into a permanent track. Charles Sturt led one of these expeditions and, with his previous experience, he could see that overlanding was regarded by Indigenous groups as an invasion.[41]

Few overland parties escaped unscathed from the raids by the Barkindji, who were 'thoroughly roused all along the Murray'.[42] Overland parties were spooked by their ability to stealthily follow them, to watch and wait, hiding in scrub and then to mount surprise ambushes.[43] Open conflict broke out along the trail with Aboriginal people frequently shot and many killed and wounded.[44] Tensions came to a head with the massacre of Aboriginal people at Rufus River in August 1841. Subsequently, Governor Grey acceded to calls for the overland route to be brought under control.

All around the Murray–Darling pastoral districts, Aboriginal people fought a bitter campaign against white invaders such as the ones described above. Short-lived victories though they may have been, historians have had difficulty explaining such actions in military terms. Were Aboriginal nations engaged in warfare, something less organised or merely revenge raids? Historians have to rely on scattered information from Europeans sources – journals, diaries, newspaper articles and official inquiries. We have to imagine how Aboriginal people, who likely heard about the white man's capacity for killing through trading networks, perceived the wave of new settlers.[45]

The term 'frontier wars' is commonly used today mainly to describe the systematic violent actions white settlers waged against Aboriginal people. But the term 'war' can be equally applied to both sides. Historian Arthur Laurie[46] is credited with the first use of the term 'black war' in 1958 to describe the fierce response of Queensland Aboriginal people to the expansion of the pastoral frontier on the Darling Downs from the 1840s. Between 1840 and 1850, southern Queensland's Aboriginal population of between 3000 and 8000 outnumbered the fewer than 2000 white inhabitants, and consequently were in a strong position to inflict harm on the early squatters.

Evidence from across the Basin shows that Aboriginal people deployed a range of tactical measures to resist white settlers. These included cooperation among clans and nations; forcing settlers to abandon their properties; widespread slaughter and diversion of livestock; ransacking and emptying settlers' food stores; destruction of crops; cutting settlers' supply lines by attacking drays carrying supplies; picking off isolated settlers to create a state of fear; and deploying guerrilla-style raids to ambush settlers.[47]

Aboriginal leaders played a crucial role in organising and perpetrating sabotage against whites. Historian Bob Reece highlights the role played by the military leadership of a Mandandanji elder on the Darling Downs in the 1840s variously referred to as 'Possum Murray', 'Eaglehawk', 'Old Billy' and 'Bussamarai'. A commanding figure, he held 'sway over large regions where he was able to unite the Bigambul and two or three other groups with the Mandandanji in concerted efforts to drive out the whites, sometimes involving pitched battles with the Native Police'.[48]

What was the purpose behind these various military-style tactics? How did Aboriginal nations see their options? In his ground-breaking study of frontier violence, historian Henry Reynolds argued that Aboriginal people were motivated by political as well as economic reasons, 'to make whites share their goods'.[49] Others have speculated on deeper economic and political motives. 'Was it an attempt to beat the squatters at their own game,' asks historian Ray Kerkhove of Aboriginal resistance, 'by wresting the pastoral industry out of their hands?'[50] There is unlikely to be a definitive answer to his question, but the massive retaliation unleashed by squatters, discussed below, suggests they held genuine fears about the ability of Aboriginal people to threaten their interests. And Kerkhove poses another reason why the Aboriginal war of resistance has been overlooked as a military campaign: it wasn't intended to maximise the deaths of whites; rather, the aim was to undermine the pastoral economic model.

The war of extermination

When does war become genocide? An often bitter contemporary debate between historians and conservative commentators has surrounded the extent and nature of the murder of Aboriginal people on Australia's colonial frontier.[51] And the Murray–Darling Basin has been in the forefront of this debate.

Myall Creek, lying between Moree and Glen Innes in the northern part of the Murray–Darling Basin, is the site of one of Australia's most notorious massacres of Aboriginal people. Even though it has become one of the best known on the pastoral frontier, its details still have the power to shock. On 10 June 1838, 11 armed stockmen led by a young settler, John Fleming, who stood out with his commanding build and ruddy complexion, rode into Henry Dangar's cattle station in the traditional country of the Wirrayaraay people. They had planned a mass murder of the small party of 30 or so Wirrayaraay, comprising old men, women and children, living peacefully on the property. When the Wirrayaraay heard the sound of horses galloping at full speed and the shouting of men they took refuge in a nearby hut.

Fleming and his men tied up the Wirrayaraay, leaving one woman and four or five children. The intruders slaughtered 28 of them – shot or knifed, or speared with Fleming's sword, in a frenzy of violence. On the night of the rampage, Fleming and his men camped at a nearby creek and took it in turns to rape the Aboriginal woman they had abducted from the camp. The next day the murderous party returned to the scene of the carnage and burned the bodies, then scoured the surrounding bush for the remainder of the group – thought to number between ten and twelve – who had been in the bush at the time of the massacre and who were never heard from again. Later, the white perpetrators (with the exception of Fleming) were arrested, charged, convicted and hanged, making the Myall Creek massacre unique among mass killings of Aboriginal people.

The point in recalling a brief account of Myall Creek in this context is the role massacres played in appropriating the Murray–Darling for the pastoral industry. As historian Richard Broome reminds us, 'massacre' is not always the appropriate term as some mass killings resulted from battles in which one side (almost always the Aboriginal side) suffered the heavier casualties.[52] Nonetheless, the term has gained wide currency, and, as historian Professor Lyndall Ryan has argued, in each of the colonies, 'massacre was the defining strategy in the conquest of Aboriginal people'.[53] As she further points out, unprovoked attacks of the sort Fleming and his men perpetrated on the Wirrayaraay were not uncommon. In Victoria (formerly the Port Phillip District), Ryan found that most of the massacres were carried out in broad daylight by armed stockmen and settlers on horseback, in some cases supported by detachments of mounted and/or native police under the direction of white officers: 'Of the 68 incidents of massacre that I was able to identify, 24 were in reprisal for the killing of settlers, 24 for the killing of livestock, and the remaining 20 were pre-emptive strikes or unprovoked without any clear evidence of motive'.[54]

In the wake of Myall Creek, massacres followed the frontier of the pastoral industry as it headed into the northern regions of the Basin in the 1840s and east to Moreton Bay. Although the extent of collective violence perpetrated on the frontier was enveloped in a code of silence, euphemisms, denials and coverups,[55] contemporary official accounts still bristle with graphic descriptions of its deployment. Thus, Richard Bligh, the local Crown Lands Commissioner, noted of the conflict on the Liverpool Plains that a 'system of terrorism' and murder, exacted by whites, was well known to everyone and kept quiet.[56]

And, according to Ryan's research, the same blood-stained pattern occurred in the 1840s, as it had a decade earlier further south: 'As in the 1830s, the assassins usually comprised groups of heavily armed stockmen on horseback under the command of a settler'.[57] The violence that rampaged through the grassy, undulating country of the northern Basin had deadly consequences:

> The rush of squatters and their servants from the Liverpool Plains
> and the Darling Downs after 1847 quickly dispossessed and
> depopulated the Bigambul, Mandandanji and other Indigenous
> groups by sheer force of arms and with great bloodshed …
> the Liverpool Plains and then the Maranoa became one big
> battleground.[58]

Accounting for the extent of this violence was a major problem for historians until Lyndall Ryan and her team at the University of Newcastle's Centre for Humanities compiled a database in the early 21st century. For the purposes of the project, a massacre is defined as an incident involving the deaths of at least six protagonists, black or white.

Professor Ryan described the work of compiling the database as 'very confronting … [W]e find we have to walk away from it quite often. You put all those together and you get a very distressing story'.[59] The *Guardian* newspaper converted this data into an interactive map showing the location of massacre sites across the country.[60] A heavy concentration can be seen in the Murray–Darling Basin.

This data has limitations, though. It is not designed to take account of the sporadic deaths of smaller numbers of both whites and Aboriginal people – both of which would lift the figures significantly. And new sites of massacres are being added as material is discovered.

Massacres of Aboriginal people served two tactical purposes in the conquest for the Murray–Darling Basin (and beyond). They depleted the numbers of already vulnerable clans, making their survival more precarious, and they also constituted an 'organised form of colonial terror on the frontier' aimed at driving Aboriginal people out of a particular region. Settlers referred to the tactic as 'the drive' or 'bushwack'.[61] In the broader story of European colonialism, the use of such terrorist acts, often sponsored by governments, has a history extending back to the Spanish conquest of the New World and the British organisation of the transatlantic slave trade.[62]

The state and massacres on the pastoral frontier

Enlisting the help of the state was crucial in quelling Aboriginal raids across the pastoral frontier of the Murray–Darling Basin. In 1838, for example, the New South Wales colonial administration sent out a large expedition of troopers to the Gwydir River pastoral region because, over the previous year, local Aboriginal people had gained the upper hand in their conflict with squatters. The guerrilla-style tactics were described in 1839 by one squatter in an article in a Sydney newspaper:

> So nimble are these Aborigines so well acquainted are they
> with every thicket, reedy creek, morass, cave, and hollow tree,
> in which they can secret themselves, and so inaccessible to a
> horse or any white man are those rocky mountains to which the
> blacks generally betake themselves on being pursued, and from
> the summit of which they can unperceived take a deadly aim at

their pursuers, that it is sheer nonsense to talk of apprehending them. You must either shoot a few of them by way of example, or you must abandon the country altogether. There seems to be no alternative.[63]

Stockmen and vigilantes joined the troopers and together they massacred between 200 and 300 Gamilaraay people at Waterloo Creek, south-west of Moree over a three-day orgy of violence between December 1837 and January 1838. Allegations were raised that the troopers and vigilantes had used disproportionate force by killing people who posed no risk to anybody.[64]

Charles Sturt's expeditionary prowess was again deployed in an attempt to quell fears about the lack of safety for inland travellers, especially for women. In 1839, he set out on a five weeks' tour of the lower reaches of the Murray River. Included in the travelling party were three women – thought to be the first white women to journey on the river. The inclusion of Sturt's wife, Charlotte, his 15-year-old daughter Julia and a maid servant, 18-year-old Eliza Arbuckle, were meant to send the message that it was safe for women to journey into the new pastoral frontier.

The Aboriginal nations of the Basin were increasingly forced to defend their land under the all-conquering intentions of the first wave of settlers. The expeditionary force sent out by Governor George Grey in South Australia in 1841, to bring the overland route under control, also engaged in a blood-thirsty spree of murder. The force was led, ironically, by Matthew Moorehouse, the Protector of Aborigines, and his deputy, and among whose party were expert marksmen. The aim of the force was to quash the rebellious Barkindji who, even though they put up a 'stout fight', were gunned down in a volley of bullets in numbers thought to be far greater than the reported 30 killed. Aboriginal bodies lay heaped on the ground and strewn among the reeds of the river bank.[65]

In Queensland, the relationship between settlers and the state in the murder of Aboriginal people was even more systematically developed than in the southern parts of the Basin. The tradition of violence migrated north with settlers.[66] Originally created in New South Wales, the Native Police force, which comprised Aboriginal troopers under the command of white officers, patrolled the expanding Queensland pastoral frontier and operated as a well-organised military force with the specific purpose, according to historian Jonathan Richards, 'to suppress Indigenous resistance to colonisation'.[67] Native Police posts opened and closed with the shifting frontier in the same way that army posts did in other colonial wars.

Reprisal killings

As horrific as pre-emptive attacks were, reprisal killings of Aboriginal people were no less devastating because they were often undertaken on a scale out of all proportion to the damage inflicted by Aboriginal warriors. One of the most notorious examples occurred in 1842 on Kilcoy Station, about 100 kilometres north-west of Brisbane on the eastern edge of the Basin. Captain John Coley gave an account of what happened. 'For want of police protection', he told the Queensland Legislative Assembly Committee, 'the settlers had to protect themselves, and their retaliation was very severe'. He shamelessly went on to explain that in one incident on Kilcoy hundreds of traditional owners were 'destroyed' for the murder of two white men. Asked in what way the Aboriginal people were destroyed, Coley replied, by shooting and poisoning them, the latter method using strychnine and arsenic in the flour.[68]

Poisoning by ordinary settlers was apparently common in both the New South Wales and Queensland sections of the Basin[69] as was the willingness of such people to join vigilante groups 'which roamed the [Darling] Downs hunting Aborigines'.[70] The effect of such reprisal killings was part of the system of terror that brought the pastoral frontier under the control of whites. As one squatter explained as early as the 1840s, Aboriginal people in the Western District of Victoria no longer dared to mount attacks 'because they understand the system of reprisals'.[71]

Thus, whites on the pastoral frontier had been turned into mass murderers and the frontier was sufficiently anarchic to enable them to feel they could act with impunity. Such widespread acts of murder would, today, constitute a form of collective violence – violence that is carried out on behalf of one's group – the likes of which have a long and tragic history in human affairs.[72]

Pastoralism: Mass murder and terror

The literature on collective violence has much to offer a study of frontier violence in Australia, even though there have been few attempts to link Australia's frontier violence to this instructive literature.[73] It confirms the well-established link between the dehumanisation of marginalised groups and the violence that is sometimes perpetrated against them.

According to philosopher David Livingstone Smith in his book, *Less Than Human*, dehumanisation plays a crucial role in all forms of collective violence. It does so, he argues, because it acts as a powerful psychological driver operating in a process that dissolves inhibition, plays on deep cultural fears, strips the humanity from target groups and, in rendering them as subhumans, paves the way for atrocities. Racism has been one of the key drivers of dehumanisation throughout history; in fact, Smith argues that 'the concept of race is the place where the psychological, cultural, and ultimately the biological dimensions of dehumanisation all converge'.[74] The dehumanisation of Australia's Aboriginal population is testimony to this claim. Books on Australian history are littered with examples of British colonial racism and the depiction of Aboriginal people as subhuman 'savages'.[75] Both Sturt and Mitchell were perpetrators of this long and destructive tradition.

The view that Aboriginal people were 'savage', 'brutish' and, therefore, subhuman fostered widespread 'eliminationist' thinking among European settlers. Examples abound. George Carrington, an early squatter on the Macintyre River, recalled in his memoirs, written in the early 1870s, the mindset of the early white settlers in relation to Aboriginal people. He felt no shame in saying that nothing but the total elimination of Aboriginal people would have satisfied whites:

> Therefore, says the white man, in his superiority of strength and knowledge, away with them, disperse them, shoot and poison them, until there is nothing remaining; we will destroy them, their wives and little ones, and all that they have, and we will go in and possess the land.[76]

Of course, thinking that Aboriginal people should be eliminated doesn't equate with official policy nor does it mean widespread individual involvement in collective violence. However, testimonies from white settlers suggest that the prevalence of eliminationist thinking reinforced and justified those who decided to participate in mass killings. The actual number of participants will never be known, but Charles White, an early Queensland settler, confessed years later in a newspaper article that he was a 'white murderer' for his participation in dispersing [frontier euphemism for killing] Aboriginal people. Describing the Native Police Force as 'an exterminating Force', he regretted that their work was 'not more thoroughly done … we must go the whole length, and say that the sooner we clear the weak useless race away the better'.[77]

The appeal to squatters' 'natural' property rights acted as a powerful driver for the mass murder of Aboriginal people. Neil Black, a Scottish immigrant and aspiring squatter in western Victoria, acknowledged as much in his 1839 diary:

The best way [to acquire land] is to go outside and take up a new run, provided the conscience of the party is sufficiently seared to enable him without remorse to slaughter natives right and left. It is universally and distinctly understood that the chances are very small indeed of a person taking up a new run being able to maintain possession of his place and property without having recourse to such means.[78]

Black, a staunch Presbyterian, was aghast at the 'moral wilderness' of frontier life; the casualness with which 'gentleman' squatters – people from colonial elite circles – discussed slaughtering First Nations peoples in the pursuit of riches. He was disgusted by the culture of bragging and bravado, alongside the heavy drinking, that infused their social interactions.[79] Black spared his conscience by purchasing an established squatter's run where the slaughter of Aboriginal people had already occurred.

But in the 'moral wilderness' of the frontier, gentleman squatters searching for easy riches weren't the only group primed to potential violence against the traditional owners. Their convict shepherds and emancipated convicts-turned-stockmen actively participated in the murder of Aboriginal people. Many had been brutalised by the Empire and its lacerating punishment regime of the lash. Some of these damaged men were employed as shepherds in isolated locations where they became the targets of Aboriginal raids; fear played on their minds.[80] They responded with a trigger-happy attitude to any Aboriginal people who came within firing range of their huts.

Convict shepherds were both perpetrators and hapless victims of frontier violence, unlike squatters who, as Black insisted, were opportunists bent on acquiring riches. Historians agree. The squatters, writes David Cahir, 'were undertaking a risky land grab for purely pecuniary purposes'.[81] It's not surprising, therefore, that they rejected any claim Aboriginal people had to their land.

Wealthy squatters were hungry to grab as much land as they

could, while immigrant squatters, pouring in from overpopulated Britain, where all cultivated land was already allocated, were casting about for land and fortune. After surviving the rigours of a long sea voyage, they were in no mood to place the needs of 'wandering black savages' above their own.[82]

Squatters were, by necessity, rugged individuals, and their determination to protect what they perceived was theirs by force, if necessary, was a function of the extreme struggles many endured. In 1847, one squatter wrote to the press and described the toughness it took to succeed:

> At last, after days-weeks of toil and trouble, after enduring gnawing hunger and parching thirst, sleepless nights and anxious days, after frequent disappointments and perilous adventures by flood and field, adventures with the natives and misadventures with his nag, the object of his idolatry is discovered.[83]

It is not surprising that squatters were prepared for a clash with the traditional owners over land. Violence was inevitable because competition over resources is recognised as the root of intragroup conflict.[84] Neil Black saw this process at work. He couldn't countenance, he wrote, 'the prospect of having to kill for gentlemanly prosperity' that he witnessed all around him in western Victoria.[85] Because squatters had obtained their land for free, David Cahir writes that they were aware of their precarious legal position and were keen to shore up all possible credibility as legal landholders.[86] This they achieved in part with the introduction of a leasing system in 1843. Even so, their continued occupation of Crown land amounted to 'cheap pasturage'.[87] And it wasn't just squatters with a vested interest in maintaining sole rights to Aboriginal land. A system of settler capitalism – discussed in the next chapter – quickly grew around the land grab: governments were keen to attract capital to develop the pastoral industry, and colonial and British banks were keen to respond such that, together, all had a strong stake in maintaining white occupancy of land through violent means.[88]

It is important to note, too, that not all squatters in all regions of the Basin took an aggressive stand against Aboriginal people. Around western Victoria, which Black wrote about, some wealthy squatters took a conciliatory approach towards Aboriginal people and, in some cases, allowed groups access to their properties. Some of the Wathawurrung brokered working relationships with whites and were valued by them.[89] Other squatters saw the value of allowing Aboriginal people access to their traditional land, with the offer of rations, as a means of 'keeping an eye on the untamed savages'.[90] Still others appeared to have significant intercultural relationships with Aboriginal people on their sheep runs.[91]

While such negotiated relationships are a part of frontier history, they were still predicated upon the dispossession of Aboriginal lands. What motivated some Aboriginal people towards conciliation is difficult to ascertain, but, as one study showed, they waxed and waned in their attitudes towards cooperation with settlers.[92] The squatters saw these conciliatory approaches as a departure from the customary way of dealing with Aboriginal raids, described by one as 'to shoot blacks and drive the others off the run'.[93]

The ready resort to violence had moral justification in the minds of most colonials. Theirs was a calling to establish 'a higher civilisation' throughout Australia's interior; Sturt and Mitchell had proclaimed this ideal as part of their justification for promoting the appropriation of the Murray–Darling lands. It was a view widely held by others. The South Australian Legislative Councillors investigating 'The Aborigines' in 1860 asked the Commissioner for Crown Lands, JT Bagot, whether all Aboriginal people should be dispossessed. Bagot thought the answer so self-evident that he simply replied, 'Wild men coming into contact with civilized men die away'.[94]

The combination of racism, greed, perceived exclusive rights to property and appeals to cultural chauvinism swirled around the frontier like a continual dust storm, creating a diffuse but deadly ideological atmosphere justifying the widespread mass murder of Aboriginal people. Killing for a cause has been another powerful motivator for collective violence, as any student of history knows.[95]

And we can't remove entirely the role of individual personality in the perpetration of collective violence on Australia's pastoral frontier. The problem is a complex one to explain. 'Ordinary' people committing violence for political ends are not normally regarded as psychopaths, who derive personal pleasure from killing.[96] Yet the existence of psychopathic tendencies among some of the mass murderers of Aboriginal people is not easily explained away. Thomas Crampton's sadistic exploits discussed at the beginning of this chapter come to mind, as does the manner in which John Fleming perpetrated the Myall Creek massacre.

Fleming appeared to have been socialised into violence. This made the pursuit of his goal to drive Aboriginal people from his pastoral holdings all the more potent. As thorough research into his background has shown[97], Fleming was the son of a violent and lawless father who grew up on the first colonial frontier, the rich farmland of the Hawkesbury River just west of Sydney where the conflict between white settlers and the local Darug Aboriginal nation was endemic. He appeared to carry the 'dark side' of the early settler tradition for racial conflict when he went on to manage a family property in the Gwydir River region. Leading up to the atrocity at Myall Creek, Fleming had boasted of participating in recent killings of Aboriginal people on the Gwydir, and his actions at Myall Creek had a sadistic quality. He didn't only murder innocent members of the Wirrayaraay, he also raped one woman and, seemingly without remorse, left his colleagues, over whom he had exercised authoritarian control, to face their fate.[98]

It is impossible to determine how many of those who participated in the mass murder of Aboriginal people on Australia's pastoral frontier were as heavily invested in the idea of violence as was Fleming. Rape of Aboriginal women on the frontier was certainly common and perpetrated with exceptional brutality.[99]

As Black noted, frontier life in the 1830s and 1840s was a male-dominated culture characterised by heavy drinking and macho-bravado. In addition, both pre-emptive and reprisal raids used disproportionate force. But, ultimately, we have no way of assessing the psychological attachment of squatters and their workforce to indiscriminate violence as an end and not just as a means. Nevertheless, individual cases such as those of Crampton and Fleming are reminders of the complexity of this link. As David Livingstone Smith tersely reminds us, man 'is a cruel animal'.

For the combination of reasons discussed, it was easy enough for squatters to recruit parties to engage in the mass murder of Aboriginal people. In 1839, William Thomas, a landholder on the Campsie Plains in northern Victoria, noted in his journal that if he went in search of men merely to 'pacify' members of the local Daungwurrung nation, 'I should not be able to get a single man to accompany me'. However, if he made it known his intention was to 'to exterminate them', he'd have at least 30 men from the surrounding district 'who would willingly volunteer in the service'.[100]

In these various ways, violence was normalised across the pastoral frontier until Aboriginal resistance was quashed in each district. A settler who gave evidence to the 1858–59 Victorian Select Committee explained that pastoralists were 'well aware that they can only maintain a superiority in conflict by means of fire-arms'.[101]

Consequences

Not surprisingly, the 'Aboriginal Wars' were accompanied by a further decline in the population of many Murray–Darling Aboriginal groups. George Mason, the Sub Protector of Aborigines in South Australia, for example, told the 1860 Select Committee on 'The

Aborigines' about the tragic plight of 'Murray natives'. For 30 miles (about 50 kilometres) up the river from Adelaide, he said, there were only four living blacks; 'their friends were all dead, and the settlement broken up'.[102]

In the Mount Franklin region, north-west of Ballarat, the local Protector of Aborigines offered the alarming assessment in 1845 of the near total decimation of some groups: 'Some are almost extinct, having one family member left; others include from twenty to thirty individuals'.[103]

And down near the mouth of the Murray, the 'Coorong tribe [Ngarrindjeri] have been very largely reduced in numbers during the last ten or fifteen years', according to evidence to the same committee.[104] These are small, regional examples of a larger catastrophe. In Victoria, for example, the estimated pre-contact population of about 10 000 fell to 1907 in the two decades to 1853.[105]

In response to this decimation, each of the colonial governments reviewed the condition of Aboriginal people; inquiries were held between 1845 and 1861. In the Basin, the frontier wars were effectively over, although they continued to be waged across northern Australia. These committees attempted to shift the focus from dispossession to measures to 'protect' surviving populations. However, some witnesses revealed their first-hand impressions on the extent of the decimation and demoralisation among the Aboriginal populations. A few lone white voices could see the plight of Aboriginal people as the vanquished race. 'They cry out that the whites have taken away their land', one witness told the 1858–59 Victorian inquiry.[106]

Counting the dead

Numbers matter when counting war dead, especially in colonial wars that become the subject of bitter historical disputes, as has occurred in Australia's 'history wars'. Based on the research of Henry Reynolds in the early 1980s, the figure of 20 000 Indigenous and 2000 white deaths across the continent had, for several decades, become the consensus among historians. Reynolds was conscious that the publication of the estimates would be contentious: 'At the time I felt that it was risky to put a figure on it because I anticipated that others – historians, but particularly the culture warriors – would heavily criticise me for that. I thought it was going out on a limb'.[107]

However, as new research has been undertaken, the consensus figure is being challenged as far too conservative. Respected researchers of frontier violence, Raymond Evans and Robert Orsted-Jensen,[108] have compiled a figure in excess of 60 000 Aboriginal deaths in Queensland alone, a number equivalent to the deaths of Australian soldiers in World War One. In other words, as a nation we have only begun to understand the full impact of frontier violence on the Aboriginal population.

Whether or not smallpox and other introduced diseases killed more Aboriginal people in the Murray–Darling Basin than the frontier violence, it was the latter that sealed their fate as a dispossessed people.

No known records exist of any of the Aboriginal survivors of the frontier massacres. However, in 1899, the death of an Aboriginal woman named Biddy, one of the survivors of the Myall Creek massacre, was announced by the New South Wales Aboriginal Protection Board. A few sparse details were given in the press:

> The aboriginal Biddy must have been the little black girl left
> behind with two black gins, two boys, and two black-fellows, at
> the huts [at Myall Creek Station]. The aboriginal Biddy, whose
> death was reported to the Aborigines Board at its last meeting, was
> aged 70, and must have been about 10 years old at the time of the
> massacre. She was for some years in receipt of Government relief.[109]

The publication of such examples now, and in the past, revive Aboriginal people's painful memories of the burdens borne by their ancestors because of colonisation.[110]

The purpose in revisiting this history of violence has been two-fold. Reconciliation, and the broader need for 'truth-telling', remain unfinished business in Australia. The recognition of Aboriginal rights to the land and water of the Murray–Darling Basin itself remains part of this unfinished project. Aboriginal people continue to be marginalised from decision-making in the Basin. And government policy moves at glacial speed to change this dynamic. In short, Australians have done little to confront the violent manner in which the foundation of the nation's wealth was obtained and its tragic ongoing legacy.

Now, having won their war, how would the white settlers tame the land for their own purposes?

4

RICHES AND RUIN:
THE DREAMS OF
SQUATTERS AND SELECTORS

In 1885, one of the early inhabitants of Echuca wrote an article for the press reflecting on the town's progress since it was established in 1855.[1] He recalled standing on the banks of the Murray River as a boy when Hopwood's Hotel and a few shanties were all that existed in the town. The banks of the river were densely covered in timber and silence reigned supreme save 'now and again for the cooey of the blackfellow'. The arrival of the steamer drew everyone within earshot, and the appearance of the occasional sheep and cattle drovers and shearers brought the only life to the town. They 'knocked down their cheques' at the Hopwood Hotel and held 'high carnival for a few days'.

Twenty-five years on from his boyhood days, so the correspondent wrote, the 'mighty river' with its 'majestic grandeur' still swept peacefully to the ocean, but otherwise everything had changed. The forests 'have been felled'; 'the corroborea [sic] of the blackfellow ... has ceased'; the 'hum hum' of machinery filled the air; and 'smiling farms cover the land'. Echuca's population of 6000 inhabitants supported 'public halls, schools, shops, hotels and numerous private residences, all of a substantial character'. The progress made, commented the correspondent, was a 'credit on the [white] race'.

Nothing could have expressed more powerfully the realisation of the vision that Sturt and Mitchell promoted for the Murray–Darling Basin. Here was a town brimming with the benefits of British civilisation, fulfilling the economic potential of pastoralism and where Aboriginal people and the environment were pushed aside for the interests of whites. A similar story could be found throughout the Basin's burgeoning township populations.

However, the process of establishment of European settlement in the Basin proved far more complicated than Sturt and Mitchell envisaged. Who had a right to this land with the potential for such riches to be made? For the first two decades after occupation by Europeans, squatters claimed exclusive right to the Basin. The pastoral empires they established formed the backbone of the Australian economy for decades to come.

Yet, handing such a vast landmass to a few hundred powerful people was never likely to go unchallenged. A new nation-building project emerged: small, independent farmers toiling to build an agrarian society. In the battle of who owned the lands and waters of the Murray–Darling Basin, Aboriginal people, of course, weren't considered, but sharp conflicts existed between the two rival nation-building projects. Embedded in them was a conflict over class: wealth for the few or opportunity for the many. While these visons played out, little noticed were the far-reaching environmental changes that swept across the Basin's landscape.

Pastoralism

Pastoralism was Australia's first nation-building project. The Murray–Darling Basin was transformed into a vast sheep run in the furtherance of developing colonial Australia's most profitable export commodity. As the *Sydney Morning Herald* commented in 1855, prior to the discovery of gold in Victoria in the early 1850s, 'the pastoral settlers were our only great producing class'.[2] In fact, for a century, wool underpinned Australia's living standards, which were among the highest in the world. But the wealth of the industry was concentrated in relatively few hands. As historians Beinart and Hughes write: 'even in the case of the Americas, it is difficult to find a comparable example of frontier expansion in which so few people rapidly assumed control of such immense tracts'.[3] These wealthy few, of course, were the infamous squatters.

The squatters may have had a tough time establishing their runs, as briefly discussed in chapter 3, but their golden age began from mid-century. As one colonial newspaper reminded its readers, it took extraordinary largesse from the public purse to establish the nation's first export industry: free labour in the form of convict servants who worked as 'slaves without wages'. When this system was stopped, governments supplied immigrant labour paid for 'by nearly every man in the colony'. In short, 'what have the squatters received from government, but a succession of favours'.[4]

By 1849, the colonies had become the dominant supplier of wool to Britain.[5] Charles Sturt had predicted this, but even he must have been surprised by the speed with which the Murray–Darling Basin was converted from native vegetation into pasture for millions of sheep. New techniques in the textile trade, along with fine wool – the type Australia specialised in – paved the way for the development of finer clothes that appealed to expensive tastes.[6] Allied to this was the rise in purchasing power of a larger, more affluent British population.[7]

Australian conditions favoured the rapid growth of the industry. Apart from the land being essentially free, the capital costs to gain an initial foothold in the industry were not especially high, even though they were beyond the means of emancipists and most of the colonial born.[8] Pastoralism was the spur that led to self-government for the new colonies of Victoria in 1851 and Queensland in 1859.

Banks were eager participants in the pastoral bonanza. In fact, much of the banks' business consisted of lending to squatters. And why wouldn't banks want to lend to squatters who boasted of 'landed estates larger than whole English counties?'[9] As silent partners in the industry, banks reaped 'magnificent dividends' out of public lands.[10] This was 'settler capitalism' at its most basic. Between them, the squatters and the banks had, for many years, the land 'almost on their own terms'.[11] This coalition of interests made pastoralism politically powerful, a power that was exercised 'to reap their share of the plunder', as one colonial newspaper wrote.[12]

And squatters continued to enjoy the ongoing protection of government to ensure that dispossessed traditional owners did not impede the uptake of pastoral properties.[13] When, for example, in the early 1850s, Commandant Frederick Walker established a post of the Native Police on the Macintyre River, his primary aim was in 'checking the aggression of the aboriginal natives'.[14]

If large estates, easy money, a vibrant wool market and police protection were not sufficient advantages to propel the pastoral industry, the vast river system of the Murray–Darling provided access to permanent water. Well into the 1860s, few squatters ventured further than 24 kilometres from the river, giving stock easy access to water.[15]

Squatters brought their 19th-century British-derived attitudes to the Australian landscape, and this greatly aided the rapid transformation of the Murray–Darling Basin into a world-scale pastoral industry. Whether they were from the colonial wealthy elite, or recent immigrants, the squatters were 'rough country optimists' unfazed by living on one of the least fertile landscapes on earth.[16] Most were also opportunists. They had been lured by tales of the rapid fortunes to be made from pastoralism. Some wanted quick riches, hoping to return home wealthy men in the prime of life.[17]

Men dominated this wave of migration. However, the case of a Scottish woman, Janet Templeton, showed that gender was no obstacle to the gamble of finding a new life as a pastoralist in the antipodes for those with sufficient pluck. Finding herself a wealthy widow after the death of her banker husband in 1829, she decided to head for Australia. She selected a flock of merino sheep, charted a brig and set sail from Greenock, Scotland, in August 1830 with her nine children in tow.[18] While she was the exception, plenty of women accompanied their aspiring husbands on the epic voyage to New South Wales, the privations of which can scarcely be imagined today. Passengers were herded into cramped quarters to fend for themselves for the average 109-day voyage, surviving without fresh food. Travellers found the ship biscuit unpalatable owing to its 'flinty hardness', the salted beef and pork were rated as 'villainously bad' and the preserved potatoes were simply 'revolting'. Rough weather taxed the nerves of immigrants, who cursed their foolishness for leaving 'old England'. The deaths that occurred along the way – with bodies unceremoniously thrown over the side – were a reminder of the perils of transporting pioneers to the colonies.[19]

The underlying ideas behind this drive to riches were the same ones that were articulated by Sturt and Mitchell. A correspondent to the *Darling Downs Gazette and General Advertiser* revealed in an article in 1875 the cultural connection to their Empire-inspired values. 'What a startling change has the lapse of a few years made,' the correspondent wrote, 'the aboriginal natives of the country are nearly extinct; the very animals that frequented the scrubs and forests have become nearly obsolete; the wilderness has become peopled with numerous families; and cattle and sheep can be seen sporting on a thousand hills'.[20]

The *Advertiser's* comment is ladened with the cultural attitudes that shaped the development of the Basin: the racism that justified the genocide against Aboriginal people; the attachment to private property rights that drove the squatters' desire to accumulate profits; and the belief in the superiority of white man over nature derived from the ancient Greeks and from centuries of Christian theological teaching of the Creation story that man had virtually unlimited control over nature.[21]

Ignorant of the landscape and its finely tuned, but unpredictable, fluctuations in climate and alienated by the Australian bush, the squatters were untroubled by their determination to bend the land to their ambitions. 'Very few of the squatters', writes poet Judith Wright in her history of the region, 'knew anything of the components of the pastures onto which their flocks and herds were poured'.[22]

Aboriginal people and the pastoral industry

Of course, Aboriginal people had intimate knowledge of the country, but pastoralism had rendered them a dispossessed people. 'Victoria', the members of the 1858–59 Legislative Council Select Committee 'On Aborigines' triumphantly wrote, 'is now entirely occupied by a superior race, and there is scarcely a spot, except in remote mountain ranges, or dense scrubs, on which the Aborigine can rest his weary feet'.[23] In a world transformed by disease, decimated populations and dispossession of land, Aboriginal people of the Basin (as elsewhere) had to find a way to maintain their collective identity while accommodating to radically altered circumstances.[24]

Perversely, pastoral stations in the Basin relied on Aboriginal workers in the decades after occupation. The shortage of labour forced owners to employ Aboriginal men in a variety of roles: sheep washing, clearing vegetation, tilling the ground, chopping wood and, as stockmen, shepherds. Women and girls were occasionally employed in domestic duties.

These duties were performed on stations whose owners frequently embraced an Aboriginal language name. Along the Barwon from Walgett there were stations called 'Gingie', a word meaning the foam that used to gather in the waters there; 'Ulah', meaning the waves found in the nearby lagoon; 'Milrea', meaning the pipeclay found in the nearby river banks; 'Boorooma' from 'Booroomooear', meaning whirlwind; and 'Collarwaray' from *cullee woori* meaning bad water.[25] It's hard to speculate on why so many owners appropriated the names of the very people they dispossessed and frequently murdered. Perhaps owners felt the need to acknowledge the presence of the people they had so ruthlessly conquered.

However, little dispute exists that Aboriginal people constituted an exploited workforce on these stations. Payment in wages was rare; instead, most Aboriginal workers on the stations were paid in provisions.[26] Yet, relationships could be complex. 'Pastoral stations', writes historian Rodney Harrison,[27] represented a 'frontier zone' for cross-cultural negotiations and encounters. More like small villages than simply a farm, stations were a government-authorised distribution point for the issuing of blankets and provisions to Aboriginal people, many of whom established semi-permanent camps on the properties. Relations between the two groups had to be negotiated. As the 1845 New South Wales Legislative Council inquiry into the treatment and conditions of Aboriginal people heard, there were a few stations where Aboriginal people 'are more attached to the settlers than at others, and these have generally greater benefits than the other natives who only come now and then'.[28]

Again, we are reliant on observations by whites about how the dynamic between the two groups was struck during the 19th century. In a few instances, at least, amicable relations were established, at least from the perspective of station owners. In 1854, the *Sydney Morning Herald* reported that one squatter boasted that:

> The greater part of the work on his establishment was performed by black fellows ... [they] were all under regular agreements for short terms at a specified rate of wages and allowances which were paid to them with scrupulous fidelity.[29]

However, there was no escape from the reality for Aboriginal people that theirs was an unequal status. 'The Aboriginal', wrote one historian of pastoralism in Western New South Wales, 'was in no position to emulate the way of life of the station homestead and his whole cultural tradition was opposed to it'.[30] There were daily reminders of inferior status: white workers took their meals at the homestead while Aboriginal workers were given theirs to eat on the wood-heap.[31] Not only was the non-payment of wages exploitative, but a considerable number of white workers and at least some managers had sexual relations with Aboriginal women. Sexual exploitation on Queensland pastoral stations was especially rife, described by some contemporaries as a kind of slave trade.[32]

Aboriginal male workers on Queensland pastoral stations were also subjected to a harsh regime of authority and exploitation masked in the public mind with the stereotypical image of the 'benevolent station manager' overseeing faithful, childlike 'native' workers.[33] Yet, with few exceptions, Queensland stations were run on 'rough justice', including rounding up Aboriginal workers with whips.[34] Such cruelty was part of a wider culture among settlers as ruthless oppressors of Aboriginal people.[35]

Conditions were not nearly as harsh south of the Queensland border. Some station owners in New South Wales found that it was impossible to secure regular employment from Aboriginal people because 'they just work on their own inclination'.[36] Station owners often relied on the deep familiarity of Aboriginal people with the local landscape; they had intimate knowledge of the vast properties as no white man ever could.[37]

One of the early squatters on the Darling, Edmund Morey, freely admitted that he would have been unable to establish his run but for the assistance he received from Aboriginal people, highlighting why they made such valuable shepherds: they could shepherd sheep through flooded areas; they needed neither hut nor tent, but camped happily by their flocks; and their dogs kept dingoes at bay. Morey believed that sheep were better cared for by Aboriginal shepherds than by white ones.[38] In return, Morey allowed Aboriginal people on his station to frequent their 'old haunts'.[39]

Such a bargain enabled Aboriginal people living on station camps to maintain links to their traditional life styles. They could leave the station and roam the bush, living on wild foods for months at a time.[40]

On pastoral stations in western New South Wales, a degree of cordiality existed between white and Aboriginal workers. Shearers put aside their racial opposition to 'Asiatic' labour and accepted working alongside Aboriginal workers. When the pastoral trade unions were formed in the 1880s, Aboriginal workers were enrolled, out of concern that they would form a pool of cheap labour if left to themselves.[41] Outside working hours, however, the two groups remained separate, with Aboriginal workers content to socialise with kin in the camps. One shearer was on record as saying: 'Keep clear of 'em [Aboriginal people]. Say goodday to them; stop and have a talk, but keep away from their camp'.[42]

While the dispossession of Aboriginal people was thought necessary for whites to exploit the Murray–Darling Basin, Aboriginal labour was incorporated into the pastoral economy, but only as an exploited labour force. The pastoral economy represented a type of feudal relationship – permanent camps were set up on vast properties of wealthy owners who recruited Aboriginal labour for the paltry payment of provisions, highlighting the historic injustice of 'stolen wages' from Aboriginal people.[43]

Resistance to this injustice simmered, demonstrating Aboriginal people's acute awareness of their rights. As early as 1860, the Yorta Yorta people demanded compensation from Victorian authorities for the destruction of their natural fishing stock by paddle steamers. And over the next century there were 17 separate attempts by the Yorta Yorta to obtain compensation and land. Their only success was the granting of freehold title to 1200 acres (485 hectares) of the Cummuragunja Reserve.[44]

Not all Aboriginal people were accommodated in the pastoral industry or on reserves. Some continued to live in the traditional way. In 1866, for example, there were said to be hundreds of poor Aboriginal 'wretches' living along the Murray and Goulburn rivers, in dreadful conditions.[45]

In the years immediately after the European occupation of the Murray–Darling, authorities searched for answers to the problem of how to deal with the remnant population of Aboriginal people still ravaged by disease, social breakdown and loss of access to traditional lands. The chairman of the South Australian Legislative Council inquiry boldly recommended compensation for injuries Aboriginal people sustained as a consequence of 'the forced occupation of the country'.[46] But that notion went counter to the prevailing belief that Aboriginal people had no legal right to land, and it died with the report. In its place missionaries and reserves sprang up along the Murray–Darling, as they did elsewhere across the continent, establishing complex relationships between Aboriginal people and institutions run by churches and colonial governments. Some Aboriginal people adopted Christianity; others believed that institutions for their 'protection' were tantamount to prisons.

White workers on stations often fared little better than Aboriginal workers in their makeshift camps, confirming the exploitative underpinnings of pastoralism. In the second half of the 19th century, stations employed a range of full-time European workers: bullock-drivers, ploughmen, boundary riders and carpenters; some of the larger stations employing up to 40 men. Provided with an interminable diet of mutton and damper, one observer reckoned that the Australian bush worker was 'the worst fed labourer in the world'.[47] Pastoral workers were housed in huts, which, as one contemporary observed in 1870, were so dank it was as if they were merely peasants living in feudal times. Huts were typically around 3.5 by 5 metres in size with barely enough room to stand upright. Men ate, slept and cooked in the filthy single space with the carcasses of slaughtered sheep hanging on the walls. Conditions were squalid; huts were devoid of light in winter and ventilation in summer and the bark roof leaked when it rained.[48]

Battle for the land

The exploitation of both Aboriginal and white workers underpinned the wealth accrued by the largest of the squatters. Consequently, they became the first of the Basin's powerful political lobby groups. Their model of wealth extraction based on monopolisation of political power left an enduring legacy in the Murray–Darling Basin. In whose interests was this land to be developed – the wealthy and well connected, or the people at large? The battle of the squatters to retain their vast estates against a populist movement commenced in the mid-1850s, after the influx of immigrants to the Victorian goldfields. Squatters understood the stakes were high, and fended off claims from ordinary settlers opposed to their exclusive rights to their vast runs. Settlers used the rallying cry of 'unlock the land' to put pressure on politicians to reform the land laws.

New South Wales Governor George Gipps was the first to grapple with this conflict; his battles with the squatters would wear down his health. Gipps arrived in the colony in 1838, seemingly well qualified for the position. He was another veteran of Wellington's Spanish campaign against Napoleon. Whether, like Mitchell, his military career had left a permanent imprint is difficult to say, but he was widely seen as having a fractious personality: a proud, overbearing, autocratic man with an uncontrollable temper.[49] Yet he could also be a stubborn man of principle. The two sides of his personality combined when he took on the squatters.

Gipps confronted a rising tide of change. Immigrants were pouring into the country demanding cheap land; both the squatters and the new arrivals sought a greater say in the running of the colony; the frontier war between Aboriginal people and settlers was creating great anger and anxiety; and the squatters had not only shown their disdain for government regulation but were quickly turning into a wealthy and arrogant landed gentry.

Almost as soon as he arrived, Gipps got offside with both the squatters and the public in general. Bringing to justice the perpetrators of the Myall Creek massacre stirred up heated antipathy to his rule; those arrested, charged and hanged for the massacre were, for many years, regarded as martyrs by most settlers.[50] At much the same time, his focus turned to tightening up the regulations around squatting, mandating, in 1839, that newly appointed district commissioners would target those squatters who did not pay their required £10 annual licence fee in a timely manner, with powers to remove their licences without appeal. Predictably, squatters saw the measure as high-handed.[51]

Relations between the squatters and the governor deteriorated. Critics alleged that Gipps brought the battle with the squatters on himself through his 'love of disputation', which turned a political struggle into a personal one.[52] But the governor had his own pressing issues to address, namely a depleted Treasury and the consequent necessity to raise funds. Gipps sought to 'secure a larger income from the squatters'.[53] His 1839 stricter regulations were the first shot fired in this campaign.

Squatters moved to open hostility when, in 1844, Gipps bypassed the recently established Legislative Council to announce new squatting regulations, which, while establishing a fairer system, increased the costs of licensing to those squatters who owned multiple stations. Importantly, the regulations failed to deliver long-term security of tenure.[54] However, the timing of the new regulations could not have been more calculated to increase wider public hostility. In 1844, the colony was in the grip of an economic downturn caused largely by a temporary decline in the price of wool. Squatters cried 'ruin'.

Gipps wanted to better regulate the system of squatting; he saw its irregularities as indefensible and he seems genuinely to have been offended by the vast land holdings claimed by some squatters. In April 1843 he wrote to the Colonial Office: 'The lands are the unquestionable property of the Crown, and they are held in trust by the government for the benefit of the people of the whole British

Empire'. In the same despatch he wrote: 'I have long felt the necessity of entirely remodelling the squatting regulations in this colony'. And, as he further explained, returns showed, among other things, 'that some individuals hold eleven hundred times as much land as others do for the same money'.[55]

It could be argued that Gipps intermingled principle with expediency in his desire to change the system, but the effect of the regulations outraged the squatters. By 1844, their power was formidable. In fact, the Governor was taking on an entrenched power structure. Their network was built around close connections to the colony's wealthy interests, notably the Legislative Council, which operated on high property qualifications and which was occasionally derided as 'a squatters' debating club'.[56] Squatters also owned their own newspaper, the *Atlas*, which issued a torrent of criticism against Gipps, and they had an influential supporter in WC Wentworth, arguably the most powerful man in the colony other than the Governor himself. Rounding out their power was direct access to the British Parliament via the country's commercial ties to the pastoral industry and the employment of a British MP, Francis Scott, as a lobbyist.

But, as the colonial newspaper the *Argus* argued, the overt forms of power wielded by the squatters were matched by covert forms. The squatters, the paper argued, were a unified body motivated by self-interest: 'they can meet and discuss their plots and plans' protected by the Legislative Council, 'their own body'.[57]

Squatters moved to have the regulations undone and a more favourable system introduced. They mounted a sophisticated political campaign to achieve these ends. A public meeting, held in the saloon of the Royal Hotel Sydney, was called to channel public outrage. The two main speakers were Wentworth and Benjamin (Ben) Boyd, who was a recent immigrant from Scotland and descended from an ancient Scottish family. He arrived in Port Jackson in 1842 in his ship *The Wanderer* and quickly set about creating a pastoral empire comprising 14 stations and 172 000 hectares of land. Like some latter-day business tycoon, Boyd's gifts were grounded in his outsized personality. He could talk banks into lending him a seemingly endless stream of money to fund his ventures, and he had a knack for self-promotion. Even before his arrival in Australia, 'Melbourne and Sydney had heard all about the coming of *The Wanderer* from the publicity agents on his steamers. He was given an almost royal welcome'.[58]

Wentworth rallied the crowd by 'pouring forth a volume of vile and salacious abuse' at Gipps, while Boyd inadvertently gave away the squatters' game in his remarks opposing Gipps' new regulations. A journalist overheard him tell the crowd that he looked upon his stations 'as a freehold and an inheritance for him and his', which, the newspaper publishing these remarks, took to mean that the squatters desired 'to enjoy these lands free of rent … and to transmit them in like manner to their heirs'.[59] In other words, they had pretentions to becoming colonial aristocrats.

Boyd and Wentworth were instrumental in forming the Pastoral Association as a lobby group to promote their aim of gaining fixed tenure over their leases. Their aim was to convince the British government to overrule Gipps' regulations with legislation guaranteeing their right of ownership of the public lands on which they had built their dream of riches and power. A flood of petitions was sent to the British Parliament, and Boyd himself was dispatched to London to further their cause. Boyd teamed up with English and Scottish woollen manufacturers, shipping companies and other groups with a commercial interest in colonial pastoralism, to lobby members of Parliament. The end result of this campaigning was a substantial victory. In mid-1846, *The Australian Waste Lands Act* was passed by the British Parliament, giving the squatters 14-year leases and pre-emptive rights of purchase over their leases. The Melbourne *Argus*[60] lamented that the British government had 'handed over to a few hundred of men some fifty millions [of acres] of the finest lands of this fair province'.

The same process occurred in the newly created colony of Queensland where, after self-government in 1859, every effort was made for a quick uptake of settlement through land laws favouring the squatters.[61] In fact, between 1850 and 1860, the region was described as 'one vast sheep run' divided into stations of between 16 000–60 000 hectares, whose unfenced boundaries were defined by the watersheds of creeks. So vast were some of the holdings that squatters were often unable to determine where their properties ended, 'a few hundred acres more or less was of very little consequence'.[62]

In convincing the British Parliament of their cause, the squatters had effectively stifled 'the rest of the colonists … whose interests were entirely disregarded', as the *Labor Daily* put it.[63] The Act formalised the land grab envisaged by Sturt and Mitchell to serve imperial aims. It cemented the power structure around pastoralism for decades to come, for, as one historian has commented: 'The squatters had effectively stolen public land, became very wealthy … and used their influence to have their rights to the land recognised'.[64] The formation of the 'squattocracy' was complete.

The scale of the wealth and power wielded by squatters fomented a simmering class divide. Historian John Hirst writes: 'The Sydney liberals in the 1850s viewed the outback squatting country with hostility … because it supported precisely the social order they wished to avoid – a privileged class of landholders and a subservient class toiling for them'.[65] Indeed, in the decade after being granted greater security of tenure, squatters managed to cement their pastoral empires. Working conditions on stations were harsh; the relationship between squatters and their workers was akin to that of master and servant. Squatters were confident that the courts would uphold their coercive system should any worker challenge their treatment.[66]

The story of the squatters' rise to power is instructive in the history of the Murray–Darling Basin. They established the model of vested interests capturing the political system to control the resources.

The age of paddle steamers

While the battle of the squatters was noisily played out, a quieter but crucial change came to their assistance. To get their prized wool to market, the squatters on the stations needed a mode of transport from their remote locations to one of the urban areas of Sydney, Melbourne or Adelaide. Human ingenuity provided the solution in the form of flat-bottomed, steam-powered paddle steamers.

From the mid-1850s, the Murray–Darling was the lifeblood of the wool industry, the artery through which tens of thousands of bales of wool were transported yearly from the far northern and western reaches of the Basin and on to export to Britain. In fact, the spur provided by the rapid development of pastoralism, paved the way for the commercialisation of steam boats along the Murray–Darling rivers. In turn, the service provided by paddle steamers opened up the farthest reaches of the Basin to pastoralism and facilitated the provisioning of stations necessary for their survival. For the wool industry and its British clients, the paddle steamers solved the problem of the region's vast distances from urban centres.

This promise of development was foreseen when the first paddle steamer to venture up the Murray, the *Mary Ann*, left Goolwa in August 1853. Newspapers covering the event trumpeted the beginning of a new era: 'The permanent navigation of the Murray will open up for profitable occupation an immense extent of country … Runs will be taken up wherever they are available, and a great increase in cargo traffic will be the consequence'.[67]

A fleet of flat-bottomed craft was quickly developed for the trade. Shallow in draught, the stout, double-decker steamers were loaded up with bales of wool or other cargo in addition to the stacks of bales piled high on barges pulled behind the steamers. It was a sight to behold: 'No light task this towing of barges in a stream that winds like a snake through the plains', wrote one newspaper correspondent.[68] Procuring fuel for the boilers was not easy before an organised supply of cut timber was arranged. In the early days of the trade, the crew on board the boats had to go ashore and cut their own supplies, standing in up to a metre of water.[69]

On the journey up the river, steamers carried large stocks to supply the stations, but they carried news as well. When a steamer came to port for a few hours or days, everyone in the town gathered for 'a song and dance and a good glass of wine' and the latest news would be exchanged 'digested and probably exaggerated to other persons hungry for news!'.[70] Compressed bales of wool were transported by bullock and drays or camel from the stations to these ports. Towns along the way developed into lively ports where wool and other goods were loaded and unloaded. In their heyday in the 1870s and 1880s, 193 paddle steamers plied the river.

By the 1880s, towns like Wentworth and Wilcannia and even as far west as Bourke, became important local regional commercial and social centres via the river trade. In fact, their livelihoods depended on it. When the Darling River ran low in Wilcannia, for example, navigation was suspended 'and the town practically shuts up for a time'. It was not uncommon for squatters' wool to be detained in the town for nearly twelve months waiting for a rise in the river.[71] But when the Darling was flowing, Wilcannia was a magnet for shearers, squatters, boundary riders, teamsters and rabbiters from the various sheds around the district who were drawn to one of its 13 hotels to slake their collective thirst.[72]

As the steamers passed along the river from one colony to the next, they were required to stop for inspection at the border Customs Houses, a reminder that the various colonies occupying the Basin jealously protected their respective economies through tariffs on goods passing through.[73] Throughout the 19th century, arguments for free trade between the colonies were continually stymied because, as one newspaper lamented, 'patriotism finds its utmost limit within the narrow bounds of one colony'.[74]

In fact, the imposition of tariffs and charges by the various colonies on the movement of goods along the river system foreshadowed the deep divisions that engulfed the politics of the Basin for the ensuing decades and to the present. As the tariff issue intensified in the 1860s, it was likened to a 'border war' of the Middle Ages with the colonies engaged in 'suicidal bickering'.[75]

The construction of wharves on the Murray–Darling varied. This was still an age when muscle-power moved goods. However, by the late 1880s, technology was starting to have an impact. The wharf at Morgan on the lower Murray River was built above the floodplain, and vessels were loaded and unloaded by cranes worked by hydraulic power. By this technological marvel, 250 bales of wool could be unloaded each hour.[76]

Conditions were much more primitive at Bourke where the steamers merely sided up against the steep banks on the town's edge and the wool bales were hauled up by hand with the aid of planks. Nonetheless, Bourke was also an important pastoral town dependent on the river trade. In the 1880s, it was common to see a fleet of steamers tied up at its banks and as many as 1000 men wandering the main street or happily seated in one of the town's 32 wood-and-iron hotels.[77] However, the transport of wool by steam boat ceased by the end of the century, killed off by the coming of the railways and then roads.

Nowhere symbolised this change more than the town of Echuca. The river boat trade made it both a commercial and social hub. Boats 'were coming and going day and night'. The town had 50 pubs, all with dancing saloons, and the 'fast and furious life' of the town centred on free fights between the 'bullockies' and the 'steamboaties'. But when the railways were extended to Deniliquin, Albury and Hay, all the 'kick' was knocked out of Echuca. From being an important hub of Victorian trade, its glory days ended. It was said that 'hotels were given away with a packet of tea' and the town settled down, became respectable, and locals went to church on Sunday.[78]

Beyond the Murray–Darling rivers

In addition to the river boat trade, pastoralism fostered the development of towns throughout the Basin. Gundagai was one such town that rose in the 1840s on the back of land investment. Showing how little government officials and squatters knew about the unique ecology they had so quickly acquired, the town site was gazetted in 1841 on a floodplain of the Murrumbidgee. This is Wiradjuri Country, whose people had fought a bitter war with the new settlers that had ended only a few years before. Despite their defeat, the Wiradjuri warned against building on the site of the floodplain, advice that was ignored.[79] But the floods came in 1844, 1847, 1851 and 1852. Destructive doesn't adequately describe the 1852 flood; it simply washed the town away. In the darkness of night the water surged in, reaching to the tops of 10-metre trees, carrying in its wake houses and stock and human bodies. Eighty-one people are known to have died, but the actual figure was thought to be higher on account of the number of diggers camping on the flats en route to the Bendigo goldfields.

In approving the site for the town, colonial officials, including Governor Gipps and Sir Thomas Mitchell, considered the 1844 flood a one-off occurrence.[80] In a pattern that would become entrenched into the future, Aboriginal knowledge passed on to authorities that towns should never be established near rivers[81] was simply dismissed as 'unlearned' by men who considered that they embodied 'scientific' knowledge. In 1852, Gundagai was rebuilt on higher ground.

But the higher ground was no guarantee of protection from floods. As if to remind settlers that these events were a regular feature of the Basin's ecology, in early May 1870, Gundagai was struck by a flood nearly as big as the 1852 catastrophe. It, too, arrived in the dead of night after three days of persistent rain during which the town was enveloped in thick fog. On the third night of the downpour, residents could hear the river roar like a fierce storm. The following morning, with the fog having cleared, residents confronted a 'rapid stream' 7 metres wide rushing across the flats. Several people died, and losses from the flood were 'very grave and serious'.[82]

More than one hundred kilometres north-west of Gundagai, across dead-level plains and on the edge of the Murray–Darling Basin, lies Mount Gipps Station. When tank-sinkers first inspected the region in the mid-1860s, looking for a supply of water to drive stock overland to Melbourne, it was a region of sharp contrasts. When it was dry, there was little but shimmering heat, restless winds and saltbush. In a lush season it was carpeted in wavering grass and wildflowers.

Prior to the arrival of the tank-sinkers, the area had been an Aboriginal camping ground, and 'the ashes of their camp fires and the bones from their feasts could still be seen'. Folklore has it that it took tough, hard-driving men of indomitable spirit to 'fight that grim region'. The sheep moved in and Mount Gipps became a squatters' domain. However, in 1883, a boundary rider on the station, Charlie Rasp, discovered silver ore. He and other Mount Gipps' men formed a syndicate to mine what became known as Broken Hill and Charlie was soon a wealthy man – known as 'the Silver King'.[83]

'Unlock the lands'

Even with the spread of the pastoral and mining industries, the Murray–Darling Basin remained sparsely settled during the 19th century. The towns that had been established along the major river systems had yet to experience much growth. Pastoralism, based around a relatively small number of large estates, acted as a break on drawing immigrants into the region.

All this was set to change dramatically with the discovery of gold in 1851 in the Port Phillip District, widely seen as a turning point in the nation's history.[84] The surge of immigrants eager to try their luck in panning for gold quickly created a new set of political demands for a more democratic system of government and greater access to land for the ordinary worker. During this transformative period, between 1851 and 1871, the Australian population quadrupled from 430 000 to 1.7 million as migrants from across the globe arrived in search of gold. The precious mineral lured many hopefuls for their chance at wealth; some realised their dream, most did not, making little more than wages, and soon had to scratch around for work.[85]

These changes combined to create a new vision for the Murray–Darling Basin based around putting the 'little man' on the land as independent, yeoman farmers – a movement known as agrarianism. The term has a lineage stretching back to ancient thinkers but, by the mid-19th century, it had become associated with a set of powerful ideas about the importance of agriculture to a modern, thriving society. Advocates believed that it 'represented a more wholesome life for humans than urban living with all its temptations. And agrarianism offered a way for hard-working ordinary folk to gain economic independence and to demonstrate their virtues'.[86]

This new vision for the nation was not only an alternative nation-building project to pastoralism, it was a threat to the squatters' monopoly of land. The pressure for this new vision was a direct consequence of the demographic and political changes wrought by the gold rushes in the 1850s.

The influx of people from across the world spurred the other great development of this decade: the achievement of universal male suffrage in colonial parliaments. Working men finally had a voice in their future – and the future they saw was on the land. The major city newspapers agreed that land reform was needed; unlocking the land was seen as a panacea to the problems facing the country: the throngs of able-bodied men in search of employment and the necessity of attracting even more migrants.[87] The influential newspaper *The Age* championed land reform as a populist cause: land must be brought within the poor man's reach because it belonged to the people.[88]

Ordinary people had a right to obtain a block of land of their own.

Despite powerful supporters, the squatters couldn't hold back the tide. The new, democratic temper of the times was soon being felt to 'unlock the lands'. In May 1853, the *Argus* reported a groundswell of community opinion on the issue comprising 'numerous meetings' and the organisation of a 'monster petition' of 15 000 signatures. This showed, the paper argued, that free selection of lands locked away by squatters 'must now be grappled with, and decided in a manner satisfactory to the great mass of people'.[89] The paper called on government to reverse the 1846 British legislation granting squatters 14-year leases.

The call on agrarianism across the self-governing colonies that shared the Murray–Darling Basin developed into a program known as 'free selection'. The idea of placing anyone who wanted to be a farmer on the land became one of the great grassroots political movements of the second half of the 19th century. It was promoted as a path to an ideal society, one where empty lands would become densely populated by a new class of antipodean yeomanry working their own family farms.[90] The promise of developing self-sufficiency in wheat production added to the rationale of the scheme.[91]

Free selection was promoted by progressive politicians wanting to appeal to the recently enfranchised urban working class. Hence, the rallying cry of 'unlock the lands' was heard in town halls in cities and country towns. Land reform became one of the most hotly contested issues of the age; it was a fault line for rival class interests, a vehicle for populist politics, and a utopian ideal for social reformers.

Destroying the squatters' monopoly over land drove the appeal of free selection. Many grounded their support in the works of Henry George, an American newspaper editor, who advocated the destruction of land monopoly through a tax on land in its unimproved state. Busting up the big estates had plenty of local advocates who regarded them as a symptom of an unjust society. 'The large estates', commented one colonial newspaper, 'are considered by the bulk of the people as an evil, and their owners intensely disliked'.[92] They needed to be thrown open for ordinary people to select a portion.

This grand vision was to be underwritten by government through legislation, regulation and the financing of transportation infrastructure and population centres. The key to realising these goals was enacting the various Land Acts of the 1860s, which all four colonies encompassing the Murray–Darling Basin sponsored in a massive expansion of settlement that employed a 'small army' of surveyors working for expanded Lands Department bureaucracies. Millions of hectares were opened up each year for selection across the Basin.

The Murray–Darling Basin, with its vast areas of 'wastelands', became the key region for the success of the Land Acts. The scale of the vision involved in these land reforms occasionally caught contemporaries by surprise. As the Victorian newspaper, the *Leader*, wrote in 1878, the colony had achieved in a few years what had taken half a dozen generations to accomplish in the United Kingdom.[93]

Even though the separate colonial Acts – all of which were amended several times between the 1860s and the 1880s – had differently worded provisions, each was based around similar principles: selectors of limited means could pay for half of an allotment from 40 acres (16 hectares) up to several hundred acres at a fixed price (typically £1 per acre) and pay rent on the other half for a defined period (three to seven years), thereafter paying out the balance of the amount.

The simplicity of the legislation hid myriad problems. Foremost among them was wealthy squatters undermining the spirit of the Acts to protect their class interests. The big runs were thrown open across the Basin's grazing lands, but the squatters were able to exploit loopholes in the legislation to consolidate their grip on the most productive land.

Across the colonies occupying the Murray–Darling Basin, squatters used their pre-emptive rights under the 1847 British legislation to purchase the best parts of their land to protect their interests in a process known as 'peacocking'. To allow for multiple numbers of such selections, squatters put them in the names of their children.[94] They also employed agents and other third parties, known as 'dummies', to select land only to sell it later to squatters for a negotiated fee. An 1883 New South Wales inquiry into the operation of that colony's Land Act found plenty of evidence of squatters using numerous dummies to secure lands surrounding legitimate selectors, hemming them in and forcing them to sell.[95]

The abuses of the system caused continual public outcry, with numerous commentators decrying the system as corrupt.[96] In fact, according to the *Geelong Advertiser*, the Victorian Land Acts of 1860 and 1862 had done more to corrupt respectable men than any measure that was ever before enacted in the colony.[97] In Victoria, for example, it was estimated that by the mid-1870s nearly a third of the land sold by government had passed into the hands of less than 200 people.[98]

Barrister and radical Victorian politician John Quick wrote a history of the Victorian land laws, the pages of which crackled with indignation about the failures of the colony's politicians in allowing 'numerous swindles' and 'wholesale fraud' and allowing nearly a million acres of land, 'constituting the garden of Victoria' to pass into the 'powerful moneyed class'.[99] The 'land racket' was played out in the public eye for all to see: 'Taverns were kept open for the accommodation of gangs of dummies; stage coaches were with unblushing effrontery engaged from day to day to carry the dummies from sale to sale'.[100]

Similar corrupt practices were taken for granted in Queensland into the 1880s. In 1883, the *Queensland Figaro* explained to its readers 'How to become a squatter'. It all came down to the exercise of surreptitious political influence:

> [W]hen the time comes for throwing open to selection, you don't object … But you just try to get some land put to auction.

You or your friend knows the minister, or the under-secretary, or both, and its not difficult for a nice pleasant fellow like you to get a simple matter of an auction sale arranged. Of course it is an auction sale, but you have made it right so that the size or shape or the situation of the block suits you and nobody else.[101]

Squatters could also take advantage of their ability to purchase land on which they had made improvements. It was a provision ready-made for rogues: rough huts on wheels were moved around a squatter's domain. The improvements became a 'mockery'.[102] 'Squatterdom', therefore, had found a way to prevail despite the populist appeals of colonial politicians. However, unlike their fierce political agitation a decade earlier, squatters could, in addition to exploiting loopholes in legislation, bide their time, waiting for the weaker selectors to fail.[103] As late as 1909, the *Molong Argus* decried the 'shameful spectacle' whereby crowds of farmers unsuccessfully scoured the state for land while 'a greedy gang of squatters, land jobbers and sharks' were supported by a conservative government to grab what land they could.[104] In turn, the economic development of the country had been hampered because the owners of these estates used them exclusively for grazing.[105]

If the Land Acts made comparatively little inroads on the squatters, how far did governments succeed in their utopian aim of creating an agrarian society of yeoman farmers? Despite unimaginable hardships for many, such an opportunity to establish themselves as independent farmers was a feeling of 'genuine, deep joy'.[106] However, overall, the results were widely seen to have been a failure.

Problems were seen early on because the dreams of colonial politicians were largely delusionary. Most, like Victorian Gavin Duffy, the author of the 1862 Victorian Land Act, were convinced that an industrious man and his family could live on 80 acres (32 hectares) of land, mainly because he had seen farmers in Belgium and France living on less.[107] This was a case, according to the respected *Freeman's*

Journal, of politicians being allowed 'to talk glibly on topics they did not understand'.[108] And no consideration was given to the capacity of individual selectors to become farmers under demanding conditions, opening up the likelihood that many would fail.[109]

Nor did the public at large understand much about the requirements of farming in the areas being opened up under the Land Acts. Many farmers were sent onto the land with too little capital and, consequently, in possession of too small an area to farm sustainably. Conditions governing the purchase of land also proved onerous, especially the need to clear a minimum number of acres within a few years.

However, whether a selector stayed or was forced out was highly conditional on the type of land they were able to select. Heavily timbered country meant several years of clearing without the returns from harvesting a crop. 'Hasty selection', explains DB Waterson in his study of squatters and selectors of the Darling Downs, 'often meant rapid ruin'.[110] In Victoria, selectors were mostly forced to bid for sub-prime land far removed from the centres of population and situated in poor country for farming.[111]

Settlers could also be ruined by competition from native birds and animals that emerged from the surrounding thick scrub at night to eat crops. This forced selectors into a war with native animals in a ruthless campaign of extermination (see chapter 5).

Adding to settlers' chances of failure was the lack of knowledge of the environment; not much more was known about rainfall patterns, soil types and the cycle of droughts since Sturt's and Mitchell's expeditions. The risks in farming parts of the Basin became apparent by the mid-1880s in northern Victoria. The floods of 1870 and 1875 had produced abundant wheat crops but these good years were followed by dry seasons between 1878 and 1885. When officials visited the region in 1885, they found that selectors 'have had to wage a severe struggle for bare subsistence. Some had lost the struggle, succumbing to the pressure of succeeding droughts'.[112]

For many, the chance of a lifetime became a Darwinian struggle of survival of the fittest. Most selectors began with 'nothing whatever except strong hands and willing hearts'.[113] Those who purchased forested blocks for one pound per acre found that they couldn't obtain sufficient returns for their outlay.[114] Clearing blocks was time-consuming and arduous. Family members were often the only available labour to perform this work. This frequently involved women and children burning cleared scrub. A report from Queensland in 1885 revealed the extent of the struggle for survival: 'boys and girls all lend a hand; indeed many of the children are worked too hard, and their schooling is neglected'.[115]

Farming a small or modest-sized selection was a continual dance with uncertainty: too little capital meant almost a lonely slide to failure and thwarted dreams. And drought lurked as almost a constant presence.

It is impossible to tell just how many became trapped in a cycle of unviable small holdings, bad seasons, lack of initial capital and lack of access to ongoing credit. Certainly, endurance paid off for some. Around Horsham in Victoria, a large number of selectors survived three or four years of hardship and worked their way to prosperity.[116] However, such prosperity does not appear to have been typical.

Even those who stayed on their properties eked out a sparse existence. In 1880, two decades after the original Land Acts were passed, the *Australian Sketcher* gave a glimpse of the souring of the agrarian dream. It estimated that two-thirds of selectors were carrying on under satisfactory circumstances but in conditions of rural deprivation, 'squeezed into such small cottages' that townspeople would not tolerate. And, 'the opinion seems to be growing … that farming can only be carried out when the grazing of stock is combined with agriculture'. But small selectors couldn't afford to purchase stock.[117] The only way most small selectors could attempt to make a go of an impossible situation was to overuse the soil – planting crops in the same patches of ground year after year, rendering the soil in a constant state of exhaustion in what one commentator regarded as a 'suicidal system of cropping'.[118]

Around Ipswich on the Darling Downs, selectors suffered under the weight of improvements such as felling and clearing scrub and forests. In fact, one Queensland newspaper worried about the implications 'if the small farmers are turned out of the homesteads … [and] become a broken-down, dissatisfied class'.[119]

Even selectors with adequate capital and viable-sized farms found the going tough. A reporter from the *Ovens and Murray Advertiser* visited selectors in the Benalla district of central Victoria and found a well-situated selector who had commenced with the 'handsome' capital of £1600 and possessed good soil, which returned profitable harvests of wheat. But this farmer's underwhelming endorsement of the scheme took the journalist by surprise: 'If I had my money back again, I don't think I would put it into farming; but here I am, and I suppose I'll get along'.[120]

The paper found other selectors trapped in dire poverty. One family of 12 was found in difficult circumstances; their crops had failed and two of their three cows had died. To keep going they had borrowed £300 at 11 per cent interest and the repayments crippled whatever hope they had left. Their 'hut' was almost empty of furniture, other than a sofa and a bench. On the day the journalist visited, the mother was sitting on a stool, mending 'the old man's' clothes. A breeze wafted in from a broken window pane, flapping the blind about. Old sacking was the only floor covering. When the journalist looked up at the roof, he noticed openings between the sheets of bark, whereupon, 'the mother looked up, and remarked that the place was not always dry in rainy weather'.

The father of this family had 'very little to say' so it was difficult for the journalist to tell whether they had felt cheated by the free selection project, which had been so fulsomely promoted by progressive colonial politicians. As was shown in the Benalla investigation, grudging success sat side-by-side with abject failure.

Slowly, a process of 'natural selection' took place in many regions with undercapitalised farmers quitting their selections, bought out by neighbouring farmers to create larger and more viable estates. An investigation by the *Bacchus Marsh Express* in 1880 found that 'in every parish there are four or five selectors who are either going or about to go'.[121]

Those who failed often had no option but the open road. How many of the failed selectors became 'travelling men' or 'swaggies' is unknown. The term 'swaggie', which originated in the gold rush years when diggers roamed between goldfields trying their luck, broadened to designate an itinerate rural labour force comprising shearers, scrub-cutters and station hands identifiable by their shabby appearance of patched trousers and worn-out felt hats and their meagre possessions.

Their number was said to constitute a small army by the late 1880s, likely as a consequence of the failed land selection scheme. Taciturn, and mostly travelling alone, swaggies were said to be composed of two types – men travelling about the countryside looking for work, and those more like tramps, whose only business, it was claimed, was to eat at other men's expense, and who never did a hard day's work.

The former group were acknowledged as playing a useful role in the development of the pastoral industry, while the latter group were more akin to wanderers. They usually arrived at a squatter's station at sundown (hence the sobriquet 'sundowners') where, by custom, they were given a meal of damper, mutton and tea. The few women recorded as swaggies were said to be as tough and resourceful as their male counterparts. Swaggies were part of the rural life of the Basin until the late 1940s when many of the big pastoral estates were eventually cut up to make way for further free selection schemes.

The presence of so many swaggies was one indicator that the utopian ideal to create a yeoman society failed to fully materialise. There are no overall data of the number of selectors forced off the land; the process took place over three decades. Some small selectors survived until the mid-1890s when a perfect storm of economic depression, low international prices for wheat, and prolonged drought ended the hopes of many.[122]

Even by the late 1880s, it was clear that selectors had been misled on two counts: by city-based politicians ignorant about farming and by their own misplaced dreams of independence. The myth of a nation of yeoman farmers never fully squared with the reality that selectors were really small businessmen in an age of a rapidly expanding capitalist system.[123] Nor did it square with the abuses of the system: the rorting and corruption that became endemic, despite attempts to close loopholes that allowed wealthy squatters to undermine the intended purpose of the scheme. In this way, idealism had failed to take account of human nature. As Stephen Roberts, the historian of land settlement in Australia, has written: 'while a land law should not be written for rogues, it should at least take them into account'.[124]

However, it would not be the last time that the Murray–Darling Basin would act as the epicentre for social engineering. A new scheme to revise the social goals of free selection gathered pace after the turn of the century, but nothing seemed to have been learned from this first experience of selling the agrarian ideal. As historian, Michael McKernan has written, the national fixation on this ideal was 'an Australian tragedy'.[125]

Nevertheless, the agrarian ideal propelled a shift away from pastoralism to different forms of agriculture, and especially cropping, illustrated by the figures. Between 1860 and 1900, the area being cropped across Australia increased nearly eight-fold to more than 3.4 million hectares.[126] This reversed the prevailing situation whereby Australia was unable to compete in the global export market for wheat because too little was being planted and, as a consequence, wheat had to be imported from the United States.[127] Henceforth Australia saw the emergence of new farming industries that affected the growth and development of towns in the Murray–Darling Basin, facilitating both population growth and the development of a railway network throughout the Basin. In short, crop growing was a more labour-intensive industry than grazing.[128] 'A very large and important industry [wheat] has grown up with marvellous rapidity under the most adverse circumstances', wrote the *Weekly Times* in 1902.[129]

However, nation-building as a project in such a variable and often unforgiving environment proved as much an illusion as it was alluring. The allure of agrarianism had noble objectives, as did large-scale pastoralism. But both were founded on the willingness to bend the unique environment of the Murray–Barling Basin to the will of humans. And both had a common enemy: nature.

5

THE WAR ON NATURE

In mid-September 1893, Mr Samuel Melville, the manager of Trinkey, a pastoral station west of the New South Wales town of Forbes, gathered together 150 men for a ritual common in the Murray–Darling Basin in the second half of the 19th century – a slaughter of the local kangaroo population. In the preceding week, nothing had been discussed more than 'the kangaroo battue'. This was a term used for a particular type of hunt involving one group of hunters who drove designated game towards a corralled area where a second, armed group, shot them at will.

The event arranged by Melville thrilled participants. Three thousand kangaroos were slain, 'besides a great number that were dangerously wounded in the battle, and had to retire and seek a place to die in peace'. They were found later and were finished off by the scalpers who gutted the animals for their skins. Battues were held at regular intervals on Trinkey station, and Melville had supervised all of them. At 'a rough calculation', he said, he had overseen the destruction of 30 000 kangaroos. One of the participants in the battues at Trinkey couldn't speak highly enough of Melville: 'So three cheers for old Samuel Melville; and may I be there to assist at the next kangaroo slaughter which I believe is to take place the end of shearing'.[1]

Not all kangaroo battues were surrounded by such exuberance. Some contemporaries found these events brutalising. In 1897, a correspondent who identified himself simply as 'H.M.C.' wrote a two-part series on 'Kangaroo Hunting on the Darling Downs', which was serialised in colonial newspapers. He was shocked by what he witnessed. With the yapping of the dogs and the stampeding of the horses, the yard became 'one confused jumble of bounding kangaroos'. Madly intent on escape, they were 'flying off' in all directions. Some crashed into each other in mid-air and fell sprawling to the ground amid the already dead and dying animals. Then the killing spree began:

> A dozen of us were soon in the yard with waddies [Aboriginal hunting stick] amongst the thick of it. The middle of the yard was the safest and you would keep a sharp lookout for collisions; the animals seemed quite blind with fright. It was simply slaughter; the beasts were struck down right and left as they flew past us within easy reach. We killed 300 on that drive and then went off to another part of the run. As a means of extermination, those yards … were a success, but it was all too brutalising from a sporting point of view.[2]

There is nothing unusual in farmers' battling native animals as pests, but there is more than a whiff, in the case of kangaroos, of wanting the species exterminated. However, the slaughter of kangaroos was part of a larger war on nature driven by cultural and economic forces. Out on remote stations and around the properties of selectors, and even among towns' folk, a war of extinction was unleashed on native wildlife.

From the late 19th to the early decades of the 20th centuries, local newspapers openly covered this assault on native wildlife in the Basin often deploying stark language: 'extermination of the dingo'; 'wild slaughter' of koalas; 'wildlife destruction by the millions'; 'bird slaughter'; 'wanton destruction of Australia's wildlife'. The use of this language confirms that locals were well aware that a war on nature was being waged.[3]

This war was so extensive that it defies easy explanation. At its base, it reflected the centuries-old hard-baked cultural attitudes that nature was subservient to human needs. This mindset was exacerbated in the case of Australia because early settlers regarded much of the landscape as a useless wasteland. And there was the lure of quick profits by squatters and the utopian ideas of nation-builders; both saw nature as an impediment to their dreams. Adding to the mix was the attractiveness of destroying native wildlife for sport.

Consequently, the idea of conquest became deeply ingrained in the culture of pastoralism and crop growing. In fact, as discussed below, very much the same metaphors of violence that were used to describe the frontier war against Aboriginal people were employed to depict the new conquest over nature. As late as 1938, the *Courier Mail* opined triumphantly that the coming of the pastoralists in the mid-19th century had created 'a vast and wealthy territory conquered and subdued'.[4]

The ghost of William Forster Lloyd, and his theory of the tragedy of the commons, hung over the development of the Basin. Great wealth could be produced, but at what cost?

Damage wrought by pastoralism

The first signs of environmental damage were barely noticed: the failure of squatters to appreciate the value of native grasses.

Before the arrival of Europeans, the ecology of the Murray–Darling Basin had evolved to accommodate the cycle of floods and droughts. In particular, the native grasses were tall and tussocky, offering protection to the root system in the hot, dry summers and in droughts. When floods washed through the landscape, the deep roots of the native grasses were adapted to respond to occasional heavy rainfall, which soaked into the spongy soil. Marsupials were not especially aggressive grazers and their softly padded feet left little impact on the ground. Aboriginal people did affect the environment using their fire-stick agriculture – which helped produce some of the open rangeland that so captivated the first Europeans – but not in a destructive way.[5]

Within a few decades, tens of millions of sheep had invaded the landscape, and they devoured the native grasses, eating whole plants down to the roots. In their place, squatters planted shallow-rooted grasses that were not well adapted to the environment, leaving the ground at the mercy of the summer heat and rainstorms. Exacerbating these changes was the relentless pounding of heavy-hoofed sheep and cattle, which, in the areas where they were concentrated, compacted the soil, leading to long-term problems with soil erosion, the formation of gullies created by runoff and declining soil fertility.

The urge to riches drove the squatters to overstock their runs. This was widely understood to be the case. The *Singleton Argus* wrote that overstocking had been caused though the 'greed of the gambling speculator with British money too often at his back'.[6] The *Sydney Mail and New South Wales Advertiser* criticised the greed of large property owners who 'in order to get returns, urge their unfortunate managers to stock up'. It was no wonder, the paper argued, that droughts were so disastrous. The situation called for station owners to change their system, 'to get managers of a new style – men who will prepare for times of dryness, and will not overstock even at peril of dismissal for not doing so'.[7] But economic logic defied such a call.

For the first few decades, the profits generated by pastoralism pushed up the value of stations, propelling new buyers into greater debt, which then encouraged overstocking[8]. In turn, overstocking continued to have a deleterious impact on native grasses.

These changes in the environment, while cumulative, were clear to observant squatters. In 1853, John Robertson, later author of the Robertson Land Acts in New South Wales, noted the dramatic changes occurring on his property. When he arrived in 1840, it was 'splendid country' with excellent grasses and free of weeds: 'all the landscape looked like a park with shade for sheep and cattle'. For three or four years little changed, but some indigenous plants began to disappear, replaced by invasive weeds. As the deep-rooted native grasses died out, the soil began to dry out and crack and there were hundreds of landslips. As the ground became trodden down by the hooves of stock, the bare land caused run-off to muddy the creeks and water courses and caused gullies to form: 'Ruts, seven, eight, and ten feet deep, and as wide, are found for miles, where two years ago it was covered with tussocky grass like a land marsh'.[9]

Out in western New South Wales, the disappearance of tall, tussocky native grasses had a particularly destructive impact. In a region of naturally low rainfall, such grasses regenerated with the smallest amount of moisture because the root systems were protected. Consequently, droughts wrought further havoc on the landscape.

The environmental problems created by pastoralism were compounded by the pressure for quick profits and by the surge in the release of Crown lands for take-up by selectors. In 1915, one Queensland newspaper reported that native grasses had been 'seriously reduced or completely eaten out by over-stocking with sheep'.[10] In Victoria, the *Stock and Land* agricultural journal reported in 1920 that pastoralism, along with deforestation, was having a dire impact. It noted that much of Victoria had been carrying sheep for the past 70 years, and with each new wave, the land had been robbed of essential nutrients.[11]

Wheat growers were similarly pushing the soil to exhaustion through continuous cropping, which resulted in the loss of soil fertility and declining wheat yields; these halved between the 1860s and 1890s.[12]

Land and forest clearance

Native grasses were not the only part of the Murray–Darling Basin's ecology to suffer from nation-building agricultural enterprises. Forests disappeared. In fact, the wholesale destruction of the region's forests and woodlands shocked many contemporaries in the second half of the 19th century who were powerless to stop its relentless march. Squatters believed that tree clearance had economic benefits. In 1888, the *Ovens and Murray Advertiser* proclaimed that tracts of land, which, before the trees were cut down, would barely feed a hundred sheep, would afterwards support a thousand.[13] Deforestation was thought essential for a productive pastoral industry.[14] It was buttressed by a widely propagated crackpot belief, popular in the American west and Australia during the late 19th century, that human settlement and agriculture made arid regions more humid and thereby attracted more rain over time.[15]

Such confident assertions relied on new techniques to replace the human muscle supplied by the axe, in particular ringbarking. The process consisted of cutting a ring at least one foot wide around the circumference of a tree and removing the bark down to the hardwood. The tree above the ring was thereby cut off from being supplied with water from the roots and died within 12 months. A long-used technique to remove individual trees, it had not been deployed for deforesting extensive areas in south-eastern Australia until the early 1870s.[16]

The practice spread rapidly. Ringbarking on pastoral leases was 'going on to an alarming extent', wrote one New South Wales country newspaper in the early 1880s.[17] There was no shortage of observers to this destruction. One correspondent wrote to the *Argus* that people travelling about the colony couldn't avoid being struck by the 'wilful and deliberate destruction' of the forests. Squatters and selectors, the paper argued, seemed to be driven by an 'insensate hatred' of trees.[18]

What lay behind such environmental vandalism? Apart from deep-seated cultural anti-environmental attitudes, greed continued to motivate the practice. As a Darling Downs newspaper explained in 1900, the destruction of forests was seen to yield 'extremely substantial returns' on the investment outlay.[19]

But there were also wider commercial forces at work. The

steamship trade and the coming of the railways created heavy demand for timber. As one New South Wales local newspaper highlighted, any forest within reasonable distance of a railway or steamship had been 'exhausted'.[20] Forests were being torn down in the name of progress.

In fact, the insatiable demand for railway sleepers highlighted the wasteful approach that underpinned the destruction of forests through the Murray–Darling Basin. By 1900, the New South Wales Railway Department complained that so much timber had simply been burned that the department was forced to pay higher prices for wood for sleepers.[21] A few years later the situation got even worse. Railway authorities in South Australia predicted that half a million sleepers would have to be imported into the country to make amends 'for the forest destruction associated with the pioneering days'.[22]

The red gum was one species that became heavily exploited for sleepers and for use in the construction of wharves and bridges. Great stands of the species could be found for hundreds of kilometres along the Murray, stretching from 5 to 13 kilometres back from the river, where they were perfectly attuned to the periodic flood conditions. By the 1880s, the red gum had already acquired the mantle of a 'magnificent' species in the public's imagination, but this iconic status did not protect it from over-exploitation.

Commencing in the 1860s, successive Victorian governments valued the revenue-raising opportunities for the sought-after timber and divided up the resource into blocks of 200 hectares, which were licensed to sawmillers with the right to cut all the natural timber on their blocks. For the next 20 years the rhythmic thudding sound of axes echoed throughout the red gum forests, such that by the late 1880s fears were held that the red gum would disappear in Victoria.[23] This prompted governments in the late 1880s to consider measures for their conservation; but too much damage had already been done and the species would continue to decline throughout the region.[24]

Legal requirements also propelled clearing. In January 1877, a landmark decision in the Murrurundi Magistrates Court upheld the claim of a squatter against a selector who had taken up part of his run. Prior to selection, the squatter had issued a claim against the selector for 'improvements' undertaken on land comprising tree clearance, which increased the value of the land. The implication from the case was that selectors would have to pay a higher price for land where improvements had been effected. Such a higher price, it was thought, would deter selectors and preserve the landholdings of squatters.[25] Thereafter, squatters went on 'a wholesale slaughter' of timber as the easiest way to deter free selectors from going on the land.[26] Reports from districts throughout the Basin in New South Wales in the early 1880s showed that armies of workers were 'ringbarking every tree' in response to the magistrate's decision.[27]

For their part, selectors had no choice but to clear their land. This was required under the conditions of their leases. The sheer scale of the opening up of Crown land for selection hastened the destruction of forests throughout the Basin.[28] Innovation came to play an essential part.

Indeed, the agricultural sector generally took a keen interest in the development of technology to make the work of clearing more effective and efficient. While ringbarking remained the preferred method for most of the 19th century, a new piece of equipment came on stream in the early 1890s. Known as 'the forest devil', it was a contraption of taut wires and rods – one length of which was anchored halfway up a tree and another length pulled by a horse in circular movements. This method was capable of bringing trees to the ground and hauling out the stump, and could clear more than 1 hectare per day.[29]

Today's wheat fields of the vast Mallee district – four million hectares in northern Victoria – are the product of innovative technological development. Originally comprising mainly dense, dwarf eucalypt trees, stunted by the naturally low rainfall, the region was, until the mid-1880s, regarded as little more than a 'howling wilderness'; 'unproductive waste'; and the 'undisputed home of the rabbit and the dingo'.[30] But it was thought to be a suitable area for wheat growing because it was so heavily vegetated. The drawback was the lack of an efficient way to clear such a densely forested landscape.

The advent of the 'scrub roller' provided the answer to the dreams of selectors. This mechanism comprised an old, heavy boiler, pulled either side by up to six bullocks, the force of which literally rolled over the low vegetation. The process broke down the scrub close to the roots, and when it had dried out it was burned. Using this method, 2 hectares per day could be cleared.[31] Within a few years, the opening up of the Mallee – which continued to unfold over the next few decades – was described as 'one of the most remarkable developments that has taken place in the colony'.[32]

Early experiments with tractors proved disappointing. In 1909, a huge machine was transported to the Mallee with high expectations. Fitted with 'slabs' on its wheels to navigate across the sandy terrain, the tractor pulled three large rollers on axles attached with wire ropes. Despite being an imposing piece of machinery, it couldn't penetrate the dense Mallee vegetation.[33] In this quest for domination, almost everyone at the time overlooked the value of the Mallee scrub in preventing sand drifts.[34] The days of choking dust lay in the future.

In the meantime, the opening up of the Mallee was aided greatly by the development of the stump-jump plough – invented in South Australia by Richard Bowyer Smith. Farming similar Mallee scrub to that in northern Victoria, Smith realised that a typical British plough was redundant. Designed to create continuous, deep furrows, it didn't work in scrub country because of the frequency with which it either hit a stump or became stuck behind one. Smith's invention was designed to simply ride over the stump. He was derided at the start as either 'a fool or a lunatic' for such an unconventional approach, but Smith's invention transformed farming in rough country, not just in parts of Australia but in America and Canada as well.[35]

As early as 1891, the combined impact of the roller and the stump-jump plough had created a land boom in the Mallee. Selectors jostled for the chance to grow wheat amid the hype that the region would become the most productive cereal-growing region in Victoria.[36]

The lack of government regulation over the vast forest resources was a classic example of William Forster Lloyd's theory of the tragedy of the commons. His work may have been gathering dust on library shelves, but, in 1907, the *Sydney Morning Herald* invoked the essence of his theory when it wrote that the control over forests had been bandied around between different departments of the government, and that nobody was in charge. In fact, the forest resources of New South Wales had been whittled away by ignorance and by 'the Government's greed' without securing the public's right to the forests.[37]

Such widespread destruction excited a rolling debate in local newspapers. Among the persistent voices of opposition, none was more heartfelt than a correspondent to the *Wyalong Advocate* in 1900 who lamented that, through the activity of the ringbarkers, 'our sense of the beautiful in nature will be lost'.[38]

The extent of forest destruction in the Basin – which continued uninterrupted over many decades – was staggering. In 1995, the CSIRO estimated that between 12 and 15 billion trees had been removed from the region.[39]

Further destruction of Aboriginal culture

In 1902, while the destruction of forests continued apace, the New South Wales Museum made an unusual request to save a special tree on the property of Thomas Campbell of Burrendong, near Wellington, New South Wales. The tree was a yellow box 'with curiously carved Aboriginal inscriptions'. In fact, it was one of a few surviving examples of Aboriginal carved trees – comprising intricate inscriptions – usually to mark the burial place of a revered elder.[40] The inscriptions provided a pathway for an important man's spirit to 'return to the sky world'.[41] Such sites were dotted around the country, although this cultural practice was mainly concentrated in western New South Wales where the Gamilaroi and Wiradjuri had, for thousands of years, marked their respect for elders in this way.

The tree on Thomas Campbell's property marked the burial site of Lowrie, a respected local elder who died some time in the late 1850s. It must have been one of the last such burials in western New South Wales because Aboriginal carved trees became bound up with the dispossession of Aboriginal people after colonisation; almost all were destroyed by land clearing.[42] During the 1930s and 1940s, anthropologists campaigned to save the remaining trees by collecting them and sending them to museums, as was the case with the carved tree on the property of Thomas Campbell.

Forest destruction and drought

Ringbarking was aesthetically ugly. Great stands of trees stood like ghostly skeletons on the landscape until they were burned. However, during the second half of the 19th century, the stark appearance of so many ringbarked forests invited deeper questions about the impact of this practice. Was this level of destruction having an effect on the climate? The debates over the impact of ringbarking signalled the beginnings of the long journey of denialism and obfuscation of science in relation to the environment.

The Basin had been settled so quickly that squatters had little idea of how to manage their land for drought because it was difficult to estimate the average rainfall when records had not been kept long enough to enable them to do so with any degree of certainty.[43] And, in any event, weather forecasting continued to be little more than 'daring prophecy'.[44]

Nevertheless, speculation surfaced from the mid-1860s that such widespread forest destruction worsened droughts. In 1876, the Reverend WB Clarke read a paper to the New South Wales Royal

Society on the topic, in which he criticised the indiscriminate practice of ringbarking because it was increasing the 'evils' of drought.[45]

Despite his passionate interest in the issue, Clarke lacked professional qualifications to substantiate his claims. Consequently, they were dismissed by prominent landholders and politicians.[46] Nevertheless, by raising concerns about ringbarking, the practice became a contentious public issue from the 1870s onwards. Also, others with more convincing connections to science than the Reverend Clarke came to champion the issue of drought and its relationship to land clearing. The mid-1880s proved to be a turning point.

Drought struck western New South Wales in 1885 with a severity that nobody had previously experienced. It highlighted the extent of environmental mismanagement throughout the Basin's pastoral districts. Station owners had continued overstocking and clearing land. In fact, nearly all the edible trees between Bourke and Brewarrina had been cut down, exacerbating the effects of the naturally low rainfall. When the drought tightened its grip, sheep ate the foliage from the remaining trees, while men were employed in further tree clearance in order to keep starving sheep alive.[47] On Wonbabbie Station, 80 kilometres from Dubbo, sheep numbers had to be reduced from 60 000 to 12 000, and even the remaining numbers were dying fast.[48]

Parched by the dry, the area was turned into 'an unhappy grassless, waterless, stockless country', in the words of the *Daily Telegraph*.[49] Every day, sheep died by the thousands, and the toll on animal suffering was impossible to ignore. All along the railway extension to Bourke, gangs of contractors were confronted with the bodies of horses, cattle, sheep, dingoes and emus. The remaining stock staggered about like 'walking skeletons'.[50] In northern Victoria, the blisteringly hot conditions whipped up dust storms, which, locals reported, were as high as mountains and driven by hurricane-strength winds.[51] They were a portent of worse dust storms to come.

In 1885, the New South Wales Royal Commission into Water Conservation called on scientific evidence from around the world. It concluded that a growing body of evidence showed that the wholesale clearing of forests reduced rainfall – by up to 50 per cent in some districts – and caused salinity, which, together, rendered some districts desolate.[52] Such scientific evidence filtered up to parts of the colonial bureaucracy.

In 1889, for example, GS Perrin, the Victorian government's Conservator of Forests during the 1880s, issued a stinging rebuke against the relentless drive to cut down forests, and made the link not only to drought but to the economics of greed behind the pastoral industry. For over half a century, he said, Victorians had been driven by 'a mad desire' to clear forests. Forests had been 'sacrificed to the insatiable greed of the pastoral tenant and selector'. It was no wonder, he said, that drought stalked the land.[53]

Despite the dire impact, the warnings about land clearing were not heeded. And worse was to come. The Federation Drought of 1895–1902 greatly magnified the concerns that Perrin and others had raised (see chapter 7).

Pastoralism and native animals

The history of pastoralism had been about struggle: against Aboriginal people, remoteness, the weather, fluctuating prices and animal pests. Sentiment hardly came into the battle to make a living, let alone a fortune. Yet in the cities, opinion was divided on how this struggle against pests should be waged. Plenty of opinion supported the pastoralists – and the selectors – that 'vermin' had to be destroyed. Vermin was any animal that ate the grass, the grain seed or the livestock, and there was quite a tally on that score. It seemed a pity, commented the *South Australian Chronicle*, that animals good for food and their skins had to be destroyed indiscriminately, but society had 'to choose whether the country shall be possessed by sheep and cattle'.[54]

Out on the stations, controversy simmered about how best to deal with the two principal enemies – dingoes and kangaroos. Dingoes had a reputation for attacking the sheep, and kangaroos for eating the grass. Overlooked was the reality of nature, which dictated that dingoes kept the kangaroo population under control. As a correspondent from Warwick noted in a letter to the *Queenslander* in 1872, squatters, who were anxious to get rid of dingoes on their properties, would find a worse enemy in the rise of kangaroo numbers.[55] In fact, a few observers noted the lack of any logic to destroying both dingoes and kangaroos; it was simply self-defeating. As a correspondent to the *Brisbane Courier* noted in 1876, the 'marsupial plague' was caused by a disturbance to the 'natural balance in the animal world'.[56]

Those familiar with the bush pointed out that squatters were involved in a destructive dance with nature: the invasion of rabbits pushed up dingo numbers because they were given an assured food supply, and rabbits were attracted by the pastoral grasses. Some thought the task a hopeless one; stations were simply too large with so much rough country in which animals could take refuge: 'the extermination of the dingo is almost as hopeless a task as that of getting rid of the rabbit'.[57] European settlers had worsened the threat posed by dingoes. Domestic dogs gone wild joined dingo packs and bred with them, and the resulting half-breed was thought to be even more dangerous to sheep than the dingo.[58]

Nonetheless, the campaign to exterminate dingoes was waged as relentlessly as that against kangaroos. As early as 1853, plans were hatched in New South Wales to allocate government funding to 'effect the expiration of the native dog'. A system of paying for scalps was introduced – the first such payment system to eradicate a native animal.

Dingo hunting was a lonely occupation. Typically, hunters ranged over an area of between 200 and 250 kilometres checking on up to 250 traps. Special bush skills were required; the dingo 'could test the best bushcraft'. Out in the 'back country' dingo hunters had to live off wild game and sleep under the stars with 'a spring mattress of Mallee tussock'.[59]

Squatters also took matters into their own hands. They took advantage of the exemption granted to them under the *Sale of Poisons Act* to procure unlimited quantities of poisons – such as strychnine and cyanide. In 1888, a country chemist was horrified by this provision and wrote an indignant letter to the editor of the *Sydney Morning Herald* in which he argued that squatters shouldn't be allowed unlimited access to poisons, which they then not only scattered about themselves but also passed on to others who wanted to purchase them.[60]

Some thought poisoning a waste of time because dingoes seemed to be able to use their powerful scent to detect poison.[61] Not surprisingly, such a practice had a deadly impact on the wildlife of the Basin – likely on some dingoes, but certainly on birds and on carnivorous marsupials. But the campaign went on relentlessly. In 1896 in the Warwick district of the Darling Downs, for example, £1856 in 'scalp money' was paid out on 1562 dingoes in just the first six months.[62]

Despite the numbers killed, it's not entirely clear what impact the attempt to exterminate the dingo had on their overall numbers and distribution. Recent research conducted in New South Wales, however, has shown that, by 1930, the animal had largely been eradicated from the state. Between 1883 and 1930, 286 398 bounties had been paid.[63] But it is unclear whether this figure included dingoes poisoned by squatters. Nevertheless, dingoes continued to be a problem in Queensland well into the 1930s and a Royal Commission in 1930 found that the scalp system had been a failure with much of the money wasted.[64] Recent research has confirmed the conclusion that, in Queensland, larger marsupials and dingoes continued to proliferate, although the population of smaller marsupials was hard hit.[65]

The destruction of dingoes throughout the Basin encouraged kangaroo numbers to increase, and 'battue' hunting parties remained a favoured method to try to wipe them out. Yet such killing sprees seemed to have had little overall effect on the kangaroo population, and authorities resorted to more drastic measures. By the late 1880s, colonial governments covering the Basin had all introduced some form of pest destruction Act. The Queensland government called their 1877 measure the *Marsupial Destruction Act*; Victoria (1890) and South Australia (1882) each introduced a *Vermin Destruction Act*. The Victorian Act foreshadowed a government takeover of pest eradication measures; existing measures were labelled a failure. Vermin included rabbits, kangaroos, wallabies 'and all marsupials', dingoes and, indeed, 'any animal or bird proclaimed as vermin'.

The Acts gave the government the power to enter and inspect any property and, if vermin were found, order the owners to destroy the pests under threat of a fine. Inspectors could order the laying of poisons and the erection of new fences.[66] The result was a long and frequently fruitless war against so-called vermin.

The reclusive and largely nocturnal wombat was also regarded as vermin in the pastoral districts. It was hunted mercilessly because it allegedly stumbled into and damaged fences and posed a risk to livestock, which were thought to be prone to falling into wombat burrows, toppling over and breaking their legs.[67] However, few people in the country had actually seen a wombat, according to the *Wagga Wagga Advertiser*, which, in 1909, noted that destruction of the unique animal was motivated by commercial reasons – trapping wombats for their fur was a lucrative business.[68] By the mid-1920s, wombats were rapidly disappearing; their burrows 'wantonly destroyed', while traps and guns did the rest 'in a pitiless war' against the animal.[69]

Pastoralism and native birds

The Basin provided a rich habitat for a plethora of birds. Some became scarce through loss of habitat, some were turned into pests by squatters and selectors and were targeted for destruction, while other species were casualties of poisoned baits laid to kill both rabbits and dingoes. Others still fell victim to heedless hunting on stations. In the last decade of the 19th century, a flourishing export trade in feathers had also developed. By this time the small but growing band of naturalists became concerned over the prospect of many species vanishing from the landscape of the Basin altogether. However, their concerns were based on observation rather than scientific study, so we don't know the extent of the decline.

Forest clearance was a chief cause of the decline in birdlife. 'The settler', wrote the *Snowy River Mail* in 1913, 'regards the forest as his natural enemy against which a war of extermination must be waged'. With such a mindset, the paper noted, it was too much to expect 'from the average pioneer any intelligent appreciation of the beauty of plumage, or song of our native birds'; 'wanton destruction' went on 'in ordinary circumstances'.[70]

Mallee birdlife was particularly hard hit by the rolling over of the region's unique native scrub forest. Prior to the region being opened up to selectors, birdlife abounded: rose-breasted cockatoos, chattery flocks of jays, bronzed-winged pigeons, magpies and parrots of varied colours.[71]

One of the chief victims of the land clearance was the mallee fowl. These birds were renowned for their unique breeding habit of laying their eggs in large mounds – three metres by two metres – and their cooperative group behaviour in tending their young. By the early 1870s, the birds seemed to be retiring further into the bush as the country became more heavily stocked.[72] By 1913, the mallee fowl was assessed as being practically extinct, and birdlife in general in the Mallee was said to be vanishing.[73]

Squatters had two species of birds clearly in their sights. They regarded both the wedge-tailed eagle and the emu as vermin. Both were the subject of extensive campaigns of eradication.

In the mid-1890s the *Australasian* reminded its readers what a noble and imposing bird the eagle was and lamented that, in the absence of any protection by law, squatters offered ten shillings per head for its destruction because the birds sometimes killed lambs. The squatters, it was argued, had a short-sighted view about the threat posed by the species; that killing a few lambs overlooked their role in clearing squatters' runs of pests during the year.[74] In fact, the widespread killing of eagles showed how little squatters understood the ecology of the land they occupied. As one correspondent wrote to the *Queenslander* in 1880, wedge-tailed eagles formed a key cog in the balance of nature: 'The fact of eagles killing young marsupials is not sufficiently known, or surely we would not see such a wholesale slaughter of these noble birds by poison and guns'.[75]

In colonial times, emus were regarded as the 'monarch' of Australian birds. One correspondent wrote to an Adelaide newspaper in 1918: 'What grander sight or what spectacle more typical of the real old-time Australian scenery than there is of a mob of these fine birds'.[76] They were not popular with the squatters, though, because they ate so much grass.[77] Before Europeans arrived, the dingo kept the emu population under control by stealing and eating eggs from the nest. It is not known what effect the campaign to kill dingoes had on emu numbers, but squatters were worried about the swarming of the birds on pastoral stations along the Darling River, maintaining that there would be many more sheep than at present if the emus were destroyed[78]. Settlers broke their eggs and destroyed the birds at every opportunity. Some emu skins found their place as floor mats in squatters' homes and there was a large market for their feathers.

Out on the stations in the Basin, a silent war was waged against the emu. One 'bush naturalist', in an article for the *Brisbane Courier*, highlighted the 'senseless desire' among young station hands, jackeroos and visitors to hunt them down.[79] The birds were the target for the same battue-style mass killings directed at kangaroos. Hessian was strung out for up to two kilometres, after which 30 or 40 horsemen drove emus from the surrounding bush to crash into the hessian, which 'extremely frightened' the birds. These emu drives were 'exciting events' because 'the culling out was so heavy'. One account described the aim of the drives as 'to exterminate the birds'.[80]

Such was the determination to be rid of emus, they were exempt from any legal protection. Some feared that they would become extinct.[81] But when protection came late in the 1890s, it simply meant that the birds could no longer be shot; squatters got around this imposition by continuing to destroy emu eggs.[82]

From the late 1880s, squatters had an additional reason to eradicate emus. The birds became the chief culprit in the squatters' war against a rampant plant pest: prickly pear. Like rabbits and foxes, prickly pear was an introduced species that went rogue. It came to New South Wales via Rio de Janeiro in the 1820s as a garden specimen. As a member of the cacti family it was valued as a 'showy plant' in the gardens of wealthy landowners.[83] Emus were believed to be fond of the fruit and spread the plant's seeds through their droppings.

The devastation wrought by prickly pear was slow to materialise. In 1885, only 2000 hectares were affected, but this figure jumped to over one million hectares by 1911.[84] By this time, out on stations in the Murray–Darling, the campaign against emus had intensified. For example, on Callandoon Station, on the Queensland–New South Wales border near Goondiwindi, two 'emu drives' in 1909 slaughtered 601 birds and destroyed 2000 eggs.[85]

Wheat farmers had different native birds in their sights than squatters, notably galahs, cockatoos, magpies, brolgas and crows. Each was regarded as vermin because of the threat they posed to crops. Cockatoos were especially feared. Farmers could see them winging their way across the sky in large flocks, knowing that, at seeding time, they would be there taking the grain from behind the seeding drill.[86] Grain laced with arsenic and strychnine was widely used, but to little avail because the birds were just too cunning. Brolgas, loved in some circles as the dancing bird, were also a target for extermination. With their long beaks and keen sense of smell they were able to find every gain of wheat at planting time. Hundreds were killed at a time by strychnine baits.[87]

Other creatures were likely to have been killed by such indiscriminate baiting, and larger carnivorous native birds were poisoned when they picked over the dead bodies of poisoned rabbits and dingoes.[88] When poisoning didn't work, farmers resorted to shooting birds. It was estimated that many thousands of magpies were shot by farmers in Victoria and New South Wales.[89]

Rabbit eradication and the war on nature

Scenes worse than any modern-day road kill could be seen along country roads in the late 19th and early 20th centuries. A correspondent to a country newspaper reported in 1901 of seeing 'hundreds of dead birds' along one country road, including 27 dead magpies along a three-mile [five-kilometre] stretch.[90] In fact, millions of birds, including kookaburras, magpies, bower birds, larks and plovers, were being destroyed each year by pastoralists and farmers using poison baits to kill rabbits.[91]

From the early 1880s, rabbits invaded Australian farms in waves like plagues of locusts. The infestations are lodged in the nation's collective memory. However, the menace deserves re-telling here as part of the wider story of Europeans' mismanagement of the Murray–Darling Basin's ecology, which was at the epicentre of the plague. Rabbits did untold damage to the region's ecology.

Rabbits, as already mentioned, were merely one species of vermin with which squatters and selectors had to do battle. As short-sighted as it was to bring the quick-breeding, grass-devouring animal to Australian shores with the First Fleet, pastoralism, with its extensive grasslands facilitated by widespread forest clearance, enabled rabbits to reach plague proportions.

The rabbit plague that infested the Murray–Darling Basin

from the 1880s was, at heart, a crisis of the model of pastoralism – the removal of deep-rooted native grasses, overstocking and the mentality of high profits at all costs. The balance of nature had been firmly tipped in favour of rabbits. Ringbarking and the provision of water, *Queensland Country Life* acknowledged as late as 1939, had made conditions better for the rabbit as well as for stock.[92] So great was the threat to the pastoral industry that colonial governments groaned under the weight of the revenue spent trying to eradicate the problem. Selectors weren't spared either. They were more vulnerable than pastoralists, having smaller holdings and less capital, and rabbit infestation ruined many; they were, literally, 'eaten out of house and land'.[93]

Rabbits were declared a pest in Victoria in 1880. In the same year, the invasion of New South Wales began, and rabbits spread so rapidly that concerted action had to be taken against them within a few years. Between May 1883 and the end of 1886, the New South Wales government paid out £361 492 in the purchase of 7 852 783 rabbit scalps. After crossing the Murray, the rabbits travelled steadily northwards, spreading east and west as they advanced, and crossing the South Australian and Queensland borders between 1886 and 1887.[94]

By the late 1880s, the rabbit invasion had also gripped the vast pastoral district of western New South Wales. From Nyngan to Bourke, the land was completely denuded of grass and other fodder. Controlling the rabbits created a small industry; in excess of 2000 people in New South Wales alone were employed on a bonus system to deal with the invasion. Good wages could be made. Throughout the back country, rabbiting was known as 'about the best line going'. In fact, it was a common thing to find a rabbiter driving to work in a buggy and pair.[95] So good were the returns, that some rabbiters weren't in a hurry to abolish their mode of living by eradicating the plague. Claims were made that they deliberately placed rabbits in unaffected districts.[96]

Extreme measures were taken by squatters to rid stations of rabbits. During the 1880s invasion, poisoning with phosphorus-laced pollard, a finely milled brand of wheat, was common. It was laid on bare patches in paddocks, but its very lethality showed how disconnected some squatters and selectors were from any understanding of the environment. Phosphorus was known to be a dangerous poison to all creatures.[97] Its indiscriminate application also caused death to poultry, domestic animals and stock and, additionally, was a significant contributor to summer bushfires.[98]

An attempt at mass killing of rabbits began in the early 1900s with the invention of a horse-drawn 'poison cart', which was fitted with a lever attached to a cylinder that enabled baked pollard baits to be automatically spaced in furrows and back-filled to protect stock from eating them. Wide areas could be laid with baits and the carts became an indispensable piece of farm equipment for decades.

The carts were promoted as 'rabbit destroying machines',[99] but birds frequently got to the baits before the rabbits with devastating consequences for bird numbers and with damaging flow-on effects to local ecologies. 'Birds have been swept away in their thousands' since the carts were introduced, noted the *Euroa Advocate* in 1914;[100] whole areas were left without any birdlife. With the birds gone, there were yearly increases in numbers of grasshoppers, caterpillars and other insect pests.[101]

The deployment of the poison cart was not just a story of misplaced faith in technology. Its use illustrated the depth of the war being waged on nature. The *Bulletin* magazine called for the carts to be banned in 1908 because they were an 'eradicator of birds',[102] but they continued to be used right up until the 1940s with government approval.

Another common method in the war against rabbits was to fill tanks with water poisoned with strychnine. This, too, exacted an enormous toll on wildlife, killing large numbers of snakes, birds and goannas (known as iguanas in the 19th century). Lamenting this toll, a 'Backblocker' from Nyngan, New South Wales, wrote to a local newspaper complaining that 'these squatters can do just as they choose because they are too lazy to adopt proper precautions … to prevent the wholesale destruction of game'.[103]

Attention was drawn to the decimation of goannas because of their role in keeping rabbits under control; they found rabbit warrens and killed the young. In addition to being poisoned, goannas were also caught in rabbiters' traps. On one station near Wentworth, New South Wales, the owner found that he had to take the traps away, such was the damage being done. On his property, the rabbiters were trapping a thousand goannas per week. Without the use of traps, 'the iguana would increase rapidly and would be so plentiful that no young rabbit would escape them'.[104]

The Murray River fishing industry

The war on nature extended to the Basin's aquatic life. The region's rivers teemed with life – fish, turtles and frogs and the birds that fed on them, pelicans and cormorants. But all species were ruthlessly targeted by commercial and sporting groups, with dire consequences.

The most prized fish was the Murray cod, which quickly became the favoured freshwater eating fish in south-eastern Australia. Living up to half a century and more, and weighing up to 27 kilos, it soon became known as 'the king among fish'.[105]

In the late 1850s, entrepreneurs eyed the opportunities of establishing a fishing industry on the Murray by transporting Murray cod down to the restaurants of Ballarat, Bendigo and Melbourne.[106] Even before the industry became established, recreational anglers targeted the fish. As early as 1859, the *Ovens and Murray Advertiser* worried that Murray cod were being caught by nets, spears and lines all year round without restrictions. This, the paper argued, was symptomatic 'of the short-sightedness of the age'.[107]

By the 1880s, the population of Murray cod had declined alarmingly. The banks of the Murray and its tributaries were lined with fishermen, and the methods many used to maximise their catch included dynamite.[108] Commercial fishermen also used seven-metre-long drum nets, which enabled large quantities of the fish to be caught for the restaurant trade. While there is no overall data on the amount of cod taken from the river, in 1883, 150 tonnes was taken from just one port, Moama.[109] Victoria introduced a closed season to try to protect fish stocks, but that made little difference when New South Wales failed to follow suit. But what good would regulation be anyway, some asked? Such was the popularity of the fish that it would take a small army of officials to watch the length of the Murray and 'snatch wriggling fish off the lines', warned the *Bendigo Independent*.[110]

Consequently, regulation proved ineffective. In 1892, amid fears that the fish were being grossly over-exploited and faced extinction, a South Australian ministerial party undertook a tour of inspection of the Murray River and found that the destruction of the fish and their habitat was ongoing. The party attempted to engage fishermen in discussion of further regulation to protect the Murray cod but were rebuffed because additional regulation, the fishermen said, would constitute an unwarranted interference with their liberty. As one old fisherman curtly replied, 'the best regulation you can make is to leave us alone altogether'.[111] The party came away from the trip realising the complexity of protecting the Murray cod involved not just opposition to regulation but also the various colonies pursuing different agendas in managing the river. And that's where the matter rested until after Federation when new attempts were made to deal with a further decline in Murray cod fish stocks. In the meantime, Melbournians continued to indulge their epicurean passion by having access to an unregulated fishery on the Murray River.

But there were wider environmental consequences than just depleted fish stocks. Anglers and commercial fishermen believed, like squatters and selectors, that threats to their interests from any other species made them fair game for destruction. Turtles, cormorants and pelicans, which had inhabited the Murray for millennia, became the maligned destroyers of the Murray cod. 'Periodically', wrote the *Land*, 'people in the country districts organise cormorant shoots, in the belief that by so doing they are helping to reduce a pest and to give protection to the fish'[112]. Turtles fared little better. The traditional place they had in the ecosystem was not even considered; they were 'the worst enemies' of the Murray cod by following the fish into the waters to feast on the cod spawn. Fishermen, it was claimed, destroyed millions of turtles.[113] Fishermen also regularly shot pelicans on the river. Naturally tame and curious, the birds came right up to the fishermen's camp, where they would be shot at close range.[114]

Native wildlife hunted for sport

In an era of open slather on all flora and fauna, it was not surprising that sporting shooters in the Basin acted in a similar fashion. Indiscriminate shooting was widespread and shocked some contemporaries. The practice cut across social class lines. Bird shooting, known as 'gunning parties', was a favoured pastime of South Australia's social elite. In an episode that earned bragging rights among his friends, Lord Kintore and a party of 12 shooters, operating out of Murray Bridge, killed 1270 birds over two days, and it was reckoned that 'fully 1000 must have come to grief' without being bagged.[115] Gentlemen shooters, agreed the *Ovens and Murray Advertiser,* 'are in the habit of mercilessly slaughtering all the small birds they see' in the quest to become 'crack shots'.[116]

On the Murray River itself, 'pot shooters' were a common sight. These were opportunistic hunters interested only in killing birds for the sake of it. In 1894, the *Bendigo Independent* regretted that, in the breeding grounds of the lagoons and lakes on the New South

Wales side of the Murray River, pot shooters took advantage of female birds protecting their young to take a close range and easy shot at the birds, killing large numbers and generally creating havoc among the population.[117]

Another favoured pastime for recreational shooters was to take aim at pelicans from paddle steamers plying up and down the Murray. In 1913, an indignant correspondent wrote to an Adelaide newspaper about the experience of witnessing such callous behaviour. When a solitary pelican was seen on the river, the correspondent reported, some of the men reached for their pea rifles and repeatedly shot at the bird but without being able to kill it. Flocks of pelicans, the correspondent was certain, were becoming rarer on the river because of such indiscriminate killing.[118]

'Many people do not respect the game laws', lamented the *Bendigo Independent* in 1914: 'These persons shoot protected birds and animals as readily as they do rabbits'.[119] By the mid-1920s, Australian native birds were still being subjected to 'wholesale destruction',[120] according to *The Age*, with little respect shown for laws to protect them.

Farmers, gun clubs, holiday shooters and 'bird nesters' – people who robbed eggs and young chicks – were all part of a ruthless and widespread culture of destruction.[121]

The trade in skins, fur and feathers

When not slaughtered as pests, native wildlife in the Murray–Darling Basin formed a prime source for a global trade in furs and feathers for apparel. In 1888, the growing appeal of fashion made from fur was on display at the Melbourne Centennial Exhibition, which offered a 'tasteful display' of coats, foot warmers and caps made mainly from American-sourced animals. However, Australian marsupial skins were a growing part of the international fur trade. In 1887, 1.7 million possum skins had been exported to London, along with 150 000 kangaroo skins and thousands of bales of rabbit skins.[122]

As these early numbers indicate, the slaughter of marsupials for the fur trade was staggering. And it's hard to escape the view that this massive trade was another form of colonialism: Australia exporting its raw materials – in this case its native animals – to supply the London fashion industry and then importing the manufactured goods.

A rollcall of Australian marsupials supplied a trade in the manufacture of fur coats in England and America: possums, kangaroos, wallabies and koalas. They were valued because their coats were soft and would lie in any direction, like plush. Wallaby skins were also converted into shoe leather.[123] Thousands of people were employed in trapping the animals for export, with some bush towns depending on the trade. Trapping was lucrative as well as offering an attractive pastime for people in the bush, but it was callous too. Trappers went out in the early morning to check their traps. And when they returned home, the children and wives would often help in the task of skinning and pegging the pelt. Even though they could make good money as trappers, some resorted to the use of cyanide poisoning because it saved the small amount of effort involved in operating traps. However, other animals of no value to the hunter, together with birds, were destroyed in the process.[124]

The demand for marsupial skins threatened to exterminate most of the species, commented one Queensland newspaper.[125] For 20 years between 1886 and 1916, over 100 000 possum skins were sold at the Albury market, on the New South Wales–Victorian border, every fortnight.[126] And that was just one regional town in the Murray–Darling Basin.

Possum shooting by moonlight was a popular pastime.[127] It was a fond memory of grown-up country boys and girls.[128] Out on the stations 'all hands are at it', a naturalist wrote to a local newspaper, 'including squatters with their sons and daughters; and I even seen [sic] a governess with three young pupils doing the rounds and clearing up a few snares'.[129] The export trade in skins offered bushmen a lucrative living.[130] Even the squatters valued the extra money earned, some reaping £1000 worth of skins per year. But the temptation to use poison was irresistible to some. Poisoning, it was claimed, could kill more possums per night and, as mentioned, there was very little to prevent squatters from getting as much of this 'dope' as they wanted.[131]

The reclusive platypus was highly valued for its skin, which was made into expensive rugs. Typically, five or six skins went into the making of a single rug, although one turned up in London in the 1940s with 44 skins. The skins were prized for being 'thick and heavy and the fur denser than any other Australian animal'.[132] Many rugs were made in London and, as platypus became scarce, the rugs' value continued to rise.[133] The animal was declared a protected species in 1905, but skins continued to turn up in the Sydney market, which seemed to indicate that people either didn't know about the protected status or didn't hold any fears of being prosecuted for selling skins.[134] In any event, experts today believe that the fur trade had such a catastrophic effect on platypus numbers that the species never recovered. 'There was one record of a single furrier selling up to 29,000 platypus skins before the First World War, so we think that has caused long-term impacts across their range', researcher Tahneal Hawke explained in 2019.[135]

Koalas were so plentiful across eastern Australia at the time of European settlement[136] that it was inevitable their soft fur would also become a prime target for the export trade. Hunting koalas provided a source of rural income, especially for small selectors.[137] Some graziers opposed the trade, worried that trappers would harm stock; the animal posed no direct threat to pastoralists. Hunting mainly occurred on moonlit nights, and shooting koalas was not for the squeamish. A few lone voices recognised the cruelty involved. It was said that a koala was hard to kill because of its massive skull, and when being dispatched, it uttered 'a most pitiful and almost human cry'.[138] Moreover, when shot, the koala often gripped the bark of the tree tightly and did not fall to the ground, depriving the hunter of its quarry.[139]

To meet export demand, the number of koalas killed continued to escalate. America became a favoured destination for koala skins, where they were manufactured into cheap coats for working-class men toiling in the freezing winters. Demand was said to be 'practically unlimited'.[140] In fact, fur trappers in Arctic Canada were reported to favour koala skin coats as the best fur to keep out the cold.[141]

By 1924, two million koala skins had been exported from the eastern states alone.[142] The marsupial was said to have been practically 'shot out' of Victoria and was increasingly rare in New South Wales; Queensland contained the last available commercial supply. Although spread widely throughout Queensland, the Warwick district in the Murray–Darling Basin was one of a few regions in the state supplying large quantities of skins.[143]

By 1910, millions of marsupial skins had been exported to Britain and America to supply the fur trade. Few Australians, it was claimed, had any conception of these enormous figures.[144]

Native birds were targeted for the fashion trade. From the early 1890s, the British millinery industry created the plumed hat initially using the feathers from birds of paradise from across the tropical world. But as the industry boomed, virtually no bird was safe from the plume hunter. By 1905, it was estimated that between 200 and 300 million birds worldwide were slaughtered annually to supply the millinery trade.[145]

The new fashion delighted many women but horrified members of the British Society for the Protection of Birds, who slated it as 'murderous millinery'.[146] However, the fashion flourished for decades, creating an insatiable demand for birds from around the world. Australia became a key player in the trade and the Murray–Darling Basin was a prime source of feathers harvested from emus, egrets, herons, lyrebirds and peacocks.

The hunt for egrets, which one newspaper wrote amounted to a 'butchery', was carried out in the Riverina swamps and billabongs bordering the Murray River.[147] Species were disappearing and others were close to extinction.[148] In 1907, for example, word arrived in Melbourne that 'plume hunters' were busily at work in an egret rookery in the swamplands of the Upper Murray. Receiving the news, Mr Maltingley, a prominent member of the Australian Ornithologists' Union, rushed up country, but he was too late. The dark waters of the swamp were strewn with the carcasses of birds 'floating silently in death, or slowly sinking in the dismal slime'.[149]

Emu feathers also became a prized part of the trade because they were 'just as pretty' as the feathers of actual birds of paradise. Consequently, many of the tufts that nestled cosily on the side of 'tiled hats' were from Australian emus.[150] Thus, in the first years of a federated Australia, the nation had its chosen national symbols – the emu and the kangaroo – ruthlessly killed for an export trade to Britain.

For years after the turn of the century, Australians continued to have a deeply contradictory attitude towards emus: revered but ruthlessly destroyed. Nothing summed up this contradiction more starkly than the military use of emu feathers. The tradition began with a contingent of Queensland troops heading off to fight with the British in the Boer War in South Africa where the troops stood out by wearing emu plumes in their hats. As the *Brisbane Courier* proudly noted: 'an emu plume in the hat is a badge of honour … a distinctive … sign of the colony of origin'.[151] The tradition continued into World War One with the Queensland Light Horse. This prompted patriotic emu hunts to be organised in outback Queensland to meet demand.[152]

Appeals for the conservation of birdlife went unheeded for many years. The solution, as always, was regulation, as theorised by William Forster Lloyd. If women were made to realise, commented a spokesperson for the Australian Ornithologists Union, that the wearing of plumes was an offence against the law, the destruction of birds merely for their feathers would stop.[153] But it was not until 1923 that the Commonwealth banned the export of native birds, after years of pressure from groups including the Ornithologists' Union.

The war on nature fails

The decades-long war on nature had the principal objective of increasing profits from agriculture. But it had the reverse effect: rabbits continued to proliferate from such an upending of the natural world, while many species were driven into a spiral of decline.

The rabbit invasion of the early 1880s crippled the pastoral industry. Some contemporaries observed that, eventually, nearly all rabbits died out from sheer starvation. Nevertheless, the future for squatters looked gloomy; some had no money to start over again and the banks wouldn't lend to many. Yet after a few years, the country recovered and squatters started breeding up from remnant stock.

Just as flocks began to recover, disaster struck the pastoral districts again in the early 1890s with another drought and a second rabbit invasion.[154] In fact, throughout the 1890s, squatters in the Murray–Darling Basin faced a nightmare of financially ruinous factors: the price of wool declined under competition from Argentina; a severe drought stalked pastoral districts between 1890 and 1893; and a crippling economic depression hit Australia at this time, partly caused by the drought.

The second rabbit plague blighted the land. In 1891 most of the Basin was overrun by rabbits. They consumed any grass as fast as it grew; even the roots in the ground had been laid bare. The *South Australian Register* commented that it looked as if 'the whole area must speedily be reduced to a wretched barren waste till even the rabbits themselves perish of starvation'.[155]

In country towns, rabbits were everywhere: servants in hotels brushed them off the doorsteps early in the morning; boys hunted them going to and from school; and people squashed them with the wheels of their buggies.[156]

The rabbit plague was the last straw for British banks. They descended, circling like wedge-tail eagles for prey. British banks and their shareholders – along with those in Australia – had invested heavily in pastoralism and had come to expect annual returns of between 12 and 30 per cent. They took a dim view of their future returns in the face of the rabbit plague and the drought. Action was swift. Banks added pressure on demands for greater effort to exterminate the rabbits, and they repossessed hundreds of squatters' runs.[157]

In a perverse way, nature had extracted its revenge on pastoralism.

Alternative voices

The history of environmental destruction that accompanied the development the Murray–Darling Basin in the first half century after settlement worried conservation-minded people who fought for better protection of the natural world. Among this group were the growing number of colonial- or state-based naturalist groups, scientists, newspaper columnists and ordinary Australians who wrote letters to their local papers.

The number of such people may have been small, but they spoke with a collective voice. By the first decade of the 20th century, three voices in particular stood out: New South Wales government etymologist Walter Froggatt; and two authors and newspaper columnists, ES Sorenson and TP Bellchambers. Collectively, they argued that the nation had no answer to the destruction of nature centred in the Basin.

Firstly, regulation had failed because governments had not taken implementation of legislation seriously. As Froggatt argued, protection Acts amounted to little more than 'dead Acts', because the responsibility had been passed onto harassed local police officers who had neither the time nor the knowledge to implement them.[158]

Secondly, implementation failed because the extractive model of agriculture was just too embedded in the culture. The 'old stockman', argued Froggatt, destroyed the country by looking upon every native animal that ate grass as an enemy.[159] Sorenson was no less strident in his criticism of pastoralism. Squatters, he wrote, had destroyed the forests, and the native animals and birds, so that the 'land might carry a sheep or two more to the acre'.[160]

Lastly, all were concerned about the flagrant ignorance of the need to preserve the balance of nature. Native birds and animals, Froggatt pointed out, were adaptable and if their natural food sources were destroyed they would regard crops as a suitable alternative. Bellchambers agreed. Pastoralism, he argued, was destroying the 'valuable links in nature's chain on which man's very existence depends'[161]. He revived an uncomfortable reminder of the frontier war. 'The blackfelllow', he wrote, 'was never a wasteful killer. His life depended on reasonable conservation laws … a perfectly fitting cog in nature's scheme of balance'.[162] It is not hard to imagine the distress that the widespread destruction of native wildlife caused Aboriginal people.

By the time these conservation ideas percolated into the public domain, progress and its environmental consequences had continued to unfold in the Basin. A revival of agrarianism followed the drought of the early 1890s, with waves of new settlers taking up blocks. A visionary scheme to introduce irrigation along the Murray River was being constructed to support this influx of people, while at the same time, the region was brought to its knees in the Federation Drought of 1895–1903.

It is to these developments that we must turn, against the backdrop of the toll of environmental destruction, about which a handful of contemporaries had so courageously tried to warn.

6

IRRIGATION EMPIRE: THE RISE AND FALL OF THE CHAFFEY BROTHERS

On 3 June 1896, George Chaffey, the elder of two brothers who had been invited to Australia from the United States to establish the country's first large-scale irrigation settlements in Victoria and South Australia, gave evidence before a Victorian Royal Commission into the collapse of the settlement at Mildura. The financial scandal threatened to drag the town down with it. Such a development came as a complete surprise. Across the various colonies, the Chaffeys were heroes; people hoped that the Mildura and Renmark projects would pave the way for the future prosperity of the nation's agriculture.

Alfred Deakin, later three times Prime Minister of Australia (1903–04; 1905–08; 1909–10), had invited them to set up operations in Victoria as a private company in the mid-1880s when he was Water Minister in the Victorian government. And John Downer (later Sir John) – from an old established Adelaide family – had enticed the Chaffeys to set up a second operation at Renmark. Farmers from England had been lured by the bright prospects of the schemes and, over the next few years, the new settlements attracted visitors from around the country and around the world who marvelled at the progress achieved in turning dusty plains into models of agriculture and human settlement.

Yet here was Chaffey having to account in the most public manner for his and his brother's failures. In addition to being financially ruined, Chaffey was said to be a broken man.[1] He was certainly an angry man. He began his evidence by saying that he had been 'wilfully' misunderstood, 'abused and slandered', and accused of deception. He dismissed most of the allegations of financial and project mismanagement and focused, instead, on a malcontent among the settlers who had whipped up agitation and created chaos. But he did concede to one deeper problem; settlers had been demanding free water.[2] Soon afterwards, George returned to America, penniless, never to return; his brother, William (known as 'WB') Chaffey, resisted the storm of criticism, staying on to help rebuild Mildura, where he remained for the rest of his life.

Despite the financial collapse of the Chaffeys, over time their story became part of the national mythology, especially as Mildura and Renmark went on to become key parts of Australia's great nation-building project: irrigating inland Australia. Along with their political backer, Alfred Deakin, the Chaffey brothers became the 'fathers of irrigation', and their brush with the Royal Commission became 'a grievous blot' on their reputations. Thus, by 1929 the *Sydney Mail* wrote that 'the story of the conversion of Mildura from "a God-forsaken wilderness" into a comparatively prosperous closely-settled irrigation colony is one of the romances of Australia'.[3]

But how did Australia's first major irrigation scheme go so wrong? Why were American entrepreneurs given the right to develop it? And what role did the Victorian government play in its demise? In a searing report, the Royal Commission highlighted public policy failings in the design and execution of the Mildura scheme. The scheme survived the Chaffeys' mismanagement only through government intervention. The story of its establishment illustrates an emerging pattern of flawed decision-making for the development of the Murray–Darling Basin.

The quest for irrigation

A wave of technological advancement in the second half of the 19th century – specifically, mechanical pumps and concrete piping – opened up new possibilities for 'scientific' irrigation on a scale hitherto unimaginable. The potential of irrigation attracted visionaries with utopian ideas of adapting this form of agriculture to new self-sustaining yeoman colonies. At first fringe ideas, they had, by the late 19th century, found influential supporters in both America and Australia.

By the 1880s, there was an urgent imperative driving irrigation: finding a solution to drought, the constant adversary of the Murray–Darling Basin's farmers. This was not the silver-bullet solution advocated by those who had explored the science of drought. As mentioned in the last chapter, increasingly that advice was to halt – and, by implication, reverse – land clearing. But politics dictated nation-building over the environment. The 1880s marked the first sustained effort to solve the problem of providing water in a dry continent. Deakin and the Chaffey brothers were the first big water entrepreneurs to put their aspirations into action. Irrigation promised to transform the interior of Australia, which held a forbidding reputation among settlers as a place where 'only lost souls would venture unasked or unassisted'.[4]

In Victoria, the drought of the early to mid-1880s, discussed in chapter 4, spurred large-scale development. It was the beginning of the quest to drought-proof inland Australia.

In the previous two decades, large areas of northern Victoria had been opened up to free selection. Following good seasons, however, dry conditions returned with a vengeance. Rainfall over the region slowly declined,[5] most likely as a consequence of large-scale land clearing. Selectors in the drought-stricken areas were reduced to a parlous state. Some went bankrupt and had to abandon their land altogether, while the rest were forced to wage a struggle for bare existence.[6] Water was brought in by rail in an attempt to stave off even further losses.[7] Churches in Melbourne offered up prayers for rain.[8] Unfortunately, providence didn't intervene and farmers became angry that, while they suffered, water from the Murray River flowed past their properties and ran into the sea. They clamoured for action on irrigation.[9] So did Victoria's premier newspapers, *The Age* and the *Leader*, both published by David Syme, said to be one of the most powerful newspaper owners in the English-speaking world.[10]

Amid the clamour, doubters warned the government that the benefits of large-scale irrigation schemes might not produce the expected results. Two early irrigation experts, G Gordon and A Black, prepared a report for the Victorian government in 1882 in which they wrote that optimistic assessments of the profitableness of irrigation 'are often entertained from an under-estimate of the costs and an over-estimate of the results'.[11] In throwing such cautionary warnings to the winds, the Victorian government began a long tradition in Australian irrigation policy of sidelining rational analysis in favour of reckless extraction.

Irrigation attracts an apostle

Closely watching the clamour for irrigation was a young, talented and ambitious politician. From the time Alfred Deakin entered politics as a 22-year-old protégé of David Syme, who had employed him as a writer, he attracted an extraordinary aura of destiny about him. Effusive accounts of his qualities poured out in the columns of the press, and there is little doubt much of it was deserved. Deakin, as Judith Brett, his most recent biographer eloquently attests, had a rare combination of talents – intellectual curiosity, boundless energy and integrity.[12] Yet Deakin's championing of irrigation had a proselytising quality about it, and he was referred to as 'the apostle' of irrigation. Such a stance seemed odd in a young, urban-based politician with no background in agriculture.

Deakin came from a privileged, middle-class family and was educated at Melbourne Grammar and the University of Melbourne. A dreamy, restless young man, he fixed on a direction in life only when he came under the notice of David Syme. Deakin became a progressive, liberal politician under the stern guidance of his employer. He took up the cause of irrigation with gusto, becoming a national authority on the subject. As an emerging progressive, liberal politician Deakin was drawn to nation-building and concerned about long-term economic development.[13] As he explained to a newspaper in 1887, 'the capacity of the country to carry a large population depends entirely upon the amount of irrigation that can be successfully carried out'.[14] Behind such a goal was a utopian dream, 'to make the deserts and waste places flourish'.[15] And Deakin had big dreams about the potential of irrigation. He envisioned ten million acres (about four million hectares) in northern Victoria available to agriculture, delivering a £10 million rise in national wealth.[16]

As a progressive, Deakin was also interested in how people lived, and not just in the wealth that society produced. He was a firm believer in the virtues of rural life and saw in the development of irrigated agriculture the ability of a man and his family to make a good living on a small plot of land by combining different kinds of activities: orcharding, bee-keeping and dairying. Family life, he believed, was strengthened when all members could help in one way or another. Better off socially and economically, irrigated agricultural communities would be able to access education for their children.[17]

The Chaffey brothers

The failure of the Mildura irrigation colony – and the scandal that surrounded it – inevitably led to questions about the real motives of the Chaffey brothers in coming to Australia. At the time of the Royal Commission, some newspapers depicted the brothers as 'penniless adventurers who had come to this country to exploit a credulous people for their own sole advantage'.[18] While this overstates their flawed characters, the Chaffey brothers were both visionaries and opportunists.

George was the dominant of the two brothers. He described himself as an engineer, but, at heart, George was an entrepreneur, steeped in post–Civil War American self-starting business culture. Australians noticed the restless pleasure with which George approached business matters.[19] He was charismatic, a risk-taker, an innovator and a self-promoter with a high regard for his own capacities. But with his engineering background, he could also turn his mind to solving problems in a practical way.[20] In business, he was a shrewd operator prepared to deploy practices that ranged from the innovative to the shonky and, some say, fraudulent. Possessing a strong streak of rugged American individualism, he was disdainful of government.[21]

To Australians, George was an American, but to Americans he was a Canadian. The blurring of nationalities reflected the restless spirit of adventure in the Chaffey family. Born in 1848 in Ontario, Canada, George was described as a delicate boy. Taken out of school at 13, he began tinkering in his father's workshop before he began his working life as an engineer alongside his father, designing and building boats on the St Lawrence waterway.[22] By his early 20s, he was a noted designer and builder of boats and inventor of marine equipment.[23]

Sometime in the early 1870s, George Snr sought a warmer climate for health reasons and landed at Riverside, an innovative irrigation colony in southern California. George followed his father there in what proved to be a turning point in his life. It was through his experience at Riverside that George Jnr embraced the 'irrigation philosophy': the opportunity to develop idyllic societies of self-supporting yeoman farmers living in well-designed, healthy communities.[24]

George struck out on his own, purchasing 600 hectares of land on the arid Santa Fe Trail where he was joined by his younger brother,

William, a trained horticulturist. Together they developed 'Etiwanda', which became a pioneering irrigation colony. Critics scoffed at their plans to grow fruit trees in the desert, but through the development of a concrete piping and hydro-electric pumping system, the land blossomed. The ten-acre blocks they released sold well.[25]

Soon after, the brothers plunged into an even more ambitious scheme at Sierra Madre, east of the then little-known town of Los Angeles. They called the 3230-hectare property 'Ontario' and it became renowned as a model irrigation colony, comprising a town with broad streets, a school, a post office, a railway station and a college of education. Saloons were banned, reflecting the brothers' strong temperance philosophy. From an engineering perspective, George's achievements were substantial as they involved piping water from the melting snows of the nearby 3000-metre range for 42 kilometres to the blocks that the brothers sold. The scheme was so successful that, within a few years, $4 million worth of produce was being sold to neighbouring states and the value of the land had risen nearly four-fold.[26] 'We were laughed at for tackling it', George later told an Adelaide newspaper.[27]

Both the Etiwanda and Ontario colonies were founded on the same business model, which the brothers then imported to Mildura. These ventures pioneered by the Chaffeys were pure American capitalism – land and water turned into profitable speculation. The brothers developed an innovative approach around the individual ownership of land and water.[28] Californian law permitted individual ownership of public water. By the 1890s, southern California had become 'an orange empire' of fruit growing.[29]

The Chaffeys' plan was deceptively simple: desert land was bought cheaply and water was piped in. Blocks were sold to settlers and the money raised paid for the further development of the irrigation works and the township that formed the nucleus of the colony. So long as the land kept selling at an ever-increasing price and the goods kept being produced, all was well. Any interruption to the flow, and the lack of underlying capital, could expose the fragility of their business model.

The success of the Chaffeys' operations highlighted their entrepreneurial skills. Ontario became the most famous irrigation town in America.[30] Its success was underpinned by fierce marketing through printed materials and pre-arranged tours for prospective buyers, all produced in the 'booster' style advertising of the time, relying on flowery language and exaggerated claims: 'The rivers run over golden sands and over golden sands run rivers of gold into golden hands'.[31]

It was Deakin's guided tour of the Chaffeys' property in 1885 that opened a new chapter in the Murray–Darling Basin.

Deakin's involvement

In 1884, Deakin was the newly installed Minister for Water Supply in the recently elected Gillies–Deakin government. One of the first actions of the government was to appoint a Royal Commission into Water Supply, and Deakin was given the job of heading up the inquiry. In effect, he was a one-man Royal Commission. In this capacity he headed to America on a fact-finding mission in December 1884. Accompanying him were his wife Pattie, two journalists and an engineer. The party arrived in San Francisco in January the following year. Everything about the three-month trip – which took him by rail from coast to coast – was done at break-neck pace. They visited irrigation schemes in several states and in Mexico. Deakin must have been in a buoyant mood throughout knowing that his fact-finding mission was going to help shape one of the great issues of the day. He was just 28 years old. He kept a diary of his journey and the intensity of his observations have been described as 'if a tornado were touching paper.'[32]

The visit to the Chaffey's operation at Ontario came at the beginning of the trip when, on inquiries made in San Francisco, he was directed there. From the moment they arrived, Deakin and his travelling party were immensely impressed.[33] They were driven through a paved, 60-metre-wide avenue 11 kilometres in length, extending from one end of the settlement to the other. It was lined on each side with poplar, eucalypt, magnolia, orange and palm trees. Set back a few metres were villas surrounded by lawns, orchards and flower-gardens.[34] Taken on a tour of the property by William, Deakin later said that the Chaffey brothers' colonies were the best that he had seen.[35] He was also impressed with the character of the Chaffeys. Of William, Deakin said, 'It amazed us [the travelling party] that W.B. Chaffey, a man scarcely out of his teens, could so personify that American determination to do things'.[36]

At the end of the day, Deakin's party were sitting in William's office waiting for a train to take them east. Exactly what happened in this meeting has become part of the mythology surrounding the role of the Chaffeys and Deakin in the history of Australian irrigation. One version has it that a member of Deakin's party casually remarked that it would be 'an excellent thing' if the Chaffeys could be induced to come out to Victoria to give a practical demonstration of irrigation 'on the latest scientific method'. William was said to have smiled and replied that their operations in California would prevent the offer being taken up.[37]

Another version of the meeting has Deakin playing a decisive role, using all his rhetorical skill to persuade the reluctant brothers. In this version, George also attended the end-of-the-day meeting. Deakin turned to George and 'talked of Australia's greatest river flowing uselessly into the ocean through an arid, almost uninhabited Basin, nearly one-sixth the size of the United States'.[38] In response to Deakin's stirring imagery, George was supposed to have 'become fired by the possibility of new deserts to conquer'.[39] (Not surprisingly, the rights of Aboriginal people were not even considered in these negotiations, and the historical record is silent on how the advent of large-scale irrigation affected Aboriginal groups.)

The reality appears to have been far less romantic, but no less curious. Clearly the Chaffeys' interest was piqued by the enthusiasm of the Victorian visiting party, but it was not fully realised until the intervention of a Californian of dubious background. Stephen Cureton proved to be the key to the Chaffeys' decision to come to Australia. 'Colourful' seems the most apt cliché to describe this fellow Californian. Said by one commentator to be a 'fourth rate Pressman' and an 'American adventurer'[40], little is known about him other than he had first visited Australia in 1882 because, on his own admission, he had got into a 'shooting scrape' and came 'here for it to blow over'.[41] At some point he had travelled down the Murray where the idea occurred to him of its potential for irrigation. He had heard about Deakin's fact-finding trip to America from the reports in the Australian press and wrote to the Chaffeys that he could negotiate a deal for land for them by using his influential circle of friends.[42] The brothers subsequently authorised Cureton to enter into tentative negotiations with the Victorian government.[43]

Although there are gaps in the account, questions arise from the early interactions between the Chaffeys and Deakin. Had Deakin invested too much emotion in the impressions he had formed about the Chaffeys? Had he seen in them the way to realise his dream for nation-building irrigation? And, again, were the Chaffeys merely opportunists out for the deal of a lifetime?

It's important to note that Deakin's utopian attraction to irrigation was widely shared. At one level, the appeal to nation-building as enunciated by leaders including Deakin was a key part of that appeal. But at another level, the popularity of irrigation captured prevailing 19th-century religiosity. As historian Melissa Bellanta has written, the promotion of irrigation during the second half of the 19th and early 20th centuries 'was heavily freighted with religious and millennial imagery'.[44] Through such imagery, irrigation promised 'to revive the lost garden of Eden'. Thus, Deakin earned the reputation in the popular press as the 'apostle' of irrigation who 'preached' the development as if it were a 'gospel'.[45] And Deakin himself was prone to such religiosity, being a keen advocate of spiritualism.[46]

Cureton reveals his hand

Early in 1886, and after Deakin had returned from his trip to the United States, he submitted a report to Parliament which, in addition to compiling a vast array of technical details about irrigation in the United States, laid out his policy approach. The contents of the report were widely covered in the press.[47] His ideas were an amalgam of his fascination for American-style capitalism and his Australian-informed liberal principles requiring a strong State. Thus, he wrote that Australia should adopt the private sector approach that had been so successful for America, but the State should retain control over the sources of water and protect the public interest by preserving the supply and thereby prevent all irrigation from being controlled by capitalists. Was such a hybrid framework workable, and how could he implement its principles? In the same year, the energetic Minister for Water laid the legislative framework for irrigation in Victoria with the passage of the *Irrigation Act*.[48]

Not long after Deakin had laid out these approaches, Stephen Cureton called on him. Cureton had arranged with the Chaffeys to have a financial share in their scheme. We have Deakin's recollections of this meeting, which he gave as evidence to the Mildura Royal Commission. According to Deakin, Cureton didn't waste any time unveiling his plan. The Chaffeys were seeking somewhere between 200 and 400 thousand hectares as a land grant and £250 000 in cash. This was an audacious claim given that the Chaffeys held only 3000 hectares at Ontario. It reflected Cureton's belief, expressed to the Chaffeys, that they would be able to get an easy deal from the government.[49] Cureton had probably formed an impression that Deakin was an idealist anxious to get results and, therefore, an easy target. When Cureton confirmed this version of events himself to the Royal Commission, one of the commissioners blurted out that 'this looked like plundering the country'.[50]

How reliable Cureton was as a witness is difficult to know. He pulled out of the Chaffey project after a few years but made money on the deal so he doesn't appear to have harboured malice. His view about the Chaffeys is supported by others. In 1898, a journalist from the *Adelaide Observer* paid a visit to the still struggling irrigation colony at Renmark where he was told by a dozen of the farmers that the Chaffeys were 'out on a money making job'.[51] As a private scheme, it was obviously designed to make money; the salient point is the scale of the Chaffey/Cureton ambitions. One of the underlying reasons for the collapse of their venture was simply the scale of the operations that they were unable to manage.

Deakin had to wind back George's expectations of free land and unlimited control over water. Negotiations went back and forth between February and October, 1886. The Chaffeys made a number of proposals, which implied that they had substantial capital, and it was assumed that a good portion of this was their own. Inquiries were made in California by the Cabinet that suggested otherwise but were inconclusive.[52] Deakin's due diligence on this crucial issue was sloppy. As matters transpired, the Chaffeys had little working capital to devote to a large, private irrigation scheme. Claims that George instructed William to sell their American operation for a fraction of its value are unverified, but, if true, seem to suggest they regarded Australia as an El Dorado of irrigation and wanted to jump while they had the opportunity.[53]

George felt he needed to quash rumours that he had misrepresented himself as a wealthy man in his evidence to the Royal Commission. Nevertheless, the fact remained that the brothers had little capital between them. The Royal Commission was forced to the conclusion that the brothers had 'obtained an enormous concession … with capital practically amounting to nothing'.[54]

The deal that finally emerged, after Deakin had pressed upon George Chaffey that things could be done the same way in Australia as in America, still came down to a large and generous scheme. The essence of the deal was that in return for a grant of 50 000 acres (about 20 000 hectares), the Chaffeys had to spend £300 000 constructing irrigation works over 20 years and that the land had to be cut into blocks of not more than 80 acres (32 hectares). The Chaffeys could purchase an additional 200 000 acres (about 81 000 hectares) at 1 pound per acre, so long as they guaranteed to spend £120 000 on improvements. Of this land, the Chaffeys could not cultivate more than 5000 acres (about 2000 hectares) for themselves.[55] In terms of irrigation projects, this was hugely ambitious. William John Allen, formerly a manager of a fruit farm in California, told the Royal Commission that the average farm in California was 12 000 acres (about 4800 hectares). 'I never saw any settlement there as large as Mildura', he told commissioners.[56]

But, it could be argued, Victoria had nothing to lose from the project because the agreement bound the Chaffeys, under penalty, to accomplish all that they undertook to do, and all losses fell on the shoulders of the two brothers. In the event of failure, the land reverted to the Crown.[57]

News of the negotiations between Deakin and the Chaffeys filtered across the border where the 'old lion' of New South Wales politics, Sir Henry Parkes, was incensed at developments. 'The Murray is ours', he thundered.[58] There couldn't be two politicians with such contrasting backgrounds and temperaments: Melbourne Grammar versus the school of hard knocks. While Deakin's talents were nurtured by powerful men, Parkes was a self-made man, rising out of poverty in England before migrating to Australia. But the two men shared strong egos and a talent for oratory. It was perhaps inevitable that Parkes would oppose Deakin's pet project. The New South Welshman had a reputation as a political firebrand, using every opportunity to create divisions between his colony and Victoria.[59] And Deakin had initiated the Victorian scheme without, apparently, considering its impact on either New South Wales or South Australia, despite the simmering tensions across all colonies with a stake in the Murray–Darling Basin.[60]

The crippling drought of the 1880s, together with the advent of the Chaffey scheme, brought to a head the economic stake each colony had in the river system, but efforts to get the respective premiers to meet to discuss a joint framework of 'rights' to the river failed to materialise.

In the absence of any agreement, Parkes maintained that he was on strong constitutional grounds in opposing the irrigation colony in Victoria. It was his view that the legal settlement separating the two colonies granted the waters of the Murray as part of New South Wales. He cited Section 5 of the *New South Wales Constitution Act 1855,* which stated that the whole of the watercourse of the Murray, from its source to the South Australian border, 'is and shall be within the Territory of New South Wales'.[61]

Of course, Victorians disagreed with this interpretation, pointing out that the convention of riparian rights – that is, restraints on upstream users – restricted the powers of New South Wales on the Victorian side. And South Australians, occupying the last stretches of the river system, felt vulnerable, especially because the advent of the railways in the 1880s and 1890s, had reduced the importance of South Australian ports to the transport of wool and other goods. The Chaffeys were dragged into the dispute. They made a statement through their spokesperson, Stephen Cureton, that the outbreak of intercolonial jealously was 'beyond our comprehension'.[62]

But Parkes was undeterred. In mid-1889, he took another verbal swipe at the Chaffeys, labelling them 'trespassers', and he made vague threats to disrupt their operations if the company could not get the quantity of water they needed.[63] With his talent for political invective, he labelled the Chaffeys 'water pirates', and predicted that it would not be long before the Murray 'disappeared into the Mallee, leaving the paddle steamers sticking in the mud'.[64]

The intercolonial spat over the Chaffey project was a foretaste of the conflicts over irrigation and the management of the river system that would flare during the debates over Federation and fester for decades to come. In failing to respond to Parkes' intercolonial jealousy, Deakin lost the opportunity to resolve the sharing of the Murray–Darling waters while irrigation works were in their infancy.[65]

Meanwhile, in Victoria, conflict also broke out over the Chaffeys' proposal. While the press overwhelmingly endorsed the deal, the Victorian Opposition was outraged when the proposal came before Parliament. Deakin didn't help the government's cause by introducing the Bill in an evening session and without warning. This excited suspicion that the arrangement was somehow underhanded.[66] In an all-night session, vitriol flowed from Opposition members, led by Thomas Bent who lashed out that the proposed legislation was a 'downright swindle' and a 'gigantic fraud upon the country'.[67] Adding to the raucous debate, Bent alleged that Cureton had been stalking the corridors whipping up support for the measure.

According to American historian Frederick Kershner[68], a good deal of this vitriol was anti-American sentiment in a decade when the first stirrings of an Australian nationalist movement unnerved English-born colonials, who regarded the American model of independence as a threat to the ties of kinship with Britain. Therefore, it was easy to accuse Chaffey of 'Yankee graft and greed'. In any event, Bent forced the government into a compromise that required the offer to be put out to tender for a period of two months. The Chaffeys felt betrayed.

Watching these events with a keen eye was South Australia's Attorney-General, John Downer. He invited the Chaffeys to Adelaide, offered them an expenses-paid trip along the Murray and closed a deal with them to establish a colony at Renmark.[69] Meanwhile, the two-month tender period in Victoria closed and the Chaffeys had emerged as the only bidders. Even so, Deakin had to undertake some swift persuasion to get them to take up the offer at Mildura. The effect of the intercolonial competition had a significant bearing on the collapse of the Mildura project: the brothers became too stretched managing both projects at once.[70]

A dodgy beginning

With the deal signed, the Chaffeys threw themselves into the task of developing the Mildura site and attracting prospective farmers. Their approach to promotion revealed, again, the Chaffeys' questionable business ethics. Reasoning that they needed to attract interest from overseas, they mounted an extensive public relations campaign in both Great Britain and India as well as throughout Australia. In addition, agents were appointed in almost every major town and city in Britain to handle the promotion campaign. Glowing information about the prospects of the scheme was compiled in what become known as the 'red book'. Two controversial claims were made in this promotional material. Firstly, that the scheme was backed by the government and, secondly, that the water would be free, having been purchased with the land.

On the matter of government backing, a journalist, who interviewed English migrants settled on the Renmark project, reported that all had been induced to migrate from the guarantees in the red book. 'Are we fools', they told the visiting journalist, 'We knew nothing of the Chaffey Brothers in England':

> They issued a red book, and scattered it throughout the English world. On the frontispiece there were the colonial coat of arms and the words 'Regulated by Government'. All through it was stuffed full of references to the powers of supervision reserved by Government. We looked upon that as a prospectus, with all its flowery and picturesque painting; but it was never contradicted.[71]

Incorporating the terms 'regulated' and 'supervised' by government was a deceptive use of language made more so by the inclusion of the official stamp of government. While Deakin had issued guidelines around the dispersal of land and maintained state control over water, the actual operation of the Chaffeys' business was not controlled by government. But it was not surprising that the brothers would blur the facts about the operation of the scheme because it replicated the 'boosterism' they had adopted in America. It had its desired effect. In August 1890, William Chaffey returned from a trip to Canada and England and gushed to a journalist from the *Mildura Cultivator* about the impact of the red books:

> I found that Mildura was talked about pretty much everywhere.
> Our [i.e. Australia's] Chief Commissioner in London has pushed
> the scheme … in every hotel and steamer I found it talked about
> … I was kept busy in London day and night by people who
> wanted to interview me, and if I had been able to stay there and do
> business I could have sold thousands of acres of Mildura land.[72]

Stephen Cureton, in his evidence to the Mildura Royal Commission, was aware of the deception involved in the red books. When the first books were printed and distributed, he suspected that the government would order them to withdraw the claims of government control and supervision, 'but nothing was said and we let it go'. He impressed on their London agent to draw attention to the guarantee and reckoned that most of the people who came from outside Australia were induced to come by seeing the advertising of a government guarantee.[73]

Similarly, some settlers gained the distinct impression from the promotional materials that they would not have to pay for water, because this would be covered in the purchase price of their blocks. Free water! The Chaffey brothers reiterated this claim in an interview they gave to an Adelaide newspaper in January 1887 in which they stated clearly that, 'we sell the water with the land'.[74] Yet, in his evidence before the Royal Commission, George refuted that the red book stated that the water would be free but then admitted that free water was given at the start of the project.[75]

These deceptions didn't become an issue until the brothers' management of the operation ran into problems. Their early efforts were little short of heroic and became the backbone of the mythologising of their story. Europeans derided the area around Mildura as a wilderness. Critics questioned George's choice of an abandoned pastoral property as 'a hissing Sahara of hot winds and red driving sand ... strewn with the bleached bones of sheep and cattle.'[76]

Undeterred, the brothers launched a company – Chaffey Brothers Limited – based on £2500 in cash and over £200 000 in shares issued to the public. These funds, together with money raised from the sale of land to settlers, formed the basis of the cash flow needed to fund the colony and meet the Victorian government's obligations as set out in their agreement.

All went well in the initial development phase. Settlers came flocking into the two river settlements to make their livelihoods out of fruit. Tent towns sprang up in the cleared Mallee ground. Large areas were enclosed with rabbit-proof fences, and pumps were installed on the river banks. And there was an unexpected bonus. The land proved richer than expected: loam, more than seven metres deep in places, and rich in nutrients.[77] The centrepiece of the town plan was to be called Deakin Avenue.

Mounting problems

In 1887, after only a year of operation, the township was gradually taking shape with homes, shops and a school under construction. Irrigation channels had been cut and orchards planted. At the end of two years, just over 320 hectares had been sold; around 800 hectares had been ploughed and a similar amount planted with trees.[78] Then things started to turn sour. Many of the settlers had no background in farming, let alone orcharding; they barely 'knew a melon from a pumpkin', as one newspaper report put it.[79]

With little capital at hand, and a massive expanse of land to irrigate, the Chaffeys couldn't afford to install the concrete piping that had been one of their engineering feats in California. Instead, they dug open drains. However, they had so little understanding of the soil structure at Mildura that much of this water was lost as seepage. Not only did this deprive the orchards of water, the seepage caused salts in the soil to rise to the surface, creating the problem of salinity. The connection between irrigation and salinity, through a rise in the water table, was known at the time, even if the science of its dynamics was not fully understood. Thus, HG McKinney, a New South Wales government engineer and keen proponent of irrigation, stated to the Royal Society in 1883, that, 'irrigation is likely to cover the ground in salt'.[80] It is not known whether the Chaffeys had access to this information.

Meanwhile, the funds that were expected to be raised through shareholdings did not materialise, resulting, as the Royal Commission found, in an insufficient amount to carry through the onerous responsibilities associated with an undertaking of this magnitude.[81] This obviously had a ripple effect throughout the entire operation.

Mismanagement by the Chaffeys was a critical factor in the collapse of their company. The Royal Commission documented the shoddy practices at Mildura. The settlement was too spread out for an efficient operation. This necessitated extensive channelling, exacerbating the seepage of water, and powerful pumps that required expensive upkeep. The pumps were also faulty and sometimes incapable of performing the work. The first batch of fruit trees supplied to settlers were of poor quality. And the Chaffeys themselves were overstretched managing both colonies. However, the colony at Renmark caused fewer problems because it was more compact in layout and, the Royal Commission found, because it was better supervised by the South Australian government.

By 1892, the settlers were becoming agitated at the Chaffeys' mismanagement of the colony. David Gordon, who had come to Mildura induced by the promise of government backing, gave evidence to the Royal Commission, and explained the causes of the upset. The trouble, he said, began in 1892 when the Chaffeys introduced a payment for water usage for the first time. Then the pumps broke down. Settlers started to complain that they had been misled. When they approached the Chaffeys, they were told that the problems with the scheme lay with the government, not them, and when they approached the government, they were told 'you must go back and approach the Chaffeys'. They were frustrated, too, that the Chaffeys' company board met in Melbourne, which meant that the settlers knew nothing of what was going on. Their frustration culminated in the appointment of a committee of the settlers to investigate the management of the scheme. Thus, Chaffey's statement that the whole trouble was caused by one agitator was incorrect.

In the end, the Chaffey project collapsed. The tipping point was the end to Victoria's long land boom. From the late 1880s, large amounts of British capital had flowed into Melbourne, and money was so plentiful that everyone thought land values were bound to rise continuously. The boom ended and land sales at the Mildura settlement declined and revenue dried up, exposing the limited credit behind the Chaffeys. One-third of the settlers defaulted and couldn't carry on. Pumping ceased and channels fell into disrepair. The remaining settlers demanded government action.[82]

Mildura survived and went on to thrive, but only after the Victorian government stepped in by legislating for the Mildura Irrigation Trust to take over operations. Deakin was out of Parliament, having lost a fortune in the property crash of 1893, and he had had to return to the Bar to restore his finances.

Deakin explains his actions

At the end of July 1896, Deakin appeared before the Mildura Royal Commission. He was still smarting from a stinging attack made on him for his handling of the Mildura colony by the conservative *Argus* newspaper more than two months previously.[83] The paper was no friend to liberals like Deakin, but it delivered some pertinent points in blunt language. Deakin had been sucked in by the Chaffeys. He had gone out of his way to assure the people of Victoria that they were capitalists who could be trusted: 'What are the facts? The Messrs Chaffey found a credulous community under the spell of a mere political gusher'. The barbs behind the *Argus* attack continued. It was Deakin's 'crass ignorance' and his 'aerated oratory' that had misled settlers and ruined many, and for whom the state now had a moral responsibility.

Deakin began his comments to the Commission by complaining about the 'political assassination' mounted by the *Argus*. He appeared thin-skinned and defensive. No doubt the collapse of the scheme for a man of Deakin's high self-regard came as a blow. Not surprisingly, then, there was no *mea culpa* in his appearance before the Commission. Yet Deakin admitted to some failings.[84] He said that the government was 'anxious' to get an agreement with the Chaffeys, but that they could not get them to outline their plan of operation. The Chaffeys, he further explained, were told that so long as the expenditure was their own and the state lost nothing they would be left alone. These admissions go some way to explaining why the scheme collapsed, but Deakin wasn't pressed by the commissioners, nor did he offer them any greater insights into the reasons behind the collapse. In fact, he refused to accept any responsibility for the deceptive advertising campaign mounted by the Chaffeys. This, he said, 'might have misled some people who were in the habit of attaching great importance to very little'.

Deakin went on to play a decisive role in Federation and to serve three times as Australian Prime Minister, confirming his place as one of Australia's foremost statesmen. But in developing Australia's first major irrigation scheme along the Murray River, Deakin revealed contrasting leadership qualities. On the one hand, he had used his talents to develop a vision for irrigation and was instrumental in placing this on the agenda of government. However, he failed to see the shortcomings in his hybrid private/public model. In a wider sense, too, he failed to grasp the opportunity presented by the series of droughts, to articulate a sustainable vision for irrigation into the future. As mentioned in the previous chapter, the debate over land clearing and drought overlapped the debate over irrigation.

Yet Deakin failed to ask deeper questions about the place of irrigation in a system of agriculture already causing great damage through overstocking and excessive land clearing. In so doing, he helped perpetuate the dominant paradigm that national development and the environment were unrelated fields. While he was not alone in being a single-minded nation-builder, as a former journalist, Deakin would have been aware of these broader environmental debates. Deakin also played his part in not adequately foreseeing how the first large-scale irrigation scheme in the country necessitated a new legal framework between the colonies over the Murray River. And, more broadly, allowing private companies to drive irrigation projects was seen for many years as mistaken.[85]

The failure of the Chaffey scheme gnawed away at Deakin for years afterwards. In 1903, when he was federal Attorney General, he gave a public address in which he returned to the issue. He told the audience that he had initiated great schemes in Victoria, 'but those who were to help him failed him and he was largely blamed'.[86]

Mildura did recover from its near collapse. William Chaffey stayed on to 'see it through', paying off all his creditors. In 1913 a newspaper recorded: 'The fight he [William] participated in with the settlers who remained was a hard one. But there are men at Mildura today who own two or three motor cars and can write 10,000, 20,000 and 30,000 pound cheques'.[87]

The newspaper quoted above headlined its story 'Success after Failure'. Such triumphalism spurred further nation-building land development, exposing the brave souls who lived and farmed in the Murray–Darling Basin to further environmental disasters.

7

A NATIONAL CALAMITY: THE FEDERATION DROUGHT, 1895–1903

By the turn of the century, drought had been a constant, lurking presence in the Murray–Darling Basin. Between the mid-1830s and the mid-1880s, five major droughts had affected parts of, or the entire, Basin, lasting between two and five years in duration (see appendix). In that half century, pastoralists and farmers groped for an understanding of the region's weather patterns. As a correspondent lamented to the *Queanbeyan Age* during the drought of 1877–78, 'this young country' has limited experience in understanding 'the law of recurrence of seasons of drought and flood' compared to 'older countries' where weather patterns have been long observed and 'where no such law [of droughts and floods] is known'.[1]

Not surprisingly, the unpredictability and ferocity of droughts wore heavily on a largely unsuspecting population. New waves of British settlers had to contend with a force they had never before experienced. Droughts evoked deep emotional responses to the landscape. Graphic descriptions, such as the one published in the *Riverina Grazier* in 1884, were attempts at coming to grips with a shockingly unfamiliar experience. The drought, the paper wrote, left the land 'a naked waste'; it dotted the landscape with 'the bleached bones of perished herds'; it caused birds to 'to fall exhausted from the wilted branches'; and it left the gum trees 'fairly hissing for rain'.[2]

With the capacity to torment settlers, each drought stood out like a gravestone in the collective memory.

The ruinous drought of the early to mid-1880s was broken by drenching rains, which returned to southern Queensland in 1890 surging down the Darling as they had since time immemorial. The local settlers recorded the event as the most damaging flood since white settlement. When the waters reached Bourke, the town was in danger of being swept away. Alarm bells rang out around the town to enlist all the able-bodied in a desperate attempt to save the town by erecting an embankment around it, but to no avail. The water broke through and inundated the town. While there was no loss of life, damage was widespread. Hundreds of people gathered on the few dry spots, along with their stock and domestic animals. With the railway line cut, the town was isolated. Towns further down, including Walgett and Brewarrina, were damaged with heavy losses to stock and property.[3]

But in 1895 the rains stopped again and a dry season slowly settled on the land. For the first few years, colonial politicians scarcely noticed the slow baking of the earth; they were preoccupied with querulous debates over Federation.

Water and the movement for Federation

By the time the rains failed in the mid-1890s, the debate over Federation had become a wearisome topic for many Australians. They were torn by its potential and its problems. A shared history as British subjects vied with colonial parochialism – each colony had its own distinct history of settlement and different economic interests. This was exacerbated by the vast distances that separated them. Thus, the debate about a unified Australia had, for years, become bogged down in intercolonial jealousies and rival interests. Among the many obstacles in the way of creating the new nation was control over the Murray–Darling. The topic had given rise to the 'most excited controversy' in the meeting rooms of the Federation Convention in February 1898.[4] Some described it as 'the great stumbling block', such were the polarised positions between the various colonies.[5]

The dispute, in particular, between South Australia and New South Wales reinforced the difficulties that lay ahead in developing a cooperative approach to managing the Murray–Darling river system. Not only did the two colonies have fundamentally different economies, each recognised that the river system would struggle to provide for both their respective interests. Apart from the irrigation settlement at Renmark, South Australia had not developed plans for large-scale irrigation works, and it therefore relied on the river trade as a key part of its economy. Consequently, it wanted a guarantee that the river would be navigable at all times. It felt that this naturally fell to the Commonwealth as a national responsibility.

The priorities of New South Wales, on the other hand, were in developing its agricultural lands and attracting further immigrants. Their position was put by Joseph Curruthers, one of that colony's delegates. Implicit in his argument was that the river was a finite resource. Developing the country, he argued, 'could not be attained by making rivers navigable; it would be in making waters available to settlers'. He warned that the people of New South Wales would not join a Federation that handed over the arteries of the colony to federal control.[6]

South Australian delegates responded by pointing out that people in their colony were haunted by the prospect that the irrigation schemes in New South Wales and Victoria would result in the river being 'pumped dry'. Commenting on the impasse at the Convention, the *Adelaide Observer* noted that 'a river which may be reduced practically to nothingness will be useless as an irrigation reservoir.'[7]

Again, the bigger colonies opposed South Australia's renewed attempt to secure federal control over the Murray–Darling. New South Wales Premier George Reid led the counterattack. New South Wales, he said, was bound to maintain its rights to 'the supreme control' over the river system. Alfred Deakin, with an eye, no doubt, to protecting Victoria's still struggling Mildura settlement, agreed with New South Wales. He would not back federal control. And so, South Australia lost the argument.[8] With hindsight, it was an unfortunate fight to have lost.

The return of drought

By the time the heated discussions over the Murray–Darling subsided, the situation with the drought had become dire. Although coastal areas generally, and some of the more productive lands, were spared, the dry had become the longest drought 'any white man had ever seen'.[9] Spanning the years 1895 to 1903 it covered most of the east coast, but was heavily concentrated in the Murray–Darling Basin. Initially referred to as 'the long drought', it was later renamed the 'Federation Drought'.

The drought couldn't have come at a worse time. During the 1890s, Australia was faced with the after-effects of the drought of the mid-1880s, the confrontational shearer's strike of 1891, and the economic depression of the early 1890s. But the Federation Drought would test national resilience like no previous event; it was, without doubt, the greatest calamity to befall the country since the early struggles of Europeans to establish themselves on the continent.[10]

Local newspapers gave vivid accounts of its extent and impact on the land. 'The whole of western and northern parts of Victoria', cried the *Kilmore Free Press*, were 'more or less one huge desert'. Stock died in their thousands, their desiccated bodies strewn everywhere. The land looked to have been 'swept bare'.[11] Up around Charters Towers in Queensland, the situation was starkly similar. 'For hundreds of miles in the interior', wrote one correspondent to the local paper, the *Evening Telegraph*, 'not a trace of herbage is to be seen'. The country had been turned into a vast expanse of sandy soil. Even the rabbits were suffering, having perished in their millions.[12] Indeed, much of Queensland was 'one long stretch of withered wilderness', with bleary-eyed beasts staggering pathetically around.[13]

The interior of New South Wales had been reduced to the appearance of a moonscape. 'A traveller from Sydney to Broken Hill', reported the *Western Grazier* in 1901, 'would encounter nothing after leaving the coast range but treeless prairies, devoid of grass, the earth baked hard under the pitiless sun, with a scanty population struggling to endure a frightful existence without hope for the future'.[14] One newspaper described western New South Wales as 'a pastoral holocaust' of deserted homesteads, abandoned stations and decimated flocks.[15] Exacerbating the death toll was the lack of transport for agistment; railways departments didn't have the rolling stock for a mass movement of animals. However, emaciated stock was no use even for the knackery. Consequently, the stock was trapped on properties, forcing station owners to strip paddocks and tree foliage in the forlorn hope of saving their animals from an agonizingly slow death.[16]

Images of wholesale destruction in south-western Queensland on the edge of the Murray–Darling Basin shocked observers. Such regions were totally remote from the experience of nearly all Australians. But in 1900, at the height of the drought, travellers brought back to the cities reports of an environmental catastrophe:

> Far as the eye could see in all directions were the bleaching bones
> or the shrunken mummified skeletons of dead sheep and cattle
> … Gaunt, starving emus, in sombre grey and black plumage,
> stalked past us like shadows, and great kangaroos hopped
> mournfully away, or stood and gazed at us a few yards distant,
> hunger and thirst subduing all fear … The amount of animal
> suffering was something too terrible to contemplate. We had
> fallen into a desert land.[17]

The severity of the Federation Drought was different in one key respect from previous droughts; it was the first to seriously awaken the consciousness of city people to life on the land. As the *Adelaide Observer* noted, at the time the majority of Australians wouldn't have thought that droughts affected them: 'To the man in constant work, the artisan and Government employee, a drought was a matter of supreme indifference'. But that attitude changed as the Federation Drought had ripple effects throughout society. As the rural economy contracted, household budgets were hit with rises in the cost of basic food items, unemployment went up and businesses experienced difficulties staying afloat.[18] Even so, it was country people who bore the brunt of the devastating psychological impacts. 'The vastness of the scene, the immensity of the dryness, the unending misery', one correspondent wrote to a local newspaper, had to be seen to be believed.[19]

Causes of the drought

By the time of the Federation Drought, the idea that human factors worsen drought had gained greater currency. Hence, criticism of the 'suicidal' rates of both land clearing and overstocking were blamed for the return of drought. The idea that trees were essential for attracting moisture from the clouds was well aired in newspapers.[20] 'If our forests are to go on disappearing', one newspaper declared, 'our rainfall must inevitably be less'.[21] Overstocking of pastoral stations was also decried in similarly strong terms. No less an authority than the *Sydney Stock and Station Journal* highlighted in 1896 that speculative practices were baked into the thinking of most pastoralists. They reasoned that while their paddocks may be getting bare, their stock was looking well and, 'it's sure to rain in November'.[22] The trouble with such a gambler's approach was that when a bad season came knocking 'the destruction is frightful.'[23]

The gamble pastoralists waged against the weather was made worse by the decades-long shift from native to imported grasses. The gradual disappearance of Mitchell, blue, mulga and corkscrew grasses was acknowledged by the early 1880s to have been a mistake, yet little interest was shown in their cultivation.[24] By the onset of the Federation Drought, the 'foreign' grasses were found 'piled against wire fences after a few weeks of hot and windy weather'.[25]

To survive the Federation Drought, many station owners removed what little vegetation was left on their properties to feed their stock. Edible trees, shrubs, and bushes were chopped down by gangs of men especially employed for that purpose. But as the *Sydney Stock and Station Journal* highlighted, this practice only added to the overall environmental destruction wrought by the drought: 'sheep were compelled to travel long distances for water and to feed, thus cutting up and destroying the country by constant traffic, leaving it a dust-bed to be blown away by high winds'.[26]

Competing with the explanations of land clearing and overstocking was the emergence of the 'cyclical theory' of Australian droughts – that they descended at regular intervals and little could be done to mitigate their impact.[27]

Today, scientists regard the Federation Drought as an example of an extreme El Niño weather event exacerbated by anthropomorphic changes to the environment, including land clearing, degradation of native grasses, overstocking and overcropping, and the introduction of feral species.

Impacts on society

For many people on the land, the severity of the drought forced them into a primeval struggle against the forces of nature. In north-eastern Victoria, for example, a journalist found weary and grimy-looking men toiling day after day to pump water, cut scrub and haul emaciated stock out of the drying and boggy water holes. They were living on the rotting offal of dead sheep, washed down with tea made from putrid water. All around was a scene of death reminiscent of a battlefield – carcasses 'wherever you go and wherever you look'. The countryside was silent save for the low, continuous bleating of slowly dying sheep. The smell at night of bonfires built to burn the dead stock sickened the stomach. Across the horizons, dusty bare paddocks lay as far as the eye could see.[28]

The scale of stock deaths awakened a consciousness about human responsibility to animals. A few linked the system of pastoralism to the systematic cruelty that the drought laid bare. As one country newspaper reflected: 'If such a vast and horrible cruelty is a necessary adjunct of Australia's great pastoral industry, it may be seriously asked whether the millions won from our shearing sheds are worth the cruelty which their getting involves'.[29]

Nature had had its revenge on both pastoralists and farmers, and many families were ruined as a consequence. Those with little capital who had taken up blocks of Crown land as selectors were especially vulnerable as they had been since the Land Acts came into being. This was the last straw for some.

Selectors in Victoria's Mallee were especially hard hit. The high hopes of the first few years of settlement had turned to dust. Around 4000 selectors had moved into the area, some attracted from other colonies, to take up a block to farm. For several years, returns were promising and the region became an important centre of agricultural activity. But the Mallee's environment had been changed beyond recognition. Years of land clearing had turned the area 'dreams of golden fields ... to the realities of drought'.[30] Wheat yields were already in decline due to over-exploitation of the soil.[31] Then rainfall dried up.

By 1902, many of the settlers had sold what little they could, left their homes and headed south, because to them, the area had become synonymous with hard work and disastrous failure.[32] Most of these bush people had 'worked like slaves' at their chance to become independent farmers.[33] Those who remained on the land now faced an even worse monster. Every day, haggard eyes stared longingly for any sign of a cloud – 'day after day, week after week, month after month, until people cease to hope', as the *Daily Telegraph* put it in 1903.[34]

The New South Wales Lands Department, on instruction from the minister, took a hard line against selectors falling behind in their interest payments. Controversy was sparked when the notification for payments sent out by the Department became public. According to one newspaper, the terms in which these were couched 'were sufficient to spread terror among the recipients'.[35]

As a consequence, some smaller country towns were emptied of their population as men, and sometimes their wives and families, went 'on the track'. At intervals along the country roads, small groups of 'sullen, hopeless-looking men' could be seen who had, almost overnight, become 'swaggies'. They were a pitiful sight; some were even bootless in the blistering sand aimlessly looking for work, which they had no hope of getting.[36] In addition to failed selectors, some of these men were likely to have been station hands who had been let go. As one newspaper reported, large stations that only a few years previously had employed 20 people, had become practically deserted with just a caretaker in charge.[37] As all Australians know, the struggles of the swagmen were immortalised in the national ballad, 'Waltzing Matilda', written in 1895 at the start of the Federation Drought.

Among those who grimly hung on to their properties, few escaped a crushing sense of desperation. For some, that moment arrived when they were denied credit at the local store, which traditionally had kept 'bushies' going in bad times. But fending off calls for extending credit turned many country shopkeepers 'grey and haggard' as the Federation Drought wore on.[38] Alongside the cry of 'No credit', farmers knew they were in desperate straits when the last of their working horses died or they were forced to scrounge for food on their properties, the wallabies being so weak that they were hardly worth shooting. Some resorted to making soup from galahs and cockatoos.[39]

Little is known about the extent of food shortages, but, by 1902, it was clear that some form of social disaster was unfolding. Pockets of dire poverty and near-starvation appeared across the Murray–Darling Basin. In the mining town of Cobar, in far western New South Wales, for example, several families were discovered on the threshold of starvation, their only means of subsistence for the previous several days being birds with the occasional piece of dry bread.[40] In the same year in Charters Towers, the local *Evening Telegraph*[41] discovered the children of one settler's family clothed only in sugar bags and another family living on boiled prickly pear and damper.

Hunger stalked the Mallee, where hundreds of settlers lived on the edge of starvation. In 1902, the Reverend ES Bickford, Secretary of the Home Missionary Society of Victoria, returned from a visit to the region worried about the deprivation he had seen. He described 'a famine-stricken people' with many living on mutton shank soup and clothed in sack cloth.[42] His observations were backed up by newspaper reports. The *Bendigo Independent* reported in 1903 that most of the settlers in the Mallee were 'on the verge of starvation'.[43] Particularly vulnerable were large families who had no means of obtaining food and clothing and families living without easy access to the railway. Storekeepers couldn't help out these people by extending credit because there were too many of them. It's no wonder that staring such devastation in the face, selectors, both men and women, had a 'worn-out and despairing appearance'; one selector spoke of his wife 'wasting away before him'.[44]

Some people feared a wider catastrophe unfolding. South of the Mallee, in the Goulburn Valley, a local doctor was quoted in the press in October 1902 that time might be running out for the district: 'It is no longer drought that is to the north of us, but famine! Credit is being stopped; food is becoming scarce … It is only a question of a few weeks when this will reach down to our district'.[45]

Aboriginal people living on their traditional homelands in the Murray–Darling Basin were especially hard hit by the drought. Those formerly residing and working on stations had this source of livelihood cut off, with a consequent rise in the number applying for relief to the Aborigines' Board.[46] Others lived in camps along the Darling River. Two Aboriginal men from one camp found themselves in the Broken Hill Magistrates Court in August 1900 after they were caught stealing sheep. The Court heard that there were extenuating circumstances arising from the drought, namely that all the native game had been 'swept away', and they could not get any rabbits or kangaroos.[47]

For those living in the larger country towns in the epicentres of the drought, conditions caused widespread deaths. In 1892 in Bourke, for example, a six-week heatwave that descended on the town like an inferno pushed temperatures up to nearly 50 degrees Celsius and over 38 for 24 consecutive days. Residents dropped dead in droves; 66 people were reported killed from 'heat apoplexy'. Memories of the event were still vivid nearly half a century later, when it was recalled that:

> Apoplexy stricken persons dropped ill in the street. Hansom cabs laden with ice patrolled the streets. When a subject fell over he was placed in the cab, ice packed around him, and he was rushed to the hospital. At the hospital the victim of the heat was placed in a room full of ice.[48]

A madness afflicted the residents of the town. Sleep in the insufferable heat was impossible and those suffering the first signs of 'heat apoplexy' behaved in abnormal ways, including shedding their clothes in public and walking around in circles. Some were found entangled in rabbit-proof fences; their skeletons left to be found later.[49] Those who could fled to the coast, but the cost of a train journey was out of reach for many.

In 1896 an unprecedented heatwave suffocated Sydney. Temperature records were smashed. Data compiled from cemeteries showed that, in one intensely hot week in January 1896, the mortality rate more

---

than doubled, with 250 deaths recorded within a short radius of the city – a number said to have exceeded that of any period since the outbreak of the influenza epidemic of four or five years previously. The funeral trains were crowded to their utmost capacity.[50] Across the city hundreds of people slept in parks, and on beaches, to escape from the smothering conditions indoors. And, as a reminder of the drought, a scorching wind swept the city coming in hot gusts from the far west, which seared the face, neck and arms.[51] Across the east coast of Australia, it is estimated 435 people died in the 1896 heatwave, ranking it as the nation's deadliest.[52]

Out in the towns across the Basin, a spike in diseases occurred. In January 1896, the *Sydney Morning Herald* compiled reports on the drought from country towns across the state. From places including Dubbo, Forbes, Grenfell, Wilcannia and Mudgee came reports that the heatwave was causing sickness and death: 'There is much typhoid fever, many children, chiefly babies, are dying of the effects of heat'.[53] In the same heatwave, the *Wellington Times* reported that in many parts of New South Wales, the water supply was running short and that the hospitals were full of people suffering from either typhoid fever or sunstroke.[54] Outbreaks of typhoid were common, but the apparent spike in typhoid deaths during the Federation Drought was likely linked to the severity of the drought because of the deteriorating quality of the water, which could then become contaminated.[55]

Not surprisingly, the economy suffered. The country's reliance on primary industry exposed its vulnerability. Starvation thinned out the number of sheep in Queensland by about 60 per cent; nationwide sheep numbers nearly halved, while cattle numbers dropped by one-third.[56] The dairying, meat export and wheat industries were paralysed. In the larger country towns, workers were left idle because the drought closed butter factories, and tradesmen like shearers, blacksmiths and wheelwrights were left with little or no work.

The paralysis across agriculture created food shortages in the major cities, which, by the turn of the century, had resulted in steep increases in the cost of bread, meat, butter and milk. Complaints became so loud that the issue flared in the metropolitan press. Although city people knew about the drought from newspaper articles circulated from country newspapers, the spike in the cost of staple foods brought the drought's effects firsthand to the cities.

Not surprisingly, the price rises and scarcity of supply hit low-income earners the hardest. To manual labourers, meat formed a chief part of their diet and, as they began to buy sparingly, or seek out cheaper cuts, like shin bones, retailers started going out of business.[57] These developments came as a shock to city people. By custom, Australians were big meat eaters. 'One idea prevalent among Australians', wrote one newspaper in 1901 'is that animal food is a necessity at every meal'. It was, the paper explained, a custom originating from the earliest days of white settlement when the development of vast flocks and herds made meat so cheap that it became the staple item of food.[58] Thus, in a country as large as Australia, many people couldn't have imagined that a time would come when the nation could not provide people with a superabundance of meat at reasonable, if not cheap, rates.[59]

Exactly how engaged city people were in the drought is difficult to estimate. It was a common refrain from people who lived in the vast drought-ravaged regions, or who visited to report on them, that city people didn't realise the extent of the suffering and the damage. Part of the problem was the difficulty for urban-based artists and photographers to travel to the worst affected areas. Consequently, few images of the drought came to the attention of the urban population.[60] The written word thus became the only medium through which people learned of the drought. Part of the problem, too, lay in the uncomplaining nature of bush people. Reverend Bickford, on his previously mentioned trip to the Mallee, noted the sturdy independence of selectors 'and their silence regarding their privations'.[61]

Poems and stories, circulated in metropolitan newspapers, helped engage city-dwellers in the drought. A poem by Will H Ogilvie, which was widely circulated in newspapers at the height of the drought in 1902, captured its menacing grip. Ogilvie, a Scottish immigrant, was a jackeroo and drover captivated by the outback, which he described as having 'a peculiar witchery of its own'.[62] 'King Drought' began with the stanza:

> My road is fenced with the bleached white bones,
> And strewn with the blind white sand,
> Beside me a suffering dumb world moans
> On the breast of a lonely land.

And it ended with the lines:

> I am the master, the dreaded king drought,
> And the great West Land is mine.

Ogilvie became a noted poet, but his work was outshone by several of his contemporaries, all of whose work was shaped, in part or in whole, by the great drought. As historian Don Garden has pointed out, some of Australia's best writers such as Henry Lawson, Banjo Paterson and Steele Rudd, spent long periods of time in the bush and depicted the hardship, struggle and mateship of the Federation Drought.[63]

Ecosystem collapse

The crippling drought not only threatened human populations, it had a catastrophic effect on the environment. Native animals and birds died in large numbers; dry creeks and water holes were strewn with dead birds and the surviving native wildlife were 'merely living skeletons'.[64] This decimation would have had a major impact on the lives of Aboriginal people.

Howling dust storms, some lasting two or three days, became a major problem throughout the Basin, their frequency and severity heralding a new phenomenon. A correspondent to a newspaper in 1902 blamed pastoralism:

> Dust-storms in the district where I resided were practically unknown 20 years ago. Not until the great drought of 1884 did they begin to be noticeable … During 1884 the natural herbage and scrub was eaten out. This scrub had served to bind the surface, and when it was gone the sand commenced to shift. Since then, the trouble has increased with each dry season, until now it has reached a calamitous stage.[65]

The Mallee region was particularly affected by dust storms, given the hundreds of square kilometres flattened to grow wheat and sheep. Omitting to leave continuous broad belts of the original Mallee scrub was described by the *Leader* newspaper in 1902 as one of the 'gravest mistakes' of the Lands Department because witheringly hot winds swept across the whole landscape of the Mallee, bringing with it drifts of sandy top soil.[66] Drifts of sand in this and other areas filled houses knee-deep, blocked front doors, clogged water tanks and engulfed fences and vegetation.

Catastrophic bushfires also broke out several times during the drought. In the summer of 1898, fires raged across Victoria, causing devastation in the Gippsland region where hundreds of settlers were burned out and once-thriving homesteads were reduced to ashes. Several towns were practically destroyed. The smoke of the fires was so dense that it paralysed shipping along Victoria's coast for four days.[67] The destruction of property was so great that many people were thrust into poverty, necessitating a public relief fund to be established.

For the rural settler population of the Murray–Darling Basin, the Federation Drought must have conjured an image of the Four Horsemen of the Apocalypse. Indeed, the Bishop of Melbourne, delivering a sermon in March 1903, proclaimed that God had withdrawn the gift of rain because people had become too slothful and too 'feverish' in their desire for pleasure.[68]

But among nature, the long drought inflicted an 'ecosystem collapse' on the Murray–Darling Basin (and beyond). This was the conclusion of a 2019 CSIRO study in which scientists reconstructed the environmental impacts of the 'megadrought' – established as one of the world's worst – from thousands of contemporary written records. Among the findings were the mass mortality and collapse of edible shrubs and grasses. The subsequent onslaught of dust storms and land degradation was a 'clear case of ecosystem meltdown'.[69] In the worst affected areas, native fauna, including kangaroos, koalas, emus and predatory birds, suffered 'apparent population collapse'. The drying up of rivers and water courses decimated fish populations. Of course, naturalists had been warning of the slippage towards extinction of many species of birds and animals for decades, but neither governments nor primary producers listened.

The implications of the CSIRO study are profound. The Federation Drought stands as a warning about the capacity for megadroughts to inflict long-term environmental damage. Climate change is likely to inflict more droughts of the scale of the Federation Drought.

What did contemporaries understand to be the lessons of this catastrophe?

Were lessons learned?

It is not often acknowledged that the Australian nation came into being in the midst of the worst crisis it had ever experienced. By 1902, it was widely acknowledged that the country was facing a disaster without comparison.[70] The death and destruction from the Federation Drought, along with the squeeze on living standards and rising unemployment, were at their height when, on 1 January 1901, white Australians celebrated their new nationhood with a typically patriotic rallying cry of a bright future awaiting the country.[71] But by then, the overall death toll – directly and indirectly – from the effects of heat, bushfires, disease and malnutrition – was likely to have been in the thousands, given that nearly 500 have been estimated to have died in the 1896 heatwaves alone.

When the drought finally lifted in 1903, a lively debate filled the pages of newspapers across the various states about what lessons had to be learned. Some problems were well known: the destructive practices associated with pastoral production, the relentless clearing of forests, the loss of soil quality, and the destruction of drought-resistant native grasses and shrubs. In particular, pastoralists continued to overlook the potential of saltbush as an effective protection against future droughts. Americans discovered the drought-resistant qualities of this native plant and began to import large quantities of seed. Graziers in Australia's arid lands, however, continued to be lulled into a false sense of security whenever good seasons returned, and failed to cultivate 'the most valuable shrub in the country', one which would save stock from starvation when the next drought swept the grasses away.[72] Such short-sightedness, a quintessential example of the Australian attitude of 'she'll be right', prevented pastoralists from confronting the environmental damage they were causing.

Yet action on these pressing problems of the nation's pastoral and agricultural industries did not form any part of the Commonwealth's first administration, which was led by Edmund Barton. There are a number of reasons for the inaction. The new federal government was focused on the enormous task of establishing its administrative structures and responsibilities, and Barton himself was neither a particularly capable or inspiring leader. In the estimation of the *Darling Downs Gazette*, Barton was more focused on 'coining phrases' than providing vigorous leadership.[73] In fact, Barton left for Britain in 1902 for an Imperial Conference, just as the drought was reaching its peak. While there, he went to considerable pains to explain that the drought had been exaggerated by the newspapers, a position he apparently felt was necessary to articulate in order to protect Australia's credit standing in Britain's financial markets.[74] Denial of the adverse effects of extreme climate started early in Australian politics.

The Federation Drought was predominately a rural crisis, sparing urban populations its worst effects. Although pastoral production greatly suffered, the nation as a whole was quick to recover. In 1904 – the first year after the drought ended – Australia's terms of trade were favourable, with exports (£89 million) exceeding imports (£71 million).[75]

Consequently, entirely the wrong lesson was learned from the Federation Drought. This is clear from the campaign mounted by government and the press for an expanded system of irrigation that would 'drought-proof' agriculture. Echoing the political evangelism of Alfred Deakin, the *Daily Telegraph* declared that every 'spare penny' should be spent

> in sinking tanks and putting down bores, in locking our thousands and thousands of miles of rivers – almost at sea level – where oceans of water waste away after each flood time. To attend to these things is a national work, for the benefit of the whole nation; to neglect them is a national crime – it is suicidal.[76]

Australians continued to rally around such a nation-building idea and let go the real lessons of the Federation Drought. Arguably, the lasting cultural impact of the Drought was Dorothea Mackellar's poem, 'My Country'. Her story is well known but requires a passing reference here because of the power her imagery had on the public consciousness about Australia's variable climate – her love of 'a sunburnt country'; 'a wide brown land'; and a land of 'droughts and flooding rains'.

The Mackellar family owned a station in the Hunter Valley during the years of the Federation Drought. The poem is thought to have been inspired by 19-year-old Dorothea witnessing the breaking of the drought on the family property. Written on a trip to England with her father, and first published there in 1908, the poem came to be regarded by white Australians, who were slowly shedding their British identity, as 'a universal statement of our nation's connection to the land'.[77] Mackellar made no reference to prior Aboriginal occupation of the continent.

Instantly embraced as 'a stirring patriotic poem', 'My Country' was said to have 'cured Australia's inferiority complex'.[78] It launched Mackellar as the Australian poet everybody knew, especially as school children learned the poem by heart. Yet, the cultural impact of Mackellar was felt not just on national sentiment, but on how white Australians viewed the environment. Mackellar helped foster an uncritical cultural acceptance of the natural cycle of droughts and floods, as if no human hand were intervening to alter the natural balance. By the 1920s, there was a 'general impression among landholders' that droughts were becoming more frequent and more severe since the early days of settlement, an impression that Mackellar's poem failed to capture.[79] She was a typical product of her time but, perhaps due to the years she spent living in England, she had been sheltered from the debates about how the pastoral industry had been contributing to the worsening of the continent's environment. Two years after the poem was published, the Australian Bureau of Meteorology was established.

If 'My Country' romanticised the Australian climate, Mackellar's poem, 'Burning Off', was a triumphal celebration of the clearing of a native landscape for agriculture. It evokes the awesome power of fire – the flying sparks and the intense glow – to reduce mighty trees to white ash, so that 'wheat shall bow to the wind'.

Mackellar undoubtedly reflected the pioneering spirit that infused the settlers, who, through sheer hard work, opened up the Murray–Darling Basin to agriculture. But she was, too, a contributor to what Don Garden has pointed out as the silence that crept over Australia's worst national disaster. The drought didn't, he writes, 'accord with the image that the new nation sought to portray of itself as a land of agrarian opportunity'.[80] Prime Minister Barton had taken this approach on his trip to England. In other words, the political system was not predisposed to grappling with the causes and catastrophic effects of drought. Rather, every effort was made to protect the prevailing economic model.

The debate about the deeper lessons of the drought petered out. Those who had been concerned for a number of years about the loss of fauna and flora due to pastoralism and land clearing continued to advance measures for greater protection. But few critiqued the nation's founding cultural ideas as did the Sydney tabloid newspaper the *Sun* on one occasion in 1922, offering these observations:

> When we came to this country our first impulse was to ruin it by extracting, in the crudest and quickest way, its natural wealth. Coal and gold were torn from the earth; the fertile land was exhausted by continuous cropping; wide acres were over-stocked with sheep and cattle ... vast forests were ruthlessly ringbarked. And, to a somewhat lesser extent the same spendthrift progress is going on now. We are a hasty and an improvident people. Our forest wealth is being systematically destroyed in our quest for easy money. We are drawing with increasing heaviness upon our natural resources; we are deforesting a continent.[81]

That a mainstream newspaper, such as the *Sun,* could question the adverse effects of Australia's economic system of resource extraction shows that popular opinion was not always on the side of politicians promoting this model. However, the concerns raised by the paper were also an aberration, and we must now turn to reconstructing the early 20th-century mindset that favoured development at all costs.

8

POPULATE OR PERISH: CHASING THE AGRARIAN DREAM

In the early months of 1908, WA Craven, the Chairman of Committees in the Victorian Legislative Assembly, had a meeting with the President of the United States, Theodore Roosevelt. Such an honour had fallen to few Australians. But why would the President take time out of his busy schedule to meet a regional politician of no international standing? Craven, who hailed from Bendigo, had a background as a surveyor and inspector of mines, hardly the sort of character who would appeal to the worldly Roosevelt whose image of vigorous masculinity was carefully crafted around his time as a rancher, adventurer and big game hunter. But Craven, in addition to having a connection to a retired American senator and good friend of the President, also had luck on his side; Roosevelt had an intense interest in Australia, its history of settlement, land policies and geo-political location in the Pacific. 'Australia appeals to me, and interests me immensely', he wrote to an Australian touring the United States in 1905.[1]

It's not known how much Craven knew about the President's interest in Australia and, specifically, whether he had read Roosevelt's best-selling four-volume history, *The Winning of the American* West. In a rollicking account, Roosevelt paid tribute to the waves of non-British European immigrants to the United States, who, contrary to prevailing racist sentiments, had, in Roosevelt's telling, earned an equal place as Americans because the physical strength and courage they had shown in taking up unknown lands and taming the wilderness.[2] In the introduction to volume one, Roosevelt saw the parallels between the colonisation of America, Australia and Canada by the British as a project of English-speaking imperialism. During the past three centuries, he wrote, the spread of English-speaking peoples 'all over the world's wastes' had been 'far-reaching in its effects and importance'.

Roosevelt particularly admired the speed with which Australia had dispossessed its Indigenous people: 'The natives were so few in number and of such a lowly type, that they practically offered no resistance at all, being but little more hindrance than an equal number of ferocious beasts'.[3] America, he said, had had to fight more valiantly to ensure 'white conquest'.

Roosevelt, therefore, maintained an active interest in how this 'colonising conquest' was taking shape in Australia. But, as Craven later reported their conversation, the President first felt obliged to offer some advice: 'People your vacant lands. Fill up your waste spaces with settlers and the towns will fill themselves up fast enough. But you must have population if Australia is going to hold its own in the South Seas'.[4] Roosevelt asked about the White Australia policy – enacted by the new federal government in 1901, to prohibit non-European people from migrating to Australia – as if the two goals were linked in his mind.

Craven informed the President of the Victorian government's efforts to promote settlement by breaking up large private estates and opening them up to settlers, a process known a 'closer settlement'. Craven was particularly impressed with the President's level of interest in the matter: 'He asked a great many questions about the Riverina country, which for some unexplained reason appeared to interest him very much and he was pleased to get a lot of facts from Mr Craven with regard to the Mallee country'.[5]

Here was the meeting of two minds across two continents: Craven and Roosevelt agreed that nature must be subservient to Western values and Indigenous peoples conquered.

New waves of settlers in the Basin

Craven was able to inform Roosevelt that considerable efforts were in train in Australia to extend the reach of population across the continent. A new movement to revive the agrarian ideal, battered from the failure of the free selection Land Acts, was taking shape with the advent of Federation and a new century. Closer settlement would dominate Australian politics for the next half century. Settling new waves of people on the land became a panacea for the challenges facing the new nation and a 'plaything' for politicians.[6] It was an easy sell in a land of such limitless horizons as Australia. 'The parrot cry of the moment', wrote one newspaper in 1908, 'is for closer settlement ... We have three million square miles of territory and four million inhabitants'.[7]

But the timing of the revived policy said much about Australia's fixation on economic growth at the expense of the environment. When the first of the state Closer Settlement Acts was presented to the New South Wales Parliament in 1901, drought still stalked eastern Australia. As outlined in the previous chapter, the country was in the grip of an unprecedented ecological crisis. But according to the state's politicians, there was no lasting damage. Eager new settlers could move in, take up a block, clear the forest, shoot the marsupial 'pests', and engage in continuous cropping and overstocking, as if no lessons had been learned about the environmental problems associated with the development-at-all-costs model.

When introducing the legislation to Parliament, William Crick, the Minister for Lands, extolled the virtues of the measure by reviving the populist pitch that the government would press forward to compulsorily acquire the big estates. It was disgraceful, he explained, that much land situated near centres of population 'should be in the hands of a few people, while there were thousands of people waiting to settle on it'. And besides, closer settlement would be a fillip to the development of the country.[8]

Crick was typical of the type of early 20th-century politician who championed land development. Raised in Wellington, New South Wales, this self-made man became a lawyer and built up a large police court practice before entering Parliament in 1889. He was a knock-about sort of bloke, blessed with wit, charm and a lawyer's knack for subtle sarcasm. A racing enthusiast, he had twice entered a horse in the Melbourne Cup, without winning the grand race. As a debater, he knew how to rough up a political opponent, and he had the tenacity of a British bulldog.[9]

Crick was clearly not a man to deviate from his set path, and he certainly didn't when visited by a group of pastoralists in the course of the debate over the Closer Settlement Bill. They wanted his ear on two matters. Firstly, they were keen to point out the extent of their suffering during the drought, and, secondly, they wanted to issue a warning that it would be useless to throw land open for settlement while the drought continued: 'defer it until the drought breaks up', they insisted. Crick would have none of their warnings. It would be cruel, he said, to delay people taking up land until rain fell.[10]

In the meantime, the potential for further ecological crises mounted. Existing settlers continued the relentless clearing of bush. The *Snowy River Mail* broke with the prevailing ethos to criticise settlers who 'regard the forest as a natural enemy against which a war of extermination must be waged'.[11]

Rabbits remained in plague proportions. The early decades of the 20th century witnessed a boom in the demand for rabbit skins. Traditionally, the British and American fur markets had been supplied by Russia, but this source ceased after the Russian revolution of 1917 forcing suppliers to search for other sources of fur and looked to the Australian rabbit as a replacement. Such was the demand that farmers found difficulty securing men to harvest the crops; they had 'all gone rabbiting'.[12] The 'rabbit boom' might have provided a lucrative trade for trappers, but they made little overall dent in rabbit numbers.

Rabbits weren't the only indicator of a stressed ecosystem. Big dust storms, which had begun in the Federation Drought, continued to plague Basin communities periodically. On 19 January 1915, for example, the farming community of the eastern Riverina woke up to a fierce wind blowing from the north, bringing with it clouds of dust. It continued to blow with menacing intent all day until 5 pm when, in an instant, the whole town and the surrounding countryside was enveloped in impenetrable darkness. 'The effect', one local newspaper wrote, 'was as if night had suddenly fallen over the landscape'. In houses and shops people began groping about blindly until they could secure an artificial light. Outside nothing could be seen but a wall of blackness, fringed with 'a lurid yellow'. As the wind raged with cyclonic fury, businesses shut their doors.[13]

Against a background of threats posed by rabbits and dust storms, pro-developers like William Crick dismissed concerns about the state of the environment, demonstrating the disconnect of decision-makers in the first half of the 20th century on this issue – a situation that would recur later. As minister, he was well aware of the scale of the failure of previous agrarian schemes. In a public speech he pointed out that six and a half million acres of Crown land had been abandoned and returned to the state. 'What must have been the condition of things', he rhetorically asked his audience, 'to have brought about the abandonment of these six and a half million acres?' His answer was to double-down on another round of settlement. But what drove such faith in the agrarian ideal in the face of its obvious shortcomings?

Crick himself came to a sticky end. After overseeing the introduction of the first of the state's Closer Settlement Acts, he was charged, along with a land agent, WN Wilson, with corrupt dealing in land sales in 1905, which led to the appointment of a Royal Commission into the Lands Department. The two had been trying to 'work the system'. Crick died of a heart attack before court proceedings were concluded. Wilson fled the country.

Irrigation development

The advent of Federation and the push for closer settlement brought with it a renewed commitment to develop the irrigation potential of the Murray–Darling. As was seen in the debates leading up to Federation, the colonies had been tangled up in who had rights to the water and how the resource might be shared equitably. The post-Federation era intensified these debates, and especially as Victoria embarked on new, major irrigation works.

The long march to a shared agreement between the states – begun in 1902 and not reached until 1915 – was bedevilled by legal complexity and parochialism. One of the stumbling blocks continued to be the sharply differing views on riparian rights, the just allocation of water among landholders who shared the water's path. But did this common law concept apply equally to states? Victoria and New South Wales continued to reject the idea that riparian rights applied in Australia when each state was a sovereign entity; South Australia took the reverse view. The latter's position was dealt a blow when two eminent lawyers, John Quick and Robert Garran – who had both attended the Federation Conventions – produced the first legal text on the new Australian Constitution. As they set out in the *Annotated Constitution of the Australian Commonwealth* (1901), which quickly became the leading text on the subject, there was no such thing as riparian rights between independent states.

The states, therefore, needed to reach mutual agreement. With the Federation Drought continuing to blight Australia's agriculture sector, the states were compelled to try to set aside their differences and negotiate a settlement. The survival of Murray–Darling farms and towns was threatened. In 1902, frustrated farmers, backed by a newly formed lobby group – the River Murray League – organised a conference in Corowa on the banks of the Murray in New South Wales. A hundred delegates pledged to attend, among them politicians such as Prime Minister Barton and several state Premiers.

The goal was to try to see the issues of riparian rights and the harnessing of the Murray waters from a national perspective. The work of achieving Federation had shifted parochial sentiment, at least in spirit. As the *Wagga Wagga Advertiser* acknowledged, prior to the opening of the conference, politicians had candidly admitted that the Murray was a national stream in which the three claimant states (Queensland had yet to develop major irrigation projects) had joint interests.[14]

Yet Australian politicians couldn't reach a consensus on a way forward. The Commonwealth government was reluctant to come to the table. Prime Minister Barton felt constrained by the constitutional provision that irrigation was a state matter.[15] So, at a crowded meeting on the last day of the conference, state Premiers agreed to the appointment of a Royal Commission, with one representative from each state, to consider the just allocation of the Murray waters. Comprising also three engineers, the Interstate Royal Commission focused on finding practical solutions and, when it reported later that same year, it attempted to strike a balance between the rival interests of the states. It devised a formula to determine the just allocation of water each state could take out of the river. It also recommended the establishment of a central body to regulate water allocations.

However, the states wrangled over the implications of the report, setting back the signing of any agreement.[16] Inertia set in, as the *Sydney Morning Herald* observed:

> We hold Cowra conferences, and Federal and State Ministers travel thither and elsewhere to iterate the same truths and the same warnings. Then the drought breaks and, following our usual happy-go-lucky Australian custom, we straight away proceed to forget all about it.[17]

Victoria races ahead

While the states bickered on how to share the water, Victoria jumped ahead to grab the lion's share. The state moved in 1902 to begin diversion works at the head waters of the Murray. South Australians were incensed. The state's location at the bottom of the river system continued to make them feel vulnerable about irrigation plans developed by the two upper river states. 'If they [the South Australian government] sat down and allowed Victoria to go on with these works', one Adelaide newspaper, the *Register,* wrote, 'that State would say that she must have water for the works already carried out, and she would share what was left'.[18]

Not that South Australian anger bothered Victorians; quite the contrary. Victoria saw its role in developing irrigation as paving the way for Australia to be 'a great country', showing the world what can be achieved with irrigation.[19] In 1905 the Victorian government passed the *Water Act,* which centralised all existing irrigation works under a new body, the Rivers and Water Commission. The lack of centralised planning and management was seen to have retarded progress in developing irrigation.[20]

The following year, and in a major coup, Victoria secured the services of Elwood Mead to head the Commission. Mead, an American, was widely regarded as probably the foremost living authority on irrigation settlement.[21] He had been Chief Irrigation and Drainage Engineer to the United States government and, later, Professor of Irrigation at the University of California. He was an 'irrigation enthusiast' and was drawn to 'straighten out our irrigation tangle'.[22] When he arrived in Victoria, the state boasted over 120 000 hectares under irrigation, concentrated in the Goulburn, Loddon and Campsie rivers, which all drained from the Murray.[23]

Mead found a model of irrigation that was innovative but costly. After the debacle of the Chaffey brothers, the state had replaced private enterprise in the development of irrigation projects. It was government's role to purchase land, by compulsion if necessary; build the irrigation works; ready and even plant the land; construct roads and lay out towns; prepare house plans; build fences; and locate prospective livestock before the settlers were invited to the project. The government assisted in purchasing and building houses, providing agricultural advice, and establishing cooperatives for marketing and sale of produce.[24]

Such state paternalism deeply affected Mead's outlook. He wanted the United States to give up the idea that the state was purely a political institution with no concern for human development. In Victoria, he witnessed that the state could act as a business partner with the people.[25]

By 1913, Mead had overseen the release of over 4000 hectares of new irrigated blocks with an additional 7000 hectares in the process of purchase and preparation.[26] And Mildura orchardists continued to make a good living, but only off the back of subsidised water involving considerable losses to the public purse in the form of interest payments on borrowings for irrigation works.[27] Ever the enthusiast, Mead maintained that there was room in the irrigated areas of Victoria for thousands of new settlers.[28]

Populate or perish

The perennial call for new settlers reached a new peak after Federation. The national ambition around land development and settlement was given the urgency of national survival. 'We need to get forty million people on the soil', wrote the *Sydney Stock and Station Journal* in 1908, 'and they must come from abroad'.[29] The paper's sentiment raged as a political rallying cry for decades to come. 'The salvation of the country', wrote one newspaper in 1921, 'depends upon getting the waste places filled, converting the idle acres into busy acres'.[30] The continued use of the word 'waste' to describe the natural environment shows how deeply embedded the 19th-century worldview remained in the 20th. The same terminology was used to describe the water that flowed down the Murray and Darling. The popular perception was that it was simply a 'waste' to let it run to the sea.[31]

The Closer Settlement Acts introduced in each of the four states sharing the Basin in the first decade after Federation were extremely popular with the public. They spoke to both the fears and aspirations of the newly federated country. And there was no greater fear around Australia than the country's proximity to Asian 'hordes' and, correspondingly, no greater aspirations than to develop the country and to keep it white. Aboriginal people were not seen as part of the white nation; racial theory held full-bloods were expected to die out and others assimilated into white society.[32] Thus arose the need for large-scale British immigration and the spread of population to the regional and remote parts of the country. Closer settlement was the answer to the nation's future needs. It represented a fusion of agrarian and immigration policies. Consequently, up went the cry of 'populate or perish'.

The emergence of this captivating slogan requires a brief history. It is commonly credited to Arthur Calwell, the gruff, gravel-voiced and passionate Minister for Immigration in the years after World War Two. After the country had been bombed by the Japanese and threatened with invasion, Calwell expressed Australians' sense of vulnerability about its tenuous grip on large parts of the continent.[33] But the slogan was actually coined in the 1920s when it was used to bolster the ideals of closer settlement, immigration and White Australia.

British newspaper tycoon Lord Northcliffe is credited with devising the slogan that Calwell so successfully revived. Northcliffe, a colossus of the British press, and a maker and breaker of governments, successfully deployed his renowned 'exaggerated opinion of himself' to become one of the most familiar names in the English-speaking world.[34] Known as an advertising genius, he was one of the chief enthusiasts for British involvement in World War One, and became the UK government's chief propagandist behind the British war effort.

Northcliffe came to Australia on a three-week tour in August 1921, visiting Sydney, Melbourne, Brisbane and Townsville. The few critics of his visit lampooned the way he skilfully 'foisted his balloon-like estimation of himself on the Australian public'.[35] As the *Brisbane Courier* recalled several years after his visit, when Northcliffe was touring Australia, 'he received much applause because of his picturesque phrase, "populate or perish," which he repeated again and again'.[36] The slogan took off.

Thus, in 1923, the Anglican Archbishop of Bathurst, Dr Long, told his parishioners that, 'the alternative to which Australia is faced is clear for anyone to read – populate or perish'.[37] And the *Newcastle Sun* gave the headline 'Populate or Perish' to its account of the 1924 Pan Pacific Conference in Sydney at which delegates discussed the level of population that Australia could support. These estimates were devised out of thin air, as if the participants were bidding at auction. The consensus arrived at was 63 million 'at current standards of living', although others suggested a doubling of the figure or even higher.[38] Prime Minister Stanley Bruce adopted the slogan.[39]

Thus, the policy of closer settlement came to be the key vehicle to achieving the broader goals of immigration, defence and White Australia. Declaring, 'We must populate or perish', the *Farmer and Settler* enthused that rural life produced 'healthy types … apt and ready for the defences of the nation'.[40] George Waite, a New South Wales trade union official, also supported closer settlement on the basis that 'the vacant inland areas must be the homes of millions of people if Australia is to remain a white man's country'.[41]

Political support for closer settlement around these broader goals of defence and White Australia was aided by the sudden alarm created over publicity about Australia's declining population, which was first raised in a statistical analysis by TA Coghlan, government statistician for New South Wales. In 1903, Coghlan grimly warned that there was 'no hope of a teeming population springing from Australian parents'.[42] The spread of contraceptive methods was believed to be the culprit threatening the nation's future. Similar concerns were raised in America where President Roosevelt coined the term 'race suicide' to draw attention to the consequences of a declining proportion of Anglo-Saxons in the country. The concept gained popularity in Australia. 'The terribly menacing spectre of race suicide', warned the *Riverina Herald*, '[was] sapping the life of the nation'.[43]

In contrast to these dark forebodings was the countervailing idea that Australia's potential was unlimited – that the nation should have ambitions to match the size of the continent it was fortunate to inhabit. A slogan was born to capture this ambition: 'Australia Unlimited'. It was the brainchild of Edwin Brady, journalist and aspiring Labor politician, whose book by the same name, published in 1918, enthused about Australia's boundless fertile farmlands, capable, he argued, of supporting 200 million people. Politically well connected and gregarious by nature, Brady's genius was in capturing the ethos of the times and devising a catchy title to promote his ideas. Largely overlooked for his contribution to Australia's interwar fixation on land development schemes, he was, according to one recent historian, influential in shaping the pro-development policies of both sides of federal politics.[44]

This striving towards a nation filled with white people toiling on the land to bring prosperity did awaken a debate about humanity's relationship with nature. As mentioned in chapter 5, the continuous destruction of nature, centred around the Murray–Darling Basin, increasingly worried naturalists concerned about the preservation of native wildlife. But the advent of massive new agricultural schemes after the turn of the century shifted the debate to justifying this development ethos. Newspaper headlines such as 'Man's War with Nature', seemed to reaffirm the idea that the conquest of nature was the natural state of affairs.

Christian thinking continued to assert this traditional view, which buttressed the policy of populating the land. Thus, the *Methodist* wrote in 1926 that

> Man and Nature in the economy of existence, are at war. Man fells the forests, tunnels the mountains, makes the soil yield him harvests … And nature answers with her pests and other oppositions, and once in a while with her earthquakes, fires and floods.[45]

The *Newcastle Morning Herald* was even more bullish in upholding this idea. 'Man', it wrote, 'develops a culture which places emphasis upon nature's own subjection'.[46]

These comments are a sharp reminder that the mindset of 'mastery' or 'domination' over nature remained deeply entrenched in Western thought.[47] It continued to have particular application in Australia.

Breaking up the big estates

Bolstering the general enthusiasm for closer settlement and the inevitable 'war' with nature was the appeal to social equity. For decades, the squatters' land grab in the Murray–Darling Basin was seen to be both unfair and against the national interest. The nation-building project of Federation stimulated renewed commitment to tackle the problem.

Legislation associated with closer settlement in each of the states finally contained sufficient teeth to take on the challenge of breaking up the squatters' estates. The process was helped by the passing away of the original generation of squatters and the financial difficulties the succeeding generation faced after years of drought and declining wool prices. Government-appointed Land Boards were empowered to identify estates for purchase, value these at market prices and enter into negotiations with owners on fair and just terms. Governments poured millions of pounds of borrowed money into acquisitions. Surprisingly quick results were achieved in some districts of the Basin. By 1912, the landscape had taken on a different appearance in many parts of the interior of New South Wales:

> In place of the station home and men's quarters with the shearing shed in the distance, are now to be seen scores of smiling homesteads; in places where hundreds lived, thousands now are found. The wool that grows on the back of the sheep is no longer the sole source of wealth.[48]

Success in breaking up the big estates also occurred in Queensland, where, between 1906 and 1920, 130000 hectares were purchased from pastoral properties, mainly in the highly productive Darling Downs. The number of farms rose from 18000 to nearly 27000 over the same period.[49]

Adding to the momentum for redistribution of land from rich to ordinary people was the introduction by Andrew Fisher's Labor government in 1910 of a federal land tax on wealthy landed estates. Labor had advocated such a tax for several years amid criticism in the press that it was merely a grab for revenue and that it would not hasten the settlement process, which the same papers actively supported. The effect of the tax was to force large landowners to consider whether they wanted to pay the tax or to avoid it by selling off a portion of their estate. Twelve months after the tax's introduction, the Land Tax Commissioner prepared a brief for the government showing that sales of big estates were proceeding and that the principal reason was that 'many owners have cut up their estates'.[50] Three years later it was reported that 'subdivision [of estates] has been greatly accelerated by the tax'.[51]

Desirable though it may have been to break up the big estates, the policy came with underlying environmental consequences. The boom in wool prices after the end of World War One led to inflated land prices and, out in saltbush country, men of modest means were ever eager to get the chance to 'ride to prosperity on the sheep's back'. Their financial situation forced them to overstock and disaster lay around the corner, as it always had.[52]

Despite attempts to break up big estates, the Murray–Darling retained some whose size and wealth represented an Australian version of the English manor house with its attendant village. In parts of the Riverina and the Western Districts of Victoria, the 'old stations' were a world apart well into the 1930s. However, despite the optimism about breaking up the big estates, all was not well with the grand nation-building dream of closer settlement and irrigation.

Staring at failure again

It was inevitable that the closer settlement movement would run into administrative, social and financial problems. The flaws should have been obvious because the design of the legislation across the various states was fundamentally similar to the land selection schemes devised by both the land selection Acts of the period 1860 to the 1880s and, later, the Chaffey brothers' scheme.

Few lessons had been learned from the problems these schemes ran into, specifically that widespread failure would result from over-promotion of the schemes, which attracted people with inadequate capital and little experience and who set out to farm blocks that were often too small in country that was often marginal. These were the findings of a Victorian Royal Commission into Closer Settlement, which reported in 1916.

Commissioners were critical that settlers were often pawns in a grand scheme in which their chance of success was often low. The 'inevitable hard struggle', commissioners wrote, of men with little capital, saw them 'pivot on the see-saw of destiny' burdened by debt and unrelenting sacrifice.[53] The occasional visiting male journalist who peered into the lives of struggling selectors found that women bore the hardships with a steely resilience. Often living miles from the nearest railway line, along a rutted track that became an impassable quagmire with the first heavy shower, they eked out their lives 'starved for company' in 'two room humpies'. Brave enough for these privations, wives often 'did the work of men, drawing water and cutting scrub for stock, in addition to their domestic duties'. And the long hot summers brought 'torments of flies and dust and heat'.[54]

No statistics were kept on the number of settlers who failed to make a success of their blocks. However, the Royal Commissioners calculated the success/failure rate on the dry land farming areas by classifying the land upon which settlers took up blocks. They divided these into four categories – 'Unadaptable', 'More or less failure', 'More or less success' and 'Successful'. The latter two categories represented nearly 60 per cent of settlers, giving a failure rate of around 40 per cent.

The Commission did not consider the impact of large-scale agricultural development on the environment, consistent with the prevailing ethos. However, one insight into the ongoing scale of deforestation associated with closer settlement was the grievance settlers had at the high-handed actions of the Forests Department. As the settlers cleared their blocks, 'the Forests Department entered their allotments and took the settlers' timber and milled it without their consent causing a serious state of unrest and uncertainty among them'.[55] It appeared to the Commission that the Forests Department and the Land Board were using the forests as a way of recouping the costs of the scheme. Inept administration resulted in estates being over-valued and a consequent drain on state funds. In Victoria, the losses amounted to four million pounds.[56] 'Purchase values of resumed land', commented the *Leader* 'have been determined in a very haphazard manner'.[57]

In the meantime, the states maintained their bitter feuding over water rights. Negotiations over the water agreement waxed and waned. While New South Wales abandoned its claim of absolute ownership of the Murray, Victorian politicians operated under the assumption that they were entitled to divert whatever water from the river they wanted.[58] A hoped-for breakthrough in signing an interstate agreement fell apart in 1908 amid mutual recriminations. South Australia remained the most aggrieved of the states. By 1910, it laid the blame for the impasse squarely on the Victorian government, which had negotiated 'in accordance with their own views and without regard to any other party to the arrangement'.[59]

South Australians had good cause to be angry at the stalled negotiations. By 1912, flows into South Australia from the Murray were being affected by the up-river irrigation schemes in Victoria and New South Wales. In 1912, the water from the Murray that flowed through South Australia was as low as if it were in the grip of one of the severest droughts.[60]

In 1914, the wrangling stopped. The outbreak of drought again forced the states' hands and Elwood Mead took a decisive stand in moderating the hitherto intractable position of the Victorian government. But drought alone was not responsible for the breakthrough; the Commonwealth proposed spending one million pounds to undertake a capital works program of locks and weirs along the upper Murray. Out of the agreement, too, came the revived proposal for a River Murray Commission to regulate the use of the waters between the states. It was pretty much the same agreement that had originally been put forward in 1902.[61]

The year the agreement was signed, irrigators in Victoria became alarmed when the Murray ceased to flow. The drought was partly responsible, but as Elwood Mead confirmed, too much water was being extracted above Swan Hill, leaving those below unprovided for.[62] It was the first time that over-extraction became a recognised problem.

By the time these developments were being played out, war was tearing Europe apart. Four years later, in the wake of the terrible carnage of World War One, the Murray–Darling – along with other parts of the country – was set to receive another wave of settlers.

The World War One
Soldier Settlement Scheme

Planning for returned soldiers to go on the land began in Australia in 1915, a year after Australian soldiers were sent to Europe. A survey showed a strong interest among many troops to become farmers.[63] This was not surprising. Many of the soldiers were the sons of selectors.[64] And because the war became the defining expression of Australian nationhood, there was much greater urgency to settle soldiers on the land when the war ended in 1918 than occurred in similar schemes in other English-speaking countries.[65]

In addition to the nationalist idea of 'a land fit for heroes', a Soldier Settlement Scheme fitted neatly into the culturally entrenched agrarian ideal of building a nation of yeoman farmers.[66] Although soldiers were placed on land across the Australian states, the lands along the Murray River in New South Wales, Victoria and South Australia saw a concentration of settlers because irrigated farming was regarded as ideal for mass settlement on small blocks. The findings of the Victorian Royal Commission of just a few years earlier, which had criticised the operation of small, under-capitalised irrigation schemes, were lost in the midst of patriotic fervour. Victoria settled over 11 000 ex-soldiers and New South Wales over 9000.

State paternalism drove the scheme: state governments provided loans of up to £500 for buildings, clearing, fencing and stock at low interest rates. Land was made available through subdivided Crown lands, unsettled or leasehold holdings, farming allotments carved from state government–purchased estates, and individual farms bought by the state governments.[67]

Within a few years the scheme ran into difficulty, forcing several official inquiries at state and Commonwealth level. There was by now a familiar ring to the reasons for the failure, as set out in the Commonwealth inquiry headed by Justice Pike in 1929:

> The unsuitability of settlers due to war service and want of training in farm work was one of the causes of many failures, but perhaps the chief cause was the placing of returned men on [small] farms which, … in many instances, were made up of poor quality or inferior country.[68]

Pike's bureaucratic language didn't fully capture the years of fruitless struggle to which many returned soldiers were condemned by the land settlement scheme. Poet and writer Kate Jennings described her grandparents' 'soul-shrivelling soldier–settler farm', that so wore down their spirit that they were 'almost mute' by the time she spent school holidays with them. Straddling a stony ridge, the farm developed 'erosion gullies deep and wide enough to bury a Melbourne tram'. And this was her grandfather's reward for serving in the Australian Light Horse Brigade in the Battle of Beersheba. He had already known hell.[69]

Documenting the extent of the failure proved difficult for historians because of the lack of data kept on the number of soldiers who left their blocks. Failure was also a relative term. Some soldier settlers like Albert Abbott struggled on like a peasant farmer, accumulating debts and never getting his head above water. Abbott received his block of land in the Wyalong Land District in the heart of the Murray–Darling Basin in March 1919 with an advance of £625. Abbott had only one arm (presumably as a result of a war injury), but this was not considered an impediment to him being a success on the land. He was judged to be a 'good steady fellow'.

In the 1926–27 season, Abbott's crops were a failure and his debts for the land and the advance amounted to just over £490. He wrote to the Closer Settlement Board asking that the interest he was required to pay be deferred until seasons improved. However, the seasons did not improve and as well as having to contend with drought, his crops were badly damaged by grasshoppers. He was still on the land in

1931, but his debt had increased to a over £1400. Thereafter, official records on Abbott fall silent.[70]

Settling tens of thousands of soldiers increased the pace of land clearing in the Murray–Darling Basin. The same reckless attitudes prevailed as in previous decades. In 1932, the *Daily Telegraph* acknowledged that ringbarking had had more effect on Australia 'than any other invention'.[71] With thousands of square kilometres already cleared, soldier settlers were vulnerable to the clearing mania. Every patch of ground had to become 'payable' such that in some places farms were reduced to 'salt blocks' or overcome with drift and sand ridges. Many settlers had their hearts broken from such relentless environmental vandalism.[72]

While over 80 per cent of soldier settlers in Victoria remained on their holdings in 1929,[73] many continued to struggle on into the 1930s. By 1934, only 39 per cent of the original Victorian soldier settlers remained on their blocks.[74] Nonetheless, the successful soldiers helped extend the dairying and fruit-growing industries in the Murray–Darling Basin, although it came at great financial cost. By 1927, the Victorian government alone had borrowed £23 million to underwrite the scheme.[75] As with the closer settlement movement in general, World War One soldier settlers were not just heroes society wanted to repay, they were foot soldiers in the domestic campaign of agrarianism, an ideal perpetuated by nationalist urgings.

Bigger dreams still

Just as it was becoming clear that many returned soldiers were floundering, the promotion of closer settlement received another injection of enthusiasm. In November 1921, the former Premier of New South Wales and member of its Legislative Council, Sir Joseph Carruthers, launched his campaign, 'A million farmers for a million farms',[76] which became abbreviated to the Million Farms campaign.

With a background as an advocate of free trade, a businessman and a lawyer, Carruthers had a modest record as a reforming minister and Premier. As a former Minister for Lands in New South Wales, he was well versed in the populist appeal of closer settlement.

The Million Farms campaign tapped into the zeitgeist for immigration and securing the country's defence by white people. It was less a proposal for legislation than a slogan for action. Carruthers had always intended his scheme would be an Australian project rather than simply one pursued by individual states. The praise he received from the press, the public and, ultimately, the Prime Minister, Billy Hughes, is testimony to Australia's deep insecurity about its place in the world and its preparedness to regard the environment as simply a resource to exploit at will. Could the landscape support a million farmers? According to the *Daily Mail*, the question wasn't worth posing. In its endorsement of Carruthers' scheme, it wrote:

> Australia has 1,903,000,000 acres [about 770 million hectares] and only 163,000,000 [about 66 million hectares] have been sold which means that the people still own 92 per cent of the whole area in the form of unsold Crown Land. What a lure must such a vast empty continent be in the eyes of the congested Orient whose Pacific stepping stones reach near to our northern shores … It is to increase Australia's population that Sir Joseph Carruthers puts forward his 'million farms' plan.[77]

As part of his publicity drive, Carruthers went on a tour of inspection of the Murray and Darling rivers and returned energised by the 'vast, rich areas' that were available for settlement. On his return, he met with Prime Minister Billy Hughes, a polarising figure who had formed his Nationalist Party after splitting with Labor over conscription for World War One. Hughes expressed strong support for the Million Farms campaign,[78] despite the press recognising that the plan involved 'insuperable difficulties'.[79] Like many Australians at the time, Hughes was a keen imperialist and advocate of white Australia. But some thought the diminutive, Welsh-born career politician a populist demagogue.[80] As William Crick's career showed, closer settlement was irresistible to political opportunists.

Intended as a goal, rather than a strategy, the Million Farms campaign spurred governments around the country 'to catch the idea' and maintain their commitment to open up new country for settlement.[81] The Railway Commissioner of New South Wales, for example, submitted a map to the government outlining an area of 1 379 200 hectares within 20 kilometres of the state's extensive railway network, which was thought to be suited to wheat growing and closer settlement. Yet, as more sober analysis pointed out, opening up such a huge area 'would involve a vast loan by the State and would cripple its finances and credit'.[82] Nonetheless, the campaign was influential in drawing Commonwealth government attention to the potential of settling thousands of British immigrants on Murray irrigation lands across the three states.[83] Within its first year, nearly 24 000 British had emigrated to Australia attracted by the land settlement scheme.[84]

The planning and capital works for this expansion was undertaken by the River Murray Commission, whose main project after its establishment in 1915 was construction of the Hume Dam. Set for completion in 1930 (in fact, it opened six years late), the dam expressed the dreams for irrigation development in the Murray Valley. The vast concrete edifice provided water storage during the summer and in dry years. With a surface area more than twice the size of Sydney Harbour, it was set to be the third biggest reservoir in the world with a capacity to irrigate nearly 17 million hectares.[85]

Calls to halt the scheme unheeded

A few influential voices derided closer settlement as a hopelessly unrealistic scheme from an environmental perspective. Harold Swain,

Queensland's Director of Forests during the interwar period, used his position to oppose the continual clearing of forests for agriculture, championing reforestation. He repeatedly clashed with governments promoting agricultural expansion.[86]

If Swain was an example of the bureaucratic insider trying to influence the 'system', Griffith Taylor was a public intellectual who critiqued the prevailing obsession with closer settlement. English-born, he emigrated to Australia as a child with his family and, when he returned to England to study at Cambridge University, he developed a passion for Antarctic exploration. Joining Robert Falcon Scott's ill-fated Terra Nova expedition as a young man (1910–13) brought him lasting recognition. Scott's team vied with Norwegian explorer Roald Amundsen in a 'race for the pole'. When Scott and several others lost their lives in the frozen wastes, a powerful aura surrounded every Antarctic adventurer.[87]

Between 1912 and 1920, 'Griff' Taylor held a senior research position with the Weather Service where he produced some of his most significant work on meteorological conditions and 'climatic controls' in Australian agriculture and settlement expansion.[88] He was the first to scientifically map the interaction between climate and human settlement in Australia. He became an ardent critic of what he described as 'optimistic politicians who talk about our vast unexploited but fertile land'.[89] He realised that politicians were motivated by expediency rather than scientific knowledge and he was unafraid of using his considerable public profile to take them on, especially as he believed that it was incumbent on politicians to show some knowledge of the physical nature of the continent over which they governed. He was, by the 1920s, 'one of the outstanding figures of Australian science'.[90]

By the time he weighed into the debate on closer settlement, Taylor had just been appointed as professor and head of Australia's first geography department at the University of Sydney. There, he soon found himself intellectually at odds with both the geography profession and the other senior staff in the department. In the debate over 'man versus nature', Taylor had become an environmentalist and a visionary.

His work on Australia had led him to some profound insights: 'Man might imagine that he is a free agent; able to shape his future', but 'nature's plan', exerted a force of its own, and would always shape the future of human endeavour.[91] Taylor had developed other controversial views about which he wrote regularly and which he collated into a book titled, *Environment and Race*. In it he examined the influence climate had exercised on humanity across time and place, and dismissed the doctrine of the superiority of the white race. He also provided a corrective to 'the super optimism' of enthusiasts 'who believe[d] that Australia's "empty spaces" can carry a considerable population'.[92] Taylor was an iconoclast prepared to tell the truth based on science. As such he represented the emergence of a new phenomenon: the expert prepared to weigh in on issues of public policy.

However, his views ran counter to the prevailing intellectual trends in geography. In the early 1920s, most geographers emphasised human ingenuity and its capacity to overcome the limitations of the physical environment.[93] In Australia's first geography department, such ideas ran in parallel with those of government. As historian JM Powell has highlighted, the 'Australia Unlimited' catchcry won considerable support: 'Respected scholars holding Imperialist views, including Professor John Walter Gregory, publicly challenged Taylor's efforts to dilute the appeal of Australia as the Empire's major field for White Immigration'.[94]

Thus, Taylor knew that many of his views were unpopular when in 1921 he submitted a lengthy critique of Sir Joseph Carruthers' Million Farms campaign to the *Sydney Morning Herald*.[95] 'The promoters of the scheme', he wrote soberly, 'seem to have little conception of the scientific factors which control future settlement but no progress will be made if these factors are ignored'. Having asserted his claim that science should dictate decisions over land policy, he moved on to attacking the hubris of politicians who backed such a grandiose scheme:

> It seems absurd to state that as Australia contains three million square miles [about eight million square kilometres] therefore each member of a total population of six million can have as much as 320 acres [130 hectares] to support him. Yet this is something like the crude reasoning to which we are treated. There are two arguments which are always cropping up … which have little value … The first states that we have only to irrigate our arid regions and all will go well; the second is that our arid and desert soils are remarkable for their fertility.

Taylor went onto dispel these common misconceptions, pointing out that irrigation would be a valuable, but limited, contribution to Australian settlement and that agriculture in the vast regions with scanty rainfall would, like the pastoral industry, prove precarious. He calculated that Australia had 616 000 square miles (about 1.6 million square kilometres) for agriculture, not the several million continually promoted by politicians.

Taylor's interventions in the land settlement debate were dismissed as 'pessimistic' and 'unpatriotic'. They infuriated the 'settlement boosters' behind the scheme. Consequently, he paid a price for dismissing the grandstanding of politicians and the greed of business. After being passed over for promotion, Taylor decided to quit Australia in 1928 to take up a professorship at the University of Chicago. His departure left a powerful message. According to Carolyn Strange, it convinced subsequent geographers that, 'notwithstanding their expertise, it was unwise to become ensnared in national debates'.[96] More immediately, the departure of Taylor removed a persistent, expert voice publicly warning of the environmental limits to large-scale, scientifically unplanned agricultural development. The dismissal of expert opinion without any consideration of their views was, by now, an established tradition in Australian policy-making in regard to land development and its impact on the environment.

Environmental consciousness, embryonic though it may have been, was coalescing around the desire to preserve native wildlife and its habitats. However, such concerns were no rival for the populist pitches driving the promoters of large-scale agricultural development.

Conditions for Aboriginal people

The onward march of closer settlement affected Aboriginal people in the Murray–Darling Basin. The shift from big estates to smaller, family-sized holdings reduced the demand for Aboriginal employment: 'Family-sized blocks needed few if any permanent workers and had neither the means, nor need, to support an Aboriginal camp – as the larger pastoral properties had done in earlier periods'.[97] This trend accelerated with the introduction of mechanised farming methods.

Aboriginal people were not considered eligible for Soldier Settlement blocks in the 1920s and 30s, despite the fact that a number of Aboriginal men had been recruited for the Australian Imperial Force. Indeed, the defence force applied the same racist assumptions that Aboriginal people were subjected to in the broader community. In 1917, for example, a group of 16 Aboriginal soldiers from Barambah Settlement in south-east Queensland were summarily dismissed from the army when it was discovered that they were, in the racist terminology of the time, 'full bloods'. The men complained that, instead of an orderly discharge, they were handed over to police 'like a lot of prisoners'. The army would only accept 'half caste' Aboriginal recruits, because 'full bloods' would not make soldiers, although it is not clear why they thought this. Nonetheless, the 16 men suffered the indignity of an examination by an army medical officer to determine their racial classification.[98]

Adding to the injustice, dozens of Aboriginal returned soldiers were denied an old age or war pension throughout the 1920s and 1930s.[99]

The pastoral industry continued to exploit Aboriginal workers and did so with the willing support of governments. In 1939 the New South Wales branch of the Australian Workers Union (AWU) spoke out against the repressive and exploitative system of sending Aboriginal children out to work:

> [The] Aborigines Protection Board owns 10,000 aborigines in this State, body and soul. It can, and does, take young children away from their parents and send them to work, and it can send the parents to the other end of the State away from their children's place of work. Young girls who work as domestics on pastoral stations are supposed to get 1/0 a week, but actually they only receive 6d a week, the rest supposedly being put away in a trust fund by the Government for the time the gin comes of age. In fact, however, the girls rarely see the money again, and certainly never see the full amount deducted from their weekly pittance.[100]

With the outbreak of war in 1939, some Aboriginal people were called upon to fill labour shortages, although they continued to be denied equal pay. In 1944, Justice Kelly of the Arbitration Court rejected an application made on behalf of Aboriginal pastoral workers by the AWU on the basis that 'natives … neither needed nor desired the so-called standard of living claimed by Australian and European workers'.[101]

In New South Wales during the 1930s, the policies of the Aborigines Protection Board hardened into one of systematic segregation as it aimed to concentrate Aboriginal people throughout the state into a limited number of reserves. Occasionally, reports surfaced about the conditions Aboriginal people experienced on these country reserves, temporarily shocking white society. Situated conveniently away from settlements, reserves were typically shanty towns often without electric light, proper ablution facilities or children's playgrounds; overcrowding was endemic.[102]

Although the policy of segregation was ostensibly aimed at paving the way for Aboriginal people's assimilation into white society, few thought this realistic and, of course, it was imposed on Aboriginal people. Reserves put Aboriginal people out of sight and out of mind, as one contemporary observed in 1931:

> Many stories have been told of the customs and peculiarities of the black fellow in the early days, but little is heard of the present-day aboriginal, who, robbed of his native land, is relegated into some reserve where the authorities endeavour to care for him as best they can and educate him on modern lines. In this endeavour to civilise and train the black, one meets many amusing situations.[103]

When efforts were made to assimilate it was directed at children. The Pooncarie Reserve in western New South Wales was unusual in having a school provided by the Education Department. Children were taught only to third grade by Miss Trench, who had 'a great fondness for the young natives'. When the *Sydney Mail* visited in 1931, Miss Trench told the visiting journalist of the lesson she had given on postage stamps, explaining to her pupils the significance of the King's head on the stamps. Three days later she repeated the lesson, asking the children whose head was on the stamps. One answered 'Jesus', another 'the devil' and a third 'the boss where you live', meaning Constable M'Evoy.[104] Many other Aboriginal children were forcibly removed from their families and placed in missions, where they suffered terribly in the white cause of assimilation.[105]

For their part, Aboriginal people continued to campaign for their rights, including in the Murray–Darling Basin. At a meeting in 1937, Aboriginal people from Dubbo formed the Dubbo Aboriginal Progress Association. The meeting carried motions advocating the abolition of the Aborigines Protection Board, full rights of citizenship and direct representation in Parliament.[106]

Some Aboriginal people lived away from reserves and close to their traditions. Groups continued to live and fish on the Murray River. Writing in 1908, a journalist found Aboriginal fishing camps every few miles between Tocumwal and Echuca. The people moved slowly from place to place with their canoes. Sometimes their camps were a gunyah of boughs, at other times a few sheets of bark, a tent or a lean-to.[107] Overlooked, of course, was what their continued presence should have said about the traditional rights of Aboriginal people in the Murray–Darling Basin.

The rise of the tourism industry

In the early decades of the 20th century tourist operators began taking visitors along the river. The industry began around the turn of the century, redeploying the old paddle steamers for a week-long return journey from Adelaide via Morgan to Mildura. By the mid-1920s, the trip was becoming popular for those seeking a relaxing holiday. It offered 'relaxation and beauty, sunshine and rest', and arresting views of wildlife, homesteads shaded by tall gums, station life and orchards.

Tourists could see the enormous amount of money Australian governments had sunk into the river – the elaborate system of locks installed in the hope of making the river navigable all year round. And there were glimpses, too, of the strange world of 'river types' – those who erected permanent camps along the river.

The Murray had, for decades, become home to groups of itinerant workers – woodcutters, fishermen, dingo scalpers and kangaroo hunters.[108] They lived in rough shacks or in tents and came and went with whatever work was going around. 'Who lives in these lonely tents with the delicate blue smoke from their fragrant fires drifting through the trees and across the water?', wondered one wistful traveller. By the 1920s, the lives of these itinerant workers became an attraction in itself for tourists meandering up the Murray. 'Almost more enthralling than the river itself', wrote one traveller, 'are the people who live along its edges'.[109] As unemployment rose during the 1920s, heading into the Great Depression, the New South Wales government established unemployed camps along the Murray and put men to work cleaning and thinning the remaining forests.

However, the itinerant group that created the most interest for tourists was the largest one: the 'Murray Whalers'. These fishermen derived their nickname from the huge size of the biggest of the Murray cod they caught. Were they 'Murray Cod or Murray Whales', was the standard quip when a big fish was landed.[110] Hundreds of Whalers took up living along the banks of the Murray, Murrumbidgee, Lachlan and Darling rivers. Wherever they were, they formed close communities, a 'camaraderie so characteristic of the Australian bush'.[111]

Each of the Whalers had his own favourite spot where a humpy was built out of bark, boughs and bags, and, among themselves, they regarded each other's 'mansions' as conferring exclusive rights as if they were private property.[112] Living on the river banks, they eked out an existence fishing for Murray cod or perch for the Melbourne and Adelaide markets or just to feed themselves. Another group of European Australians was identified as 'vagrants' or more caustically as 'professional loafers' also eked out a living on the Murray. Unlike the Whalers, these social dropouts didn't live in semi-permanent habitations. Instead, they spent years on the banks of the river, 'following it up one side and down the other'. The river could sustain these itinerants: 'the Murray River tramp can always hook a fish – he's therefore independent to some degree'.[113]

Observers saw no contradiction in attitudes towards blacks and whites living rough in much the same way on the river. And while little interest was shown in the lifestyles of Aboriginal people on the river, the gypsy-like lifestyle of the Whalers attracted the attention of journalists and writers, adding to their mystique. ES Sorenson, a renowned writer of bush life, was familiar with the Whalers' lives. He injected colour, humour and pathos into the daily existence of these largely forgotten men. One of the characters Sorenson brought to life was Bill the Battler, whose refuge was a small bark gunyah, pitched in a secluded bend along the Murrumbidgee:

> He had dwelt so long in that one spot that he was not contented anywhere else. The spot … frequented by friendly birds, sweetened with the perfume of wild blossoms, and fronted by a running river that he almost regarded as his mother, was his only home. It did not look a very cheerful place to fade away in, after a strenuous life in many parts that had earned him the name of Bill the Battler. He had worked hard for anything he had ever possessed, and in his old age his possessions could all be rolled up in an ordinary swag.[114]

Outsiders tended to see Whalers as derelicts, but the few who got to know them, and wrote about their lives, including Sorenson, saw them as harmless, eccentric, semi-hermits – people forced to, or who wanted to, drop out of society. As one writer noted, among their ranks were 'disqualified jockeys, carpenters, station hands, a mechanic and even a broken-down lawyer'.[115] However, most were said to be retired bush workers. In the dry seasons, when station work became scarce, the community of Whalers grew with the influx of shearers and drovers, who broke camp when times got better. But for the permanent Whalers, the river was 'their twilight home'.[116] So long as they had a little 'tucker', observers noted, nothing seemed to worry them much and that seemed to be the fascination for tourists.

However, this watery haven was succumbing to a steady toll of environmental changes. Murray cod were getting scarcer, and certain species of birds were disappearing. The continuing use of strychnine baits for dingoes, wild dogs and wedge-tailed eagles 'have killed most of our small eagles and hawks', reported *Freeman's Journal* in 1923.[117]

The problem was exacerbated by the continuing loss of forests around the Murray River. Into the 1920s, wood continued to power the steamers: the annual consumption of firewood between Murray Bridge and Echuca was estimated at 100 000 tonnes a year. As one travel writer noted, wood was being used up more rapidly than it is growing: 'When the trees disappear much of the beauty of the Murray will go. The birds will be forced to seek sanctuary elsewhere'.[118]

By the late 1920s, the region had established itself as the county's food bowl: wool, cereals, dairying and orcharding were important domestic and export industries. Establishing these industries took grit and hard work by settlers, and the social costs had been enormous. Thus the dreams of countless ordinary men and women foundered on the hopelessly optimistic expectations promoted by politicians and the press. And in continuing to dismiss environmental warnings from acute observers and experts, it was always likely that disaster would revisit the region.

9

NATURE'S VENGEANCE: AUSTRALIA'S DUST BOWL

On 11 May 1934, a disaster struck Washington DC with a mighty force that reverberated all the way to Australia. A gigantic wall of dust, which had kicked up days before on the Great Plains of the Midwest – breadbasket of America – had lifted into the air and roiled east, carrying with it three billion tonnes of topsoil and dumped it on the capital and the wider region. The dust blotted out the sun in Washington. People on the streets of New York tasted grit from the fields of Kansas and the Dakotas. Residents of New England states found layers of dust sprinkled around their houses. And topsoil fell on the decks of ships hundreds of kilometres out on the Atlantic.[1]

The epic story of America's dust bowl, the largest environmental disaster in the nation's history, had begun years earlier on the Great Plains, but the scale of the disaster was inescapable when the East Coast was unexpectedly blacked out. Storms known as 'black blizzards' or 'dusters' were fuelled by topsoil unleashed by years of clearing native vegetation and the impact of drought, which, together, had changed the landscape of the Plains. Nature's revenge was brutal. Whole communities were buried in sand drifts, ruining the lives of tens of thousands of farming families. With the land laid bare, stock perished, crops wilted and people died from a crippling 'dust flu', a condition similar to silicosis. Others suffered hacking coughs and other painful breathing and throat ailments. Some went mad from the unrelenting seepage of dust into their homes and the fear that 'black blizzards' could appear, as large as mountains, out of nowhere.[2]

Australians, especially those in the Murray–Darling Basin, followed the unfolding crisis in America's Midwest with a grim interest that was disconnected from their own reality. During the 1930s and early 1940s, few newspaper reports on the American crisis drew the parallel story that Australia already had a history of mega dust storms going back to the Federation Drought. Consequently, it was vulnerable to a recurrence of the phenomenon, because, like America, Australia shared the same destructive agricultural practices that created conditions for the storms. In a rare acknowledgment in 1940, *Pix* magazine wrote that while Australians were 'interested, appalled at drought and erosion conditions which created the American dust bowl, few realised that our own country is drifting in a similar condition'.[3]

In fact, only six months after the American disaster in 1934, a record dust storm hit Burra in the South Australian section of the Murray–Darling Basin. The morning of 19 December 1934 began hot and sultry in the small town. By 10 am a dusty haze had replaced the clouds and by lunchtime the temperature reached a scorching 38 degrees Celsius with dust blowing furiously. By 2 pm the intensity of the storm plunged the town into semi-darkness. A sudden thunder-clap of lightning added to the eerie atmosphere. It began to rain, and with it, the dust turned to mud, coating the town. Out in the pastoral country beyond the town, 'nothing but a deep, fiery wall of dust could be seen'.[4] The Burra storm, although localised, marked the return of Australia's dust bowl years during the 1930s.

However, history has treated the 1930s dust bowl era in each country very differently. In the United States, it is immortalised in the nation's historical memory as a defining event and treated with the cultural gravitas it deserves. John Steinbeck's classic novel *The Grapes of Wrath*, published in 1939, is considered a true account of the experience of a typical dust bowl refugee family and was made into an equally popular film directed by John Ford and staring Henry Fonda. Folk singer Woody Guthrie was called the dust bowl poet after he released his album 'Dust Bowl Ballads' in 1940.

By contrast, Australia's dust bowl years have, until recently, been lightly passed over by historians,[5] and, with the notable exception of acclaimed artist Russell Drysdale's graphic work on soil erosion, little of Australia's own catastrophic experience of erosion and dust has endured in the public imagination. To be sure, the social impacts in the United States were especially grave, with between 300 000 and 400 000 farmers – known as 'Okies' – forced to leave the land and travel to new lives in California.[6] As Australian newspaper readers learned, the position of these people was pitiful: 'their land is useless, their crops are ruined and they are faced with illness and poverty'.[7] However, evidence of a dust and drought exodus by Murray–Darling Basin farmers in phases from the early 1930s to the mid-1940s has received scant attention. And, in terms of the area affected by erosion and the length of time over which dust storms erupted, Australia's dust bowl was greater than America's.[8]

Australians learn a lesson

Unlike in Australia, action from the federal government in America was swift. A Soil Conservation Service had been established in 1933 headed by Hugh Bennett, a charismatic son of the soil and fierce advocate for action on soil erosion. Days before the disaster unfolded, he had been called to Washington to testify before Congress on the work of his agency. Bennett came to the Service with a message that was as profound as it was unfamiliar. Governments, he warned, had encouraged 'an exploitative farming binge', and that a man-made epic disaster was unfolding, that change was needed from the ground up, and that humans would have to accept the blame for changing nature.[9]

Just as he was about to testify before Congress, Bennett heard that a monster storm was on the way and he used every stalling tactic he could to keep the committee in session until the skies darkened on the Capitol. Bennett then grabbed the attention of members of Congress, many dozing in their leather chairs. In a dramatic gesture, he raised his hand and sighed, 'Gentlemen. This is what I have been talking about'. The Bill enacting funds for remedial action passed less than a month later, in April 1935.[10]

Australians looked on as America's dust bowl was covered extensively in the media. Readers of country newspapers in the Murray–Darling Basin, and across the nation, were given a history lesson on the causes behind the ravages of America's mid-west. Thus, the *Macleay Chronicle* informed its readers that the dust bowl was a man-made disaster – a wide treeless swathe from the Dakotas to the Texas panhandle – 1.6 million square kilometres blighted by wars against Indigenous people and a model of extractive agriculture. Ranchers over-ran the region, profits were high and the plains were over-grazed and the soil loosened.[11]

Another country newspaper rounded out the history lesson with a pithy account of the misguided impulses of wheat farmers who completed the transformation of the Great Plains by 'making the land yield its maximum wealth in as short a time as possible'.[12]

After the first of the great dust storms to hit the East Coast signalled the start of the dust bowl, the local newspaper in Albury, New South Wales, reported, without a trace of irony, that America's farmers now realised that 'they should have husbanded the soil they so heavily mined ... the dust storms ... are the bitter fruit of the American policy of reckless land exploitation'.[13]

Locals in the Murray–Darling Basin simply couldn't see the connection between the re-emergence of dust storms in their region, and the calamity that befell the Great Plains. Nevertheless, the historical parallels were striking.

As in the Murray–Darling Basin, the influx of settlers onto the

Great Plains was encouraged by a government policy of agrarianism. The Homestead Acts, commencing in 1862, offered settlers 160 acres (about 65 hectares) to head out west. And both regions shared similar complex ecosystems and volatile weather patterns. The Great Plains were characterised by 'unyielding droughts and torrential floods'. Like Australian's European settlers in the Basin, farmers in the Great Plains showed little interest in understanding this intricate ecology, describing it as a desolate waste.[14] And they were unreceptive to the warnings from science and dismissive of Indigenous cultural knowledge.

As high wheat prices spurred expansion in the Great Plains in the early 1900s, calls to heed advice about the complex ecology of the Plains were overlooked. The soil was regarded as an indestructible asset, despite a warning from the US Geological Survey, which, in 1901, wrote that if ploughed, the region was vulnerable to rapid erosion.[15] As in Australia, the fragile soils of the Great Plains were exploited to secure the high prices then available.[16] Both nations embraced the same Western ideas of development, oblivious to impacts on the environment.

And, in both countries, farming methods exacerbated the problem of dust. The annual practice of burning wheat stubble after the harvest fuelled dust storms, because it left nothing to anchor the soil. Agricultural Departments advised farmers that 'a good stubble burn' was the best way to kill fungus spores prior to the next planting. Yet, it was recognised in Australia as early as 1914 that the practice of leaving paddocks fallow and burned bare after harvest created ideal conditions for drift sand.[17]

Warnings about impending disaster

From the mid-1930s, a small body of Australian scientists predicted the return of mega dust storms throughout the Murray–Darling

Basin. By this time, Australia had created a fledging yet robust body of scientists who could link the systems of weather, agriculture and the environment to analyse potential disasters. They comprised experts in state agricultural and forestry departments, academic geographers and meteorologists. This body spoke with a unified voice in warning governments, the public and farmers that the nation faced a massive problem with soil erosion in the form of dust storms, sand drifts and 'red' rain unless far-reaching action was taken. Yet, as the Brisbane *Telegraph* reported at the end of 1935, the 'new conditions' generating dust storms, 'were generally *disregarded*'[18] (author's italics). Consequently, the nation sleepwalked into an environmental and social disaster.

In fact, in 1933, the year before the Washington DC and Burra dust storms, soil scientists in Australia had called for action. Dr Tom Guthrie had been chief chemist with sugar company Colonial Sugar Refinery Co between 1917 and 1931 before joining the Queensland government to study soil erosion. He called for a national stocktake of the problem. The absence of a full and impartial scientific inquiry, he warned, was 'nothing less than a national calamity'.[19]

One of Australia's most prolific authors of the post–World War One era, Ion Idriess, warned as much. As a young man he had ambled about western New South Wales as a rabbit poisoner, boundary rider and drover. In 1936, sensing the impending disaster posed by dust storms, Idriess wrote an article on the issue for the *Sydney Morning Herald* in which he proclaimed that it would be 'our fault if we do not endeavour to prevent a catastrophe'.[20]

As Australians ignored these warnings, they read regular reports on the unfolding crisis in the United States and continued to turn a deaf ear to scientists. In 1937, soil conservationist Samuel Clayton warned that Australia was likely to experience a similar disaster to that of the US. Addressing the Agricultural Instructors Conference in Sydney, he said that drifting sands were already creating a menace, even in fertile country, and warned of the creation of semi-deserts. He called for ringbarking and overstocking to be stopped. In fact, out in far western New South Wales, sand ridges between 4.5 and 6 metres high had covered great tracts of land.[21] Clayton was the latest expert to argue that the model of agriculture needed to change.[22] He declared that if disaster was to be averted, conservation measures would have to take precedence 'for many years to come'.[23] He decried Australia's attitude to the land, which was based on over-exploitation.[24]

Also in 1937, Dr Tom Guthrie set out on a world tour to study erosion, visiting North and South America and South Africa. On his return, he pointed out that the losses from erosion were greater in Australia than in any other country in the world, and that losses from erosion were greater in New South Wales than in any other state. He described as 'licensed butchery' the destruction of forests.[25]

Not long after Clayton and Guthrie issued their stark warnings, Melbourne was blanketed by red rain for an entire weekend. It splattered the buildings and streets and household and car windows. 'It was a striking omen', wrote one newspaper, of the steady advance of erosion. But even more so, 'it told the nation that erosion was not merely a popular catchcry but a serious national problem which must be treated as such'.[26]

In 1938, dust storms were on the march again. The worst in 20 years hit much of New South Wales, causing a thick haze over Sydney. The towns of Hay and Nyngan were shrouded in darkness. In Hay, several men out cutting wood were caught in the storm. Enveloped in the dense dust they couldn't find their truck and were shouting to each other from only ten paces away. For people in the towns affected, the dust formed scales on their lips and made breathing difficult.[27] When drought returned the following year, desperation also returned.

To those living in the Basin, a mega dust storm was a frightening experience. Invariably they occurred on very hot, dry days. Once the storms became normalised during the 1930s, many residents in the Basin were on edge at the first sign of gathering dust. An approaching storm was heralded by a thin, dusty haze; some described this as a dense curtain of dust billowing high in the sky.

As the storm gathered speed, the atmosphere darkened as the dust blotted out the sun. Raging dust soon overwhelmed the bush and towns, forcing residents to seal themselves in their homes. The storms often lasted all day and well into the night, and houses were bombarded with pebbles, doors were pounded and windows rattled in the face of the 'hysterical screaming' of the wind. Nervous occupants peered through cautiously parted curtains 'at the howling of the spectacle outside'. At sunset, a dust storm produced 'a red glow of flashing flames' as if the sky were on fire. Not surprisingly, these big dust storms 'put fear in the hearts of timid folk'. One farmer wrote that he and his family cowered while the second dust storm in eight days blasted his home and farm.

Once the wind died down, people surveyed the damage. A policeman living in country New South Wales described the scene in his home as almost unimaginable: 'The dust lay inches thick on the floors; it got into the food; it seemed to penetrate through the walls'. Predictably, it fell to women to perform the arduous job of cleaning sand from homes. With dust storms sometimes wreaking havoc two or three times a week, women's role was 'heroic', according to a report in the *Herald*.

Out in the bush pubs, dust storms were a ready topic of conversation, with a sprinkling of bush humour: 'That storm' one drinker quipped to his mate, 'reminds me of one day back in the nineties. The dust was so thick the crows flew backwards to keep the dust out of their eyes'.[28]

What effect were dust storms having on people on the land? One of the enduring images from America's dust bowl was the exodus of farmers in their thousands, captured in heart-rending photographs. In fact, photography was instrumental in defining the dust bowl as a human disaster. A team of 'documentary photographers' was established as part of the relief effort to re-settle the Okie refugees.

The photographers didn't want to just churn out propaganda photos of bread lines, vacant farmhouses and barefoot children caked with dust. They also wanted to capture the raw emotion behind the drudgery and bring empathy to the suffering of ordinary Americans.[29]

One particular photograph captured the power of the medium. It was Dorothea Lange's iconic shot, 'Migrant Mother', which depicted the vacant expression on the lined face of a forlorn-looking woman (identified as Florence Thompson) surrounded by her unkempt children. She appeared to be utterly without hope. The photograph came to symbolise not just the dust bowl but the Great Depression itself. Travelling around the dust bowl states, Lange realised that she was witness to a historic event. 'This shaking off of people from their own roots', she wrote, 'started with these big storms and it was like a movement of the earth'.[30]

There were no photographic studies on this scale during Australia's dust bowl years. Perhaps the most graphic photograph showing the destructive nature of wind erosion was published in the *Australian Women's Weekly* in late 1944. The photograph shows two men struggling up a steep incline, the size of a small hill. The accompanying caption reads: 'Tragic spread of dust-bowl conditions is indicated as these two farmers scramble up a sand-drift 50 feet high on what four years ago was wheat land producing bumper crops at Nangiloc, near Mildura'.[31]

The Mallee was one of the worst erosion-affected areas, yet it remained important to Victoria's agricultural economy, producing a third of the state's wheat. However, the ravages of sand drift during the 1930s had pessimists including WO Brown, an engineer with the Railways Department, gloomily predicting that 'the Mallee will undoubtedly lapse into a Sahara'. Yet, this seeming paradox of riches alongside ruin was not that difficult to explain. Most of the successful farmers in the region had developed pioneering agricultural practices that mitigated erosion.[32] Many farmers thought such measures beyond them because of the costs, but others disagreed. SM Wadham, Professor of Agriculture at Melbourne University, and appointed in 1943 as a

Commissioner to the Rural Reconstruction Commission (discussed later) believed that most rural people were badly educated; that they lacked an appreciation of the balance of nature and, especially, 'the way in which the forces of nature have worked and given the land its present form'.[33]

Throughout the 1930s, the cost to both state and local governments and individual farmers from all forms of erosion steadily mounted. There were scattered references in the press to abandoned allotments[34] during the 1930s and the growing incidence of paddocks that had to be taken out of cultivation. 'Whole paddocks have been swept away throughout Gippsland by erosion', reported the *Horsham Times* in 1939.[35] And, as another country newspaper recorded, some of the most highly productive farming districts, with high average rainfalls, were affected by gully erosion. Although less spectacular than wind erosion and dust storms, gully erosion still constituted a serious problem because it swept the rich soil away as silt into streams and reservoirs.[36]

Keeping railway tracks free of sand drifts required the permanent employment of gangs of workers who took a full day to clear a typical one- to three-metre-high drift. Victoria alone had 9600 kilometres of irrigation channels, which required continuous clearing of sand blockages at significant cost. Farmers' incomes were hit by the loss of productive land, the loss of access to roads inundated with sand drift many miles in length, and the destruction of fences.

And sand was difficult to shift. 'Scooping is about the only means of removing the drift', reported one country newspaper in 1936, 'but the trouble is, the work is slow, and the drift again follows in behind the work'.[37] It's not surprising, therefore, that some farms could no longer support the number of people they used to, or that land values across New South Wales fell by more than half by the early 1940s.[38] By that time, Samuel Clayton, now head of the state's Soil Conservation Service, estimated that 60 million acres (about 24 million hectares) of New South Wales – comprising virtually the whole of the state's agricultural area – was affected by erosion. And Victoria was faring no better.[39]

As far as can be discerned, farmers started leaving the land in the early to mid-1930s, before the sand drift crisis worsened the trend. The romantic ideal of agrarianism finally came face-to-face with reality: year by year, young people were leaving the country because there were no jobs for them. Many were forced to find work in the cities where some 'became forgotten cogs in the remorseless metropolis', as the *Farmer and Settler* newspaper put it.[40]

Then came those who were increasingly affected by the twin problems of drought and sand drift. They weren't given a recognisable name like Americans gave to the 'Okies' and no government department was on hand to capture the expressions of those forced to quit. Little documentation exists to detail this exodus.

Ern Ruchel is among the very few farmers who gave an account of his experiences. Interviewed in 1952, he explained that he took up wheat farming in Millewa in the Mallee in 1926 and became a model farmer, winning prizes for his clean-fallowed paddocks. As the years advanced he saw his land blown away by the relentless farming. At 4 pm on some afternoons Mrs Ruchel had to light a lamp in the house because of the raging red sand swirling outside, completely blanketing the windows. The Ruchels hung on, but around them other settlers were quitting Millewa 'in droves'.[41]

There are no records of what happened to these environmental refugees; surely that is what they were. Thrust onto the world during the Great Depression, it is likely some joined the growing ranks of swaggies among whom some were already close to starving.[42]

The dust bowl exodus continued thoughout the 1930s and into the early 40s. Out in far western New South Wales, some pastoralists abandoned farms in the early 1930s. The *Land* reported in 1932 that shovels had to be used frequently to prevent the 'lonely homesteads from burial, and many of these houses, abandoned by their drought-ruined owners, were buried to such an extent that the simplest way to enter them when the drought had ended was to remove a sheet of iron from the roof'.[43]

Reports surfaced in 1940 that some Mallee farmers had packed up goods, sold their horse teams and set out in search of work, effectively abandoning their farms.[44] In the following year the *Argus*[45] sent reporters on a journey of thousands of miles throughout Victoria during which they spoke with hundreds of people. What they discovered were 'ghost towns' in the Mallee and those in other districts which had lost hundreds of people, and half-deserted shopping centres in country towns around the state.

By this time, World War Two was in deadly progress across Europe, Africa and the Pacific. Young farm labourers were drawn into the munitions industry, which paid good wages. But war alone did not account for the exodus; a combination of failed agricultural policies and soil erosion represented the fuller picture. The *Argus* observed that

> There were … genuinely hard workers, who are tired of a losing struggle against heavy burdens of interest on property taken up at fictitiously high prices, tired of trying to survive on farms too small to support them, tired of drought and swirling sand …[46]

As happened in the Federation Drought, nature was exacting its revenge on European ideas of extractive agriculture.

America sets the example

Franklin D Roosevelt showed the way with his bold New Deal approach of using the powers of the national government to deal with the critical issues of market failure that arose during the Great Depression, including those related to agriculture. As one American historian has commented, when Roosevelt became President in 1933, saving America's farms was one of his priorities, his actions considered a blueprint for how government should respond to an environmental disaster by combining science, community involvement, business incentives and environmental policies of soil and water conservation.[47]

However, Roosevelt also brought great empathy to solving the dust bowl crisis. In 1936, he undertook a tour of the nine affected states, spoke with families, and devoted one of his frequent fire-side radio chats to speak to the American people from the heart about the human distress he had witnessed and the impact it had on him.[48]

The scale of the crisis that the Roosevelt Administration confronted continued to come before the Australian public. Newspapers in the Murray–Darling Basin carried a syndicated article by British journalist Robert Wild, who, in 1940, travelled to the region to witness for himself 'the drama and tragedy of dust'. By then, an area as large as the United Kingdom had been turned into a 'grim desert'. As Wild wrote, two million people lived in the affected states: 'Two million pioneers who thought they were going to inhabit the greatest granary in the world. Two million people whose labours were broken by dust, strangest enemy of man'.

Driving around, eating and choking on dust, Wild was struck by the social tragedy before him. The shabby-looking families all around him had answered the call to 'go west, young man' on borrowed money only to be left destitute.[49]

Newspapers in the Murray–Darling Basin wrote extensively about the bold measures taken to arrest the problem: the 'colossal undertakings' of planting wind breaks across the Great Plains and the growing consciousness of farmers to engage in their own tree-planting measures.[50] In fact, 220 million trees were planted in a belt stretching from Bismarck in North Dakota to Amarillo in Texas. Readers were also informed of the far-reaching measures taken by federal authorities: paying farmers compensation to reduce their acreage under wheat and to replace it with grasses and legumes to bind the soil.[51]

As the local Charters Towers newspaper informed its readers at the end of 1942, a 'conservation miracle' had been performed in the Midwest. The United States Agriculture Department had, over the previous six years, worked with farming families to turn the dust bowl into a region of stable farm homes – a transformation depicted by the press as a quiet, effective revolution.[52] The cry for similar national action was made frequently in Australia. 'Dealing with sand drift is a national job', declared the *Ouyen Mail* in 1940.[53]

Australia dithers

In 1939, soil scientists VG Jacks and BO Whyte published *Vanishing Lands,* a survey of erosion across the world. Establishing the global seriousness of the issue, the authors had some caustic comments about the situation in Australia. They criticised the policy of closer settlement and described the extension of pastoralism into marginal country as the equivalent of carrying out an experiment. And they criticised the lack of action from Australian governments. Noting that a great deal of damage has already occurred in Australia, the authors highlighted that no conservation policy had been developed for the country as a whole.[54]

Pastoralists had already felt the impact of past policies of reckless overstocking. In 1939 it was reported that stations that had once carried 268 000 sheep were now carrying 35 000.[55] The topsoil from these stations had literally blown out to sea.

The various states took some action. By the late 1930s, all Basin states had passed some form of soil conservation legislation. In 1938, New South Wales passed the *Soil Conservation Act,* which established the Soil Conservation Service, with the forceful voice of Samuel Clayton as its head. The Service's biggest task was to undertake a state-wide survey of the problem of erosion but, as one newspaper reported, 'it does not appear that the Soil Conservation Service is adequate for the size of the battle'.[56] The country would pay, the paper went on to declare, for the lack of Commonwealth action. The *Argus* newspaper also weighed into the debate over the lack of Commonwealth action. 'Here is a striking lesson for Australia', it wrote. 'The United States … is tackling the problem on a national basis and spending billions of dollars.'[57]

However, Australian federal politics couldn't summon up a visionary of the calibre of Roosevelt. Joseph Lyons was Prime Minister as the erosion crisis unfolded during the 1930s. He won the 1931 election in a landslide under the new, conservative United Australia Party, which had been backed by powerful business figures. However, despite his commanding position in Parliament, neither Lyons nor the UAP had the fortitude to tackle the twin crises of economic and environmental disaster.

Lyons had earned the moniker 'Honest Joe' from his reputation as an open, trustworthy man of the people. He was genuinely popular with the public. According to contemporary critics, however, Lyons was 'a born railsitter', 'a plodding patriot' leading a party united only by a rejection of the Labor government's financial policies and vaguely expressed patriotic ideals. His government lacked the necessary vision, boldness and purpose to tackle the unfolding soil erosion crisis. One of its leading ministers, RG Casey, candidly described the government's approach as akin to ambling along as a collection of individuals, doing the obvious things that came to hand, 'but doing no forward thinking' and side-stepping difficult problems 'until they are on our doorstep – then we make a snap line-of-least-resistance decision'.[58] Casey could have been describing Australia's history of inaction on the environment and climate policy.

Ditherers though they may have been, Lyons and his ministers faced no political pressure to act on erosion. Rural producer groups were state based with only loose federal affiliations and were focused on protecting specific commodities rather than representing farmers as a group with common concerns.[59] With the defeat of the UAP government in 1941, federal Labor came to power under John Curtin. Facing an ever-threatening military situation, it would be understandable had the government decided to put long-term domestic issues aside. However, with an eye to post-war reconstruction, the government appointed a Rural Reconstruction Commission in a far-reaching attempt to examine 'the reorganisation and rehabilitation of the rural economy'. Among its ten reports and 330 recommendations on every aspect of rural production, management, marketing and lifestyle, wind erosion and agricultural sustainability figured prominently.

Space prevents a full consideration of this attempt at long-term government planning; others have undertaken such studies.[60] But on the matters of erosion and sustainability the Commission had some notable comments to make. Two of the Commission's members – ES Wise, a former farmer who was Western Australian state Labor Minister for Lands and Agriculture, and Melbourne University's SM Wadham – gathered evidence about soil erosion in all states and reported on the matter in 1944. They concluded that the magnitude of the problem was considerable and that the people of Australia as a whole did not realise the extent to which it 'was a very real menace' and that, if a national calamity was to be avoided, drastic action would have to be taken in the following decade.[61] The Commission proposed the establishment of a national soil and water conservation service to combat the problem.

The Curtin government committed only to considering the recommendation, prompting one newspaper to criticise its lackadaisical attitude: 'No amount of leisurely discussion will arrest or divert the drifting sand and which is turning considerable areas of this country into a horrifying desert'.[62] Wadham, in particular, was concerned about how to strike a balance between the rights of farmers and their responsibility to the wider community to prevent damage on their properties. Given his generally low estimation of farmers' knowledge and appreciation of the environment, Wadham advocated 'effective statutory powers to restrain the individual ... not prepared to cooperate in a general scheme designed to prevent or stop erosion and wastage of soil fertility'.[63]

But the bold step in calling for a curb on the rights of farmers highlighted the gap between the Commissioners and the government; few of their recommendations were implemented. In fact, in their study of the Commission, social scientists Whitford and Boadle argue that the Commissioners' concern for long-term planning, education and government control to achieve sustainable agriculture (although that term was not used) did not seem to please the government, which was concerned with short-term and practical measures.[64] The Commissioners certainly didn't endear themselves to government by criticising the failings of the World War One Soldier Settlement Scheme; the government was actively planning a scheme for returning World War Two soldiers.

And so another opportunity was lost. The ideas raised by Wadham and Wise, though circulated widely, were dismissed by the Curtin government, highlighting again the endemic problem: that when it came to matters of the environment, scientific experts were given a lukewarm reception by their political masters.

The big blows

As the federal government vacillated, the cycle of weather again took a turn for the worse in 1944. The public had been forewarned of the disaster to come. In the previous year, *Truth* newspaper described western New South Wales as the 'lands of the Red Blizzards' where windstorms swept fertile soil 'off the neglected and abused land', carrying it off into the air.[65]

Then, at the beginning of 1944, one local resident wrote to the *Singleton Argus* to express his concerns about the 'ominous signs' of the return of Old Man Drought, giving him 'the gravest apprehension' about the season ahead. Whatever intuition he had summoned, it proved to be unerringly accurate. The years 1944–45 were among the worst droughts recorded in large areas of the Murray–Darling Basin. The return of such searing, dry conditions were ideal for the outbreak of dust storms. By 1944, Australian newspapers had regularly referred to 'Australia's dust bowl'. And the problem was set to dramatically worsen.

In mid-October that year, Sydney was swept up in a mid-afternoon blackout from a dust storm, which, a day or two before, had swarmed over towns in far western New South Wales. Vast quantities of top soil fell as mud over the city and suburbs. An outraged *Smith's Weekly* criticised the state's pathetic response to preventing erosion. It was still only 'fooling about' with the issue, the paper argued, because figures showed that, in the previous year, the Soil Conservation Service had only spent £14 000 on the problem. Preventative work in other states was even less developed, relying on one or two officers in Departments of Agriculture.[66]

A month after the soiling of Sydney, federal politicians in Canberra had a rude reminder of the lack of national action on the issue. On 13 November, in the midst of a state-wide, week-long heatwave, a heavy pall of dust enveloped the capital and much of the wider region after sweeping in from the interior. It was the worst dust storm for half a century. The scale of the storm staggered pilots flying from Adelaide to Sydney who later reported that dust more than two kilometres high blotted out the landscape from Mildura on the Murray to the Blue Mountains just west of Sydney – a distance of nearly 1300 kilometres. Afternoon quickly turned to twilight, with Black Mountain invisible from the balconies of Parliament House. A coating of dust settled on the inner courtyards of Parliament House. The member representing Broken Hill blurted, 'my electorate is being blown into the sea'.[67]

It was exactly a decade on from the mega-dust storm that blanketed Washington DC, and *The Age* was scathing of the lessons Australia had failed to learn regarding the country's agricultural practices. 'Any people', the paper argued, 'that fails to put a high value on its forests and natural watersheds, by guarding and improving them, rather than being passive witnesses to their destruction is destroying the basis of their own prosperity'.[68]

In fact, between October and November 1944, dust storms erupted across the Basin. A monster dust storm blanketed almost the entire state of New South Wales in a savage reminder of the power of nature that could be unleashed by widespread erosion. One eyewitness to the tonnes of dust in the atmosphere exclaimed, 'half the country is in the air'. In Broken Hill, an epicentre of the storm, residents were 'holed up like rabbits'; those caught in the streets had to grope their way through pitch darkness. Subjected to regular dust storms, Broken Hill residents couldn't even plan a picnic ride in an open truck. One resident explained that townsfolk were 'prisoners of the Great Dust Bowl of the Far West'.[69]

In Mildura, locals feared the end of the world was coming when the sun appeared in the red sky as a ball of yellow fire. In Sydney, a sunny summer morning was suddenly transformed by a strange orange glow. The Qantas flying-boat from New Zealand arrived late in the day, having experienced a foggy haze of dust and smoke 800 kilometres out to sea. The day after, Sydney's *Daily Telegraph* editorialised that this was a matter for the Commonwealth to rectify and that it should immediately despatch experts to the United States.[70]

At the height of the drought and dust storm crisis of 1944, the *Sydney Morning Herald* convinced Russell Drysdale to accompany one of its journalists, Keith Newman, on a tour of western New South Wales, the worst affected region. The words and images were published in two feature articles headlined: 'An Artist's Journey into Australia's Lost World: Our Western Inferno'.[71] During the two-week trip, the duo travelled over 3000 kilometres ostensibly just to cover the drought, but in the course of which they discovered the broader ecological crisis of drought, dust storms and sand drift.

Newman described their experience as 'one long tragedy over

scorched earth'. When the dust was blowing, it took eyes narrowed to slits to peer into the baked earth. The land was completely devoid of life. The few trees left standing were all dead, ghostly apparitions that looked as if they had died in an agony of thirst. The duo found countless creeks buried in sand drifts; they would never run again. Strangely, though, there weren't many dead sheep to be seen – most had been buried by the sand drifts, often while they were still alive. And if the sheep survived the onslaught of the storm, their fleeces could be so weighed down by sand that they were not able to get back on their feet, and so they died a slow death from starvation.[72]

These must have been distressing sights for Drysdale and Newman. Yet more was to follow. The two travellers came across an eerie reminder of the impact of Europeans. The howling winds had scooped away the earth from Aboriginal burial grounds revealing the skeletons of long dead Aboriginal people. Few locals wanted to talk about this grim reminder of the tragedy that had befallen the original owners of this land; they just weren't interested. Yet the land was being haunted by the past.

Newman rejected the claims that a mass exodus had occurred in the region. He talked to farmers who were hanging on with the optimism of the habitual gambler; they had seen their paddocks waist-high with grass before, and they were sure they'd see it like that again. So why worry? The pastoralists with whom Newman talked were tempted to regard the drifting sand as no more than a nuisance, and resented use of the word 'menace' as 'alarmist nonsense'.

Yet there were unmissable signs of human flight – 'gaunt houses' with their doors flapping on rusty hinges, along with the skeletal frames of windmills, whose rusting weather vanes had blown off. Out of this Hades-like world of heat and barrenness Drysdale produced one of his most acclaimed works, *Crucifixion* (1946).

All around the country, the storms of late 1944 were front-page news. The tabloid newspaper *Truth* best summed up the prevailing sentiment with its headline, 'Australia Gets a Dustbowl, No Action!'[73]

Commentators searched for culprits and scapegoats. Predictably, some pointed the finger at a familiar class. The old settlers, argued one newspaper, had caused the disaster through their 'reckless policy of deforestation', which was motivated by little more than, 'Here's a tree. Let's kill it and grow more crops'.[74]

Others saw the fault lying in the economic system: 'Capitalism breeds greed in town and country alike', wrote the *Tribune*, because it fostered a culture for profit-hungry squatters to overstock the country. And the small farmers were also beholden to the banks and faced the grinding necessity to meet high commitments.[75] The *Tribune's* ideological bent is, perhaps, obvious, but its views were shared by sections of the mainstream press. The *Mail* argued that a financial industry had been constructed

> based on the production of wool and meat from the inland.
> Any State-wide reduction in the amount of production from
> the saltbush country must be reflected throughout the financial
> structure of the State. Hence – our unwillingness to recognise the
> necessity for any reduction in the rate of stocking on that country.[76]

And governments? 'Short sighted', was the left-leaning *Tribune's* curt response. But the problems also went to the heart of the democratic system, argued the *Western Mail*: there were few urban votes in heavy expenditure on soil conservation.[77]

The big dust storms of 1944 dissipated quickly from the atmosphere but they hung for longer in the collective consciousness. Out in the Murray–Darling Basin, opinion favoured owning up to the reality that Australia had a dust bowl. And the obvious comparison was made. 'Australia is menaced', argued the *Scone Advocate* in 1947, 'by a dust bowl more terrible and likely to be even more far-reaching in its effects than that in America'.[78]

The exodus from the land continues

There was, of course, a price to be paid for Australia's neglect in tackling erosion and sand drift, in the billowing dust storms and the red rain that had choked the land and blanketed towns and capital cities alike. And that price continued to be paid mainly by the small farmers. The combination of drought and sand drift in the years 1944–45 forced another exodus from the land. 'Veritably an army of land men', wrote the *Western Grazier* in early 1945, 'is drift-driven and ruined in the Wimmera and Mallee districts ... on both sides of the Murray for thousands of square miles'.[79] In this vast, drought-stricken and sand-clogged area, Mildura was the only bright spot thanks to its irrigation infrastructure. But even this had been badly affected by dust.

In every direction, lands were desolate and barren. The old generation of Mallee farmers had battled away for decades mostly on their own. Farms between one and 2000 hectares typically had no labour other than the family that owned the property, and many felt it had become impossible to do the job effectively.[80] They were 'robbed of all their energy and initiative'.[81] And beyond the Mallee, right through to Broken Hill, were pastoral properties that yet again had been turned barren by large stretches of sand drift.[82]

Mega dust storms equal in size to those of 1944 and 1945 returned again in 1948. Out 'Back O' Bourke' they lasted for nearly five continuous weeks and ravaged cities on the east coast once again.

'Dust storms are driving settlers out of parts of north-western New South Wales', reported the *Daily News* in 1948. Repeated storms had 'laid waste' to thousands of square kilometres of country. House cleaning was being done with shovel and wheel barrow and 'cooking was almost impossible'.[83]

The scattered evidence from the dust storms of the 1930s and 1940s suggests that they had a significant human impact. However, unlike the Roosevelt Administration, which took the ecological crisis seriously, governments in Australia appeared to regard affected settlers as somehow expendable; they remain ghostly victims of one of Australia's worst environmental crises.

The consequences

Australia's dust bowl was not solved by a grand, redemptive scheme of intervention as occurred in America. Rather, political neglect and lack of ambition allowed the problem to reach crisis proportions, despite the warnings from experts and the tragic example of America's Midwest. Each storm depleted the fertility of the soil. Repairing the damage was left to a new generation of farmers and the slow, steady adoption of better farming techniques, which eventually stabilised the soil. Thus, in 1951, the *Weekly Times* celebrated this shift with the headline, 'New Generation of Farmers Fights Drift'. The paper glossed over the mistakes their fathers had made and the challenge facing them in 'reclaiming large areas which were left desolate by unsuccessful settlers'.[84]

Henceforth, Agriculture Departments ceased recommending burning off the wheat stubble and gave advice to farmers on planting supplementary crops of rye corn and oats as a way of binding the soil. Government-funded soil conservation measures increased, with Samuel Clayton continuing to be a leading voice in this effort. Moves were made to convince pastoralists to re-plant saltbush. After decades of being chopped down and eaten out, the humble native plant was now hailed as Australia's agricultural saviour in dry country.[85] But any move to compel farmers to adopt soil conservation measures was strenuously opposed by the Country Party.[86] Consequently, approaches to soil conservation were largely voluntary in the years immediately after the big dust storms.[87]

While erosion was stabilised during the early 1950s, experts agreed that 'the improved pastures of the 1950s and 1960s were not improved enough'.[88] The reluctance of the states to hand control of soil conservation to Canberra acted as a restraint on progress.[89] And individual farmers complained that they faced difficult challenges in redeeming the large areas that 'needed to be sown to hold the country together'.[90]

Australia's dust bowl lodged, for a time, in the national consciousness, but it failed to do so in the same enduring way that occurred in the United States. There were no recognisable heroes like President Roosevelt and Hugh Bennett. Australia seemed marooned in its cultural narrative of building the dream of an agrarian nation and in a Dorothea Mackellar–inspired love of a romanticised landscape.

The debate over Russell Drysdale's *Crucifixion* highlighted this tension. It was one of several oil paintings to come out of the artist's 1944 trip, each depicting tortured trees in grotesque form. Connoisseurs of art hailed *Crucifixion*, in particular, as an allegorical painting that powerfully suggested that Australian soil was being crucified on the cross of erosion. Drawing a large audience when first shown in 1946, the painting also sparked a fierce debate about the accuracy of his image 'and the appropriateness of revealing what was wrong with the country'.[91] To critics, Drysdale's erosion-inspired work descended into 'realms of unutterable gloom'.[92] But the political inference was unmistakable – farmers were 'flogging the country' and governments lacked an environmentally sustainable land policy. It was a message that many Australians were reluctant to hear.

One especially searing poem came out of the nation's dust bowl. Titled simply 'Dust', it was written in 1947 by Henry Pryce, a World War One veteran and poet. He had already achieved acclaim for his collection of war poems, *Your Old Battalion*. He was motivated to write 'Dust', he explained to the *Sun* newspaper, when thinking about his digger mates: 'we want to see the homeland they fought for made a clean and fit place wherein to live'.[93] In 'Dust', Pryce conjured the image of 'a dying continent':

What have we done for the Great South Land?
Filled it with cows and sheep,
Fought with its forests, axe in hand,
And given it eyes to weep:
Wounds that gape in the grassless hill
And death in the shrinking stream

…

And the trees have gone from the runnelled Down
And the grass is going too;
The falling shacks that were once a town
Show what the dust can do;
And the townsfolk? Some are dead, some broke
And gone to the cities' dole
But Canberra sleeps in the poppy smoke
Of its dream-filled empty soul.

Pryce didn't see his words as pessimistic but rather as a challenge to the 'Australian spirit' represented by his fellow diggers. Nonetheless, his was a withering critique of the country's culture of environmental vandalism. As far as we know, schoolchildren were never asked to consider the meaning of his poem as they continued to be encouraged do so with Dorothy Mackellar's 'My Country', which was a centrepiece of the curriculum during Australia's dust bowl. On school celebrations of Empire Day, in School Essay Competitions and in the Children's Corner of newspapers, the romantic image of the 'sunburnt country' vied with the National Anthem – 'God Save the Queen' – for children's attention. In this way, lingering doubts that the country's environment had been ravaged and that thousands of people had paid a terrible price gradually faded from view.

Initially, however, Pryce was not alone in his concern that the country's soul had been eroded along with its landscape. The dust bowl encouraged calls for a national program of reforestation and for deeper thinking about the responsibility to future generations. This spirit of reckoning captured the attention of people in the Murray–Darling Basin. 'A freehold title does not give land-owners a right to destroy the land, they are only trustees for the land', argued the *Horsham Times* in 1939.[94] Articles published in Murray–Darling newspapers carried a recognisably new debate: 'The Urgent Need for Forests'; 'Closer Settlement evils'; 'Urgent Demand for Scientific Forestry Policy'; 'Tragedy of the Past', 'Our Diminishing Rainfall and Forest Destruction'. These articles spoke to a new awakening among Australians to European impact on the landscape. America's experience with its dust bowl had helped foster these more sympathetic Australian attitudes towards the environment.

The *Land* newspaper wrote in 1951 of a 'spirit of conservation' taking hold among the public. Letters were pouring into its offices

> for advice on tree planting, pouring into the Forestry Advisory Council for free tree seed, pouring into … the Epping Public School for free trees and school plantings, pouring into Forestry Commission and Soil Conservation Department about trees, trees, trees! Does this new spirit indicate we are seeing the light, the need to conserve our forests, plant new ones?[95]

Inevitably, perhaps, the counter narrative of big development vied with conservation for the public's imagination. Throughout the 1940s and early 1950s, Australia's water dreamers had been trying to whip up support for the most ambitious scheme yet to drought-proof inland Australia. The so-called Bradfield Scheme was the grandiose idea of Dr JC Bradfield, an acclaimed engineer among whose credits included designing the Sydney Harbour Bridge. In the late 1930s he proposed diverting north Queensland rivers to flow into the Diamantina River and Cooper Creek and, eventually, into Lake Eyre in South Australia, which would be converted into a permanent inland water supply.

Backed with 'stupendous' figures of water to irrigate pastures for three million sheep, promoters saw it as a way to develop the north and stop the spread of desert.[96]

For a few years, the proposal captured the public's imagination, although it was panned as unviable by the Department of Post-War Reconstruction. Although never intended as a solution to the Murray–Darling Basin's water supply shortages, it was a reminder of the eternal lure – pushed by optimistic nation-builders – that Australia's geography could be altered by massive engineering projects.[97]

The Murray–Darling was, however, set to be a major beneficiary of the largest public works project ever undertaken in Australia – the Snowy Mountains Hydro-electric Scheme. Inaugurated in October 1949, the 25-year, £200 million project proposed to trap the melting snows of Australia's alpine region to provide 3 million kilowatts of power and over 20 million acre feet of irrigation water for the Murray and Murrumbidgee rivers (an acre foot is the volume of water that would cover an area of one acre to the depth of one foot). The vast addition of water was expected to increase food production in the Basin by £25 million annually.[98] The Snowy Mountains Hydro-electric Scheme soon became known simply as 'the Mighty Murray Scheme'.

But would the Murray River be able to fulfil the expectations of these dreamers?

10

PROSPERITY AND ITS PROBLEMS

In November 1950, Arthur Helliwell, a columnist for the British Sunday newspaper *People,* with a circulation of 4.5 million, was sent out on a hurried trip around the British Commonwealth to investigate how migrants had fared since they left Britain. It was an infinitely more pleasant assignment than the one he had reported on a few years earlier when, as a war correspondent, he witnessed the British recapture of Rangoon, the capital of the British colony of Burma, after three years of Japanese occupation. He found 'a nightmare city'; the broad, tree-lined boulevards afflicted with hunger, filth and misery.[1]

On the jaunty tour of Australia, however, he reported from the sleepy, dusty towns of the Murray–Darling Basin where he discovered something he found quite staggering – 'the wildest wool boom' imaginable. 'Everyone who has anything to do with sheep', Helliwell wrote, 'has hit the jackpot'. The worth of the nation's wool clip had risen from £43 million before the war to £400 million by the late 1940s. Pastoralists were awash with money. Almost overnight, many had acquired 'near-millionaire tastes'. One 'crazy' character at the local pub shouted the bar and went straight out to buy a sports car that had caught his eye in a nearby showroom.

The wages of white shearers had tripled. They were now 'plutocrats who rode to work in hire cars', wrote Helliwell. And 'gun' shearers earned even more than the inflated going rate. These lean, tough, taciturn veterans, many of whom could neither read nor write, were earning six times their wages of only a few years back. Farm hands and cooks working on stations, other than Aboriginal people, were also enjoying the boom times. One British migrant told Helliwell that she had 'written to half a dozen people back home suggesting that they move here'.[2]

The wool boom may have lasted only a few years, but it mirrored a wider growth in post-war Australian agriculture of which the Murray–Darling Basin was a prime driving force. But little had changed. Triumphalism surrounded the economic benefits, while the environmental consequences were largely ignored; there would be a price to pay later on.

The proponents of the post-war agricultural boom of land clearing and irrigation in the Murray–Darling Basin showed they had learned little from past mistakes (exactly how little was not fully understood until the 1980s). From the 1950s to the 1980s, the economy boomed, and in 1964 Australia was given its nickname 'the lucky country' by author and social critic Donald Horne in his book of the same name. Although the phrase neatly summed up the country's good fortune in the post-war period, Horne used it with lashings of irony. Largely forgotten is the full quotation: 'Australia is a lucky country run mainly by second-rate people who share its luck'. It would not have surprised Horne that Australia's leaders mismanaged the agricultural boom.

The agricultural revolution

To contemporaries, the growth in Australian agriculture in the post-war era represented a revolution in production processes.[3] The advent of plant research, chemical weedkillers, aerial seeding, the availability of bulldozers, new methods of tillage, superphosphate fertiliser and myxomatosis to kill off rabbits all underpinned an increase in productive capacity and a rosy future for pastoralists in the Basin. As more land came under production, however, a continued assault was mounted on native vegetation and forests.

Superphosphate became an elixir for depleted soils. The phosphorous-laden chemical fertiliser not only increased wheat yields, it also improved pastures, helping to bind the soil and prevent erosion.[4] The work to prevent erosion was also the ongoing mission of the various state-based soil conservation agencies, which recruited newly graduated agricultural science professionals who spent decades educating farmers and developing farm plans with them.[5]

Protection against foreign competition on some rural goods helped underpin the good times for Australian farmers. Consequently, they received prices substantially above world markets, which, while locking in a high cost structure, boosted the incomes of efficient farmers.[6] In other cases, farmers were subsidised to export commodities, including beef and canned fruit. And commodity-based marketing boards and growers' associations conferred with governments to keep the system ticking over to the benefit of farmers. To aid efficiency, farmers in selected closer settlement areas were paid a subsidy to walk off the land, enabling remaining farmers to enlarge their holdings.[7]

The boom quickly wiped away the stark memories of the dust bowl years and dampened down calls for conservation of forests and wildlife. With new techniques to keep the soil relatively stable, land clearing continued its relentless pace. Until the 1980s, farmers could obtain a full tax deduction for expenditure on the destruction and removal of timber, scrub or undergrowth.[8] And the Commonwealth Development Bank, established in 1960, enabled landholders to obtain loans to undertake development work, including land clearing. In fact, the bank was established with a philosophy to encourage a resurgence of a 'pioneering spirit'.[9]

This optimism spilled over into 'development fever' across the country, exemplified by the commitment to build the Snowy Mountains Scheme, the introduction of a post–World War Two Soldier Settlement Scheme, the expansion of irrigation projects and a revival of closer settlement, which, by now, had become 'something of a sacred creed in the nation's consciousness'.[10]

Alongside the quest for development, the Murray was increasingly being appropriated into white Australia's national mythology as the quintessential Australian landscape through the appeal of its pioneering history, its physical beauty and the freedom it offered in the midst of nature. As George Farwell wrote in *Walkabout* magazine in 1947, the Murray offered a near spiritual experience:

> To camp by its lonely reaches; to fish off the steep, clay banks; to listen to the rush of water over a weir on a moonlit night; to penetrate the silent red gum forest, or fry the sweet Murray cod at the floor of an ancient stout-fibred river gum; to have known these things is to have discovered the quiet and the strength of Australian earth.[11]

The Murray also became the central backdrop of an epic three-volume historical novel, *All the Rivers Run*, by Nancy Cato. The first volume was published in 1958 and introduced readers to the central character, Philadelphia Gordon, universally known as Delie. The story charts her life living on the Murray, during which time she becomes an artist who paints local river identities and, following her husband's death, works as a steam-boat captain. Cato based her story on Pearl Wallace, born into a family that lived and worked on the river, who in 1946 became the first woman to obtain a river boat captain's licence. In Cato's rendering of her heroine, the Murray was the central feature of Delie's life. One early reviewer suggested that Cato was so evocative in depicting scenes from the annual rhythms of the river, its connections to Aboriginal culture, its changing ecology and its symbolic links to Delie's own life journey, that the Murray was the real star of the novel.

But Cato's desire to mythologise the river went beyond her interest in depicting Delie as an independent woman taking on life's challenges. Cato herself had strong environmental interests, and through Delie she charted the transformations – and degradations –

of the river system by settlers, decrying at one point: 'You engineers! ... You love to tame Nature, to turn rivers out of their courses or dam them up. But this river's too big for you ...'[12]

Like all national myth-making, emotion and reality blurred into one another. The romantic images conjured by Farwell and Cato stood in contrast to the far-reaching changes taking place. As one writer lamented in the early 1950s, the Murray was succumbing to technological innovations:

> At times in those early years there were 1500 men working on the Echuca wharf, and it was second only to Melbourne in the amount of cargo it handled. But those days have gone long since, probably never to return. Railroads, huge trucks, semi-trailers and airplanes have wiped our inland waters off the map as a means of heavy transport.[13]

And the peace, beauty and simplicity that appealed to Farwell were at odds with the plans for the Murray to be a key driver of national wealth creation.

Aboriginal people in the Basin continued to be left out of the region's emerging post-war riches. Most country towns had an Aboriginal reserve, its very location on the edge of town designed to enforce a marginalised status on its inhabitants. But not all succumbed to this form of colonialism. Tom Trevorrow recalled his early years:

> But we didn't want to [live on a town reserve], so we stayed together in camps administered by Ngarrindjeri elders. We couldn't live on our traditional land anymore because it had been taken away from us by the Europeans so they could make money from European farming practices. They came in and they cleared the land and they put fences up and it became private property, so Ngarrindjeri had no other choice but to go and live in camps on unallocated land where there was still some native vegetation left

and kangaroos and emus, wombats, swan, duck, geese, fish etc; our traditional food, and good fresh water.[14]

Traditional values are reasserted

Old values were reasserted in the drive to clear more bush. In large areas of country Australia, land continued to be viewed as wasted unless it was developed[15] and the appeals to post-war patriotism made land clearing something of a crusade. The cry of populate or perish carried added meaning in the wake of Australia's close brush with invasion by the Japanese. The agrarian ideal of settling soldiers on the land was seamlessly revived.

Councillor Earnest Wright of Tuncurry, New South Wales, summed up the process of adaptation to the new realities of post-war Australia. With the spectre of 'menacing sandhills' shadowing his memory, he acknowledged, just before the end of the war, that the history of Australian agriculture had thus far been 'a melancholy one of exploitation for quick profits, of ruinous deforestation, of denuding the soil of its fertility, bringing with it the tragedy of erosion'. Yet he went on to say that the resources of the country must be developed and that the country must 'open our doors to an ever-increasing flow of immigrants' so that it could be defended.[16]

Bolstered by pro-development fever, the bulldozer became almost a national symbol of post-war Australia. The Caterpillar D7, released in 1938, quickly became the favourite model because of its capacity to handle challenging terrain. Imported from America, the country couldn't get enough of these smoke-belching, diesel-powered machines. Newspapers in the Murray–Darling Basin hailed its bush-crushing powers. The *Macleay Argus* wrote in 1944 that

the bulldozer must come to be looked upon as one of the greatest national assets industrial science has given us … Anyone who has seen a bulldozer at work in the forests cannot fail to be impressed with the immense part they promise to play in bringing into productive use many thousands of acres of new country ... there is virtually no timber country that the bulldozer cannot clear ... landholders are due to make a lot of money out of their idle lands.[17]

Along with the bulldozer, chemical spraying helped bring more land under production. In 1964, the *Bulletin* magazine reported that 'great areas of land at present too steep, too hard, or too wet for ploughing may be brought into production' through the use of chemical sprays.[18]

This national fixation on development brought with it a familiar lament that native wildlife continued to disappear. In the immediate post-war years, a range of public figures challenged the pro-development ethos. The South Australian Chief Inspector of Fisheries and Game noted in the late 1940s that, as more and more of the state's land was taken up and cleared for agricultural and pastoral purposes, most of the native animals and birds 'tend to be pushed further and further afield, or are entirely killed off'.[19] He said too many people still lived by the motto: 'if its growing, chop it down; if it's moving, shoot it'.

Similarly, a correspondent to the *Muswellbrook Chronicle* posed the rhetorical question, also in the late 1940s: where was Australia's beautiful wildlife? 'They have disappeared farther and farther into the vast hinterland, as our so-called civilization has advanced, destroying their cover, nesting and feeding grounds, never to return unless we embark upon an active policy of restoration and conservation.'

The correspondent decried the fact that there had never been 'a rational scheme of wild-life management' put into practical operation in Australia; overworked police remained the frontline of enforcement. Moreover, white Australians had never been taught to appreciate their wildlife. The correspondent took particular aim at schools for their failure to teach the young about the nation's unique wildlife, which had resulted in a culture of 'wanton destruction of both fur and feather'.[20]

No less a figure than Dame Enid Lyons, widow of the former Prime Minister, Joe, weighed into the debate. In 1952, the staunchly conservative defender of family values and an elected politician in her own right, wrote an article for the press headed, 'Why Do We Kill Trees?'[21] In it she argued that the country had had a 'mania' for destroying trees since the first settlement. To her it was a matter of national shame that we had failed to learn any lessons from this destruction:

> Every dusty, shade-hungry township along our sun-baked roads is a reproach to us. Every strip of country ravaged by soil erosion is a monument to our lack of knowledge or our lack of interest in the future. Every dust storm striking the city, carrying precious top soil should be a reminder of our foolishness.

Lyons concluded her tirade by saying that we had, in fact, failed to heed the lessons from the 'great dust bowls of the world'.

In the post-war era, one of the few native animals that defied this bleak record of 'wanton destruction' was the koala. But it took a unique combination of circumstances to retrieve it from the brink of extinction at the hands of trappers and exporters. Australians were stirred by the koala's dismal fate when their number fell perilously close to extinction in the 1930s. It was estimated that there were as few as 200 left in New South Wales and 1000 in Victoria.[22]

While most states brought in measures in the early 20th century to protect koalas, trapping continued in Queensland, with regular open seasons between 1906 and 1919 when opposition to the killing of the animals began to grow rapidly. The decision by the Queensland government to mount another open season in 1927 sparked an outcry across Australia.[23] Despite this being the last official open season on koalas before Queensland imposed a ban, conservationists received reports that trappers and dealers were evading the ban by labelling koala skins as wombat skins.

Naturalists sent deputations to government, and a public campaign was mounted by organisations including the Australian Koala Foundation and the Australian National Travel Association around the theme of 'The Lovable Koala'[24] in what was one of the first public conservation campaigns mounted in Australia. Conservationists had a stroke of good fortune when they appealed to American President, Herbert Hoover, who, as a young man, had spent time as a mining engineer in Kalgoorlie (1897–98) where he had become an admirer of koalas. Hoover agreed to impose a ban on the import of both koala and wombat skins, effectively extinguishing demand and reinforcing the restrictions imposed earlier by the states.[25]

Thereafter, koala numbers recovered through long-term, government-initiated conservation measures. By the early 1960s, these efforts turned into an impressive success story. In Victoria, the growth in koala numbers was claimed as 'one of the most successful mammal management projects undertaken anywhere'.[26] Today, as most people realise from the catastrophic summer bushfires of 2020, the koala is again under threat of extinction and continued loss of habitat.

In the 1960s the koala success story was exceptional. Wildlife continued to be mindlessly destroyed. Wombats, which had provided convenient cover for trappers exporting koalas, remained unprotected in New South Wales until 1951 and much longer in other states. Up until that time they continued to be shot for sport and by farmers. But, asked *Walkabout* magazine columnist, Nan Hutton in 1965, 'can we afford to exterminate them?'[27] She was responding to claims that bounty money had recently been paid out on 7000 of the animals that had been 'trapped and clubbed'.

Public acknowledgment that the species faced extinction was no cause for restraint; in fact, the reverse was the case. As one newspaper reported in 1934, 'everyone wants to shoot one … just because it is now rare it is hunted as a curiosity'. The psychology of the 'sportsman', the newspaper added, 'is hard to fathom'.[28]

The same psychology of mindless destruction was behind the ongoing decimation of the bustard, or bush turkey, which once roamed widely throughout the Murray–Darling Basin and beyond. By the 1950s, its numbers were at perilously low levels in many districts.[29] With a two-metre wingspan, it was an awesome sight in flight, but, like a domestic turkey, it provided delicious meat and was hunted remorselessly by pioneer pastoralists; as well, its slow reproductive rate imperilled its long-term survival. Despite giving the species protected status, governments appeared powerless to prevent the bird from being continually slaughtered, and there seemed little prospect of averting what, in the 1950s, 'threatens to be a tragedy of extermination'.[30] Much diminished in numbers, the bustard survives today in scattered parts of Australia but mostly in the north.

By the early 1960s, however, change was in the wind. The formation of the Australian Conservation Foundation in 1964 represented an important step in lobbying governments for the protection of native wildlife and their habitats. Its first President, High Court Chief Justice Sir Garfield Barwick, was given a sharp reminder of the daunting challenges facing the national organisation when, in the same year, the Victorian government bowed to pressure from the state's farmers for an open season on black swans. In a familiar story, farmers alleged the birds were pests, and that was all that was needed. As a correspondent to the *Canberra Times* noted despairingly, what could be said of 'a public that reaches for a gun or poison whenever it thinks that an animal or bird is a pest'.[31]

Changing attitudes and policies in relation to native wildlife proved an uphill battle. In 1966, AJ 'Jock' Marshall, foundation Professor of Zoology at Monash University, published *The Great Extermination*,[32] a graphic record of the extinction of animal and plant species in Australia from the time of European settlement, and written for a general audience. Marshall, a tall and powerfully built figure with a ruddy complexion from a life spent in the outdoors, was, perhaps, just the person to shake Australians out of their complacency about the ongoing loss of the country's biodiversity. He was in equal measure engaging and combative, and a popular media figure, but, tragically, he died the year after his book was published.

The election of the Whitlam Labor government in 1972 – with its sweeping agenda for change across government – promised more action. This was especially so in the early years of the life of the government when Moss Cass, the urbane and self-described 'soft-hearted conservationist', was the relevant minister. Harbouring an affinity for kangaroos, he took up the challenge of creating uniform laws for their management. Cass explained that he was under pressure from the public to stop the slaughter of kangaroos. 'We receive … hundreds of thousands of complaints about kangaroo shooting from all around Australian and all around the world', he told the *Bulletin*.[33] Cass further explained that the government was facing increasing pressure at meetings of international bodies to ban trade in threatened species.

But New South Wales would not entertain any Commonwealth interference in its regulation of wildlife nor Cass's sentimentality about farming and killing kangaroos for the export meat trade. The slaughter of kangaroos and wallabies continued on a large scale. The animals had become an industry that deeply divided public opinion. Defenders, including the National Farmers Federation, argued that numbers were plentiful. Opponents described the industry as 'a holocaust of licensed and illegal slaughter' that was beyond supervision.[34]

The dingo and the wombat continued to fare poorly in several states in the Basin. In Queensland and Victoria, while Cass was Minister for Conservation, it was possible to kill a wombat on sight; and nobody cared much about the dingo – the exception being the CSIRO's Wildlife Division, which had formed the view that to 'slaughter wholesale the dingo was … to upset the ecosystem'.[35]

Queensland governments, in particular, were, during the 1970s, 'stubbornly indifferent to the disappearance of its wildlife heritage'.[36]

While the rise in community sentiment in favour of measures to protect koalas and kangaroos highlighted complexities in the glacial shift of Australian community attitudes towards wildlife, the status of these species as public favourites did not herald a significant retreat from the dominant culture of destruction, despite the calls from naturalists and like-minded groups.

Further irrigation expansion

While post-war land clearing was one pillar of the post-war boom in agriculture, an expansion of irrigation was the other. Leading into World War Two, engineers had big dreams for the Murray. The schemes for irrigation recommended by an Interstate Commission of Engineers, for example, when fully developed, were estimated to comprise about 560 000 hectares of land, representing an economic asset of £70 million and providing a living for about 70 000 families.[37] And the Murray was just one of the rivers in the Basin targeted for large-scale irrigation.

War only partially interrupted these dreams. The opening of the Hume Dam in 1936 had been a boon to irrigation on the Murray. The vast concrete structure was an impressive engineering feat. Through pressurised jets embedded in the wall of the dam, water surged out on a month-long voyage to Mildura and the Sunraysia irrigation district, 640 kilometres downstream.[38] There, as one writer waxed lyrical, 'the Murray River pours wealth upon the soil'.[39] The rationale of wealth-generation is sufficiently clear, but, as Deakin enunciated in the 1880s, and as recent historians have highlighted, irrigation also served nationalist purposes – a collective vision of which Australians could be proud.[40] The Murray–Darling was often referred to as Australia's Nile, a descriptor that gained popularity after Federation and was deployed regularly across the country well into the 1940s as if to signify that the very existence of the river system underpinned the greatness of Australia.[41]

At the commencement of this post-war expansion, there were glimmers of hope that development would take account of environmental values. At the forefront of this effort was the newly established Murray River League (MRL). At its inaugural conference in 1944 at Yarrawonga, Victoria, it promoted the conservation of the river's environmental assets, along with the massive development of the Murray Valley. The 250 delegates who attended the MRL conference represented 40 municipalities from Victoria, New South Wales and South Australia. The conference was opened by federal Labor Attorney-General Dr Bert Evatt. Delegates identified the key goals as securing the 'overall development of the Murray Valley through the development and utilisation of its natural and potential resources to the maximum extent consistent with their wise conservation'.[42]

Most of the delegates would have been well aware of the sporadic warning signs of problems with the quality and quantity of water available in the Murray River. As early as the 1920s and 1930s, the problems associated with salinity appeared to worsen. In 1923, Murray River crayfish were found crawling out of the water to die on the banks triggered by the high salt content of the river.[43] Concerns that too much water was being diverted to irrigation were raised periodically.[44] And the damage wrought to irrigated crops from the use of saline river water and a rising water table was widely aired.[45]

However, a 'cowboy' mentality had pervaded the development of irrigation even before the war ended. The *Cobram Times* warned in 1943 that the ambitious expansion of irrigation had occurred without due consideration of the suitability of the environment for growing particular crops, and projects were wasteful in their operation. Both rice and cotton became established industries in the Murray–Darling Basin before the war and both were heavy users of water. Without mentioning these two crops, the *Cobram Times* claimed that twice as much water was used as was needed, leading, inevitably it believed, to restrictions on irrigators. In effect, the paper foreshadowed the protracted fights ahead over allocation of water. Irrigators, the paper warned, 'will no doubt fight hard for the retention of what they call the "open go" now prevailing'.[46]

And, on the eve of the MRL conference, RR Pennefather, a Council for Scientific and Industrial Research officer, issued a stark warning about salinity. He said there was a 'dark side' to the development of irrigation. In fact, the south-eastern third of the Basin lies on top of ancient ocean sediments, which lie just below the surface. In pre-settlement times, Mallee trees and red gums, acting as pumps, kept the ancient salts, dissolved in groundwater, below. Then farmers – backed by government schemes – removed the trees, resulting in a rising water table bringing salt deposits to the surface, which killed plant life.

Behind the canneries, wineries and citrus packing sheds were areas where salt had formed a crust on the surface of the soil, killing the roots of plants. Pennefather explained that his organisation – the forerunner of the CSIRO – had found ways to prevent the problem, through better managed watering, but farmers were not applying the findings.[47] In fact, Victorian farmers remained locked into a wasteful system of water use based around a fixed low cost for the water, which acted as a disincentive to innovation and contributed to salinity.[48]

Warnings such as Pennefather's were hard to ignore, so it is not surprising that delegates to the MRL inaugural conference sought to strike a balance between development and the environment. Nevertheless, it was the first time such a balance had been entertained. Certainly, the League gained a reputation for being ahead of its time in advocating for something akin to sustainable development. But it was little more than a veneer. The MRL was never able to resolve the contradiction between its economic and conservation aims because its prime motivation was in advocating for a large-scale increase in population and production in the region.

In any event, others did not share the League's concern over environmental values. Dr Evatt set the tone about the priority for development when he described the MRL delegates as 'dreamers with shovels'.[49] Agricultural and water bureaucrats shared this pro-development ethos. Irrigation enthusiasts, like FB Harden from South Australia's Agricultural Bureau, visualised 'the time when not one drop of water would be allowed to run wastefully to the sea. The Murray Basin would be transformed into a great inland sheet of fresh water capable of being used for the dry arid areas of Australia'.[50]

The press referred to the 'open go'[51] and the 'development-at-all-costs'[52] approach to the expansion of irrigation projects. In addition to the prevailing enthusiasm favouring large-scale development, the MRL faced the problem that the body governing the river – the River Murray Commission – did not have water quality as part of its charter until the early 1980s, at which time it was realised that the 'management of water quantity without regard for water quality was a recipe for disaster'.[53]

However, in the immediate post-war years it was easy to get caught up in 'development fever' and ignore inconvenient warnings. The Murray Valley was a hive of activity with its own distinctive culture. The 'valley settlers', remarked one observer, had a unique combination of qualities: a 'vigorous belief' in the rights of private property with firm convictions about the value of collective effort. Thus, the cooperative model of business was found everywhere – in hotels, shops, packing houses, wineries and community facilities. Such extensive community endeavour had attracted worldwide attention. At the same time, the settlers were 'hard-headed' agriculturalists and 'canny conservatives' who resented any whiff of the socialist planner.[54]

In New South Wales, the Murrumbidgee Irrigation Area (MIA) extended across nearly 100 kilometres from Leeton to Griffith. Its expansion was facilitated by the opening in 1928 of the Burrinjuck Dam, which was located south of Yass on the Murrumbidgee River. Like the Hume Dam, it rivalled Sydney Harbour in its capacity to hold water. During the passage of the enabling legislation, concerns were raised about its potential impact on downstream communities in the lower Murrumbidgee. Nevertheless, there was a steady uptake in irrigation licences, from 242 in 1944 to 1220 in 1971.[55]

The MIA attracted, according to *Walkabout* magazine in 1951, 'all manner of men', from lawyers to 'the rank and file of life'. The scheme had called for 'resolute and far-sighted planning', with the town of Griffith as the main commercial hub. Italian migrants became the backbone of the area's success. Living a spartan existence, raising whole families in small fibro houses or in the back of their sheds, they built prosperity season by season. The town of Griffith boasted seven fruit-packing sheds, 17 wineries, a rice mill, a breakfast food company and three fruit canneries, along with assorted workshops. Contemporaries saw in the MIA 'a pattern for progress which can scarcely be over-estimated in national importance'.[56]

The MIA was the location for the post-war expansion of rice-growing; a national goal of 40 000 acres (more than 16 000 hectares) was established in 1943. Tractors and bulldozers began work in that year converting 10–20 hectares of virgin land a day at Wakool.

But why was rice, of all crops, so enthusiastically embraced after World War Two? After all, rice required large areas to be flooded, and where would such quantities be found in the kinds of drought that had recently turned the Murray–Darling Basin into a dust bowl? The Burrinjuck Dam was not the panacea farmers had hoped for. As early as 1943 it was reported that the waters contained in the Dam were 'already insufficient for the irrigation requirements of the settlers'.[57] A few years later, rice farmers were up in arms when their water allocation was restricted.[58]

Yet despite these realities, rice-growing increased rapidly during the 1960s and 1970s, reaching 110 000 hectares annually, more than seven times the original plan.[59] Driven by engineers and agricultural scientists, the development of rice-growing gave no consideration to the long-term sustainability of the industry or its impact on the environment. This is unsurprising. The lack of long-term vision and environmental awareness has been, after all, *the* characteristic feature of the history of agriculture in the Murray–Darling Basin. Instead, an intersection of economic and political considerations propelled rice-growing. After the war, world demand for rice boomed, with consequent high prices. 'A Bigger Australian Rice Bowl?' blared a headline in the Melbourne *Herald* in 1951, with the paper predicting shortages for the next 25 years.[60]

And, since Alfred Deakin set the tone in the 1880s, irrigation in Australia had always appealed to utopian thinking; rice-growing complemented this pattern. As one newspaper confidently asserted in 1954, the 'robust men' of the MIA live within 'a scientifically controlled' river – a river 'made safe and constant in its flow by great reservoirs held secure in the mountains of two states'.[61]

By the late 1950s, rice-growing in the MIA was seen as a glowing success. As a journalist from *Walkabout* magazine wrote on visiting a rice farm near Griffith:

> Driving alongside this crop in the warm sunlight, under a cloudless sky, we caught some of the feeling of achievement that comes from successful farming, and we began to understand the bustling enthusiasm of the young men who are the core of the Australian rice industry.[62]

And, as was the established practice in agriculture, rice-growing developed its own lobbying machine. The Rice Marketing Board and the Rice Growers' Association, along with the more established Farmers and Settlers' Association, formed an effective institutional arrangement to defend and promote the interests of the industry.

But it wasn't just rice that consumed vast amounts of Murray–Darling water. Having been developed as a fledging industry in Queensland in the 1920s and 1930s, the cotton industry took off in the 1960s in northern New South Wales under a system of excessively generous water rights for which the state government was 'bitterly attacked'.[63] This state of affairs was not surprising, given the industry operated with barely a fig-leaf of regulation in an atmosphere of explosive growth. American corporate cotton growers were attracted to the region, bringing with them state-of-the-art pumping equipment, which was used to extract unprecedented volumes of water. The industry expanded west to Bourke during the 1980s.

According to historian Heather Goodall, the rise of cotton in the region saw a shift of power away from pastoralism to cotton growers, who began to make their presence felt on local councils.[64] This highly mechanised and chemically intensive form of agriculture caused tensions to rise in places like Bourke. Aboriginal groups, including the Ngemba, Barkindji, Wangkumara and Muruwari, worried about the impact of chemical spraying on waterways and, hence, their ability to fish.

Townspeople worried about the cotton industry's chemicals contaminating the town's water supply, and graziers worried about the siphoning of water and chemical contamination of meat. They had cause to worry. Cotton crops were sprayed with a dozen different herbicides and pesticides that were damaging to human, animal and aquatic life.[65] These concerns swirled around unresolved because cotton growers could extract a limitless supply of water. The New South Wales Water Conservation and Irrigation Commission was bent on appeasing the cotton growers in the pursuit of development.[66] The industry had the ear of the federal government as well, eager to address Australia's balance of payments problems and to integrate Australia's economy with those of Japan and Asia generally. Consequently, up rang the popular outcry that when the cotton growers had their pumps working overtime, 'the river ran backwards'.[67]

However, the industry became an agricultural success story, bringing wealth to outback towns. But this success caused long-term resentment about 'King cotton' and its water use; growers became known to many local people simply as 'the bastards upstream'.[68] The industry extracted a heavy environmental toll, which was simply ignored.

During the 1950s and 1960s, the New South Wales government converted the Menindee Lakes into an inland storage system, the water to be captured in floods and released in drier times. The scheme had the added advantage of creating a water playground for the residents of Broken Hill – a place to swim, fish and relax. Some built holiday homes on the lakes' shore.[69] But the ecology of the lakes was, not surprisingly, dramatically changed from such extensive construction works. Vast quantities of red gums were removed, and the construction of weirs, combined with continually low water flows, fragmented the Darling River ecosystems, isolating fish from upstream reaches and adversely affecting waterbird communities.[70]

Successive governments in New South Wales enabled this development by recklessly handing out water licences, exacerbating tensions over water allocation with South Australia. Jack Seecamp, who earned the nickname the 'Riverland legend' for being a long-time river campaigner, took the fight to New South Wales over the allocation of water licences in the upper Darling. During the 1970s, he travelled throughout the northern part of the state fighting a series of court battles in country towns against the profligate water policy of New South Wales. 'The New South Wales authorities', he recalled years later, 'had started using Queen's counsels in the tiny court rooms to argue for the increased water allocations. The South Australians countered by bringing in their own lawyers. Sometimes the hearings ran for several days'.[71]

This development at all costs left a bitter legacy, not just of environmental damage but mounting debt as governments subsidised the water users; the charges did not recover the costs of construction.[72]

Murray cod, platypus, crayfish in decline

In the midst of the boom in irrigation construction, existing environmental problems worsened, and none more so than fish stocks in the Murray River. The largely unregulated fishing industry continued to harvest Murray cod. By the 1940s, all commercial fishermen were licensed; the old days of the Whalers were passing with just a few of the colourful dropouts left living their carefree lifestyle on the river banks. The new breed of fishermen, numbering in the hundreds, built more permanent accommodation up and down the Murray and its tributaries.[73] And the fish continued to offer a lucrative living with high prices paid in the restaurant industry.

However, it was getting harder to catch Murray cod. There were likely too many licensed fishermen, given that the species had been heavily harvested since the 1860s, although the lack of historical data on numbers makes it impossible to track the cod's decline with any certainty. Nevertheless, the broad outline is clear. Before World War One, Murray cod were, if not plentiful, at least capable of supporting an industry. According to local folklore, the steamer *Invincible* made regular runs from Mildura to Swan Hill with its principal cargo of fish and rabbits.[74] By the mid-1930s, however, local fishermen complained that 'the fish ain't here now. Them [sic] locks and weirs and low rivers, bad for spawning. Too many fishermen'.[75]

After World War Two, fish stocks plummeted further. The spread of the motor car brought an influx of amateur fishermen, many of whom felt no compunction to restrain the number of cod they caught or the methods by which they harvested the prized fish. In 1946, Deniliquin's *Independent* newspaper reported that that the Murray cod was being 'rapidly exterminated' at the hands of greedy, illegal fishermen deploying illegitimate fishing methods – dynamite, cross lines, and drum and gill nets.[76] The amateur fishermen were responsible for catching 'vast quantities of immature cod'.[77] Licensed fishermen were increasingly finding it difficult to earn a living by rod and line, with flow-on impacts to Aboriginal people.

Thus, when in 1950, the *Sydney Morning Herald* posed the question in a headline – 'Is the Murray Cod Doomed?'[78] – it was repeating concerns made periodically over the decades. It was a question that would linger for decades to come.

Drum nets not only caught large numbers of Murray cod, they inadvertently caught platypus as well. Having barely survived the fur trade, the animal now confronted an increase in the number of fishermen using the nets and their number declined precipitously. Two minutes in a drum net was a death sentence for a platypus. 'Prior to the using of drum nets', a correspondent wrote to the *Riverina Herald* in 1947, 'thousands of these little animals could be seen sporting in all the rivers'.[79]

While drum nets were banned in Victoria, poachers continued to use them along the tributaries of the Murray, killing many platypus in the process.[80] In New South Wales, where drum nets continued to be used into the 1950s, the consequences were devastating. 'Drum nets have destroyed all the platypus in the northern rivers [of New South Wales]' one local told a newspaper in 1956.[81]

In southern Queensland a different threat to the platypus emerged in the 1960s. Naturalist David Fleay explained that numbers of the animal were simply 'conking out' from the insidious long-term effects of crop insecticides that had leached into the waterways.[82] Platypus were vulnerable to the chemical agents, Fleay explained, because they lived in the shallow tributary streams where pesticides were concentrated. His warning echoed Rachel Carson's seminal book *Silent Spring*, published in 1962, which documented the harmful effects of the widespread infiltration of pesticides in the American environment.[83] However, the book received only scattered references in the mainstream Australian media.

The introduction of carp compounded the damage to the river ecosystem. Carp were introduced into the Murray River by 'misguided people' some time in the late 19th century but did not become widespread until a release of 'Boolara' strain carp from a fish farm into the Murray River near Mildura in 1964. Multiplying quickly, they became an increasing threat to the survival of the Murray cod because carp fed on cod spawn and muddied the water. It was difficult for recreational anglers to catch carp because they combined the 'speed of an express train with the wiliness of a fox'.[84]

The Murray crayfish suffered a similar catastrophic decline in numbers to the Murray cod. Growing up to half a metre in length, it was both a prolific breeder and easy to catch with bated wire traps. It was prized by inland fishermen as a succulent dish. However, with the expansion of irrigation, Murray crayfish were deemed a pest because of their reputation for burrowing into, and damaging, dams and irrigation channels. In the early 1950s an export market opened up. Thousands of crayfish were taken from the Murray and its tributaries each week on the assumption that 'the supply appears to be unending'.[85] Not surprisingly, the population steadily fell and, by the early 1980s, Murray crayfish numbers were 'at dangerously low levels'.[86]

Irrigation and biodiversity loss

In the helter-skelter of post-war agricultural development, unique ecosystems in the Murray–Darling Basin came under severe threat. Foremost among these were the Basin's wetlands. Quietly but relentlessly decimated for decades by the impact of irrigation, the wetlands continued to shrink, offering a far more sparse existence for greatly depleted populations of birds and aquatic life. But against the engine of wealth-generating and job-creating agricultural industries in the Basin how are such assets to be valued?

In a rare acknowledgment of the wetlands of the Murray River, the *Advertiser* noted in the mid-1930s that these areas weren't valued at all:

Modern excavating machinery and manpower have dug huge channels and drained the swamps and billabongs. Patches of reeds – nesting places and cover of wild duck, water fowl, and other bird life – and square miles of backwater which grew succulent duck grass to feed the birds, have been transformed into dairy farms. Where ponderous pelicans with their capacious bills scooped up baby fish, and stately ibis stalked in search of food, hundreds of dairy cows now crop contentedly at lush grass, lucerne and other fodder crops. The waters of the Murray have been harnessed to the needs of man.[87]

In the 1940s, the Basin's wetlands, with their 'wonderland' of birdlife were looked upon 'with aversion or indifference by the average picknicker or hiker'. Such areas were depicted merely as swamps.[88]

The Macquarie Marshes were subject to creeping destruction. Covering more than 220 000 hectares in western New South Wales near Bathurst, this area was the traditional home of the Wailwan people, a place of abundant plant and animal life, especially birds and reptiles. In fact, few wetlands in Australia supported such diverse bird species as the Macquarie Marshes.[89]

In 1944, the New South Wales Labor government of Premier William McKell designated part of the Marshes a nature reserve. The government attempted a new approach of trying to blend economic and conservation needs, and preserving part of the Marshes made economic sense because the birdlife that preyed upon grasshoppers and other insects helped to support the grazing properties gazetted to surround the protected area. 'Only those who have seen the ibis spread out like an army', wrote the Premier in announcing the new national reserve, 'destroying an advancing grasshopper swarm can appreciate in full what the preservation of this bird means to the security of our great primary industries'.[90]

While such ecological thinking – however instrumental – represented an advance on the previous habit of ignoring the role individual species played in the balance of nature, later events undid much of the intention behind the reserve. In 1967 the opening of the Burrendong Dam, comprising an extensive infrastructure of weirs, channels and banks, siphoned off water needed for the Marshes to irrigation and town use. Before construction, about 51 per cent of the water passing the town of Dubbo reached the Macquarie Marshes; after construction this fell to 21 per cent. This reduced the wetland to half its original size, with flow-on impacts to the diversity of its birdlife, which declined due to less frequent breeding habits and smaller colony sizes.[91] Parts of the region's plant life were also seriously degraded by grazing.[92] Other small areas received too much water, killing floodplain trees. Conservationists today argue that the Marshes represent a 50-year history of decline and, consequently, have become 'an icon issue for wetland survival in Australia'.[93]

A similar pattern of diverting waters for irrigation, with consequent reduced flows, affected other wetland areas in the Murray–Darling Basin, including the Lowbidgee floodplain, the Chowilla floodplain, and the Gwydir and Coorong wetlands. All witnessed dramatic post-war declines in bird and aquatic life.[94] Such areas have been likened to 'mini Kakadu' national parks and, as one environmental scientist has highlighted, their loss will continue 'until there is widespread understanding of the long-term effects of dams and diversions'.[95]

Some of these wetlands also contained extensive tracts of forests. The Barmah-Millewa Forest stands out. Running along the Murray north of Echuca, it has, since time immemorial, been an oasis of creeks and lagoons teeming with birdlife amid a huge redgum forest. It was thought to be home to a large Aboriginal population, including the Yorta Yorta.

By the 1940s, the sensitive ecology that sustained the red gum forests was well understood. 'It is a fastidious tree' noted the *Weekly Times* in 1941, 'because it demands only periodical inundation. If it is surrounded by water all year it dies. If it does not get sufficient water it dies just the same'.[96]

Yet, by the 1960s the Barmah-Millewa Forest was on the brink of destruction from the twin threats of forestry and irrigation. When a writer from *Walkabout* magazine,[97] John Macaulay, visited the area in 1961, he found that merely a few hundred metres into the forest the silence was broken by 'a rumbling bulldozer, pouring black smoke into the sky'. Barmah was designated a State Forest, and extraction of timber continued supposedly under a policy of 'selective' logging. But because the timber was in high demand, the Forests Commission of Victoria had been felling more timber than could be regenerated. The figures are startling. In the year to June 1960, four million super feet of redgum were felled, even though there were only 55 million super feet left in the forest.

By the 1960s, the remote and wildly beautiful Coorong, on the South Australian coast and the emptying point of the long journey of the Murray–Darling's waters, was being slowly ruined by development. The construction of huge drainage schemes designed to turn the region's lakes and fens into pasture had destroyed the breeding grounds of many native birds, as well as turning the top end of the ecosystem into a backwater, which was 'becoming more stagnant and stinking each year'. Protection had come too late. Although by the 1960s, most of the sheltered waters of the Coorong were protected, the birds were just not there anymore: 'They used to follow the fish, and the fish have gone because the water is too salty'. Even the fishermen's shacks, once dotted throughout the region, were falling down.[98]

However, as was common in the Murray–Darling Basin, the extraction of resources provided employment for unskilled workers, who formed their own unique sub-cultures. They were offered the chance of a decent and, often, independent life. This was the case with the bargemen who ferried the fallen red gum trunks downstream to the mills. Red gum provided a unique transportation challenge. Because it was so dense and tough, it sank like a lump of iron in water, making it impossible to float. In the 1950s – and perhaps before – the wood was loaded onto outrigger barges – shallow wooden-hulled vessels – with logs placed cross-wise so they protruded over the sides but chained together. The barge was then towed downstream by paddle steamers, most of which were 80 or more years old and built out of the same tough-as-steel red gum.

The life of the 'bargee' – there were two manning each barge – was like a continuous, sun-drenched holiday because the flotilla plied the run in the summer months. Barges never passed anything faster than a water-hen. The bargee and his mate lolled about in the sun, or smoked their pipes after a dinner of baked Murray cod as they floated silently underneath the stars. They went to sleep and got up when they felt like it.[99] When the barges were idle, the bargees either worked at a sawmill or went to other jobs, but every year the same crews manned the barges because it was 'in their blood'.[100]

Bargees were party to one threat to the red gum forests. The other came from irrigation, a consequence of the construction of the Hume Dam. With increased water gushing down the river, the water table steadily rose and instead of the forest drying out after a flood, it was under water for increased periods. As a result, red gums died from drowning. In fact, the drowning of red gums in Barmah-Millewa through irrigation floodwaters went back at least to the 1950s when it was reported that 'many good trees had been drowned and regeneration prevented'.[101] Promises were made by the Forests Commission to better manage these waters. When this happened, new problems arose for the region's wildlife from periods of reduced flows into the wetlands birds relied on for breeding. Birds such as wild ducks, ibis, hawks, cormorants and cranes had been present in their millions prior to the commencement of the Hume Dam. They suffered from the gradual shift from flood to drier conditions in the forest. This change had a devastating impact on bird numbers, although the change took two decades to manifest as a silent ecological crisis.[102]

In the decades after World War Two, there was no political interest in modifying irrigation practices to allow for conservation values. 'For politicians, water is holy', wrote the *Bulletin* in 1971. The magazine noted that at every election it was established practice to make a flurry of announcements for water development projects, and 'ALP politicians were just as blandly in favour of development at all costs as their conservative [opponents]'.[103]

Thus, the post-war irrigation expansion throughout the Murray–Darling Basin fulfilled the cultural fixation of the nation builders who had, for a century, promoted irrigation as vital for national development. These were government-funded schemes backed by farmers and by industry organisations, which, together, formed a powerful political force to protect and enhance the economic model while marginalising conservation values, even though clear arguments existed that such protection was in the interests of wider society. People needed reminding that the health of the Murray itself was vital to the interests of the nation.

The Murray River is dying

In 1971, the River Murray Commission, concerned about the increasing salinity in the river and along the floodplain, enlisted the services of an engineering consulting firm to conduct a thorough investigation and draw up plans for remedial action. The decision didn't impress a journalist from the *Bulletin* magazine inquiring into the issue, who wrote that engineers' conceptions 'are limited to construction and they pay scant attention to biological consequences'.[104] In one pithy sentence, the flaws in the whole edifice of irrigation in the Murray–Darling Basin had been pin-pointed. The journalist's next comment was equally sage, but more far-reaching: 'we are in a tight corner and possibly the only way out is a radical change in the intense forms of agriculture practiced along the river's dry plains'. This idea might have passed as alarmist save for the accompanying figure: in an average year about 1 025 000 tonnes of salt were carried down the Murray from the irrigation drainage system.

But no action was forthcoming. Both the consultants' 470-page report calling for an additional $110 million on engineering works and the journalist's call for a radical re-think of agriculture fell on deaf ears. But in their own way, each proposal signified the growing concern over the fate of the river. The river's problems became a 'story' with regular grim updates. Even the staid *Australian Women's Weekly* compiled a feature article in 1971 headlined 'The Murray: Tragedy of a Dying River'.[105] It used the 'hook' of a boy's death in Whyalla from amoebic meningitis, found in the town's water supply, to highlight the problems with the quality of the water from the Murray. The deadly organism lurked in the supply of practically every South Australian country town; the water piped in from the Murray was getting 'dirtier and dirtier'. In fact, a war-chest of agricultural chemicals, including weedicides, pesticides and superphosphate, all applied by farmers in Queensland, washed down the river.

The *Women's Weekly* also raised the issue of the damage to agriculture from the application of dirty, salty Murray River water. It spoke to fruit grower Dudley Marrows, whose exasperation was clear: 'It's damn near a disaster already', he said as he walked through his apricot orchard pointing out trees killed by salt. He was critical of the lack of vision and coordinated action in the management of the river. Experts were also called on for comment. Dr Peter Davis, a biological scientist at Adelaide University and author of a 1978 book titled *Man and the Murray*, also pulled no punches. The Murray, he said, was no longer a majestic river flowing to the sea. It was a series of man-made pools walled by weirs and locks and suffering the effects of what he termed, 'ruthless surgery'.

A decade later, South Australians were in uproar about the poor quality of the state's water, especially for the million citizens living in Adelaide who didn't like its taste, smell or appearance. However, unless they could afford rain water tanks or quantities of bottled water, they had no option 'but to shut up and drink it'. In 1981, two journalists from the *Bulletin*[106] investigated the issue and confirmed that the water exceeded the World Health Organization's standards for salinity. The journalists also encountered an outraged Premier, the normally even-tempered David Tonkin, over plans in New South Wales to extend irrigation projects in that state, while in South Australia, new projects had ceased in 1967.

The *Bulletin* was on something of a crusade to bring public attention to the problems of the Murray, because in the following year, 1982, it dispatched two different journalists to survey much the same issues.[107] They found a growing awareness of the problems but a reluctance to accept them. On an optimistic note, they talked to experts who believed that with proper drainage of saline water, the problem could be rectified. But solutions were as distant as a shimmering horizon, given the institutional dysfunction in the management of the river, which the *Bulletin* article neatly summarised:

> Most people on the river say the answer lies in doing away with the interstate blame shifting and strengthening the powers of the River Murray Commission to control water quality. Since 1981, following agreement with the premiers of the three river states and the Prime Minister, the commission's powers have been extended to monitoring water quality. And that, say river folk, is a lot short of control.

And control over the river system was not even on the minds of state National Party leaders. Throughout the 1980s, the New South Wales Nationals handed out water licences like they were 'confetti'.[108] And as Tony Windsor, later an Independent member for the federal seat of Tamworth, observed, 'no one had done any homework on how sustainable the system was'.[109] In fact, experts later claimed that the state had handed out more water than it had available, mainly to service the cotton industry.[110] The government was barely interested in the environmental consequences. The River Murray Commission, for example, started thinking about the health of wetlands in the 1980s, but their strategy documents had tame objectives such as 'to support community initiatives' and 'increased awareness'. In other words, there was a lack of will to tackle the issue of over-extraction.[111]

While industries like cotton and rice flourished, others struggled due to changing economic conditions. By the mid-1980s, the 'blockies' of the Sunraysia irrigation district of Mildura fell on hard times. The embodiment of the original yeoman ideal, these family-operated farms struggled on the 10- to 15-hectare blocks growing mainly sultanas. Facing growing international competition, over-production and low prices, one-quarter of the 2500 growers faced foreclosure, while most of the rest had exhausted any access to further credit. The banks began circling. However, the blockies had hitherto stubbornly refused to face the new reality because of their attraction to the lifestyle of closer settlement: families ran their own operations; children helped out after school; neighbours formed close ties; and the sunny climate and outdoor life were inviting.[112] The slow demise of the blockies showed that the yeoman ideal, one of the greatest failed social and economic experiments in the nation's history, was finally, and agonisingly, on its knees.

The demise of the blockies was simply a harbinger of bigger challenges in the Murray–Darling Basin. By the late 1980s, 84 large dams and weirs had been built in the Basin for regulating the river for water supply, river navigation, flood mitigation and hydro-electricity. Thousands of small dams had been constructed on farms for private use, and levees and channels were built to transport water to farms. This infrastructure provided for the rapid expansion of irrigated agriculture. Water use more than doubled in the period between the 1950s and the 1970s, and continued to grow steadily through the 1990s.[113] Growth in the 1980s and 1990s came despite the first warning from the CSIRO on the impact of climate change in the Murray–Darling Basin.[114] Years passed and governments remained paralysed and polarised. The Murray–Darling seemed almost too big to fail because of the size of its infrastructure and its importance to the national economy.

However, in 1987 the federal Labor government of Prime Minister Bob Hawke responded to calls from South Australia for better coordination of the Murray–Darling Basin and to halt the deterioration of the Basin's natural resource base and the preservation of its 'sensitive eco-system'.[115] It established a Murray–Darling Basin Commission for this purpose, but little changed in the short-term. 'The Murray's Ecology Left High and Dry', ran the headline of a feature article written by David Mussared in the *Canberra Times* in 1989, part of a series of articles based on his travels down the river. His focus on the ecology of the river was something of a fresh angle. He quoted Adelaide University zoologist Lance Lloyd, who said that there was too much concern with the salinity issue – which was a problem for human use and agriculture – 'and not enough concern for the threatened river ecology'.[116]

Land degradation and the environment had suddenly reached the top of the political agenda. The Hawke government introduced the Landcare program and committed to planting one billion trees. The program came on the back of a CSIRO report calling for the 'Regreening of Australia' to combat land degradation, 'our most serious environmental problem'. The report carried a further, prophetic warning; regreening was necessary to address climate change, which would in the next century, it predicted, aggravate the problem of land degradation.[117] The federal Environment Minister, Graham Richardson, had also weighed in on the debate about land degradation with a typical pithy assessment, warning that large areas of marginal land would have to be abandoned if Australia was to have a sustainable agricultural industry. He criticised state governments for doing little to discourage destructive farming practices.[118]

While Hawke's Landcare program was visionary in intent, its practical application was something else. Its critics included Bob Beale and Peter Fray, who in their 1990 book *The Vanishing Continent: Australia's Degraded Environment* found to it be 'long on rhetoric and short on money and resources'.[119] One billion trees across the entire country didn't stack up as terribly significant, given that the Hawke government had released the estimate from the CSIRO that 12–15 billion had been removed in the Murray–Darling Basin alone. And, by the late 1980s, it was estimated that 96 000 hectares of the Basin's irrigated land were salt-affected and 560 000 hectares had water tables within two metres of the land surface, with the dire consequence of increased salinity.[120] By the early 1990s, the Landcare program had resulted in a flurry of local Landcare groups in places like the Mallee, Mildura and the Riverina – often where none had existed before – but only 500 million trees had been planted across Australia.[121]

Just as the Murray was soaking up all the public attention, the Darling burst into the national spotlight. In November 1991 it was discovered that a 1000-kilometre stretch of the Darling River was covered in an algal bloom, a thick green blanket of algal scum and toxic chemicals, similar to the outbreak that the McBrides were to encounter nearly 30 years later. The toxic bloom arrived suddenly 'like a triffid invasion' and certainly scared many farmers already plagued by debt, drought and recession.[122] Like some modern-day plague, the fear of large-scale human poisoning was real, and the New South Wales Premier, Nick Greiner, was forced to declare a state of emergency.

Local graziers were the first to notice something was amiss. Malcolm and Alister Fraser discovered that cows and calves had died in a paddock beside the Darling River. Not far away they saw several of their merino rams lying dead in the grass. Momentarily perplexed as to what had killed their stock, they noticed that a thin green film had begun to form on the surface of the river; it was the beginning of the algal bloom. And, as it would 30 years later, the bloom revealed a river under stress, from siltation caused by soil erosion, low inflows of water, and excessive use of nitrates and phosphates. The problem of low inflows, local residents believed, resulted from excessive water use by upstream big cotton growers.[123]

The Darling algal bloom, rated at the time as one of the largest algal blooms on record anywhere in the world,[124] stirred up a hornet's nest. As the *Canberra Times* editorialised, the bloom was a warning sign that the land was not coping with the demands humans made of it and that Australia could not survive too long without its rivers.[125] In fact, a century and more of unrestrained growth had resulted in the river being starved of water flow; in the early 1990s, median annual flows through to the Murray mouth were only 21–28 per cent of what they would have been in natural conditions.[126] This diminished flow was the consequence of the construction over the decades of an estimated $30 billion worth of irrigation infrastructure.[127]

When a Senate inquiry investigated algal blooms in the wake of the Darling outbreak, the overuse of water in the Basin was a key issue aired by witnesses who gave evidence. Several told the inquiry that over-allocation was a major factor that led to the algal bloom and that the cotton-growing operation at Cubbie Station was using floodwaters to keep water on-farm in extensive dam storage.[128]

But it didn't need a Senate inquiry to confirm to local graziers the cause behind the mess that the river had been reduced to, although it took them a few years to articulate their concerns. Successive governments had handed out too many licences from the 1960s to the 1980s, allocating more water than it was possible to take out of the system with little concern to the graziers downstream, the environment in general, and the impact on Indigenous people's cultural rights. The consequence had been great ecological damage to the floodplains, billabongs and creeks.[129] The bloom had opened a new front in the environmental battle in the Murray–Darling Basin.

11

THE STRUGGLE FOR REFORM

In late December 1992, Prime Minister Paul Keating, who had replaced Bob Hawke as Labor leader a year earlier, visited Adelaide to announce his government's environment statement, a key focus of which was to be the Murray–Darling Basin. Only months earlier, the world's nations had gathered in Rio de Janeiro for an Earth Summit, which helped put the natural world squarely in the face of political leaders. Keating's statement was directed at boosting the government's environmental credentials in the face of the rise of the Greens and a deepening rift between Labor and the environment movement.[1] By this time Keating's political persona was firmly established. Loved by the Labor faithful for his fighting spirit, cutting wit and 'big picture' vision for Australia, he was loathed in equal measure by conservatives for his progressive social and cultural policies, his perceived arrogance and his aesthetic interests. And conservatives feared Keating; he was both a brawler and a dreamer.

At the time of his environment statement, Keating and the federal Labor machine were all too aware that the Greens had saved the government at the 1990 election through the allocation of the party's preferences in key marginal seats. But in the lead-up to the 1992 election, Keating was on the horns of a political dilemma. The Greens wanted old growth logging to end, among other demands, which he refused to endorse. Keating had to hope, therefore, that his environment statement would placate the Greens while keeping the logging industry happy.[2] The era of reform in the Murray–Darling Basin began as a political tradeoff.

In characteristic evocative language, Keating described Australia's largest river system as the 'artery of the nation's economic health, and a place where Australian legends were born'. Then he attacked the cultural attitudes that had produced the nation's economic wealth. He said that far more environmental damage had been done to Australia's environment in the past 200 years than in the previous 60 000. Keating may have been merely stating the obvious, but none of Australia's political leaders had ever dared acknowledge Australia's exploitative and destructive relationship with the environment. The Prime Minister further confounded political convention by describing this relationship as 'our war with the environment'. By now, Keating had a long-earned reputation for cutting through to the core of intractable political issues, none more so than when as Treasurer in 1990 he called out Australia's sclerotic economic performance as akin to 'a banana republic'.

And, just two weeks prior to his speech on the Murray–Darling, Keating had given his ground-breaking 'Redfern Speech' in which he acknowledged the nation's genocidal treatment and dispossession of Indigenous people. Again, no previous political leader had dared open the pandora's box of Australian racism. This speech has been regarded as a defining moment in Australia's torturous journey towards reconciliation with Indigenous people.

In important ways, the two speeches evoked a similar sentiment – to move forward as a nation, white Australia had to acknowledge its past mistakes and their impact. They reflected Keating's capacity to grow as a politician and his interest in forging a new Australian identity.[3] The two speeches were similar in the roles they ascribed to historical understanding. In Keating's mind, history was central to his vision of reconciliation. He cut straight to the heart of the matter when he said that it was white Australians who 'did the dispossessing. We took the traditional lands and smashed the traditional way of life.

We brought the diseases. The alcohol. We committed the murders. We took the children from their mothers'.[4] And, in the speech on the environment, Keating acknowledged that the present condition of the inland rivers 'spoke of generations of foolish neglect [which had] led to ecological disaster and economic degeneration'. His government was determined to restore the region 'to its former stature'.

But there was also a subtle difference in the depth of historical understanding Keating believed existed between the Indigenous experience of colonisation and European treatment of the environment. 'That part of the national character and the national economy', he explained, 'which was created out of the conquest of nature is secure'. He went on to say that 'our war with the environment is well and truly over' and that future economic growth would go 'hand in hand with environmental protection and renewal'.[5] In other words, there wasn't much the nation needed to reflect on in relation to the environment in moving forward.

Keating's environment speech was like the proverbial curate's egg: good in parts. His acknowledgment of the ecological disaster unfolding in the region was politically ground-breaking and his commitment to restore the region's environmental integrity put it squarely on the national agenda. Nevertheless, Keating's statement was laced with ambiguity. How could he say that the war against the environment was over, especially with the recent grotesque Darling River algal bloom as a testament to this destruction?

Furthermore, how could he be so confident that economic growth and restoring the Murray–Darling rivers would be easily compatible when so many vested interests had a stake in the scarce resource? And what about the Aboriginal people of the region? Keating's speech was silent on this matter. He hadn't drawn out the connection between his Redfern and environment speeches. It was in the Basin that Aboriginal people had been ruthlessly dispossessed to secure the economic future of Australia. What rights did they now have? This was a glaring omission, given that the Prime Minister was finalising legislation that would erect a high bar for dispossessed Aboriginal people to claim their rights to their land; there was no right to negotiate over water.

Depth of the crisis

Just as Keating offered his confident assertion that economic growth and environmental sustainability were compatible in the Basin, others on the ground thought this little more than wishful thinking without systemic change to the way in which Australian agriculture operated. The Darling River algal bloom played a decisive role in focusing public attention on the scale of the problems in both the river system and the wider Basin. Coming as it did on top of a decade of media focus on the salinity problems of the Murray River, the 'idea of dying rivers entered the national consciousness'.[6]

By the early 1990s, the Basin's problems had become complex and multi-dimensional. Soils had become nutrient deficient, thin and easily damaged by drought and floods.[7] Dryland salinity continued its slow, destructive march. Half a million hectares in the Basin were affected by the early 1990s, with the area increasing by between 1 and 5 per cent per year.[8] Predictions surfaced in the early 1990s that 1.3 million hectares of prime agricultural land in the Basin would be water-logged and ladened with salt by the year 2040, and that highly productive irrigated horticultural areas would be unable to grow fruit trees.[9]

Soil salinity kills everything in its path, leaving bare, damp, white crusts where once there was soil. In January 1992, Ron Cathcart, the director of the Riverina's Soil Conservation Service, told the *Sydney Morning Herald*[10] that the 'legacy of ignorance and greed' was catching up with the land: 'salt patches are breaking out everywhere – even on two Wagga Wagga golf courses – and large areas of farmland near other centres such as Cootamundra, Young, Junee and Holbrook are likely to turn to desert in three to five years'. Cathcart maintained that Australian agriculture was unsustainable.

Earlier, the *Sydney Morning Herald* had reported on the threat to native fish in the Murray–Darling Basin's waterway, writing that they were threatened by irrigation and dams, weirs and the siltation of waterways due to clearing and logging, the removal of shelter and food-providing snags, chemical spills and run-off from farms.[11] In fact, the rivers in the Basin were 'sickened with salinity'.[12] By the early 1990s, the warnings of experts were now aired regularly in the media: the 'big fix' engineering approaches of previous decades had caused profound changes to ecosystems.[13] In 1992, the CSIRO warned that the health of Australia's rivers was reaching a dead end.[14]

Yet land clearing continued apace amid conservationists' warnings that for every 40 hectares of woodland cleared, between 1000 and 2000 native birds permanently lose their habitat, with even greater carnage for reptiles.[15]

Turning around this unfolding crisis presented governments with a challenge of unprecedented complexity. Firstly, most farmers were resistant to change. The *Canberra Times* science and environment writer, David Mussared, observed this in his previously mentioned extensive tour of the Basin in the early 1990s. The old irrigators, Mussared wrote, all thought that water was too cheap, that too much of it was being used and that too much land clearing was going on, but 'individually none of them is going to change their practices'; none is going to do 'anything which is economically dangerous on their own'. Mussared thought the situation so critical that there would be a massive loss of productive land over the next 20 to 50 years. He put the challenge facing governments in blunt terms. 'The people who live [in the Murray–Darling Basin]', he said,

> have got a huge personal and economic investment in the land and in the area. You can't ask the people in the Basin to decide who is going to stand and who is going to fall. There has to be political decisions by the wider community over water allocations, how much degradation they will accept, and which industries have higher priority.[16]

Adding to the complexity was the ongoing gross mismanagement by the states. Reports of 'massive private farm dams' surfaced amid claims that all along the Barwon–Darling, the still of the night was broken 'by the roar of irrigators pumping illegally'.[17]

Indeed, an audit report undertaken in 1995 for the New South Wales government found that cotton growers in that state were found to be abusing their licences by 'stealing tens of billions of litres' of water annually from the state's biggest rivers by tampering with their meters. The North West Rivers Audit found that the situation had been caused by the incompetence and understaffing of the New South Wales Department of Water Resources.[18]

Aboriginal people continued to watch on with deep sadness as their capacity to practise their spiritual connection to the Murray–Darling was being eroded after decades of greed and mismanagement by Europeans. The Ngarrindjeri people were among the Indigenous groups dramatically affected by the extraction of vast amounts of water for agriculture. Their traditional lands are the Coorong at the mouth of the Murray River on the South Australian coast. Classified as a Ramsar site, the area is protected under a treaty of the same name that recognises wetlands of international importance. The Coorong historically contained the greatest number of waterbirds of all Basin Ramsar sites; there are descriptions from times past of the sky over the Coorong being black with birds.[19]

By the 1990s, freshwater no longer made it that far. Artificial barriers were erected in a desperate attempt to prevent seawater from entering the river system. But these, too, changed the local ecosystem.

Ngarrindjeri elder Tom Trevorrow provided an all too rare Aboriginal perspective on the debate over the river. When interviewed by a journalist from *The Age*, he looked sadly towards the river and said that he thought it was dying. And because Aboriginal people are an integral part of the environment, Trevorrow said, 'the Ngarrindjeri were also dying'.[20] Such a cry from the heart was a warning to Europeans – but who was listening? The Ngarrindjeri elder knew what was wrong: 'We believe everything in the environment is connected. Whitefellas . . . they just try to do repair jobs. They create the problem, then they try to repair it after it has happened'.

Clearly a national strategic plan was called for that addressed the integrated dimensions of the crisis: over-allocation of water, salinity, land clearing and ongoing species loss, and the impact of these losses on Aboriginal people. The crisis also called for resolving another, big question: how could agriculture be made sustainable in Australia's food bowl and in a way that preserved the tradition of family farming that underpinned the history of the region? Livelihoods depended on answering this question. In fact, the Australian Conservation Foundation called for just such a strategy: 'a really nationally concerted effort' among government, the community, landholders, environment groups and the scientific community.[21] It was a message endorsed by scientists attending the Horizons of Science forum in Sydney in August 1993. They called for 'a massive sustained rehabilitation program and a change of national attitudes'.[22] But nothing of the sort happened. The region was sold out to the politics of vested interests.

Keating shies away from real reform

Paul Keating's environment statement received a mixed reception. The *Canberra Times* criticised it for being a political exercise – a 'grab bag' of issues, most of which were already in train and, therefore, 'not an attempt to plan for Australia's environmental future'.[23] The Prime Minister responded with his trademark invective, but in a manner that undermined his central message: 'The environment movement', he said, 'is basically not interested in brown issues. They are not interested in dirty water. They are not interested in salinity and they are not interested in land degradation. They are interested in trees'.

In trying to score a political point, Keating not only missed the role that removal of trees had in creating salinity in the first place, but contradicted his own commitment to 'a corridor of green' along the length of the Murray. Just over three million dollars was allocated to Greening Australia for this task, judged by David Mussared to be as inflated as Hawke's 'One Billion Trees' program.[24] Critics accused Keating of a 'failure of nerve' by not introducing wide-ranging environmental legislation.[25]

Meanwhile, another vision for the future of the Murray–Darling water resource was being shaped in the corridors of power. A new policy paradigm was devised from the ideas of economic rationalism. This held that the free market was the best way to decide what society produced, and its advocates in the Canberra bureaucracy had moved from the wings to centre stage, becoming the driving force behind the development of the National Competition Policy (NCP) in 1992.

Assessing the long-term outcomes of this controversial policy lies outside the scope of this work, save for its implications for the Murray–Darling river system, which was included in the NCP by the Keating government. This occurred via an intergovernmental agreement signed between the Commonwealth and the states in 1994 known as the National Water Initiative (NWI). This agreement provided the framework for the reforms, while the states were given until 2004 to finalise implementation. Critics of the water reform process, including Ian Douglas representing the lobby group Fair Water Use (Australia), have observed that the 'prevailing mantra' of the free market was seen as 'the ultimate panacea for under-funded and inefficient public utilities'.[26] Water was henceforth to be commodified through the creation of a national water market and the opportunity for investors to trade in water. This, it was argued, would direct water to its most productive uses.

While there is little doubt that something had to be done to redress the overuse and wastage of precious irrigation water, policy ideas drawn from economic rationalism were a blunt tool for the complexities of the Basin. There is no evidence, for example, that any consideration was given to the long-term implications of such free market thinking on a large public asset such as water. What were the implications of treating water as a commodity rather than a common good?

Compounding the NWI's ambiguities was the accompanying decision to allow the states a decade to ready themselves for its implementation. The urgency of the problem was kicked down the road.

In the following year, the Commonwealth and the states followed up the NWI with an agreement to cap the water taken out of the Murray–Darling Basin. In an historic decision, the imposition of a cap ended more than a century of treating the Basin's rivers as an inexhaustible supply of water for agriculture.[27] Keating no doubt thought the two measures – the NWI and the cap – made good policy and good politics.[28] Yet the economic rationalist ideas he had trumpeted were, at their heart, philosophically at odds with a sincere commitment to the environment. As prominent economics correspondent Ross Gittins once commented at the height of Australia's embrace of radical free market ideas: 'Everyone knows that economic rationalists don't care a fig for the environment. They're so obsessed by "efficiency" and cutting government spending that anything to do with the environment is airily dismissed an as "externality"'.[29]

There is no indication that Keating himself had resolved these apparent contradictions. In any event, the combination of the two water measures initiated by his government had the reverse effect than those intended; they exacerbated the binge use of irrigation water. One observer commented:

> Farmers who owned water rights but had never used them proceeded to sell their now coveted 'sleeper licenses' to others who would. Industrialists were offered tax incentives to create superfarms and introduced vast olive and almond groves to the Basin. Meanwhile, the governments of New South Wales and Queensland routinely flouted the extraction cap and continued to hand out licences.[30]

Queensland, in particular, saw itself as a Johnny-come-lately to large-scale irrigation. Consequently, the state's agricultural bureaucrats behaved like mavericks where the prevailing attitude was: 'Well, we haven't fully developed everything and we're going to get in and go like hell to get it developed'.[31]

Keating was long out of office before the NWI came to fruition. However, he had laid the foundations for radical changes in water-resource management in Australia, which, as the *Canberra Times* acknowledged, were 'introduced largely without public debate or detailed examination of their consequences'.[32] Ultimately, Keating's tenure as Prime Minister was a lost opportunity for the Murray–Darling Basin.

In March 1995, as Keating entered the last 12 months of his period in office, Noel Fitzpatrick, the head of the Murray–Darling Basin Commission, retired. On leaving the position he offered up a verbal spray to state and federal politicians, who, he said, had done 'too little to save the basin from the degradation', which 'will wipe out its most productive regions by the middle of next century'. The Basin, he went on, 'was one minute to midnight'.[33]

John Howard's balancing act

John Howard won the March 1996 election, defeating the incumbent Keating government by pursuing a small target strategy and declaring that Australians had a right to feel relaxed and comfortable about the world. On assuming office, he inherited both the extent of the crisis in the Murray–Darling Basin and what can only be called federal Labor's half-baked initiatives, the Landcare program and the NWI.

Stridently conservative, and with an innate hostility to environmentalism, Howard had no intention of following Keating in depicting the Basin as a crisis caused by destructive European agricultural practices. He saw his task as reasserting conservative

Australian values and repudiating federal Labor's program, developed under Gough Whitlam in the 1970s, to modernise Australia around an agenda of multiculturalism, Aboriginal self-determination, gay rights, environmentalism and recognition of rights for refugees.

Howard's strength was his ability to mobilise 'ordinary' Australians around his conservative agenda; his weakness was to conflate his vision of Australian identity with the national interest. Howard was, in the words of historian and commentator, Robert Manne, a 'conservative populist'.[34] For conservatives like Howard, to acknowledge the full extent of the crisis in the Murray–Darling Basin was to admit the long-term failure of European settlement of Australia – our failure as a society to adapt to the unique characteristics of the environment. It was a step too far.

But the in-coming Prime Minister had access to information that should have made him take a different course: a recently completed audit of the Basin revealing the extent of the region's decline due to over-development. The report showed that the median annual flows through the Murray mouth were only between 21 and 28 per cent of what they would have been in natural conditions. It also found that drought occurred in the lower Murray in 60 per cent of years compared to 5 per cent under natural conditions and that, in most years, water was drastically over-allocated.[35]

Coming into the March 1996 election, Howard showed his willingness to use the environment as a bargaining chip for his ideological agenda. He linked his pursuit of the privatisation of Telstra, the publicly owned telecommunications company, to a $1.1 billion environmental package focused on repairing the Murray–Darling; the proceeds of the sale would be used to fund the National Heritage Trust (NHT) to carry out the work. Howard used the establishment of the Trust as policy blackmail, warning that the Trust would not go ahead if the legislation failed to pass the Senate.[36]

In one fell swoop, Howard had succeeded in neutralising the environment lobby, diluting public concern over the sale of a public asset, and putting Labor on the back foot on both the environment and Telstra. But, in the longer term, the policy turned out to be deceptive because, while the NHT funding for the environment was welcomed by environmentalists, it was offset by the cuts the government made to environment programs once it got into office and pursued its 'small government' agenda. Kenneth Davidson, economics columnist for *The Age*, commented: 'Howard is open to the charge that the trust is the classic pea-and-thimble trick, that the Government has financed the trust by cutting back the environment priorities of the previous government, rather than providing additional net funding from the sale of Telstra'.[37]

In any event, only $163 million of the NHT was to be earmarked for the Murray–Darling, far short of the amount needed to address the crisis that the government had inherited.

The rise of Cubbie Station

Once Howard was in government, he had to confront the over-allocation of irrigated water in Queensland. How were Cubbie Station and other big cotton irrigators around St George and Dirranbandi allocated such vast amounts of water? The answer lies somewhere between maladministration and the leveraging of the political process by vested interests.

Originally a grazing property, Cubbie was planted with cotton in 1983. Situated in the vast, monotonous landscape of south-western Queensland, Cubbie is breathtaking in size: it covers 96 000 hectares, or 960 square kilometres. Its landscape oscillates between oceans of green cotton plants and hard-baked earth. From the start of its cotton operations, the business model was brutally straightforward: harvest the huge floodplain waters after the periodic heavy rains and store them in massive dams to irrigate the crop. It took a decade of operations before controversy flared.

In 2000, investigative journalist Phil Dickie showed just how much Cubbie's rise owed to the reckless handing out of water licences by the Nationals in the late 1980s. This unregulated approach to water policy set the scene for Cubbie to pursue its business model of extracting the overland flows, flood events that would otherwise enter the Balonne and Culgoa rivers. These waters were not only unregulated but free.

The election of the Queensland state Labor government of Premier Wayne Goss in 1989 continued the policy of reckless water allocation, paving the way for the biggest expansion of Cubbie Station as a cotton grower. Dickie wrote that the 'genius' behind this expansion was its 'gritty' general manager, John Grabbe, a former Water Resources Commission officer who moved on to overseeing the largest privately owned irrigation operation in Australia and possibly the entire Southern Hemisphere.[38]

Grabbe exploited Queensland's lax water allocation and planning laws to establish vast dams, while the company developed close relations with both sides of Queensland politics. Grabbe was a National Party stalwart, while the Goss government's Treasurer, Keith De Lacy, went on to become chairman of Cubbie Group, while Peter Forbes, a former executive of the state government–owned investment company QIC, became a director.

Through these appointments, Cubbie was, according to journalist Bernard Keane, 'plugged straight into Queensland's business elites'.[39] These elites included a powerful set of industry lobby groups: the Australian Irrigators Association, the Queensland Irrigators' Council, the Dirranbandi Irrigators' Association, the National Farmers' Federation and the Queensland Farming Federation. Many of the representatives from these organisation sat on government committees. There is a long history of such closed networks of power influencing and even capturing the political process.[40]

The closed model of politics surrounding Cubbie served the company well. However, when stories started circulating about the extent to which Cubbie and other cotton growers were extracting the floodplain waters, the operations became viewed as 'vast mysterious no-go zones'.[41] Cubbie became a metaphor for all that was wrong with the Basin's water management, 'a vast cancer on the Balonne-Culgoa', as online newspaper *Crikey* described the station.[42]

Despite the controversy, Cubbie and cotton continued to receive high-level political backing. Cubbie's powerful connections resulted in considerable favours from governments, including 'a willingness to bend over backwards to interpret rules in Cubbie's favour'. Paramount among these was the willingness of the Goss government to turn a blind eye to internal legal advice that the company's dam proposals were so vast that they needed to be subjected to an environment impact assessment. However, as Phil Dickie commented, '[that] did not happen and the record is obscure as to the reasons why not'.[43] The other favour extended by government was simply eye-watering: of its 51 water extraction licences, Cubbie paid $3.70 per megalitre for the first 1000 megalitres and received the remaining 4000 megalitres free.[44]

No less a figure than highly respected Justice Tony Fitzgerald, who had conducted a ground-breaking corruption investigation into the Queensland National Party government led by Joh Bjelke Petersen, criticised the Goss government for failing to consider the environmental, social and economic impacts of Cubbie's dam building. As Phil Dickie colourfully explained: 'in rural Queensland an outdoor dunny can need more planning permission than a 50,000 ML [megalitres] dam with walls more than 4.99 metres high'.[45]

This lack of proper planning and transparency resulted in Cubbie being able to construct 28 continuous kilometres of dams with enough storage capacity 'to swallow the waters of Sydney Harbour'.[46] A CSIRO report later found that this vast and over-allocated system resulted in half the water of the Balonne–Culgoa rivers being extracted before it reached the Darling River in New South Wales.[47] Not only did this adversely affect the flow down the Murray–Darling, but Cubbie's extraction of water also led to the death of thousands of hectares of trees on the Culgoa floodplain.[48]

In 2006, Rory Treweeke, a grazier from New South Wales, told a Senate inquiry into water that from his personal observations going back over 20 years, 'any point of view that has been contrary to that which was pro-development to the ultimate extreme was derided, ignored or refused to be accepted'.[49]

A similar process of floodplain harvesting had become embedded in the northern New South Wales Murray–Darling Basin where, by the 1990s, there were 1400 registered private dams and storages and more than 600 individual and corporate properties eligible for harvesting. Flood works had become 'embedded in the spreadsheets and business models of most of them', as one critic put it. As was the case in Queensland, no one knew exactly how much water was being harvested by these powerful networks of corporate interests.[50]

Reform or regression?

In the meantime, Howard continued his tactic of bargaining his ideological agenda for modest environmental gains. In 1999 he agreed to an update of the Commonwealth's environmental laws. As has been noted throughout the history of the Murray–Darling, Australia has had an appalling record of protecting native wildlife habitats, especially in this region. While the culture of extinction had slowly abated and given way to a widespread concern to protect native flora and fauna, little had been done to address the problem.

Howard's approach was expedient and lacked conviction. He was prepared to update Australia's environment laws when he needed the support of the Australian Democrats, a minor party with a controlling block of votes in the Senate, to achieve his signature taxation measure – the Goods and Services Tax. But it was clear from the start that the government was firmly in control of the process and, therefore, the final shape of the legislation. The Australian Conservation Foundation and the Wilderness Society were locked out of the negotiations, and, as one commentator noted, 'both groups maintained the rage over the undemocratic nature of the process for years'.[51]

The overarching goal of the *Environment Protection and Biodiversity Conservation Act 1999* (Cth) (EPBC Act) was to protect and manage nationally and internationally sensitive ecological communities and heritage places. The Howard government hailed the legislation as a 'landmark reform' and 'the most significant environment legislation' ever introduced into federal Parliament. In reality, the government had managed to engineer legislation that gave a fig-leaf of protection to the environment while allowing almost unimpeded ongoing development. The key structural weakness of the legislation was its narrow focus on individual projects, which could overlook wider cumulative, environmental impacts. It did not lay down mandated standards.[52]

The Howard government did not list the critically endangered 654 species it had initially committed to protect under the EPBC Act, and it failed to give protection for 'endangered ecological communities'.[53] As a later investigation confirmed, Howard's EPBC Act failed to stop the continued destruction of Australia's landscape and wildlife.[54] Researchers from the University of Queensland found that, between 2000 and 2017, 7.6 million hectares of habitat had been destroyed around the country and at least 90 per cent of destroyed habitat was never even the subject of an application under federal law. Land-clearing figures showed that more than 500 000 hectares of land had been cleared in the Murray–Darling Basin between 1999 and 2002.[55]

Thus, Australia continued the long tradition of developing weak environmental laws. In the 1990s most politicians – indeed most people – didn't question this tradition.

Howard tackles salinity ... or does he?

The failure to control land clearing had been the major cause of the ongoing salinity crisis, which the Landcare and NHT programs, however worthwhile, had barely addressed. Howard had relied on extolling the virtues of the Telstra-funded NHT to burnish his environmental credentials, but, as Canberra-based journalist Phillip Coorey observed, the results were 'pitiful because there has been no government backing or strategy'.[56]

By the late 1990s, there was growing awareness that dryland salinity was a national 'timebomb'.[57] Dr Graham Harris, chief of the CSIRO's Land and Water Division, estimated that the cost of fixing salinity exceeded the annual value of farm production.[58] The National Dryland Salinity Audit revealed that 20 000 kilometres of main roads and 1600 kilometres of railways were at risk from the effects of salinity.[59]

At the beginning of 1999, Howard was briefed on both the urgency and seriousness of the salinity problem by his Science and Engineering Innovation Council, an august body established in 1977 and comprised of leading scientists and industrialists. It also pressed him to publicly acknowledge the problem. However, as Phillip Coorey observed, nothing happened. Howard offered 'only a few glib lines at press conferences during regional tours about needing a solution which is fair to everybody'.[60]

In January 2000, Howard established a high-level Cabinet taskforce on the issue, but it failed to meet in the first six months of the year. The CSIRO fed scientific material into the taskforce, but, as John Williams, the organisation's deputy chief of Land and Water, told the press, 'stakeholders were concerned that the Government would find the problem too big and walk away'.[61]

What explains Howard's inaction? The answer lies partly in the priority Howard had given to promoting and fighting the culture wars since his election to office in 1996, which hampered his ability to acknowledge the depth of the crisis of land water management in the country. Denialism was one of Howard's most potent political weapons: denial of the science of climate change as he fended off pressure to sign the United Nations Kyoto Climate Protocol and denial of genocide committed to the nation's Indigenous people. Howard waged a continual war against calls for a national apology to the Stolen Generations of Indigenous children who had been removed from their families in the era of assimilation.

Howard was uncomfortable talking about the environment; his conservatism was forged in the post-war era before the rise of the environment movement. It was unfamiliar territory, disruptive to his belief in economic progress and his need to affirm the heroic view of Australian history. As one observer noted, the environment remained 'a nuisance rather than a challenge' to the Prime Minister.[62]

Raw politics also played a part too. As Coorey observed: 'Cracking down on farmers, telling them they have to stop clearing native vegetation and using so much water is a sensitive political issue, especially among the bush-paranoid Coalition'.[63]

However, with growing concern among a wide range of organisations declaring that salinity was the nation's most pressing environmental issue, Howard clearly thought he had to act. And when in May 2000 the National Farmers' Federation and the Australian Conservation Foundation issued a joint call for more than $60 billion over ten years to address land degradation,[64] the Prime Minister had little option but to respond.

When Howard announced his National Action Plan on Salinity and Water Quality (NAP) in October 2000, it comprised only $700 million in Commonwealth funding with a commitment by the states to match the figure. The Australian Conservation Foundation's campaign director, John Connor, provided the inevitable critique when he said that that strategy would 'soon run out of puff' unless Howard 'digs a lot deeper into his pockets'. He accused Howard of 'shirking the issue'.[65]

In fact, as a later parliamentary inquiry found, recent salinity research from several disciplines was not reflected in the design of the NAP.[66] Evidence from hydrological studies had concluded that effectively managing water tables and containing salinity in most locations throughout Australia required the establishment of perennial vegetation on at least 50 per cent of the landscape. Applying it to 5, 10 or even 20 per cent of the landscape would not have much of an impact. As one witness to the inquiry explained, such limited coverage 'might buy you a little bit more time, but it does not solve the problem. It just delays the onset of the problem'.[67]

Many farmers were concerned about land degradation. A 2006 Australian Bureau of Statistics report found that 'most Australian farmers make a conscious effort to look after their natural resources', with nine out of ten farmers engaged in natural resource management (including weed and pest control, native vegetation protection, and land, soil and water management) on their properties.[68]

Yet such preventative work was frequently undone by continued land clearing. In fact, a major oversight of Howard's salinity strategy was its failure to address the problem, which the federal government declared to be a state issue. Consequently, the bulldozers continued to roar in parts of Queensland and New South Wales.

Criticism didn't deter Howard from leveraging his government's funding of the salinity package for political purposes. In mid-2001 he gave a speech to the National Press Club in which he declared that the environment would form a key pillar of his government's future policy agenda. Even the conservative *Daily Telegraph* could see the hypocrisy in Howard's stance. Journalist Simon Benson wrote that the Prime Minister's speech at the Press Club

> was lacking in content and did nothing to encourage people to
> believe anything is about to change … It was perplexing that
> the PM could stand before the nation claiming a concern about
> biodiversity and salinity and claim a commitment to fixing these
> problems yet ignore their major cause – land clearing.[69]

Howard receives inconvenient advice

While Howard continued to play politics with the Murray–Darling Basin, an influential scientific group was formed to tackle the government on its environmental record. The Wentworth Group of Concerned Scientists was established in 2002 by Peter Cosier, a former adviser to federal Liberal Environment Minister Robert Hill. It comprised 11 distinguished scientists, including two high-profile media commentators: Professor Peter Cullen, who had been named scientist of the year in 2001, and Professor Tim Flannery, palaeontologist, explorer, environmentalist and best-selling author on a range of scientific topics.

Cullen, with his scientific background in water issues, was the driving force behind the group. A brilliant communicator with a sharp mind and a courageous public speaker, Cullen set the tone of the organisation when, in November 2002, he delivered its defining statement: 'You can't drought-proof Australia. We need to learn to live with the landscape, not try to fight against it all the time'.[70] Early on in its life, the Wentworth Group, called for a national water plan and campaigned around the impact of climate change on the future of agriculture. Flannery conceptualised this in blunt terms: 'Australians are engaged in a struggle for their own long-term survival. We are effectively fighting a slow-burning war for future clean water, air and fertile soil. We will only find ourselves, and our shape as a nation, through reconciling ourselves with our land.'[71] If we failed this test, the legacy, according to the Wentworth Group, would be a dust bowl.[72]

At the end of 2002, Peter Cullen advised Howard directly on the need to mobilise a fully funded national response to tackle the 'national landscape crisis' – the combination of salt, dust, algae, erosion and soil depletion. But Howard didn't budge any further than the existing and modest National Action Plan on salinity.

While conservative groups liked to frame the Wentworth Group as alarmist, this was a more difficult line of attack against Bill Heffernan, a Liberal Senator and farmer. He also gave Howard blunt advice on the impending water crisis. With discussions on water reform continuing, Heffernan let Howard and the government know that he was sceptical about the benefits of privatising Murray–Darling water. His concerns were social rather than environmental, although he would later ridicule the policy on the latter grounds as well. For now, he told Howard that 'the first nightmare is going to be the creation of water barons', investors who made large profits from water trading. Water will be sold to anyone, Heffernan explained, 'and farmers will have to rent water. It will be a disaster. People have not thought through the consequences'.[73]

By 2002, Howard had been playing defensive politics on Murray–Darling Basin for seven years, reacting to events and hyping his intentions without any material advances in addressing the underlying issues driving the crises in the region. But so had other politicians. The wily Labor Premier of Queensland, Peter Beattie, might have declared that 'salinity scares the hell out of me',[74] but he refused to act on the state's atrocious rate of land clearing, maintaining the erroneous argument that it was a national issue.[75] And in South Australia, action didn't match the fighting words of incoming Labor leader Mike Rann, who, in 2003, passed the *River Murray Act*, which granted ultimate power to the responsible minister to protect the river. However, as Mark Brindal, a former Liberal Minister for Water Resources, candidly admitted, the legislation proved to be 'empty' because any minister 'who dared to utilise those powers would go the way of the dog that bites the hand'.[76] As matters stood, therefore, it appeared as though the Murray–Darling Basin was too complex for the political system to fix. The long history of ignoring science and contrary opinions to development were proving hard to shake.

Further inaction

One of the earliest issues championed by the Wentworth Group was the need for big water buybacks by the federal government to release more environmental flow into the Murray–Darling. In mid-2002 an opportunity to fulfil this goal emerged when Premier Peter Beattie entered into discussions with the Howard government to buy Cubbie Station so that his government could fulfil its water target under the NCP. With his ebullient nature and a talent for apologising for government stuff-ups, Beattie entered the negotiations believing that he could sell such a deal to the Queensland public. He had the support of New South Wales Labor Premier Bob Carr, for whom Cubbie was 'a source of rage'. Carr wanted the property taken out of production for the national good.[77]

Beattie, who had seen satellite images showing one-fifth of Queensland could be affected by long-term salinity, had the courage to face the townspeople in the cotton-growing towns of St George and Dirranbandi and press for the buyout of Cubbie. Declaring that 'we can't do nothing' about the salinity threat he urged locals to work with the government to find solutions. In return, the Premier received the blunt message: closure of Cubbie would send both towns to the wall.[78]

Nationals federal leader John Anderson quickly moved to head off any purchase of the station. Beattie was incensed. He accused Anderson of leaking information about his talks with Howard on Cubbie, with the effect, Beattie said, of 'stabbing me in the back'.[79] The bitter politics of water policy had flared up again. He went on to accuse Howard of a failure of leadership, holding the Prime Minister responsible for caving in to the 'myopic self-interest' of the National Party. He appealed to Howard to 'over-rule John Anderson and lead'.[80] Howard declined. 'We're not buying into it', a spokesperson for Howard told the press. 'We're leaving it up to John Anderson who has the running on the issue for us.'[81] As the move over Cubbie revealed, the Nationals were steadily moving towards a party that prioritised agribusiness over small family farmers.

Untroubled by accusations that he had failed the test of leadership over Cubbie, Howard declared in 2004 that he would personally intervene to save the Murray River. He announced his intention to call a special meeting of the Council of Australian Governments (COAG) – comprising premiers from each of the states – to push through a plan to return 500 gigalitres of water to the river. He vowed to 'cut through red tape and backbench obstinacy' to do so.[82] But again, Howard fell far short of the mark. While 500 gigalitres is an immense amount of water, equivalent in volume to Sydney Harbour, the Murray–Darling Basin Ministerial Council advised that a further 1500 gigalitres was necessary to provide considerable whole-of-river and local ecological habitat benefits; anything less would not make much impact on the health of the river.[83] And, in any event, Howard's measure was intended to take five years to achieve.[84]

One crucial area overlooked in the COAG reform process was the rights of the Basin's Aboriginal people. At the time the reforms were being finalised, Australian human rights agencies, Aboriginal organisations and Aboriginal Local Land Councils advocated for Aboriginal water rights to be included in the national discussion, but 'little interest was shown for First Peoples' water rights'.[85]

The residents of Broken Hill also felt left out of the water reform process. Fed up with the poor quality and unreliability of their water supply from Menindee Lakes, in 2004 they formed the Darling River Action Group and started a campaign. Marie Wecker, the group's spokesperson, knew who they were up against. In a letter to the local newspaper she wrote:

> You tell us about the worst drought in 100 years, but what about the huge growth in irrigation in the past 20 years. When one irrigator can hold enough water to supply Broken Hill (at today's usage) for 75 years, one can clearly see who are the greedy.[86]

Nonetheless, the Howard government pressed on with the NWI, bringing to fruition the economic rationalist ideas first set out by Keating in the 1992 National Competition Policy. In essence, the NWI created a national system of property rights for water, and allowed for permanent water trading between the states and a Commonwealth buy-up of existing water in order to return 500 gigalitres to the river system. And it created a National Water Commission to establish the infrastructure and policies for the shift to privatisation.

All aspects of the NWI were controversial. In fact, the measure exacerbated the tensions over water that had been simmering away, as Daniel Lewis reported for the *Sydney Morning Herald* in August 2003:

> Farmers and environmentalists have long been at each other's
> throats over the issue, as have the Federal Government and the
> states. But water divides supposed allies. Liberals are at loggerheads
> with their National Party colleagues and even within the Nats,
> water can be a schism like no other.[87]

An informal trading market had emerged in New South Wales in the late 1990s as the Labor government of Bob Carr imposed a cap on extraction of water. Shortly afterwards, the first company was formed explicitly to trade water – National Waterbank Limited. Although the volume of trading remained relatively small, some farmers could see that the system would end up as a commercial plaything of wealthy interests. As one irrigator explained: 'I don't mind being out bid [on water] by my neighbours, but if I'm trumped by Babcock&Brown [an investment bank] putting together a groovy trust, that would upset me.'[88] But already, National Waterbank Limited was in the market raising millions of dollars to buy up water licences to sell back to the highest bidder. Some of these were so-called 'sleeper licences'; that is, allocated water that nobody was using. However, other water was coming from small farmers battling the worsening drought and lacking cash flow. For some it offered flexibility; for others it was an act of desperation. Some farmers were facing bankruptcy, with water prices skyrocketing by 300 per cent.[89] The great experiment in water had begun.

The attempted Commonwealth takeover

Howard might have thought that he had achieved his goals of privatis-ation of water together with a commitment to increased environmental flow with the final agreement reached on the NWI in 2004, but he found that the states were dragging their feet on implementation. New South Wales and Queensland, in particular, were accused of delaying the release of more water into the environment.[90] Some state leaders harboured reservations about the long-term implications of turning water into a commodity.[91]

In fact, fault lines were deepening everywhere on the water issue. While the states dragged their feet, Cubbie Station found a stalwart defender. Barnaby Joyce, a brash accountant from St George with talent for quick one-liners, won a seat in the Senate for the Nationals on the back of financial support from Cubbie.[92] Even though he saw himself as a staunch defender of small-town regional Australia, Joyce would tie the Nationals even closer to Cubbie and the flood harvesting irrigation industry of southern Queensland. In doing so, the Nationals began to witness a fracturing of their rural base – cotton or grazing? The two industries shared the same region. Pop and Peter Petersen, who ran a grazing property straddling the Queensland–New South Wales border, were fed up with the water-guzzling cotton industry by the time Joyce was catapulted to Canberra. They were convinced that Cubbie was drying out the floodplain, which they relied upon to survive. The regular floods had stopped seven years ago, they told the press, 'and the Culgoa River is barely running'. They weren't alone in their concerns. Husband and wife graziers Karen and Owen Betts explained:

We all know why we're not getting water … A lot of people
won't survive this. It is in effect transferring wealth from many
downstream landholders to a few upstream irrigators. The river red
gums are dying and the natural grasses are dying.[93]

At the same time, far away from the Culgoa River, two well-known
personalities were planning to bring the plight of the Murray–Darling
to an Australian audience. Tim Flannery and his friend, comedian
John Doyle, decided to embark on 'a boy's own adventure' down
the length of the Murray–Darling in a three-metre 'tinnie', their
adventures filmed for an ABC documentary series, *Two Men in a
Tinnie*. As well as seeing the beauty of the river, Flannery harboured
the ambition of using the trip to reveal the politics of the water in the
area – how water was actually being used. At the time he knew little
about this, but he suspected that the cotton growers in Queensland
were able to extract large amounts without any regulation.

Early on in the trip, Flannery came face to face with his underlying
concerns. In St George, the colourful mayor of the town, 'Big Bob'
Buchan, sought out the pair. In fact, he approached the duo's tinnie,
Bismarck, on his jet-ski. And, with no prompting, he looked straight
down the camera and explained 'any drop of water that goes past my
gate is wasted'. Flannery was quietly flabbergasted at the continued
frontier mentality over the use of water resources.

Australians fell in love with the series. Flannery explained later:

For the first time people could see with their own eyes what was
happening. You could see that the system was heading for a crash
if things continued. You could see that the system could die; that it
could turn into a Cooper's Creek – only flowing during exceptional
years.[94]

The series had an impact on public opinion and served to increase
political pressure for action. By 2006, Howard had become frustrated

with the lack of progress on the NWI, warning of the need to 'put a bomb under the process'. But to what end? The Wentworth Group's Peter Cullen uttered the words the government did not want to hear. It was time to stop 'drip feeding' farmers to keep them on unviable land, he said, suggesting some drought funding be diverted to exit payments to help producers leave those properties with dignity. 'Keeping them there maximises their misery and maximises the land degradation, which is what a lot of our current strategy seems to be doing', he said. The Nationals were outraged, seemingly oblivious to the fact that the party's continued support for cotton, Cubbie and floodplain harvesting had contributed to the degraded state of the river.[95]

The Prime Minister made good on his promise to force the pace on water reform at his 2007 Australia Day speech to the National Press Club. It was set to change the face of water management in Australia. As he took to the lectern, Howard was only too aware of the crippling Millennial Drought gripping the country, especially in the Murray–Darling Basin. Claimed to be the worst drought since the Federation Drought, it had led to a cut in irrigation flows, forced dairy farmers to leave their properties in droves, and led rural businesses to slash jobs. The land was parched and scorched again. Talk of climate change and its role in drought supercharged the culture wars. Water – the lack of it – had become a national crisis.

But it was not just the ongoing drought that presented Howard with both a problem and an opportunity. He needed a circuit breaker to Opposition leader Kevin Rudd's increasing popularity on the issue of climate change. That, according to Tony Windsor, appeared to be Howard's prime motivation in introducing a $13 billion plan for national water security: 'and because Howard wasn't too interested in climate change they needed a diversion. I think it was as simple as him saying let's find something on the environment'.[96] Seasoned Canberra journalist Glenn Milne agreed. Howard's Murray–Darling announcement 'was unquestionably a reaction to Rudd', because he was 'the most potent opponent Howard has faced in 11 years in office'.[97]

Howard planned to take over management of the Basin from the states, to create a new governing authority for the Basin and to return water saved from irrigators to the environment. The states, he said, had failed to manage water efficiently.[98] Included in the $13 billion program was provision for $3 billion to be spent on buying out irrigation licences to address over-allocation of water supplies, and almost $6 billion on a huge upgrade of irrigation infrastructure. The latter was intended to address the estimated 50 per cent loss of water through evaporation from the 70 000 kilometres of unlined and uncovered irrigation channels.[99]

Howard called on the states to look past their parochial concerns to the national interest. 'This is the Commonwealth assuming responsibility for a problem created by the states', he explained. However, given the history of parochialism over the Murray–Darling, Howard's push for national control, despite its obvious merits, was always likely to fail. It was fiercely resisted by Victoria, and the Commonwealth takeover was dropped. Today, Howard regards the failure to achieve such control as 'a great policy tragedy' because it was likely to have returned more water to the rivers.[100] The veracity of this claim is unclear, however, given the power of vested interests bent on limiting any return of water; this aspect is discussed in the next chapter.

Nevertheless, the subsequent *Water Act 2007* (Cth) embodied some ground-breaking environmental principles. In fact, as one parliamentary inquiry found, there are 'few examples in Australia's history of reform on the scale set out in the *Water Act*'.[101] The foundation of its sweeping power was Commonwealth law upholding international treaties to protect wetlands crucial to the survival of migratory birds under the Ramsar Treaty. However, the Act embodied potentially contradictory provisions, which, on the one hand, enumerated the need to 'optimise economic, social and environmental outcomes', while on the other, providing for environmentally sustainable levels of water extraction.[102]

The new body created by the Act, the Murray–Darling Basin Authority, had responsibility for preparing a Basin plan. The *Water Act* made it clear that this must be 'based upon the best available scientific knowledge' and without any political interference: 'The Minister must not give a direction in relation to any aspect of the Basin Plan that is of a factual or scientific nature'.

Because the *Water Act* included a separate objective to take account of social and economic impacts, it was a veritable minefield of potential disagreement. Which of the requirements in it should prevail: water science or the broader mandate to optimise economic and social outcomes? And, shouldn't governments have ultimate authority, rather than unelected government agencies? In political terms, the Act was like an unexploded arsenal, ready to blow up when ignited, in this case triggered by the heat of public disagreement.

To match the scale of his ambitions for the new role of the Commonwealth, Howard created a new super water ministry and put Malcolm Turnbull, the multi-millionaire, articulate and ambitious merchant banker-turned-politician, in charge. The Act was broadly endorsed by the states and by the federal Opposition leader Kevin Rudd. The Nationals, however, remained wary.[103]

Despite its ambitions, little actual planning had gone into the national water security plan. Initially, the plan was little more than a series of dot points, its brevity said to be reminiscent of an episode of the ABC comedy series *Utopia*, about government folly.[104] As a senior member of the Howard government later revealed, the plan was 'hastily developed, led and nutted out by Mr Howard in mere weeks'. Tony Windsor recalls talk in federal Parliament about 'the $10 billion cigarette paper Murray–Darling package'.[105] Treasury had just two days to cost it.[106] Even Cabinet was shut out of the deliberations. Howard had simply sidelined due process to produce the plan within his own Department of Prime Minister and Cabinet.[107]

Consequently, there was little or no long-term understanding about the impact of such far-reaching changes. An independent study by the Australian National University warned of 'social dislocation from small and medium-sized farms being forced out of the market by the price of water'. Local communities, the report suggested, stood to be devastated.[108]

Howard's $13 billion plan had also been developed separately from the potential impacts of climate change. This was not surprising as the Prime Minister had spent his years in office avoiding concerted action on the issue. And, only 5 per cent of the projected $13 billion was allocated for the next parliamentary term, leading the Australian Conservation Foundation to ask: 'Have we got a crisis or not?'[109] Howard, in fact, had done little more than conjure up 'a hugely fat number in flashing lights to bedazzle voters and obscure the complexity', according to one critic in the *Sydney Morning Herald*.[110] The policy was largely spin over substance, which reflected what some commentators regarded as Howard's tendency for quick, poll-driven responses to political problems.[111]

And such a hastily developed scheme lacked a strategy to propel it forward. Potential cracks lay everywhere. Firstly, there was no indication that irrigators were on side with Howard's bold plan. As the *Canberra Times* pointed out, irrigators often opposed other irrigators selling their entitlements because they knew that it had flow-on effects for the viability of local communities and it reduced the pool of irrigators who contribute to maintaining social infrastructure.[112] And irrigators maintained significant influence in a number of rural electorates.

But even more fundamentally, Howard was advancing his plan for water buybacks before any significant amount of water had been recovered for the environment. This was forecast to result in a rise in the price of water, making buybacks more expensive for the government and, therefore, less politically palatable.[113]

For his part, the new Water Minister, Malcolm Turnbull, spent months negotiating in secret the details of the scheme with the states while pushing the benefits of the reform in further promoting the privatisation of water, explaining that the proposed Murray–Darling Basin Authority would provide a Basin-wide approach to establishing a water market and pricing.[114] However, others saw the pull of Turnbull's former business career in his aggressive push for the privatisation of water. Turnbull had made his fortune as Chairman and Managing Director of Goldman Sachs Australia between 1997 and 2001. Globally, the company had a reputation for influencing government policy by installing their 'economic hitmen' in government and central banks.[115] And Turnbull was working up the Murray–Darling Basin Plan as his former company was moving more heavily into water speculation, the merchant bank declaring it to be 'the petroleum for the next century'.[116]

Whether or not Turnbull brought with him the Goldman Sachs view of the world didn't matter; he wasn't able to complete his reform process before the November federal election that ended Howard's reign as Australia's second longest-serving Prime Minister. Turnbull liked to think of himself as the saviour of the Murray–Darling, boasting that he'd taken the issue 'out of the too hard basket' and placed it on the national agenda.[117] Of course, he wasn't the only senior politician whose statements on the issue, driven by hubris, fell short of the reality.

On the ground, conditions had steadily worsened and small farmers were packing up and leaving as they had done periodically in the Basin for generations. Would Howard's bold and expensive plan make any difference?

12

SMOKE AND MIRRORS: THE MAKING AND UNMAKING OF THE MURRAY–DARLING BASIN PLAN

The Howard government's *Water Act 2007* (Cth) had the potential to be a ground-breaking reform. However, the ambiguity surrounding whether it prioritised the environment or the needs of Basin communities, together with the lack of detail on the $13 billion budget, left ample room for uncertainty about its outcomes. Howard bequeathed these problems to the incoming Rudd government. But if the past century and more had shown anything about the Murray–Darling Basin, it was that water was a vexed problem for any government to solve. The currents of disagreement run deep – between the states and the Commonwealth, between the north and the south of the Basin, between the Nationals and the other major parties, between environmentalist and agribusiness, between Indigenous people and governments, and between the various agricultural industries. What kind of leadership would it take to address these vexed issues? Was the supremely confident Kevin Rudd up to the task?

Rudd had pitched himself at the 2007 federal election as leading a government with a policy-driven agenda and, in relation to the Murray–Darling Basin, his government achieved some early successes. In 2008, the Council of Australian Governments (COAG), chaired by Rudd, signed the Intergovernmental Agreement (IGA) for reform of the Murray–Darling Basin, spear-headed by the Murray–Darling Basin Authority. Rudd promoted the agreement as a game-changer: 'This Intergovernmental Agreement creates the vehicle for the long-term reform of the much challenged Murray–Darling Basin system,' he declared. He followed up this development with the announcement that water licences would be bought back faster, extra money would be set aside for Adelaide's desalination plant and an audit undertaken of the Murray–Darling water. But Rudd was sanguine, too, about the path ahead: 'I don't want to say there is some magical solution here', he said.[1]

Rudd was right to be cautious because behind the scenes the government's reform credentials were not as burnished as it liked to think. Firstly, only half of the saved water from the infrastructure upgrades under the COAG agreement would be available for environmental flows – the rest was to go to irrigators.

After two years in government, little actual progress had been made. This was obvious to many farmers, including Brad Fischer. His family farm lay between the Coorong and Lake Albert in South Australia. They had been forced to turn off their irrigation pumps, sell off their 700 head of dairy cows and concentrate on beef production, which required less water. This was all a result of the systemic problems in the river system, he told visiting journalist Åsa Wahlquist: 'The water in the lake now is somewhere between 5000 and 6000 EC units [a measure of salinity] which would kill your lawn. It is definitely not drinking material for cows'. Fischer thought the Prime Minister's handling of the Murray River crisis had been 'pretty poor' because he was not addressing the underlying problem with the system: 'it is over-allocated, plain and simple. The system should be able to cope with drought, but drought and over-allocation is a double whammy'.[2]

Fischer said progress on the water buyback had been far too slow, with the Victorians limiting their sales out of irrigation districts to just 4 per cent a year, and the New South Wales government refusing to sell water to the Commonwealth. 'It is ridiculous. Kevin Rudd is the only one who can override the states. He should be doing that'.[3]

By 2009, Rudd had more pressing matters on his mind. The Labor government succumbed to Machiavellian internal politics that eventually led to Rudd being torn down as Prime Minister by his colleagues in June 2010. The Labor's factional warriors charged Rudd with being a dysfunctional micro-manager heading for defeat at the next election. Rudd called them the 'faceless men'. The unprecedented move by plotters against a sitting Prime Minister heralded the beginning of a toxic destabilisation of Australian politics, with four subsequent changes of Prime Minister in the next eight years. This was not a conducive climate in which to focus on important and complex issues, such as the Murray–Darling Basin. The pursuit of power rather than good policy became the dominant paradigm of politics.

In the fevered atmosphere of federal politics, oversight of the day-to-day management of the Murray–Darling was left to the states, and chief among their concerns was to protect the industries that relied on irrigation water. Investigations by the Adelaide *Advertiser* in 2009 revealed that the state governments of Victoria, New South Wales and Queensland were 'turning a blind eye to water theft and manipulation of irrigation rules to protect their irrigators'. Upstream users were able 'to get away with the rorts because of old water infrastructure, inadequate laws and few water police to enforce standards'. South Australians felt particularly aggrieved at this rorting of the system because they, more than any other state, continued to be impacted by the water use in other states and also because all water in the state was metered for use. The state government had been lobbying to reduce the effects of unregulated water extraction, but without success.[4]

Not long after this story broke, Julia Gillard replaced Rudd to become Australia's first female Prime Minister; she inherited oversight of the development of the Murray–Darling Basin Plan. A lawyer by background, Gillard had an impressive command of detail. But a leader could drown in the details of water policy; vision had always been the missing element. In 2012 she got her chance to be the latest 'saviour' of the Murray–Darling Basin with the long-awaited introduction of the Basin Plan. It was couched in the same hyperbolic language that Howard, Turnbull and Rudd had used in their dealings on water reform. The Plan was promoted not just as the nation's largest ever environmental program, which was true, but, more questionably, as 'one of the boldest policies on record'.[5] The reality was, unsurprisingly, much different.

The Murray–Darling Basin Plan unravelled as it was being implemented. Politics triumphed over sound policy in a way that revealed the lack of commitment to environmental values hard-wired into Australian politics, the readiness with which governments sidelined expert advice in pursuit of continued development and the ongoing domination of vested interests over water issues. Such values are reflected in the relatively low status that departments of the environment are accorded in governments across the country. Environmental scientist Professor Richard Kingsford, director of the Centre for Ecosystem Science, University of New South Wales, observed:

> Environment ministers are usually low in the cabinet pecking order. Talented environment ministers are rapidly promoted up and out. Ministerial muscle lies with natural resources portfolios that serve powerful export industry lobbies, such as irrigated agriculture and mining. Where senior ministers hold environment portfolios, they often also juggle others that consume attention, such as energy.[6]

How much had really changed in the last hundred years?

Creating the Murray–Darling Basin Plan

At the centre of an unfolding drama over the development of the Murray–Darling Basin Plan was the Murray–Darling Basin Authority (MDBA), the nominally independent agency charged under the *Water Act 2007* to devise the Plan. The centrepiece was to be a figure, based on science, for the return of water to the river system in order to restore it, and its surrounding habitats, to health. The first stage in the unravelling of the Plan was the contest over what this figure would be. Rarely has a single number mattered more in the development of policy.

In 2010 the MDBA released its draft plan – *Guide to the Proposed Basin Plan* – and, in quick time, all hell broke loose. Science became bitterly contested politics.

Authority head Mike Taylor had received legal advice that the *Guide* must comply with the *Water Act* and embody the best available science. He took this to mean that the Act gave environmental considerations primacy. But as he arrived at this position, the fight to discredit the science was already underway.

Irrigation peak bodies rejected the idea that science should be the driver of a plan for the Basin. Thus, in 2010, the National Irrigators' Council told a Senate inquiry that it was

> not possible to have the 'science' tell Government what the environment 'needs'. We believe the science cannot deliver in any meaningful way and will always be open to interpretation … particularly given the highly variable nature of Australia's river systems.[7]

The Council was on safe ground. In 2010, scepticism among many irrigators about the warnings from scientists on the dangers facing the Murray–Darling rippled through communities like a strong undercurrent, as it did, too, on climate change.[8]

However, at the MDBA, scientific modelling indicated that between 3000 and 7000 gigalitres needed to be returned to the rivers. Others believed the figure needed was higher still. The environmental group Inland Rivers Network maintained that over 10 000 gigalitres was necessary to restore the river system to full health.[9] As a reminder of the volume of water being discussed, one gigalitre is the equivalent of 1000 million litres; Sydney harbour holds 500 gigalitres of water.

The Authority settled on 3900 gigalitres. Taylor then faced the challenge of convincing unsuspecting irrigation communities – who hadn't been consulted in the preparation of the *Guide* – that they faced cuts of somewhere between 20 and 45 per cent to their entitlements, representing a billion-dollar loss in potential earnings to irrigators.[10]

Whatever the merits of the science, selling such a radical change presented an enormous challenge. Taylor went on a roadshow around the Basin immediately after the *Guide* was released in the first week of October 2010. Small towns, already battling to stay alive in the drought, along with bigger towns where irrigation was the major employer, were waiting with the proverbial baseball bats.

The first stop was the Victorian town of Shepparton. From mid-morning on 11 October, people lined up outside the Shepperton Hotel to hear Taylor explain the reforms. He thought he had a ready answer to community concerns about the cuts by pointing out they would come mainly from buying back existing water licences from 'willing sellers'. Still he appeared unprepared for the tense atmosphere he encountered inside the hotel. A journalist covering the event reported that you could cut the atmosphere with a knife. One interjector called out: 'How dare you buggers sit up there and tamper with our livelihoods'; another cried out, 'They're screwing the farmers'.[11] The visceral reaction was not surprising. Hard-wired into farmers' gut response to the *Guide* was regional Australians' lack of trust in government and their perception that city-based power centres overlooked their needs.[12]

Taylor didn't help his cause at the meeting by quoting modelling which showed that businesses would adjust; alternative jobs would be available.[13] This sounded like cold bureaucratic language to a community who thought the *Guide* would cripple rural Australia.

More outrage followed the next day in Deniliquin. The local RSL club didn't have the space for those wanting to attend the briefing. Matters became tense when the overflowing crowd blocked the stairwells and foyer. When protestors started yelling, the police were called to try to maintain order. Outside the venue, vehicles were parked across the road blocking the traffic and a man burned a copy of the *Guide*.

Inside the venue, Taylor tried to reassure the angry crowd that he was listening to their concerns, but they hurled at him their outrage that the *Water Act* 'gives wildlife and wetlands a bigger say than people and jobs'.[14] It was an understandably natural reaction; humans are used to prioritising their own needs without fully appreciating the interdependence between us and nature. As this book has shown, the development of the Murray–Darling Basin has been a compelling case study of this disconnect.

As the anger over the *Guide* spilled over in Deniliquin, 200 kilometres to the north in Griffith, organisers were preparing for the roadshow to arrive the following day. They had been forewarned about a likely blowout in crowd numbers, so locals were busy putting up marquees and an outside sound system in an attempt to avoid a repetition of the chaotic scenes in their neighbouring town. A crowd of more than 4500 people turned up to the event out of a total population of 16 000. Two hundred businesses closed for the event. The assembled crowd jeered and heckled and threw question after question at Taylor. Two attendees said that they would hold Taylor personally responsible for any depression-related suicides in the town because of the size of the cuts.[15] Copies of the *Guide* were also burned as a mark of the town's anger.[16]

Placating the communities hadn't worked, but Taylor remained largely unrepentant. 'This is probably one of the most significant water planning exercises ever undertaken anywhere in the world', he told a journalist towards the end of his tour.[17] He was forced to declare, however, that he'd been having talks with the government and the banks about the precarious position that debt-ridden farmers would be put in when their water allocations were cut.[18] Why wouldn't farmers be worried?

It wasn't just farmers affected by the potential impact of the *Guide*. Aboriginal people felt left out of the planning process and were critical that the document didn't embody Indigenous cultural values. Fred Hooper, chair of the Northern Basin Aboriginal Nations, explained the failings of the *Guide* to a subsequent parliamentary inquiry by giving the example of the importance of the river red gums to the Murrawarry culture:

> Around where we call Gooramon swamp, there are ancient camp sites. That is where our old people used to go to talk through the red river gums to their ancestors. For us, spiritually, that is the most significant plant in the Murray–Darling Basin. That connects us to our ancestors … That is not considered in any of this [the *Guide*].[19]

Observing these events closely was Tony Windsor, Independent member for the federal seat of New England. Taylor, he said, 'handled the situation very badly. He went out there and said this is going to happen and if you just wanted to put people offside in the Basin, he did a very good job of doing it'.[20] As Windsor highlights, a top-down process of decision-making thrust into heated public meetings proved to be counter-productive.

Inside the MDBA, many staff were shocked at images of the public burning their *Guide*.

A quick response

If ever a protest packed a political punch, it was the irrigators' uproar over the *Guide to the Proposed Basin Plan*. It was quickly proclaimed a dead document.[21] Within a few weeks of the protests, Mike Taylor resigned, insisting on the need to put the environment ahead of social and economic issues. There was speculation he'd been forced out by the Gillard government.[22] With the federal government's plans for the Murray–Darling now in 'deep crisis',[23] Water Minister Tony Burke met with irrigators in crisis talks about the *Water Act* and afterwards gathered alternative legal advice that the government was entitled to balance environmental issues with economic and social outcomes as the latter were included as part of the objectives of the Act.[24]

The *Water Act* thus proved to be conveniently flexible. Armed with this advice, the 'triple bottom line' replaced the priority on the environment in determining the Sustainable Diversion Limit (SDL) – the amount of water to be returned to the rivers. But there was no clarity around how this could be applied to the complex issue of scarce water resources – could social, economic and environmental issues be given equal consideration? And, to cap off the retreat from the spirit, if not the letter of the *Water Act*, Burke appointed a 'Labor mate' to replace Taylor – former New South Wales Health and Environment Minister Craig Knowles – and warned that he would use his ministerial powers to override the MDBA if he was not satisfied with what he regarded as an appropriate SDL figure.[25] Thus, the independence of the Authority – supposedly guaranteed under the *Water Act* – was compromised.

Knowles was well credentialed to head the Authority, and his appointment was welcomed by some environment groups. But he made clear his change of focus by reassuring residents of the Basin that there would be 'no deliberate approach to just making the environment the only consideration in the new Basin plan'.[26]

Why did Labor cave in and make such comprehensive changes?

After all, it held no seats in the Murray–Darling Basin. In all likelihood, the party worried about the optics of so many angry hard-working farmers – producing much of the nation's food – eventually damaging the party's image in the nation's bigger towns and cities. This was especially the case as Opposition leader Tony Abbott had jumped head-long into the issue, claiming that, if implemented, the *Guide* would almost certainly increase food prices.[27] Abbott was rapidly earning the reputation as the most effective Opposition leader in living memory for his opportunistic and relentless attacks on Labor's policies. Water was becoming just another battle in the so-called culture wars – the game conservatives played to wedge Labor with its working-class base.

These pressures ricocheted back onto Knowles. He was under considerable pressure to devise a plan that stood a chance of being passed by federal Parliament, where the minority Gillard government was supported by two Independent MPs – Tony Windsor and Rob Oakeshott. But how far would the Authority go in devising a political fix on this vexed issue?

While Knowles set about revising the SDL, the Gillard government tried to further defuse anger in the Basin by appointing a parliamentary committee to inquire into the *Guide*, to be headed by Tony Windsor. The respected Independent MP came with some deep experience on water policy. In 2001 he had chaired the Namoi Groundwater Taskforce, which successfully addressed the over-allocation in that huge, discrete system. After extensive consultation, farmers agreed to cuts of between 30 and 50 per cent – with only partial compensation – in order to create a sustainable system. As Windsor says today, 'if those farmers hadn't acted 20 years ago that system would be failing them now'.[28]

The inquiry Windsor headed reflected his view that consultation and consensus was needed to deliver a successful Murray–Darling Basin Plan: 'Communities want a Basin Plan, but they want a Plan that acknowledges them as a critical part of the Basin'.[29]

In New South Wales, the state government wasn't bothered about embracing science in its management of the river system. Just as the Basin Plan was being prepared, the government enacted what can only be described as a bizarre water sharing plan. This gave major water users more reliable access to water, including scrapping restrictions on pump sizes and allowing fast large-scale industrial extraction of water even when the river was running low.[30] One farmer noted that the new pumps were so powerful 'they can nearly turn the river backwards. They were massive'.[31]

Inside the Murray–Darling Basin Authority

In the meantime, Craig Knowles and the Murray–Darling Basin Authority were pursuing a pragmatic approach to devising a Plan: making the science fit the politics. His appointment had had an immediate impact on the organisation. Several well-placed senior employees have attested to its sudden change of culture.

One of these people was Professor John Briscoe, a doyen of international water resources management studies who had been selected to play a leading role in the 2010 MDBA review of the beleaguered *Guide*. In 2011 he corresponded with the Senate's Standing Committee on Legal and Constitutional Affairs and noted his concern 'that scientists in the MDBA, who are working to develop "the facts", may feel that they are expected to trim those so that the sustainable diversion limit will be one that is politically acceptable'.[32]

Another critic of the organisation was John Bell, who was Director of Environmental Water Planning at the Authority between 2009 and 2017. He told the 2019 South Australian Murray–Darling Royal Commission that 'at some point' after the appointment of Knowles and during the lead-up to the finalisation of the Murray–Darling Basin Plan, there was a very clear understanding that the sustainable diversion limit had to begin with a number two … it was a decision of the board conveyed by the 15 senior management [and] … one of the jokes was about, well, which postcode should it be. And at the time, Tony Windsor was the member for New England, and somebody quipped, 'Well, perhaps it should be Tony Windsor's postcode'.[33]

The Royal Commissioner, Bret Walker, seemingly incredulous at such questionable practice, asked Bell whether he was aware of any published information on whether the figure could be below 3000 gigalitres as a matter of science. Bell replied he was not aware of any such information.

In fact, when the Murray–Darling Basin Plan was finally passed by federal Parliament in 2012, the jiggery-pokery around the figure '2' had become formalised as the goal to return 2750 gigalitres to the rivers, well below what the science had modelled. Even this figure had had to be massaged politically. Knowles had initially settled on a target of 2800 gigalitres but reduced it by 50 'to get Queensland in the tent'.[34]

A later and equally controversial deal, instigated by South Australia, allowed for an extra 450 gigalitres of water to be put back into the river system by 2024. However, other states regarded this deal as 'optional' if delivery adversely affected upstream communities.[35]

The Wentworth Group walked away from discussions over the Basin Plan, having worked tirelessly inside the tent trying to shape outcomes. Its spokesperson, Tim Stubbs, explained that the members maintained that the Plan provided no scientific justification for the SDL and believed that the environment would be denied the water it needed.[36]

And the compromises to reach the 2750-gigalitre figure required all parties to turn a blind eye to the potential environmental consequences. The South Australian Royal Commissioner put the following proposition to John Bell: 'But I have noticed that some of the statements about the Coorong are to the effect that it might as well be written off in order to avoid further reductions in consumptive take upstream. Have you heard such things being said?' Bell replied: 'I have heard them or read them. Yes'.[37]

Walker reserved some savage criticism for the manner in which the MDBA had forsaken science for politics: 'Instead of trying to fix the limit beyond which key environmental values would be compromised, they appear to have set out to gauge the limit of sectional or political tolerance for a recovery amount'.[38]

In fact, juggling the politics and the science of the Plan fostered a closed culture at the Authority. Walker found that it maintained a 'predilection for secrecy,'[39] in which the SDL number and the science were 'run behind closed doors'.[40] Walker also castigated the Authority for failing to take account of climate change in reaching its much-reduced SDL figure, despite the CSIRO advising the MDBA in 2009 of its impacts; that is, that surface water availability across the entire Basin was more likely to decline than increase. In ignoring this advice, Walker wrote that the Authority had engaged in 'negligence, and maladministration'.[41]

In these ways the Authority became politicised. The consensus approach advocated by Tony Windsor was set aside for raw politics, although Windsor acknowledges that, in passing legislation for the Basin Plan, 'no other Parliament before had been able to do anything of the sort'.[42]

A start or a second-best Plan? It didn't really matter because vested interests determined that something needed to be done to undermine the watered-down Plan lest it lead to the sort of cuts that Knowles and the Authority had determinedly fended off.

But who, specifically, were these vested interests?

The irrigation club

No reminder is needed that water is big business. Which groups and individuals get access to water underpins huge profits. Access to the political system is, therefore, crucial in securing the business models in the Murray–Darling Basin.

Most people realise that money has a substantial influence on political outcomes and that it is expressed through social and economic networks, political donations, lobbyists and closed-door meetings between politicians and vested interests. The fact that this institutional form of corruption of politics is well documented doesn't mean that, in the absence of thorough-going reforms, it is any less powerful or opaque in its actual workings. Water is no different in substance to any other valuable resource. However, water has been a relative latecomer to corrupted political processes because, until the 1990s, vested interests had free rein. Governments had given agricultural industries pretty much what they wanted. Once the water in the Murray–Darling Basin became capped and privatised and, hence, scarcer, it followed that powerful interests would seek to control its use.

The most obvious are the large cotton growers in the northern Basin: established families with close ties to the Nationals. With cotton using around 80 per cent of irrigated water in the northern Basin, their interests lie in the perpetuation of floodplain harvesting and in lax monitoring of water use. A second group is the water traders, or water barons, as they are often colloquially known, who have risen to prominence with the privatisation of water. Their interests lie in the preservation of the free trade in water along with the lack of transparency that has applied to this market and the system of water buybacks that has made tens of millions for a favoured few. Lastly, there are the big agricultural corporations, which have benefited from massive government subsidies for irrigation upgrades and from becoming players in the water market.

The most cohesive of these interconnected groups are the irrigators of the northern Basin. Journalist and author Margaret Simons describes them as bound by 'the old school tie'. For decades these wealthy cotton growers have sent their children to the best private schools. Here the offspring of growers mixed with the aspiring politicians from the northern Basin who go on to join and represent the National Party, forming networks where 'they all stick together'. Both growers and National politicians are 'dominant men' with the growers being big donors to the Nationals. While Simons found that the power of such networks can be over-simplified, there is a perception that the Nationals and the big cotton growers form 'a seamless web of preference and influence'.[43]

The power of the network lay in capturing key decision-making and compliance sections within state and federal bureaucracies. This pattern, of course, had gone on for decades. Normally such influence is conducted behind closed doors. Occasionally, a window into this world opens through official investigations prompted by public scandal. Such was the case with the response to the first of the ABC TV *Four Corners* programs on the Basin – 'Pumped', mentioned in chapter 1 – which in 2017 investigated the alleged theft of water by northern Basin irrigators.

After the program aired, the New South Wales government was forced to appoint an inquiry conducted by Ken Matthews, an experienced senior bureaucrat and expert in water economics. Part of Matthews' investigation focused on the claims made in the program that the chief water bureaucrat in New South Wales, Gavin Hanlon, set up a secretive group with irrigator lobbyists to discuss the Murray–Darling Basin Plan. Commenting on the *Four Corners* program, Matthews wrote that it broadcast an alleged audio recording of Gavin Hanlon from a teleconference with the group that revealed Hanlon saying:

'It worries me when you hear that, hear that beep, because you are never sure who is dialling in'. The program alleged that in the recording obtained of the meeting, 'Gavin Hanlon offers to share with the group sensitive government data'. Gavin Hanlon was allegedly recorded as stating, 'What we might do as well, is set up some sort of, something like Dropbox or something like that where we can stick documents in that we are sharing as a safe way to get information around between us'.[44]

Matthews upheld the veracity of the *Four Corners'* allegations of bureaucratic favouritism shown to irrigators. He passed on his findings for investigation to the New South Wales Independent Commission Against Corruption (ICAC). Hanlon resigned on the release of Matthews' report. In sum, Matthews found that water regulation in New South Wales lacked independence, transparency and conscientious monitoring of water, and there was an indifference to pursuing wrongdoers. As one senior Canberra journalist commented, Matthews had made quite clear in his recommendations that 'water regulators in New South Wales had been entirely captured by the interests they were supposed to regulate, and by politics'.[45]

Evidence of a revolving door between the irrigation industry and New South Wales state politics was raised when it was discovered that New South Wales Primary Industries Minister Niall Blair appointed a former irrigation lobbyist as secretary to his department.[46] Earlier, the National Irrigators' Council had named former New South Wales Labor Primary Industries Minister Steve Whan as its new CEO.[47]

The irrigation club can also rely on the 'old-style' politics of big companies running small towns. As Tony Windsor explains: 'The big contributors politically and to the economy are big irrigators. That was where the money was and the mayor of the town would say that if you take that money away from us the town will collapse, and the politics just rotates on itself'.[48]

In these ways, the pro-irrigation culture in New South Wales became entrenched. After 'Pumped' aired, the Senate held an inquiry into Australia's water market in which claims of a conspiracy of silence around illegal water theft were made by Councillor Phillip O'Connor of Brewarrina Shire Council, New South Wales. He told the inquiry that many people along the Darling River were 'too afraid to speak out' about water theft and felt that the authorities did nothing to address concerns when they were raised.[49]

David Harriss, a former head of the New South Wales Office of Water, highlighted this culture in a submission to the South Australian Royal Commission. He claimed that cotton interests were extremely influential in determining water policy in New South Wales and that he struggled to get water ministers to take steps to protect environmental flows in the Barwon–Darling. He further claimed that when he sought to implement measures to protect flow he was 'moved on'.[50]

The power and influence of the irrigation club is also felt at the national level. Barnaby Joyce, appointed as Water Minister by incoming Prime Minister Malcolm Turnbull in 2015, is seen by critics to have led the campaign to undermine the Basin Plan. Joyce embodies the traditional conservative Australian values of pro-development, anti-environment and science scepticism. With his Akubra hat, crackling laugh and florid face, Joyce styled himself as the champion of the rural battlers; a maverick drawn to microphones, populist ideas and a visceral hatred of 'greenies'. It was all part of the Joyce strategy to become a master of the media and to emulate the tortured syntax of his role model, the long-serving right-wing Queensland Premier, Joh Bjelke-Petersen.[51] Joyce cut through and established a personal brand, until his reputation took a tumble in 2018 over an affair with a staffer whom he subsequently married.

When the Murray–Darling Basin Plan was released in 2012, Joyce had expressed legitimate fears about its impact on Basin communities. Yet, his pro-development, anti-environment views were also a threat to the long-term viability of the very same communities. In 2016 he explained his boyish enthusiasm for seeing 'big, yellow things pushing dirt around. It's marvellous'.[52] Joyce, of course, knows that

'Australians have always loved big dams and irrigation schemes'.[53] On another occasion, he told the Australian Water Association that he did not have a brief to protect water; it was a resource to be exploited for economic benefit: 'water is wealth and a dam is a bank'.[54]

The ongoing damage of such a development-at-all-costs mentality is seen in the continued ruinous levels of land clearing, which, in turn, affects the Basin's river system. As the Wilderness Society pointed out to the South Australian Murray–Darling Basin Royal Commission, land clearing surrounding the Basin's tributaries in Queensland and Victoria was going on at a rapid rate, and 'is substantially reducing the amount of water flowing into the river system'.[55]

Joyce's political connections are rusted onto the irrigation club. Establishing his accountancy firm in St George, the prosperous heart of Queensland cotton country in the 1990s, Joyce built his business to over 450 clients centred around the local irrigators, cotton growers and people associated with the big cotton stations such as Cubbie. Joyce's world was, as one commentator described, 'a close-knit game of mates'.[56]

Armed with this set of fixed attitudes and networks, Joyce launched into an admission in the Shepparton pub, where he didn't realise he was being recorded, that he was doing his utmost to undermine the Murray–Darling Basin Plan (see chapter 1). In response to his comments becoming public, South Australian Water Minister Ian Hunter said he had long believed Mr Joyce was not committed to the Murray–Darling Basin Plan: 'He really is telling people what he really thinks [in the Shepperton pub] and the Deputy Prime Minister responsible for delivering the Murray–Darling Basin Plan is actually telling people he's going to undermine it. There's a deep suspicion that he's been deeply two-faced on this matter'.[57]

As these developments unfolded, the independence of the MDBA was further eroded. For several years after the introduction of the Basin Plan, Maryanne Slattery observed the deterioration of the independence of MDBA. She occupied a senior position in the

Authority as a water accountant with the task of protecting water set aside for the environment. She witnessed the damage that had been inflicted on many staff by the haste and compromise of getting the Basin Plan finalised. Encountering the continual undermining of her work and her position by certain members of the senior executive, Slatterly became a thorn in the side of a compromised system as she came to the conclusion that the numbers in the Basin Plan didn't add up; that the MDBA was trying to hide that fact and paper over the cracks.[58] She eventually took a redundancy and moved to the Australia Institute where she became chief researcher on the Murray–Darling. A quietly spoken accountant with a forensic eye for detail doesn't sound like a candidate for whistle-blower, and Slattery is uncomfortable with the term. But she has deployed her insider knowledge and professional expertise to publicly take on the MDBA.

The irrigation club exerts its power

With powerful backers at state and federal levels, and a compliant MDBA, the irrigation club set out to protect its interests in two main ways: ensuring that the Plan didn't embrace more ambitious water targets, and protecting the continuation of floodplain harvesting.

Even though the Murray–Darling Basin Plan drastically reduced the SDL, the irrigation industry wasn't satisfied. Through its major peak bodies, it continued to muddy and undermine the work of water scientists. In doing so, it borrowed from the playbook of the climate denialism campaign. Professor Quentin Grafton, Professor of Water Economics at the Australian National University, has been observing this tactic for many years. He says that the irrigator lobby groups have employed a variety of ways to put a different slant on the science in the advice they provide, including through the numerous meetings they have with the Water Minister of New South Wales, the lobbyists they employ in Canberra, and the media releases they issue critical of the work of scientists: 'the peak lobby groups see their role as ensuring that no more water gets allocated to the environment. They have been quite persistent and they have been successful in undermining the nature of the science'.[59]

From 2015, Grafton was one of several scientists working on the Basin Plan who came to the conclusion that all was not right. He began warning that the government was exaggerating the amount of water returned to the rivers, claiming that the real figure was at least half of what the government was claiming. And in the worst-case scenario, the return of water had gone backwards, not forwards. The government then tried to discredit his work:

> They just don't want to know. It's an inconvenient truth. We knock on the door, we tell them what we've done, we give them the evidence and we get pushback and the pushback is, no you're wrong. And we say fine, tell us where we're wrong. Blank. There's no response where we're wrong.[60]

Protecting floodplain harvesting

Cotton is big business in northern New South Wales and southern Queensland. Underpinning the profits and the viability of the towns that benefit from the industry is the need to access the big rains that periodically inundate the headwaters of the Basin, fanning out into all the tributaries and flowing into the entire river system. For decades a 'pirate' system had prevailed where irrigators took what they wanted and state governments turned a blind eye.

The massive undertakings by cotton growers to divert these floodwaters into huge shallow dams for irrigation was omitted from the Murray–Darling Basin Plan for political reasons. It was simply quashed in the negotiations over the *Water Act 2007* between the Commonwealth and the states; attempts by the Water Minister,

Malcolm Turnbull, to raise the issue of regulation were overruled by state premiers and his own Coalition colleagues from the National Party.[61]

It was a signal for the massive expansion of the practice. Cubbie Station, for example, has constructed capacity to store 500 gigalitres of water.[62] In 2013, the station was sold to a Japanese–Chinese consortium, raising questions about whether a foreign-owned venture would feel responsible for protecting biodiversity, as opposed to making profits for their shareholders.

No one knows just how much water is harvested by these big interests. Some suggest it might be as much as 40 per cent of any flood event. The water is free and unmonitored. And as one observer noted, 'there has been no assessment of the impacts on the environment, cultural values or downstream water users'.[63]

In these ways, floodplain harvesting was enveloped in the shadowy world where politics and vested interests intersect. There have been occasional glimmers of insight into just how powerful the irrigation club has been in protecting this resource.

In 2014, the New South Wales Water Minister, Kevin Humphries, pushed through an amendment to legislation to consider only droughts up to 2004 in assessing the worst drought on record, as taking the subsequent Millennium Drought into account 'would result in significant quantities of water being taken out of production and held in reserve in case an equally severe drought occurs'. In other words, irrigators would lose some of their allocation. This was water that would otherwise have gone to towns and to protect the river system.[64]

The issue was revisited in 2019 when another New South Wales Water Minister, Melinda Pavey, headed 'into battle on behalf of irrigators at the Murray–Darling Basin Ministerial Council in Brisbane … armed with threats to pull out of the Basin Plan unless her interstate counterparts agree to concessions that will allow the irrigators more water'.[65]

No such threats eventuated, but in the same year, Pavey made further efforts to advance the interests of irrigators. Following the breaking of the drought in 2019, the New South Wales government announced on 7 February 2020 that it would restrict overland harvesting of the floodwater because it was 'in the public interest'. But under pressure from irrigators, the government gave the large cotton-growing areas a three-day exemption from the embargo. 'That allowed several huge cotton properties between Walgett and Wee Waa, and west of Moree, to take the first flows in years.'[66]

Not all such lobbying efforts have been successful. In February 2020, Melinda Pavey's department quietly issued a regulation exempting irrigators from holding licences, and later defended the controversial move by saying that the state government had to 'carefully balance the environmental, social and economic needs of our communities', while critics 'only focused on environmental outcomes'.[67] When the regulation was later voted down in the Legislative Council, the New South Wales Irrigators' Council described it as 'a big step backwards for water management'.[68]

Pavey's other approach to protect floodplain harvesting has been to attempt to license the practice. This followed advice received from the state Crown Solicitor that the practice was likely illegal unless farmers have a development consent and a water access licence. Most do not.[69] Moves commenced to make the practice legal. But licensing remains highly contentious. 'Handing out licences now after this big water grab', argues Water for Rivers spokesperson Tracey Carpenter, 'will lock in over extraction'.[70] It would also involve 'a windfall transfer of public wealth' to big irrigators, according to the Environmental Defenders Office.[71]

Critics asserted that these moves by Pavey were shaped by the continuing influence of powerful northern Basin irrigators. Justine McClure, a farmer who is the Australian Floodplain Harvesting Association President, argues that 'the weight of pressure on politicians and senior bureaucrats alike from the top end of the system was unbearable ... powerful corporations backed by dedicated lobby groups were influencing both government policy and its interpretation'.[72]

The Association supports the ongoing purchase of water for the environment.

The Queensland government, too, has continued to support big cotton irrigators around Goondiwindi engaging in floodplain harvesting. In 2018, information surfaced about huge earth works being undertaken, funded by grants from a Murray–Darling Basin Plan program. Claims of rorting and possible criminal charges again threw a spotlight on the lack of transparency surrounding the Basin Plan.[73] Whose interests was it really designed to serve?

However, as floodplain harvesting has grown more controversial over time, a community pushback has been mounted. In early 2019, for example, the Southern Riverina Irrigators broke away from the New South Wales Irrigators' Council over floodplain harvesting. Chris Brooks, chairman of the dissenting group, explained that it was 'just insane' that large areas were allowed to harvest water 'with no metering, no monitoring, no measurement' while southern Basin farmers were experiencing water shortages.[74] Legal action against the MDBA has been mounted by the group.

The split, and associated acrimony between the northern and southern irrigators' groups, has had political consequences: the Nationals lost two seats in the 2019 New South Wales election to the Shooters' and Fishers' Party. The formation of the Southern Riverina Irrigators mirrors a broader coalition of groups opposed to floodplain harvesting, including graziers, Aboriginal organisations and environmentalists.[75]

If floodplain harvesting represented a flagrant undermining of the intent of the Murray–Darling Basin Plan, the millions of dollars of funding for upgrades of irrigation infrastructure was a case of bad public policy dressed up as a public good.

Wealthy irrigators get a boost

In 2019, two years after the *Four Corners* 'Pumped' program caused a furore by alleging water theft by wealthy irrigators in the northern Basin, the case of one of the irrigators subsequently charged finally came to court. Anthony Barlow pleaded guilty to illegal theft of water, but his sentencing submission reignited the poisonous state of water politics in New South Wales. Barlow claimed that he was given the go-ahead to pump water by the then Water Minister, Kevin Humphries, who, he claimed, told him in person that the ban on pumping due to the drought had been lifted. Humphries strongly denied the allegation.[76] At the time, ICAC was investigating the matter but opting not to hold any public hearings.

Four Corners returned to the Murray–Darling not long after Barlow's conviction. This time the focus of the program was on the alleged rorting of the $5 billion Water Efficiency Program (WEP). A centrepiece of the Basin Plan, the WEP paid irrigators to save water by upgrading their pipes, dams and sprinkler systems, in return for surrendering to the Commonwealth a portion of the savings in their water use. It looked like a simple win-win approach.

However, the WEP was the outcome of another politicised process. In devising the Basin Plan, both the Howard and Gillard governments rejected the advice of the Productivity Commission and the Australian Bureau of Agricultural and Resource Economics, both of which warned that infrastructure upgrades were costly and inefficient.[77] The inclusion of the WEP in the Plan was a result of successful lobbying by irrigation groups. For the Nationals, the public largesse to irrigators was the cost of getting the Basin Plan across the line.[78]

The WEP was ripe for investigation, and ABC *Four Corners* took up the challenge. Its program 'Cash Splash', ignited an equally fierce storm of criticism from the agribusiness industries and their lobby groups as had been directed at 'Pumped'. Focusing on the WEP operating on the Murrumbidgee, the program claimed that the value of these grants were over-estimated in terms of the water they return to the rivers; that taxpayers were paying too much for water saved; and that millions of dollars were being handed out to big business in secret deals.

A range of scientists and farmers with long experience in the Murray–Darling were quoted in the program. They didn't pull their punches. Professor Richard Kingsford explained: 'We're degrading the rivers at the same time we're handing money out to a few individuals to realise huge economic gains at public cost'.[79] And Professor Quentin Grafton called the WEP 'a national scandal'. He argued that it didn't happen by chance. The lack of transparency in the WEP, and in the implementation of the Basin Plan generally, had been 'a deliberate strategy to avoid the scrutiny and transparency that may have identified [the] weaknesses in the water reform process'.[80]

There were few bigger targets in the program's exposure in the alleged rorting of the WEP than Webster Ltd, which is chaired by the reclusive Chris Corrigan. As managing director of Patrick Corporation, Corrigan had earned the title of 'business powerbroker' for taking on the Maritime Union in the bitter waterfront dispute of 1998. By that time he was already extremely wealthy. Unlike many other multimillionaires, though, Corrigan preferred to stay out of the limelight. But when he occasionally fronted the media, he conveyed a quietly spoken and understated persona, given to delivering brief answers in a slow, considered monotone. Some observers considered him dull.[81]

Corrigan lived for many years in Europe, and it was a surprise to many when he returned to the frontline of corporate management in 2016 as executive chairman of the 180-year-old agricultural company Webster Ltd. Astute and hard-nosed, he clearly saw the potential for agribusiness when he took on the role and began a program of striking deals to expand its cropping, sheep, cotton, and walnut and almond businesses.[82] In the Murray–Darling Basin, Webster owned

230 gigalitres of water, about half the volume of Sydney Harbour.

Corrigan was asked to participate in the *Four Corners*' 'Cash Splash', but a company spokesperson for Webster declined, citing bias in the previous program, 'Pumped'. 'Cash Splash' reported that Webster had received $41 million from the WEP to help fund a $78 million expansion of its empire in the Murrumbidgee Valley, where it had purchased hundreds of square kilometres of land. Webster was undertaking a massive expansion of its nut-growing industry based on a substantial increase in irrigation. The scheme was shrouded in secrecy. As reporter Sean Rubinsztein-Dunlop noted: 'Under the scheme details of who receives the subsidies and how they are spent are not publicly available'.[83]

Chris Corrigan was part of an organised storm of criticism levelled by the industry at the ABC for 'Cash Splash'. The sector was united in condemning the program on the basis that it was biased against the irrigation industry and involved big business bashing.[84] Federal Agriculture Minister David Littleproud defended the WEP claiming it was run on 'robust systems', and that most of the funded projects were on small to medium-sized farms.[85] And the changes brought by the WEP to those smaller farms were part of a cultural change in the way water was used. Griffith farmer Terry McFarlane told ABC Regional News that 'people are more careful with their water now'.[86]

But how much of the 'saved' water is being returned to the environment? Expert opinion differs. According to recent research from the Australian Bureau of Agricultural and Research Economics and Sciences, 255 gigalitres of water has been recovered through farm upgrades at a cost of about $1 billion.[87] However, the Environmental Defenders Office maintains that 'there is little publicly available information to help the community determine whether contractual obligations are being met or water is actually being saved. Evidence increasingly suggests that in many instances more water is not being returned to the system'.[88] It's not clear why there is such a wide discrepancy in findings. The figures on how much water *is* being returned to the environment was as much disputed as the amount that *should* be returned.

In the end, the WEP was part of the politicised approach to the Murray–Darling Basin Plan. If it hadn't been, then states like New South Wales and Queensland would have introduced effective means to measure recovered water; they didn't. As Tim Flannery explains, nobody foresaw 'the foot dragging in terms of measurement ... and without measurement you can do nothing scientifically'.[89] Remote sensing technology can be used to scientifically measure recovered water, but, as Professor Mike Young of the University of Adelaide told the South Australian Murray–Darling Royal Commission, 'there are no plans to adopt this technology in the MDB'.[90]

And Webster Ltd was involved in another scandal involving the Murray–Darling Basin Plan – part of a series of water buybacks dubbed 'Watergate'.

Water buybacks

The policy of buying back water to return to the environment sounds simple enough. The Commonwealth purchases water licences from willing sellers; the licences, held in perpetuity by the Commonwealth, would help achieve the SDL set out in the Murray–Darling Basin Plan. Most water experts favoured this approach over infrastructure upgrades because, at least in principle, the water was more tangible than the WEP, with its lack of transparency.

However, buybacks contain hidden ethical and policy complexities. Should taxpayers be subsidising irrigators for licences that were largely handed out for free?[91] What price can be set for a product in the absence of any historical market, and were potential owners selling real water or merely a dry river bed where water once flowed?

When the Rudd government commenced buybacks in 2008, people living in irrigation communities opposed buybacks believing that they devastated rural towns. Not surprisingly, the rural press demonised buybacks and the National Party championed terminating them. In his role as Opposition spokesperson on water, Barnaby Joyce led the rural revolt over buybacks. As Tony Windsor recalled, Joyce was arguing that 'this was all about big brother and should never have been looked at in the first place'.[92] Joyce received support from the big irrigators, who went even further – towns would be decimated if anything was ever done about the allocation of water.[93]

When Joyce was appointed Water Minister in October 2015, he at first made good on his word to terminate buybacks but then rescinded, proceeding with three expensive buybacks. These purchases were made in secret, falling under the heading 'strategic purchases', which exempted them from the traditional government process of open tender. Each involved big cotton and its lobby groups.[94]

The purchase in 2017 of the Webster Ltd water licence by the federal government from their western New South Wales property, Tandou Station, quickly became embroiled in scandal. The company had strong connections to the Nationals, and the $78 million price was claimed to be twice the market rate. The scandal deepened when questions were asked about whether the government had actually bought any 'real' water. After all, the company secretary, Maurice Felizzi, said sale of the water was based on a decision to get out of cotton farming because of poor water security from the Menindee Lakes.[95]

In the same year, Joyce signed off on the purchase of the water licence from Tulla Pastoral Company on the Warrego River in southern Queensland. The deal was shrouded in secrecy until Senator Rex Patrick, of the Centre Alliance team, obtained documents in a Senate order, only to find the government had redacted the independent valuer's recommendation. Critics claimed that the water sold by Tulla was one-off floodwater, known locally as 'goanna water': 'The only time you get it is when the goannas are sticking their heads out of the trees [because of flooding]' explained **Ed Fessey, who served on the Northern Basin Advisory Committee**, to the *Sydney Morning Herald*.[96]

A third deal signed by Joyce was equally lucrative for another large agricultural company, Eastern Australian Agriculture (EAA), which was in turn owned by Eastern Australian Irrigation (EAI), a company domiciled in the tax-haven of the Cayman Islands. Federal Energy Minister Angus Taylor was a co-founder of EAI, although he had stood down from the company position when he entered politics in 2013. EAA had already been in receipt of government largesse – $2.173 million to line its dams with rocks to save water.[97] Not only was the price paid for EAA's licence for 10.4 gigalitres of water on its two properties in Queensland's Lower Balonne Valley twice the estimated valuation, but experts deemed the water of 'lower value'. Most of the money ended up in the Cayman Islands.[98]

A few additional twists to the plot made the EAA deal read like a script for an airport novel. An anonymous Twitter thread, created from someone claiming to have sourced information from a 'Deep Throat', went viral and, when referred to by journalists, incited angry threats of legal action from Taylor. The Twitter feed was subsequently removed. But what had actually been resolved about the ethics and accountability of the deal? As investigative journalist Michael West cheekily wrote, the EAA deal involved nothing that was illegal or corrupt:

> It is not illegal to set up a Cayman Islands company, or to be a
> director of a company in the Cayman Islands which later became a
> beneficiary of a sale of water rights in Australia ... neither is it illegal
> for a government minister ... to pay a record price for something
> which experts deemed worthless.[99]

In 2019, a spokesperson for the Commonwealth's Environmental Water Holder (CEWH) told a Senate estimates hearing that the rights bought from EAA had not yielded any water at all.[100] The CEWH reported a changed position in 2020 when good rains in February and March delivered flows that reached the Narran Lakes, one-third of which, it calculated, came from the EAA buyback.[101] But put in perspective, the deal had delivered one-third of one rainfall event in three years.

All the buybacks signed by Joyce were opaque. The result has been poor value for both taxpayers and the environment. The deals symbolise our corporatised democracy – schmoozed in the corridors of power but with a trail of unanswered questions.

So why did Joyce, the rural populist opposed to buybacks, spend $200 million of taxpayers' money on questionable deals? There are no clear answers to this question. He may have felt under pressure to meet the SDL targets, whatever his personal reservations. Alternatively, Joyce may have responded to the demands of the irrigation club; influential players leveraging the networks of influence to obtain self-interested deals against the broader public interest.

With calls for a Royal Commission growing over the buybacks, the Morrison government sent off the EAA deal (and the two others Joyce signed off on) to the Auditor-General's Office for investigation, while Joyce's reputation was said to be declining 'more quickly than our rainfall'.[102] He, of course, maintains he did nothing wrong. When the Auditor-General's report was published in 2020, the issue of any wrongdoing was open to interpretation, in that the Auditor-General found that buyback deals did not ensure value for taxpayers' money in the program, but did not find any legal breaches.[103]

In New South Wales, ICAC released its report at much the same time. Its focus was on any potential corruption by previous New South Wales ministers involved in water policy.

ICAC assesses corruption against a legislative definition, which, shorn of its technical language, involves ministers who engage in deliberate or intentional wrongdoing in ways that involve personal gain, exercising their official functions in a partial manner or impairing public confidence in public administration.[104] In its findings, the Commission found no evidence of corruption, yet it found clear evidence of the New South Wales government favouring irrigation interests going back over a decade.[105]

Thus, all the deals signed off by the federal Agriculture Department while Joyce was minister have the whiff of cronyism about them; not corruption in the black letter definition of payments to politicians, but deals that failed to uphold the public interest because they lacked full accountability and transparency. Such cronyism has been found to be endemic in the Australian resources sector.[106]

The rise of the water barons

In October 2020, the federal Water Resources Minister, David Littleproud, secretly met with farm leaders over their concerns that institutional investors with no direct interest in agriculture were hoarding water from the Murray River and driving up the price. In the process, the 'water barons' were said to be killing off the viability of drought-ravaged irrigation farmers. What Littleproud said to placate the farmers is not known.[107]

According to MDBA whistle-blower Maryanne Slattery, in the past few decades Australia has undergone one of the largest privatisations of water in the world.[108] Under the reforms, anyone can trade water – it is bought and sold by irrigators, farmers, or water investors with no involvement in farming, through water exchanges. But how do we measure its impact in the Murray–Darling Basin? Specifically, has the rise of the agricultural water market – underpinned by the idea that water will flow to its most profitable crops – marginalised or bolstered social as well as environmental values?

Answering these questions in a definite way is beyond the scope of this book, if only because experts disagree. Economists tend to favour the reforms because of the attraction of efficiency and consequent gains in economic output.[109] Some water experts also commend Australia for having one of the most efficient water markets in the world because it is capable of adjusting quickly to changing conditions.[110]

Environmentalists worry about the ethics and ecological impacts of privatising water. The Wentworth Group split philosophically over the issue. Views varied, but Tim Flannery believes that commodifying water will 'drive us into environmental and social bankruptcy'.[111]

Certainly, problems have been found to arise with the lack of effective regulation to prevent concentration of water ownership. In its 2020 review of water trading, the Australian Competition and Consumer Commission highlighted this aspect of water trading. While extolling the economic benefits of the reform, it found that the unregulated nature of the market, in which there are 'scant rules' to protect against market manipulation and a lack of transparency, favoured better-resourced and professional traders.[112]

Two agribusinesses own the bulk of the water of the Murray–Darling Basin – Webster Ltd, and the operations owned by Peter Harris and CS Agriculture.[113] Both agribusinesses are focused on cotton production, with Webster also branching out into almonds and walnuts. All are high-value crops that consume large amounts of water.

Critics worry that the environment is being squeezed by a concentrated, profit-driven system. As one critic has highlighted, the concentration of water ownership by large agribusiness strengthens pressure for short-term economic development, 'making it increasingly difficult to achieve more sustainable river management and adjust to climate change'.[114]

The views of farmers differ. Some regard the water market as a necessary evil; a means to curb the historically flagrant use of water. Others have benefited from selling their seasonal allocations of water.[115] Still others rail at the lack of a level playing field; speculators, they say, push up the cost of water for ordinary farmers. Local communities can be a casualty, as one farmer explained: 'Every day that they [investors] are in the market bidding against the irrigator means that the irrigator has got to pay more, which means that they don't have as much to spend in town, which means the whole community suffers'.[116]

And the sheer complexity of the system is geared to the bigger players.[117]

A failing Plan?

In April 2019, a few months after the Menindee fish kill, journalist Tony Wright rode his motorcycle 1000 kilometres across the flatlands of Victoria's north-east and onto the equally featureless Hay Plain in southern New South Wales. Everywhere, wheat silos dotted the landscape like church spires. A federal election beckoned, and Wright wanted to gauge the mood of farmers in the key electorate of Farrer. He discovered a quiet desperation among many because of their lack of access to water. Most blamed the Murray–Darling Basin Plan. One farmer, Mick Clark, bluntly summed up the general mood. 'So far as I'm concerned', he said, 'the supermarket shelves in the city can go empty [because] I'm not going to spend $600 a megalitre of water to keep farming just to go broke'.[118]

At much the same time, ecologist David Patton explained to the ABC that the Plan was having a devastating impact on the Coorong at the end of the Murray River. The area was dying and its internationally protected Ramsar wetlands – a haven for migratory birds – were under increasing threat. The problem was that the Basin Plan was simply not delivering enough water. The Coorong had just seen the end of a massive algal bloom, which wrought havoc on the birds' food supply; they had had nothing to eat, Patten explained. And he warned, 'rivers die from the mouth up'.[119]

As these vignettes suggest, the Murray–Darling Basin Plan was leading to some farmers going broke and key parts of the Basin's ecosystem left in worse shape than ever. Indeed, seven years after the Plan was rolled out, a range of expert opinion agreed that the Plan was sliding towards failure. David Bell, the former Director of Environmental Water Planning at the Murray–Darling Basin Authority (MDBA), in a submission to the 2019 South Australian Murray–Darling Royal Commission, claimed that 'unchecked, the current Basin Plan implementation will lead to a worse environmental outcome than would have arisen if there were no Basin Plan'.[120]

This, he argued, would give rise to the need to revisit the Plan to obtain more water for the environment. And that process, he said, would be compounded by a distrust of science and bureaucracies and governments, making it 'very hard to recover a decent outcome'.

Maryanne Slattery stated in 2019 that the Basin Plan was 'broken', her point being that the major rivers in the once interconnected system no longer seamlessly flowed from one into the other.[121] In addition, Professor Quentin Grafton has said: 'The bottom line is that the Basin Plan is going to fail in the context of the key targets'.[122] The claim is supported by the Wentworth Group of Concerned Scientists, which in 2020 undertook a study of river flows and found that, since 2012, 20 per cent of the water expected each year under the Basin Plan did not flow past most of the 27 sites they had selected for observation: 'Flows at 24 of 27 sites were lower than expected even when accounting for climate conditions. Of these, 13 received less than three-quarters of the expected flows and three received less than half of the expected flows'.[123] The volume of 'missing' water constitutes 2000 gigalitres – enough to fill Sydney Harbour several times over. The study couldn't determine whether the water was lost, stolen or simply never there in the first place.

In a similar finding to the Wentworth Group study, a team led by Professor Jamie Pittock, a water expert from the Australian National University, found that much of the Basin's extensive wetland ecosystems were not receiving the floodwaters required to keep them healthy. A key objective of the Basin Plan was to restore these ecosystems, which Australia is required to do under international law. Yet, overall, only two per cent of all the wetlands throughout the Murray–Darling Basin that could be inundated with environmental water controlled by the federal government were actually watered each year. Floodwaters were being stopped mostly by towns and private farms. The affected ecosystems, according to Professor Pittock, are 'heading towards collapse'.[124]

The list of experts who are concerned about the likely failure of the Murray–Darling Basin Plan also includes the Environmental Defenders Office of Australia. It maintains that a minimum of 4000 gigalitres of water must be returned to the system to restore the ecological values of the river system and, in the absence of such a higher return, this goal 'may not be achieved'.[125]

Not all scientists agreed with the bleak view of progress under the Plan. The Long-Term Intervention Monitoring Project, a group of scientists monitoring fish, birds and vegetation, maintain that it will be a decade before any large-scale changes become evident, but that environmental benefits are slowly but surely being seen.[126] However, this assessment doesn't equate with the majority scientific view.

To the outsider, the discrepancy between the official and the independent scientific findings on the return of water to the river system cries out to be resolved. Is the river capable of being restored under the current Plan or not? Was the Plan ever designed to be more than a smoke-and-mirrors exercise to protect the status quo? Or worse still, was it a convenient cover for powerful vested interests to make a grab for the lion's share of the water? While the evidence is elusive, there seems little doubt on one point. The river system is a shadow of its original self. According to a 2018 CSIRO study, the average inflow to the Murray River during the past 20 years was almost half the 20th-century average.[127]

The return of a good season in 2020 after years of drought will ameliorate for a time the environmental and social impacts of a declining Basin. But the long-term trends are probably inescapable without a substantial change in policy. Specifically, the lack of ambition in the SDL needs to be addressed, as do the economic rationalist ideas that lie behind the water reform process.

There is already a steady drift of small irrigators selling out to agribusiness because they can't see a future in irrigation. 'We're definitely on our knees', one small irrigator recently told the press.[128] His sentiment is widespread. 'Worshipping at the altar of competition policy', Mal Peters, a farmer and former director of the National

Farmers' Federation, wrote, 'has delivered fewer farmers, a few mega family farms, increased corporatisation and overseas owned farms with rural town disintegration'.[129] He was not alone in issuing such a bleak assessment. In 2019, rural journalist Mike Foley wrote in *Queensland Country Life* that corporate farmers are buying out family farms at an increasing rate, changing the cropping mix in the process. The consequence, Foley notes, is that the viability of many country towns is under threat, along with jobs in regional processing plants.[130] In fact, if the Murray–Darling Basin Plan had to be changed to provide more water to the system, a lot of farmers would be adversely affected; many have mortgages leveraged off their water entitlements.[131] These complex, unaddressed structural issues have been largely overlooked in the political debate over the future of the Basin. The Basin Plan appears to be a case of 'too big to fail'.

However, change rolls on regardless. Experts are worried that the expansion of the almond and walnut industries threatens to repeat the environmental mistakes of the past. Almond consumption has skyrocketed around the world as the nut variety has emerged as a superfood. In California, though, the almond industry, which for years has been the world's largest, is accused of 'sucking the state dry'.[132]

In Australia, such a warning about the environmental impacts of the thirsty crop have been ignored as 'an agricultural goldrush' has been ushered in over almonds and walnuts.[133] Webster Ltd has planted over ten million almond trees, which will require a high level of permanent water for decades to come. Investors are swooning over the future profits from the valuable crop, confirming the theory that water gravitates to the highest return. But what are the social and environmental costs? Documents obtained by Karen Middleton of the *Saturday Paper* in June 2020 revealed the risk, in terms of water shortfalls, from the increase in permanent crops including almonds, which require regular, year-round watering. There's been no application of the triple bottom line to the expansion of this industry.

It is simply another environmental experiment in the Basin's long history of development at all costs.

Quentin Grafton is concerned about the lack of planning to ensure a sustainable level of extraction around the nut industry.[134] Others are more blunt. The almond sector's growing demand for water is a 'train smash' waiting to happen, according to Centre Alliance Senator Rex Patrick, who aired his concerns at a 2020 Senate estimates hearing about the almond industry's high demand for water. He claimed that the industry's water allocations often resulted from out-bidding other farmers. During the hearing, the regulator's faith in the water market emerged in an exchange between Patrick and MDBA head Phillip Glyde:

> 'Mr Gylde, you're a man of significant power, can you pick up the red phone and say "this is not on"?' Senator Patrick asked. 'I mean, you can just see it's a disaster waiting to happen.'

> Mr Gylde reiterated it was not the MDBA's job to intervene in the market.[135]

Such buck-passing of the difficult issues has become entrenched. Maryanne Slattery has run up against repeated obfuscation about the role of the Authority: 'On any big issue we've looked at, they'll either deny access to information, give you a mountain of peripheral information that requires expert analysis to make any sense of at all, or they supply reams and reams of pages but with all the information redacted'.[136] The Environmental Defenders Office has experienced the same obfuscation in its attempts to obtain information about the operation of the Plan through Freedom of Information requests.[137]

This lack of transparency goes to the heart of the failings of the Plan. It undermines public confidence and gives rise to accusations that agendas other than the public good are being pursued, or excused, by government; that water has become another form of 'crony capitalism' in the heart of government. Such an outcome was inevitable given the politicised process begun by John Howard and perpetrated by every government since. The experience of the Basin Plan shows that too little has been learned about Australia's history of flawed environmental management and the consequent failure to confront the development-at-all-costs approach that has brought the Basin to the point of crisis.

Watching the political fight over the fate of the Murry–Darling Basin were the descendants of the traditional owners. Members of the Basin's various Aboriginal nations raised their voices against the corporate greed destroying the rivers and ecosystems, but their rights and expertise were largely overlooked. How did this happen?

13

MARGINALISING THE INDIGENOUS VOICE

Just after the Menindee fish kill in January 2019, Barkindji elder, educator and artist William 'Badger' Bates went out looking for mussel shells along the Darling at Wilcannia to use in his art work. He soon realised that the mussels were nearly all gone and the few that were left were small and blistered as if they had been poisoned. The thought struck him about the place of the humble mussel in the cosmic scheme of nature: 'Our people depend on these mussels to eat and for bait, and all other animals depend on them for food'. Bates describes what he did next: 'I was so sad that I did an art work called Fragile River, which was about 30 hanging mussel shells polished and etched with animals that depend on the mussels for food, such as water rats, goannas, cod, perch and water birds'.[1]

This vignette symbolises the stark differences in the Aboriginal and Western approaches to nature and, by extension, to the environment of the Murray–Darling Basin. Virginia Marshall, a Wiradjuri Nyemba woman and Indigenous Postdoctoral Fellow at the Australian National University, has written about this aspect in her book, *Overturning Aqua Nullius: Securing Aboriginal Water Rights*.[2] After thousands of years, the spiritual relationship of being part of Country, she writes, 'remains integral, and despite the significant political and social change heaved upon the lives of Aboriginal communities the sacredness of water shapes the identity and values of Aboriginal peoples'. Marshall goes on to say that governments do not fully understand Aboriginal water knowledge and water values. Therefore, they treat the water needs of Aboriginal communities 'as just another interest group'.[3]

As documented in this book, the continuous thread in the Western development of the Basin has been the region's relentless exploitation. European-Australian identity was forged in the nation-building optimism around industrial-scale agriculture; nature was not even an afterthought. To the nation-builders, nature was an obstacle to their dreams of wealth and security. We built iterations of a mythology around the heroic pastoralists, farmers and struggling settlers doing battle with the environment to feed the nation and build exports. This attitude was the foundation of the thinking of most European-Australians until the 1990s when the reality of an unfolding disaster in the Basin could no longer be ignored.

Action since then, as the previous two chapters have highlighted, has involved a familiar politically compromised environmental response dictated by populist politics and powerful vested interests. As a consequence, the integrity of the Murray–Darling Basin Plan has wilted like a wheat crop in a drought. Inverell farmer and former rural political lobbyist Mal Peters summed up the current state of the Basin Plan in evidence to the South Australian Murray–Darling Basin Royal Commission:

> All we've done is set ourselves up for another [water reform process] because the Australian public are going to say, you've blown $13 billion of our bloody money, and the river's worse than what it was. So away we go again. So the irrigators will have to go through – I mean, it creates a major amount of anxiety for irrigators and the communities.[4]

Governments and bureaucrats have managed to convince themselves that minimal changes to the water flows will restore the ecosystem. And they ignore further damage to landscapes by allowing ongoing clearing of native vegetation for farming enterprises, despite the clear links identified over many decades between loss of vegetation and the impact of drought.[5] The bulldozer mentality lives on, often in contravention of environmental legislation and public opinion, and with the tacit support of governments.[6]

Of all the mainstream political parties, the Nationals best represent the compartmentalised worldview reflected in centuries of European thought – that the economy and the environment are separate entities; that humans can engineer nature to their needs; and that the disappearance of the natural world is of less concern than the potential disappearance of jobs. Just as the Nationals stymied effective action on soil conservation after the great dust storms of the 1930s and 1940s, and handed out too many water licences in the 1980s and 1990s, they have helped solidify opinion in the Coalition government against effective action on both water flows and climate change. And all the while farmers suffer.

The Nationals, due to their responsibility for managing water policy at state and federal levels, are responsible for undermining the Murray–Darling Basin Plan. As Tony Windsor explains, people think that the Plan, and especially the water buybacks, are 'just a racket and a rort that's been going on'. And, the Nationals, Windsor explains, have ceased to represent family farmers and small regional businesses, and now favour the big end of town: the mining companies, big irrigators and water barons.[7] In these ways the status quo has largely prevailed since the Coalition has been in power at the federal level from 2013. But the Nationals' conduct is merely an extreme manifestation of the inability of the major parties, evident for more than a century, to grapple with the failures of past agricultural policies, to reckon with our history of environmental destruction and to seriously embrace sustainable environmental values.

By contrast, the Basin's Indigenous people have an acute emotional and spiritual response to the ravages wrought by the Western model. They have watched the slow decline of the river system within their lifetimes. They've experienced this decline as a profound 'ecological loss' – of culture, spirituality, health and wellbeing – about which most Australians are unaware. William Bates has described this sense of loss. The Barka (Darling),

> is where we teach our children and speak our language. It is where we do our artwork, take photos, make videos, make songs and dances. We walk along the river and see where our ancestors cooked mussels or cut out a coolamon or canoe, and we connect with them and use this to interpret and understand our landscape … The river is our memory, we walk along it and remember our history and our ancestors.[8]

Bates sums up the different emotional worldviews of the declining quality of the Barka/Darling River through the example of the *kularku,* or brolga, which is the totem of one of the Barkindji families. To the Barkindji, these elegant and theatrical birds are 'our relations, they tell us things and dance for us. We don't kill or eat them because they are family'. But, to the MDBA, it is fine if 'there is somewhere where the brolgas can live, but they don't understand how it breaks our heart if they can't come and live on Barkindji country like they used to. They just don't get it at all'.[9]

Aboriginal community members repeatedly told the South Australian Royal Commission that the health and wellbeing of Aboriginal people is closely connected to the health of the river. They explained that especially since 2012 when declining flows set in, Aboriginal communities have experienced a lack of social cohesion and a decline in cultural practices. The ongoing threat to cultural practice has heightened the experience of dispossession for the Basin's Indigenous people.[10]

Yet, it is Aboriginal people's holistic approach to land management and their historical knowledge of the river and its ecosystem that have been missing from the Western approach of development at all costs.

The long history of development in the Murray–Darling Basin shows the persistence and the dynamic character of the Judeo-Christian idea of the right of humans to dominate nature. As previous chapters have shown, disaster has repeatedly accompanied this model: declining ecosystem health; species decline and extinction; chronic shortages of town water; algal blooms; and increased regularity of severe droughts. As Clarence Glacken, a former Professor of Geography at the University of California, has written, the old cultural assumptions about subduing nature in the quest for development remains 'a dominant philosophy of many governments, of the developer's mentality, and of many national and international corporations and conglomerates'.[11]

A different paradigm is needed. This was the clear finding from Commissioner Bret Walker whose close sifting of the voluminous evidence in the South Australian Murray–Darling Royal Commission highlighted the extent of the management failings of the Basin. Among his recommendations were a national program of reduced water for irrigation; the environmental requirements of the *Water Act 2007* to be followed; compensation and adjustment for farmers compelled to leave the land; and a more competent system of management. The case for structural reform in the management of the Basin was simply ignored by both the Commonwealth and the other states in the Basin. Our federal system failed again to rise to the challenges of managing the nation's water resources.

Walker had something to say, too, about the need for greater Aboriginal involvement in the management of the Basin. The guidance of the original custodians, in partnership with scientific experts, seems crucial, although such a suggestion would appear threatening to most of the agricultural interests in the Basin.

However, with the Basin Plan unravelling, and the spectre of irreversible climate change looming, it's reasonable to ask – is there an alternative? That challenge appears daunting: temperatures in the Basin will continue to rise, runoff will continue to fall, and rainfall is also in serious decline.[12] These trends are already having a deleterious impact on farming, shown by a decades-long decline in the profitability of many farms.[13]

Australian farmers are adapting to these realities, through sustainable farming techniques, but climate change is likely to make adaptation increasingly difficult.[14] Predictions are grim. A study conducted by Sarah Wheeler, Professor of Water Economics at the University of Adelaide, revealed that another 0.5° increase in temperature by 2041 will halve the current number of farmers in the Basin.[15] Climate change may, ultimately, do more damage than a failing Basin Plan. Their combined impacts will take us into uncharted territory. The MDBA has scrambled to take the issue seriously, while the Morrison government's lack of ambition on tackling climate change is turning Australia into an international pariah.

Meanwhile, the Basin's Indigenous people maintain their call to be part of the solution to the region's challenges. Yorta Yorta woman Monica Morgan writes that Aboriginal people 'have knowledge and insights that are essential to a sustainable future, not least the understanding to deconstruct many of those failed notions that have separated people from nature in this modern world, such as the view that water is simply an economic good'.[16]

Given these holistic values, why haven't Aboriginal people been given a meaningful voice to guide European-Australians to repair the damage inflicted on this region?

Lack of Aboriginal people's rights in the Basin

The past is the key to understanding the present state of Aboriginal engagement in water management in the Basin. Dispossession remains a bitter legacy. Chapter 3 highlighted the racist and economically self-serving motivations of the first Europeans who occupied the Basin. Despite ongoing claims for justice, Aboriginal people remained marginalised from decisions over their Country until the 1992 *Mabo* High Court decision recognised their rights to their traditional land.

The passage of the *Native Title Act 1993* (Cth) offered a tortuous legal process for Aboriginal people to regain their traditional land, and, consequently, it has largely failed the Basin's Aboriginal nations where white settlement has a long history. In all but one case, the legal bar to determine continuous cultural connection, as required under the Act, has proved to be too restrictive. And Indigenous water rights were not considered in that judgment.[17]

This limitation was revealed in the case of the Yorta Yorta nation, which occupies a region covering the Murray–Goulburn area. Theirs was the first native title case to be heard in the Federal Court. They lost the case along with a subsequent hearing in the High Court in 2002. The judgments are widely regarded as notorious examples of the failure of the legal system to protect the rights of Aboriginal people.[18] Justice Olney in the Federal Court determined that 'the tide of history' had washed away the Yorta Yorta's traditional laws and customs. Arriving at this view, he preferred the written history of white settler and amateur anthropologist Edward Curr over the oral histories of the Yorta Yorta themselves.[19] Landowners and agricultural businesses in the area lobbied hard to have their titles validated.

The Barkindji are the only Indigenous group to have won a native title claim in the Murray–Darling Basin. Achieved in 2015 after a 17-year legal struggle, the victory conferred little real control over the waters of the Darling, essential to their survival as a culture. Control over water was denied on the assumption that, in common law, 'water in its natural state is not amenable to ownership'.[20] That is, of course, unless the water is privatised under a competing Western view of property rights, when anything can be commodified.

The national water reform process has also made little impact in changing the power relationships between Indigenous and non-Indigenous people in the Basin. On offer has been little more than nebulous and tokenistic commitments to Aboriginal engagement.

The introduction of the National Water Initiative in 2004 – which enshrined legally tradeable and transferable water use entitlements for Europeans – promised the traditional owners improved access to water for cultural reasons and increased participation in water planning and management.[21] A few years later, the 2007 *Water Act* offered much the same platitudes. It instructed the MDBA to 'have regard to' Indigenous issues in the management of the Basin.

However, in one key respect, the water reform process has perpetuated Aboriginal dispossession. Indigenous people in the Basin are effectively cut out of the water trading market through their historic exclusion from owning land when water entitlements were distributed. The Australian Competition and Consumer Commission was told in the course of its recent inquiry into the water market that 'This historic (and ongoing) lack of access to water rights not only deprives Traditional Owners of the means by which to care for Country and support economic development, but it also precludes them from participating in the water market itself'.[22]

Thus, Aboriginal people have continued to be placed in a weak position regarding their rights to water. The Murray Lower Darling Rivers Indigenous Nations explained to the South Australian Murray–Darling Royal Commission:

> Native title, in particular, has largely been held to vest in land. As a consequence, key rights and interests … in respect of water is a more unsettled proposition … In fully allocated water systems such as the [Murray–Darling Basin] there is little scope for First Nations to exercise native title rights in relation to waters, including those waters that by custom, tradition or spirituality are centrally connected to culture and its revitalisation.[23]

However, this weak legal position hasn't stopped Indigenous groups in the Basin from pressing their case for water rights. In 2005 the concept of 'cultural flows' was adopted as a means to articulate Aboriginal claims to water in the Basin. Yorta Yorta man Lee Joachim explained that, while the term means different things for each Aboriginal nation, it is about sustaining all forms of life.[24]

The idea of cultural flows is not designed to be anti-development. Rather, the river must come first, its seasons and cycles respected and, in turn, economic needs can be provided for as part of a reciprocal relationship. Of course, this challenges the Western view of nature being physically transformed to be 'useful', in a process that over time has led to the degradation of much of the Basin.

In 2012, as the Murray–Darling Basin Plan was being finalised, a group of 21 Indigenous nations, coalescing around the Northern Murray–Darling Aboriginal Nations, issued a demand that all water licences be revoked and that the river's water be dealt with from a recognition of Aboriginal sovereignty. As one commentator noted: 'For Indigenous groups to have any confidence that their interests in water will be both recognised and enforceable, they need to be supported by legislation'.[25]

While little progress has been made on these broader demands, there have been glimmers of hope for Aboriginal people at the local level. Small-scale restoration projects have been central to enabling younger generations of Aboriginal people in the Basin to reconnect with culture, and to forge a commitment to national water reform. In 2000 the Narri Narri Council began managing 11 300 hectares of Riverina land, 35 kilometres west of Hay in New South Wales. The land started out 'looking like the Sahara', but, after six years of hard work and the planting of 20 000 native trees through funding from state and federal bodies, a group of community-minded locals created a lush retreat. It became a place for the Indigenous community to relax and protect their culture and heritage. 'Families use the property to camp and fish, it has been a way for Aboriginal families to get their kids out of town when times aren't so great and teach them about the land.'[26]

Similar small-scale restoration projects on land owned or

frequented by Aboriginal people in the Basin have created mini oases in 'clapped out cotton country'. The projects reveal a powerful lesson: if only a small percentage of water could be diverted to the rivers from the vast reserves appropriated by the cotton industry, Aboriginal people would obtain a different social outcome as well as an environmental outcome.[27]

The restoration projects have also had an impact on towns, with locals coming out to inspect the changes, sparking conversations about how to do things differently. Such experiences bring to the fore a recognition that the present system is not sustainable, and underline how Aboriginal interests in water have more in common with those of ordinary townspeople than is commonly understood.[28]

Lack of consultation

Indigenous representative organisations have continued to criticise governments, especially the federal government, for their lack of meaningful consultation around the Murray–Darling Basin Plan and its implementation. Having said that, Aboriginal representative organisations have a range of views about this process.

The Ngarrindjeri, for example, have explained that, since 2009, they have been in a meaningful formal agreement with the South Australian government, which 'guides and facilitates equitable Ngarrindjeri engagement in water resource research, policy development and management processes within the SA Murray–Darling Basin region'. However, they have concerns that the Commonwealth government has failed to properly implement the Basin Plan.

Victoria also has the reputation of meaningful engagement with Aboriginal people over the management of water in the Basin. Successive Victorian governments have produced a plethora of policy documents mandating consultative processes, and two pieces of legislation – the 1989 *Water Act* and the 2010 *Traditional Owner*

Settlement Act – recognise Aboriginal people's right to access water for cultural purposes. But neither Act recognises native title rights to water.

Even with the experience of several decades of consultative processes in Victoria, facilitated through the Murray Lower Darling River Indigenous Nations, the actual level of meaningful engagement remains fraught. One observer of this process has written that: 'The different parties discussing river health at [these meetings] assumed that they were all talking about the same thing when in fact they were talking past each other'. The bureaucratic idea of 'natural resource management' was not the same thing as 'caring for country': 'Where traditional owners from the Murray River see humans as part of the continuum of "country", the water managers were by-and-large seeing humans as essentially separate to and above the river – and in control of it'.[29]

Caring for Country cuts directly across the Western concept of dominance over nature. When traditional owners speak about caring for Country, 'they are speaking about a reciprocal relationship whereby country is also caring for them', according to academic Jessica Weir.[30] Further marginalising meaningful consultation and participation is the bureaucratic process in which the current dialogue with Aboriginal people is largely constructed.

The Barkindji have faced an ever-changing bureaucracy:

> NSW water agencies and departments have faced water cycle changes and undergone widespread restructures … including the dismantling of the once 11-person Aboriginal-specific water unit. Such changes have reduced the capacity of government to address these [Aboriginal] issues.[31]

As governments control the style of consultation and participation, it is easy to consign Aboriginal views to the periphery. The experience of the Murray Lower Darling River Indigenous Nations is that:

> The actual approach taken to Indigenous consultation by government is that there is no duty to act on or accommodate Indigenous interests or views in binding outcomes, adapt government positions or policy, negotiate or bargain with First Nations, recognise at law the special connection or relationships of First Nations to waters, or construe dealings with First Nations as a unique question of the governance of water resources.[32]

These tokenistic forms of consultation highlight the remnants of a colonial attitude towards Murray–Darling Basin Aboriginal people. This is certainly the experience of William 'Badger' Bates, who says that officials from both the Murray–Darling Basin Authority and the New South Wales government rarely come to the far west of the state to consult his people. And when they do come, it's usually 'the same old thing':

> They give us hardly any notice or agenda, they turn up with maps and charts and want us to give them feedback on things without being able to think about it and understand it. They hold separate colour coded meetings for the whitefellas and the blackfellas. We never get any feedback, or minutes, so they could be reporting on anything, we wouldn't know. And they never seem to take into account what we say.[33]

In fact, between 2016 and 2018, Barkindji traditional owners organised protests, lobbied state and federal governments and sent delegations to federal Parliament to highlight their concerns. Despite this strong advocacy, 'Barkindji people's views have been consistently marginalised in negotiations over water sharing and management'.[34]

The MDBA has paid only lip service to engaging with the traditional owners of the Basin. In his Royal Commission report, Bret Walker was scathing of the MDBA's record. He pointed out that there was no requirement for membership of the MDBA Board to include an Aboriginal person. Representation of Aboriginal interests is dealt with through the Basin Community Committee and its Indigenous water subcommittee, which is required to include at least two Indigenous persons with expertise in Indigenous matters relevant to the Basin's water resources. But as Walker pointed out, this meant that although Aboriginal people are represented in an advisory capacity in Basin water management, they have no guaranteed place at the main decision-making table.

This position changed at the end of 2020 when Nari Nari man Rene Woods was appointed as the Indigenous Board member to the MDBA. However, by comparison, the New South Wales government has mandated that three positions for Aboriginal people be included in the state's top bushfire planning committee, in recognition of Indigenous cultural expertise in bushfire management.[35] Nevertheless, Indigenous people continue to press their claims for greater recognition of their water rights. In 2020 the federal government established the Committee on Aboriginal Water Interests 'to develop a new NWI element covering Indigenous people's interests in water'.[36]

Neverthless, the limited role accorded by governments to Aboriginal people's involvement in water management to date reflects the reality that there's little political will to do any more. Incorporating Aboriginal rights and values into the management of the Murray–Darling Basin would require taking water from other users in the system. And governments continue to claim the exclusive right to decide water allocations, while being held hostage to the vested interests who continue to operate in a model that most experts – along with Aboriginal people – regard as unsustainable in the long term.

CONCLUSION:
A PATH FORWARD

History is the starting point in dealing with the unfolding tragedy of the Murray–Darling Basin. There are several interrelated components to this historical reckoning. The first is coming to terms with the culture of environmental vandalism that has driven nearly two centuries of over-development. As I have documented throughout the book, the Basin has confronted a series of environmental catastrophes of which the Menindee fish kill was merely the latest. For much of the region's European history, this vandalism manifested itself in a campaign of extermination waged against native wildlife. It has been manifest, too, in a wilful over-extraction of the region's two principal resources: soil and water. Prime Minister Paul Keating came closest to a national acknowledgment of the problem, but he shied away from instigating a dialogue of understanding and awareness.

This pro-development ethos has been the driving force of a vandalism that became embedded in Australian culture from the time the squatters grabbed the opportunity to develop the pastoral industry to service the British Empire. Warnings about the adverse consequences of development from experts and scientists have been repeatedly ignored. The political system became hostile to science. Preference has been given to grand nation-building schemes and vested interests. Great wealth followed development, but so has human suffering and environmental damage, notably during the Federation Drought and the dust bowl years, both events now largely forgotten. Thus, the post–World War Two attempts at soil conservation, tree planting and salinity control were all undermined by political compromise. Science was again overlooked in the preparation of the 2012 Murray–Darling Basin Plan. Vested interests in the cotton, rice and almond industries held too much sway. For nearly 200 years we have let one crisis roll into the next without understanding the long-term lessons, or being much interested in them.

Lastly, and importantly, the history of dispossession must be addressed so that Aboriginal people are empowered to be equal participants in the future management of the Basin. Above all, Indigenous people want their rights as First Nations acknowledged. In their submission to the South Australian Royal Commission, the Ngarrindjeri put it this way:

> The Ngarrindjeri have occupied, enjoyed, managed and used our inherited lands and waters of the River Murray, Lakes and Coorong since time immemorial. Ngarrindjeri consider that Ngarrindjeri have first right attached to the exercise of our cultural rights, interests and responsibilities, that precede all other rights … the MDBA should commence their consideration of allocations [of water] without interference of these rights.[1]

Of paramount importance to the Basin's Indigenous people is the need to engage with their ecological knowledge – passed down through the generations – in determining water management.

The current top-down approach is failing both farmers and the environment. It is a process in which vested interests obtain favoured insider status in a model underpinned by a misguided faith that the free market can solve the conflict between environmental and human values. Respecting environmental values by harnessing scientific knowledge, Indigenous cultural values and regenerative farming techniques[2] hold out the best prospect that the wounded country of the Murray–Darling Basin might heal and a sustainable Basin be achieved.

POSTSCRIPT

The townsfolk of Menindee were in uproar again. In January 2021, their water supply in the local weir turned green and stank. Thick slime covered a third of its surface. WaterNSW declared a red alert for a possible toxic blue-green algal bloom in the lower Darling. The alert meant that residents could no longer drink the water. Farmers needed to watch their livestock.[1]

The townspeople claim that water from the drought-breaking rains of early 2020 wasn't flowing to them in sufficient quantities to flush the system, creating the conditions for the algal bloom. In fact, locals warned that the river was in the same poor shape as it had been in 2018, the year before the Menindee fish kill. The potential for another ecological catastrophe loomed.

Local photographer Michael Minns had been documenting the situation, posting videos and photos of the river on Facebook, showing the extent of the blue-green algae outbreak.

'They've used environmental water to help trigger extraction volumes upstream, while we are dealing with algae blooms down here,' he wrote.

'We are two years on from the worst fish kill in the Murray–Darling Basin and we are lining up for a similar set of events in 12 months' time.' It was, he said, 'beyond bizarre'.[2]

'Predictable' might be the other response.

ACKNOWLEDGMENTS

I was fortunate to have had the assistance of many people. Foremost among these are the outstanding staff at NewSouth. Phillipa McGuinness backed the project and helped shape its early stages while her successor, Elspeth Menzies, has been generous with her editorial guidance. Indeed, the entire staff at NewSouth are a wonderful team to work with, and I thank them for their interest and support. John Mapps provided valuable editorial assistance.

I was also fortunate in being able to draw upon the expertise of key participants in the debate over the Murray–Darling Basin. I would like to thank the following people who gave interviews to the project: Professor Quentin Grafton, Professor Tim Flannery, Mr Tony Windsor, Dr Virginia Marshall and Mr Paul Lane.

I was also able to draw on the comments and insights on parts of the draft manuscript from William Badger Bates, a Barkindji elder (chapters 1 and 13 and conclusion) and Maryanne Slattery and Professor Grafton (chapter 12). I thank these people for the time they devoted to the project.

Dr Virginia Marshall, a Wiradjuri Nyemba woman and Indigenous Postdoctoral Fellow at the Australian National University, acted as an Indigenous consultant to the manuscript and provided many insightful comments from her extensive historical and cultural knowledge.

My old friend Tim Muirhead came up with the book's title during a chat over coffee.

The University of the Sunshine Coast offered access to their library facilities, for which I thank them.

As has been the case with my previous books, my wife Marilyn gave generously of her time to talk over the issues and to provide extensive feedback on the various drafts. I appreciate the support she gives to my writing projects.

Of course, the author takes responsibility for the contents of the book.

APPENDIX

Droughts affecting the Murray–Darling Basin

YEAR	POPULAR NAME	EXTENT
1790–1795	Settlement Drought	Probably whole of south-east Australia – i.e. extending beyond the Basin
1797–1805		Probably whole of south-east Australia
1809–14	Great Drought	Probably whole of Murray–Darling Basin
1824–30	Sturt's Drought	Northern Basin
1836–45		Probably whole of south-east Australia
1849–53	Black Thursday Drought	South-east Australia
1861–66	Goyder's Line Drought	South-east Australia
1877–78		Southern Queensland and New South Wales
1881–86		Southern Basin
1895–1903	Federation Drought	South-east Australia
1911–15	First War Drought	Northern Basin
1926–26		South-east Australia
1935–45	Second War Drought	South-east Australia
1952		Northern Basin
1964–65		Whole of Murray–Darling Basin
1982–83	Dust Cloud Drought	South-east Australia
1990–95		South-east Australia
1997–2009	Millennial Drought	South-east Australia
2012–20		South-east Australia

Adapted from: *Australian Bureau of Statistics Year Book Australia, 1988*; *Australian Bureau of Meteorology Previous Droughts*.

NOTES

Introduction

The Murray–Darling Ministerial Council (2002), *The Living Murray*, The Murray–Darling Basin Commission.

1   Anatomy of an ecological disaster
1   ABC News, 19 July 2019.
2   Ehrenkranz and Sampson, 2008.
3   *Guardian*, 7 March 2019.
4   Interview, Radio 101.5, Adelaide, 10 January 2019.
5   Mahood, 2019.
6   See Austen, 'Power Women: Farmer Kate McBride on the Power of Going Viral', Whimn.com.au; ABC, *Australian Story*, 'The Darling of Menindee', 7 May 2019.
7   Pike, 2019.
8   *Sydney Morning Herald*, 9 March 2018.
9   NineNews.com.au, 9 January 2019.
10   Blog, 'behindenemylines', nd.
11   *Guardian*, 28 January 2019.
12   *Barrier Daily Truth*, 16 May 2019.
13   *Saturday Paper*, 19 January 2019.
14   Kingsford, 2017.
15   *Guardian*, 7 February 2019.
16   Smith, 2019.
17   Kingsford, 2019a.
18   *Guardian*, 19 January 2019.
19   Slattery and Campbell, 2019.
20   Foley, 2017.
21   Foley, 2017.
22   Farm Online, 17 January 2019.
23   Kingsford, 2019b.
24   Slattery and Campbell, 2019, p. 2.
25   Volkofsky, 2019.
26   Easton, 2019.
27   *Guardian*, 19 February 2019.
28   Cited in Smyth, 2019.
29   *Guardian*, 27 July 2017.
30   *Guardian*, 27 September 2017.
31   *Advertiser*, 8 March 2018.
32   See Beresford 2015, 2018.

33   *Land,* 10 January 2019.
34   Davies, 2019a.
35   *Guardian*, 31 January 2019.
36   Chan, 2017.
37   Forbes, 2019.
38   de Garis, 2013.
39   Smith, 2018.
40   Cattle, 2006.
41   Arnold, 2019.
42   Cited in Cockburn, 2019.
43   Arnold, 2019.
44   News.com.au, 10 January 2019.
45   Cockburn, 2019.
46   Interview, Virginia Marshall, April 2021.
47   See ABC, *Australian Story*, 2019; *Northern Star* 29 January 2019.
48   Australian Explorer, 'Menindee'.
49   Smyth, 2019.
50   William 'Badger' Bates, Statement to the South Australian Murray–Darling Royal Commission.
51   *Guardian,* 26 July 2017.
52   NITV News, 25 July 2017.
53   NITV News, 16 January 2019.
54   Thorpe, 2019.
55   Cited in Smyth, 2019.
56   *Guardian*, 17 February 2019.

2   Men of Empire
1   *World's News*, 26 August 1911.
2   Foster, 1985.
3   Cited in Genoni, nd, p. 3.
4   Cited in *Canberra Times*, 10 April 1965.
5   Weller, 2012.
6   Sturt, *Two Expeditions,* Vol 1, Chapter 2, 'Desolation of the country'.
7   Sturt, *Two Expeditions,* Vol 2, Chapter 7.
8   Reynolds, 1980.
9   Genoni, nd.
10   Genoni, nd.
11   Australian Law Reform Commission, 2010.
12   Sturt, *Two Expeditions,* Vol 1, Preliminary chapter.
13   Macklin, p. 77.
14   Cumpston, 1954.
15   Day, 1996.
16   Day, 2001.
17   Day, 2001.
18   Lang, 1875, Vol 1, p. 201.
19   Cited in Russell, 2009.
20   Sturt, *Two Expeditions,* Vol 1, Preliminary chapter.

21 Cumpston, 1951. In compiling this chapter I accessed the digital journals of both Sturt and Mitchell and also JHL Cumpston's biographies of Sturt and Mitchell. All are published by the Gutenberg project. However, none have pagination in their digital format. I have identified the quotes from Sturt's and Michell's journal either by the date of entry or the chapter.

22 Wright, 2011, p. 99.

23 Wright, 2011.

24 Weller, 2012.

25 Foster, 1985, pp. 39, 64.

26 Mitchell, *Three Expeditions,* Vol 1, 26 November 1831.

27 Sturt, *Two Expeditions*, Vol 1, Preliminary chapter, 'System of immigration recommended; encouragement for emigration'.

28 Mitchell, *Three Expeditions*, Vol 1, 27 June 1835.

29 Mitchell, *Three Expeditions*, Vol 1, chapter 1.1, and Kelly, 1980, p. 15.

30 Kelly, 1980.

31 Lydon, 2017.

32 Atkinson, 2003.

33 Cited in Cited in Atkinson, 2003, p. 117.

34 Cited in Attwood and Foster, 2003, p. 10.

35 Karskens, 2015.

36 Read, 1988, p. 5.

37 Weller, 2012.

38 Kelly, 1980.

39 Kelly, 1980.

40 Bishop and White, 2015.

41 Cited in Baker, 1995, pp. 45–46.

42 Hardy, 1976, p. 2.

43 Victorian Legislative Council, 1845, Minutes of Evidence, p. 10.

44 Sturt, *Two Expeditions*, Vol 1, Chapter six, 'Intercourse with natives'.

45 Sturt, *Two Expeditions*, Vol 2, Chapter 4.

46 Jenkins, 1979, p. 12.

47 Cited in Jenkins, 1979, p. 16, see also chapter 3.

48 Jenkins, 1979, p. 2.

49 Sturt, *Two Expeditions,* Vol 2, Chapter 5.

50 Sturt, *Two Expeditions,* Vol 1, Chapter 4, 'Effect of firing a gun'.

51 Sturt, *Two Expeditions,* Vol 2, Chapter 4.

52 Sturt, *Two Expeditions*, Vol 1, Chapter 3, 'Customs of the natives'.

53 Cumpston, 1951.

54 Sturt, *Two Expeditions*, Vol 2, Chapter 4.

55 Mitchell, *Three Expeditions,* Vol 2, Preamble.

56 Mitchell, *Three Expeditions,* Vol 2, 24 and 25 April 1836.

57 Baker, 1995.

58 Mitchell, *Three Expeditions,* Vol 2, 3 July 1836.

59 Mitchell, *Three Expeditions,* Vol 1, 11 April 1835.

60 Cited in Willetts, nd.

61 Mitchell, *Three Expeditions,* Vol 1, 29 June 1835.

62 Hardy, 1976, p. 39.

63   Baker, 1995.
64   Mitchell, *Three Expeditions*, Vol 2, Chapter 3.1.
65   Mitchell, *Three Expeditions*, Vol 2, Chapter 3.14.
66   Baker, 1995.
67   Monument Australia, nd.
68   Cited in Wilson, 1992.
69   Mitchell, *Three Expeditions*, Vol 1, 10 August 1835.
70   Mitchell, *Three Expeditions*, Vol 2, 7 October 1836.
71   Cited in Cumpston, 1954.
72   Sturt, *Two Expeditions*, Chapter 2, 'Native village'.
73   Cited in Pascoe, 2018, p. 109.
74   Mitchell, *Three Expeditions*, Vol 1, June 1935.
75   Gammage, 2011, and Pascoe, 2018.
76   Mitchell, *Three Expeditions*, Vol 1, 14 July 1935.
77   Mitchell, Three *Expeditions*, Vol 2, chapter 3.14.
78   Geisinger, 1999.
79   Mitchell, *Three Expeditions*, Vol 1, 17 June and 7 July 1835.
80   Mitchell, *Three Expeditions*, Vol 2, chapter 3.14.
81   'American Wilderness Philosophy', in Internet Encyclopedia of Philosophy.
82   Collingwood-Whittick, 2008, p. 67.
83   Ryan, 1996, p. 73.
84   Sturt, *Two Expeditions*, Vol 1, Chapter 3, 'Natives perishing from famine'.
85   Mitchell, *Three Expeditions*, Vol 1, 9 April 1835.
86   Mitchell, *Three Expeditions*, Vol 1, 9 April 1835.
87   Mitchell, *Three Expeditions*, Vol 2, 21 September 1836.
88   Sturt, *Two Expeditions*, Vol 2, Chapter 5.
89   Sturt, *Two Expeditions*, Vol 2, Chapter 7.
90   *Daily Mercury*, 9 November 1929.
91   *The Riverina Gazette*, 24 May 1929.

3   The great white land grab
1   *Don Dorrigo Gazette*, 7 October 1932.
2   Beinart and Hughes, 2007.
3   Beinart and Hughes, 2007.
4   Jervis, 1955.
5   Sturt, *Two Expeditions*, Vol 1, Chapter 2.
6   Dowling, 1997, p. 53.
7   Cited in Dowling, 1997, p. 56.
8   Dowling, 1997.
9   Poulter, 2014.
10   Campbell, 2002.
11   Mear, 2008.
12   Campbell, 2002.
13   Mitchell, *Three Expeditions*, Vol 1, 7 July, 1835. See also 28 May 1835.
14   New South Wales Legislative Council, 1845, p. 27.
15   New South Wales Legislative Council, 1845, p. 27.
16   New South Wales Legislative Council, 1845, p. 34.

17 New South Wales Legislative Council, 1845, p. 35.
18 Cited in Campbell, 2002, p. 126.
19 *Daily Telegraph,* 30 July 1919.
20 Victorian Legislative Council, 1858–59, p. 32.
21 Scott, 2001.
22 *Daily Express,* 8 October 1932; *Australian Women's Weekly*, 18 April 1973.
23 Scott, 2001.
24 NSW Select Committee, 1845, p. 17.
25 NSW Select Committee, 1845, p. 8.
26 NSW Select Committee, 1845, p. 37.
27 Wright, 2004, pp. 55–56.
28 Pascoe, 2014.
29 Riches, 2019.
30 NSW Select Committee, 1845, p. 46.
31 Pybus, 2020.
32 NSW Select Committee, 1845, p. 46.
33 Victoria Legislative Council, 1858–59, p. 30.
34 Victoria Legislative Council, 1858–59, p. 77.
35 The Aboriginal History of the Yarra, nd.
36 New South Wales Legislative Council, 1845, p. 55.
37 Queensland Legislative Assembly, 1861, p. 6.
38 Withycombe, 2015.
39 New South Wales Legislative Council, 1845, p. 39.
40 Broome, 2015.
41 Fleming, 2007.
42 Hardy, 1976, p. 51.
43 Hardy, 1976.
44 *The South Australian Colonist*, 23 June 1840.
45 Reynolds, 1974.
46 Laurie, 1958.
47 See Kerkhove, 2014; Broome, 2015.
48 Reece, 2006.
49 Reynolds, 1982, p. 69.
50 Kerkhove, 2014, p. 49.
51 James and Bain, 2016; Jalata, 2013.
52 Broome, 2005, p. 81.
53 Ryan, 2018, p. 89.
54 Ryan, 2018, p. 89.
55 Clark, 1995, and Bottoms, 2013.
56 Cited in Evans and Thorpe, 2001, p. 31.
57 Ryan, 2018, p. 97.
58 Reece, 2006, pp. 1–2.
59 *Guardian*, 27 July 2019.
60 *Guardian,* 27 July 2019.
61 Morris, 1992.
62 Jalata, 2013.
63 *Sydney Monitor and Commercial Advertiser*, 25 February 1839.

64   Lindsay, 2007.
65   Hardy, 1976.
66   Richards, 2008, p. 6; Bottoms, 2013.
67   Richards, 2008, p. 5.
68   Legislative Assembly Queensland, 1861, p. 19.
69   New South Wales Legislative Council, 1845, p. 10.
70   French, 1990.
71   Cited in Day, 2001, p. 79.
72   Littman and Paluck, 2015.
73   Michael Sturma's 1985 article, 'Myall Creek and the Psychology of Mass Murder', stands as the most explicit attempt to explore this topic. While there are parallels in our approaches, I have been able to access more extensive literature on both frontier violence and the theory of collective violence than was available to Sturma, and my focus is wider than the Myall Creek Massacre.
74   Smith, 2011, p. 165.
75   See, for example, Bottoms, 2013.
76   Cited in Bottoms, 2013, p. 1.
77   *Hilston Spectator and Lachlan River Advertiser*, 8 June 1906.
78   Cited in Clark, 1995, p. 1.
79   Russell, 2010.
80   James and Bain, 2016.
81   Cahir, 2014; see also Stone, 2019.
82   Jenkins, 1979, p. 4.
83   *The Maitland Mercury*, 3 February 1847.
84   Littman and Paluck, 2015, p. 83.
85   Russell, 2010, p. 94.
86   Cahir, 2014.
87   Weaver, 1996, p. 983.
88   Weaver, 1996.
89   Cahir, 2001.
90   *Hay Standard and Advertiser*, 25 February 1891.
91   Cahir, 2014.
92   Cahir, 2001, p. 102.
93   *Hay Standard and Advertiser*, 25 February 1891.
94   South Australian Legislative Council, 1860, p. 47.
95   Cohrs, 2012.
96   Littman and Paluck, 2015.
97   Withycombe, 2015.
98   Withycombe, 2015.
99   Davis, 1908.
100 Cited in Clark, 1995, p. 94.
101 Victoria Legislative Council, 1858–59, p. 36.
102 South Australian Legislative Council, 1860, p. 83.
103 New South Wales Legislative Council, 1845, p 79.
104 New South Wales Legislative Council, 1845, p. 94.
105 Broome, 2005, p. 91.
106 Victorian Legislative Council, 1858–59, p. 83.

107 *Guardian*, 4 March 2019.
108 *Guardian*, 4 March 2019.
109 *Burrowa News*, 27 October 1899.
110 Interview, Virginia Marshall, April 2021.

4   Riches and ruins: The dreams of squatters and selectors
1   *Evening News*, 6 October 1885.
2   *Sydney Morning Herald*, 29 June 1855.
3   Beinart and Hughes, 2007, p. 102.
4   *Morning Chronicle*, 25 May 1844.
5   Simpson, 2016.
6   Morrisey, 1972.
7   Henzell, 2007.
8   Morrisey, 1972.
9   Morrisey, 1972.
10   *Leader,* 12 December 1863.
11   *Queenslander,* 22 December 1866.
12   *Burrowa News,* 7 February 1879.
13   Hardy, 1976.
14   Cited in Hardy, 1976, p. 83.
15   *Murray Pioneer and Australasian River Record*, 19 December 1924.
16   Draper, 2009, p. 3.
17   *Launceston Examiner*, 18 March 1846.
18   Hickman, 1975.
19   *Brisbane Telegraph*, 21 November 1925.
20   *Darling Downs Gazette and General Advertiser*, 11 November 1875.
21   Thomas, 1984.
22   Wright, 2004, p. 3.
23   Victorian Legislative Council, 1858–59, p. iv.
24   Harrison, 2004.
25   *Scone Advocate*, 14 February 1908.
26   Victorian Legislative Council, 1858–59, p. 3.
27   Harrison, 2004.
28   New South Wales Legislative Council, 1845, p. 19.
29   *Sydney Morning Herald*, 10 August 1854.
30   Beckett, 1958, p. 41.
31   Beckett, 1958, p. 43.
32   Beckett, 1958, p. 104.
33   Evan, Saunders and Cronin, 1993.
34   Beckett, 1958; Evan, Saunders and Cronin, 1993.
35   *South Australian Register*, 22 June 1875.
36   New South Wales Legislative Council, 1845, p. 17.
37   Beckett, 1958, p. 36.
38   Hardy, 1976.
39   Hardy, 1976.
40   Beckett, 1958.
41   Beckett, 1958.

42 Cited in Beckett, 1958, p. 44.

43 See White, 2011, for a summary of this debate.

44 Atkinson, 2000.

45 *Australian News*, 27 June 1866.

46 South Australian Legislative Council, Report, p. 1.

47 *Advertiser*, 27 April 1903.

48 *Brisbane Courier*, 25 October 1870.

49 *Sydney Mail and New South Wales Advertiser*, 1 February 1879.

50 *Chronicle*, 31 January 1935.

51 *Sydney Gazette*, 23 February 1839.

52 *Courier*, 25 March 1846.

53 *Sydney Mail and New South Wales Advertiser*, 1 February 1879.

54 McCulloch, 1966.

55 Gipps' despatch was reported in full in the *Port Phillip Patriot and Melbourne Advertiser*, 10 July 1845.

56 *Morning Chronicle*, 28 December 1844.

57 *Argus*, 28 April 1855.

58 *The Age*, 25 June 1932.

59 *Weekly Register of Politics, Facts and General Literature*, 1 March 1845.

60 *Argus*, 14 May 1853.

61 *Sydney Mail and New South Wales Advertiser*, 7 May 1874.

62 *Townsville Daily Bulletin*, 30 December 1949.

63 *Labor Daily*, 19 March 1927.

64 Sadeghian, 2016, p. 13.

65 Hirst, 2010, p. 210.

66 Sadeghian, 2016.

67 *Shipping Gazette and Sydney General Trade List*, 5 December 1853.

68 *Sydney Mail and New South Wales Advertiser*, 29 January 1887.

69 *Riverina Herald*, 10 January 1921.

70 *Scone Advocate*, 5 May 1950.

71 *Queenslander*, 22 October 1892.

72 *Queenslander*, 22 October 1892.

73 *Sydney Mail and New South Wales Advertiser*, 29 January 1887.

74 *Newcastle Morning Herald and Miners' Advocate*, 24 June 1894.

75 *South Australia Register*, 26 March 1854.

76 *Sydney Mail and New South Wales Advertiser*, 29 January 1887.

77 Murray, 1953.

78 *Riverina Herald*, 14 September 1921.

79 O'Gorman, 2012.

80 O'Gorman, 2012.

81 Interview, Virginia Marshall, April 2021.

82 *Australian Town and Country Journal*, 7 May 1870.

83 *Braidwood Dispatch and Mining Journal*, 14 October 1949.

84 Hirst, 2010.

85 Hirst, 2010.

86 Botterill, 2006.

87 *Bell's Life in Sydney*, 5 January 1856.

88 *The Age* ran an article on its 73rd anniversary titled, 'The Struggle with the Squatters', 13 July 1927.
89 *Argus*, 14 May 1853.
90 Cameron, 2005, p. 61.
91 *Bega Gazette and Eden District Advertiser*, 31 July 1873.
92 *Advocate*, 20 April 1879.
93 *Leader*, 27 April 1878.
94 Allen, 2012.
95 Allen, 2012.
96 *Wagga Wagga Express,* 29 June 1874.
97 *Geelong Advertiser*, 16 June 1865.
98 *The Age*, 11 November 1876.
99 Quick, 1883, pp. 66–68.
100 Quick, 1883, p. 78.
101 *Queensland Figaro*, 3 February 1883.
102 Roberts, 1968, p. 240.
103 *Bendigo Independent*, 19 October 1893.
104 *Molong Argus*, 23 April 1909.
105 *Ovens and Murray Advertiser*, 29 August 1912.
106 Waterson, 1968, p. 147.
107 Quick, 1883.
108 *Freeman's Journal*, 14 April 1894.
109 *Sydney Mail and New South Wales Advertiser*, 6 June 1874.
110 Waterson, 1968, p. 147.
111 Quick, 1883, p. 85.
112 New South Wales Royal Commission, 1885.
113 *Ovens and Murray Advertiser,* 29 April 1880.
114 *Dungog Chronicle,* 1 October 1995.
115 *Bendigo Advertiser*, 29 April 1885.
116 *Bacchus Marsh Express*, 8 May 1880.
117 *Australian Sketcher*, 8 May 1880.
118 *Australian Town and Country Journal*, 16 October 1880.
119 *Queenslander*, 2 February 1874.
120 *Ovens and Murray Advertiser*, 27 April 1880.
121 *Bacchus Marsh Express*, 8 May 1880.
122 *The Weekly*, 21 June 1902.
123 Waterson, 1968, p 164–65.
124 Roberts, 1968, p. 238.
125 McKernan, 2005, p. 32.
126 Day, 1996.
127 Frost, Malam and Williams, 2014.
128 Frost, Malam and Williams, 2014.
129 *Weekly Times*, 21 June 1902.

5   The war on nature

1   *Maitland Mercury and Hunter River General Advertiser,* 14 September 1893.
2   *Bundaberg Mail and Burnett Advertiser*, 20 September 1897.

3   Headlines in sequential order: *Advertiser*, 7 February 1989; *Daily Mercury*, 31 July 1928; *Scone Advocate*, 26 August 1921; *Warwick Daily News*, 3 August 1927.
4   *Courier Mail*, 11 February 1938.
5   Barr and Cary, 1992.
6   *Singleton Argus,* 2 May 1894.
7   *Sydney Mail and New South Wales Advertiser*, 19 December 1885.
8   *Singleton Argus*, 2 May 1994.
9   Cited in Garden, 2014, p. 9.
10   *Bundaberg Mail and Burnett Advertiser*, 27 April 1915.
11   *Stock and Land*, 20 January 1920.
12   *Reeve*, 1988.
13   *Ovens and Murray Advertiser*, 16 January 1888.
14   *Brisbane Courier*, 29 June 1881.
15   Reisner, 1993.
16   *Australian Town and Country Journal*, 18 September 1875.
17   *Burrangong Argus*, 11 June 1881.
18   *Argus*, 9 May 1882.
19   *Toowoomba Chronicle and Darling Downs General Advocate*, 15 February 1900.
20   *Maitland Weekly Mercury*, 20 October 1900.
21   *Evening News,* 16 October 1900.
22   *Register*, 18 September 1908.
23   *Sydney Mail and New South Wales Advertiser*, 23 October 1886.
24   Natural Resources Commission, 2009.
25   *Sydney Mail and New South Wales Advertiser,* 27 January 1877.
26   *Albury Banner and Wodonga Express,* 10 June 1881.
27   *Albury and Wodonga Express* 10 June 1881.
28   *Ovens and Murray Advertiser*, 25 July 1905.
29   *Sydney Mail*, 19 September 1993.
30   *Week*, 2 September 1892; *Leader,* 21 January 1888.
31   *Leader,* 21 January 1888.
32   *Leader,* 25 July 1896.
33   *The Age*, 4 April 1909.
34   *Geelong Advertiser*, 16 April 1975.
35   *Chronicle*, 22 January 1948.
36   *The Age*, 2 May 1891.
37   *Sydney Morning Herald*, 18 June 1907.
38   *Wyalong Advocate*, 17 November 1900.
39   Cited in Baldwin et al., 2016.
40   *Richmond River Express and Casino Kyogle Advertiser*, 19 February 1909.
41   Creative Spirits, nd.
42   Muir, 2014.
43   *Daily Telegraph*, 13 December 1884.
44   *Leader*, 18 April 1903.
45   *Western Star*, 16 December 1876.
46   Reeve, 1988.
47   *Singleton Argus*, 15 March 1884.
48   *Singleton Argus*, 15 March 1884.

49   *Daily Telegraph,* 13December 1884.
50   *Daily Telegraph,* 24 March 1884.
51   McKernan, 2005.
52   *Sydney Morning Herald,* 21 December 1885.
53   *Australasian,* 2 February 1889.
54   *South Australian Weekly Chronicle,* 16 August 1884.
55   *Queenslander,* 21 September 1872.
56   *Brisbane Courier,* 15 November 1876.
57   *Leader,* 29 April 1905.
58   *Leader,* 29 April 1905.
59   *Australasian,* 20 October 1906.
60   *Sydney Morning Herald,* 9 March 1888.
61   *Leader,* 29 April 1905.
62   *Warwick Argus,* 19 September 1896.
63   Glen and Short, 2000.
64   Roberts, 1937.
65   Hrinda, 1997.
66   *Horsham Times,* 23 July 1889.
67   *Bulletin,* 1 June 1974.
68   *Wagga Wagga Advertiser,* 16 January 1909.
69   *Queenslander,* 26 December 1925.
70   *Snowy River Mail,* 15 May 1913.
71   *The Age,* 25 May 1891.
72   *Mount Alexander Mail,* 24 March 1873.
73   *Herald,* 3 January 1913.
74   *Australasian,* 14 July 1894.
75   *Queenslander,* 8 May 1880.
76   *Observer,* 18 May 1918.
77   *Catholic Press,* 1 December 1921.
78   *Grafton Argus and the Clarence River Advertiser,* 6 March 1914.
79   *Brisbane Courier,* 25 February 1892.
80   *Maitland Daily Mercury,* 23 October 1908.
81   *Casino and Kyogle Courier and North Coast Advertiser,* 15 January 1929.
82   *Casino and Kyogle Courier and North Coast Advertiser,* 15 January 1929.
83   *Daily Mercury,* 14 January 1922.
84   *Maitland Mercury,* 12 September 1924.
85   *Daily Mail,* 14 January 1922.
86   *Observer,* 3 June 1915.
87   *South Eastern Times,* 4 September 1925.
88   *Border Morning Mail and Riverina Times,* 22 May 1909.
89   *Border Morning Mail and Riverina Times,* 22 May 1909.
90   *Molong Express and Western Districts Advertiser,* 24 May 1901.
91   *Adelaide Advertiser,* 2 November 1903.
92   *Queensland Country Life,* 7 December 1939.
93   *Ballarat Star,* 21 March 1881.
94   *Tocumwal Guardian and Riverina Echo,* 9 May 1913.
95   *Western Herald,* 12 November 1887.

96   *Australian Star*, 12 December 1887.
97   *Hamilton Spectator*, 10 May 1881.
98   *Ovens and Murray Advertiser*, 24 February 1906.
99   *Sydney Wool and Stock Journal*, 28 April 1905.
100 *Euroa Advocate*, 30 January 1914.
101 *Wagga Wagga Advertiser*, 30 November 1907.
102 *Bulletin*, 7 May 1908.
103 *Evening News*, 13 April 1887.
104 *Riverina Gazette*, 10 April 1886.
105 *Ovens and Murray Advertiser*, 19 October 1859.
106 *Mount Alexander Mail*, 15 August 1862.
107 *Ovens and Murray Advertiser*, 19 October 1859.
108 *The Age*, 15 January 1887.
109 Rowland, 2004.
110 *Bendigo Independent*, 12 June 1896.
111 *South Australian Register*, 5 May 1892.
112 *Land*, 30 August 1918.
113 *Advertiser*, 10 July 1896.
114 *Observer*, 4 September 1909.
115 *Australasian*, 3 March 1894.
116 *Ovens and Murray Advertiser*, 31 August 1865.
117 *Bendigo Independent*, 28 September 1894.
118 *Register*, 7 October 1913.
119 *Bendigo Independent*, 9 May 1914.
120 *The Age*, 12 August 1925.
121 *Brisbane Telegraph*, 24 August 1925.
122 *The Age*, 16 October 1888.
123 *The Western Star and Roma Advertiser*, 20 March 1897.
124 *Catholic Press*, 30 March 1911.
125 *Western Star and Roma Advertiser*, 20 March 1897.
126 *Sydney Morning Herald*, 23 September 1916.
127 *Sunday Times*, 27 September 1903.
128 *Argus*, 9 June 1894.
129 *Kyogle Examiner*, 29 August 1923.
130 *Kyogle Examiner*, 29 August 1923.
131 *Kyogle Examiner*, 29 August 1923
132 *The Catholic Press*, 30 March 1911.
133 *Brisbane Courier*, 14 August 1903.
134 *Sydney Stock and Station Journal*, 27 July 1909.
135 Casben, 2019.
136 Martin and Handsyde, 1999.
137 Hrinda and Gordon, 2004.
138 *Daily Telegraph*, 11 August 1927.
139 *Telegraph*, 23 January 1924.
140 *Queenslander*, 11 February 1906.
141 *Herald*, 4 January 1941.
142 *Portland Guardian*, 24 September 1953.

143 *Queenslander,* 11 February 1906.
144 *Armidale Express and New England Advertiser,* 12 June 1903.
145 *Australian Star,* 16 December 1905.
146 *Ovens and Murray Advertiser,* 16 June 1894.
147 *Raymond Terrace Examiner,* 5 December 1913.
148 *Register,* 29 December 1913.
149 *Evening Star,* 19 June 1917.
150 *Daily Telegraph,* 1 August 1906.
151 *Brisbane Courier,* 1 March 1901.
152 *Gordon, Egerton and Ballan Advertiser,* 20 April 1917.
153 *The Age,* 30 August 1910.
154 *Freeman's Journal,* 26 January 1895.
155 *South Australian Register,* 3 November 1891.
156 *The Queenslander,* 22 October 1892.
157 *Freeman's Journal,* 26 January 1895.
158 *Border Mail and Riverina Times,* 22 May 1909.
159 *Border Mail and Riverina Times,* 22 May 1909.
160 *Catholic Press,* 2 February 1911.
161 Cited in Macgregor, nd.
162 *Observer,* 22 June 1929.

6   Irrigation empire: The rise and fall of the Chaffey brothers

1   *Daily Mail,* 20 March 1920.
2   *The Age,* 3 July 1896.
3   *Sydney Mail,* 23 January 1929.
4   *Millicent Times,* 9 May 1896.
5   Alexander, 1928.
6   New South Wales Royal Commission, 1885.
7   Alexander, 1928.
8   *Tasmanian,* 4 March 1882.
9   New South Wales Royal Commission, 1885.
10   Morrison, 2014.
11   Cited in Cummins and Watson, 2012.
12   Brett, 2017.
13   Rankin, 2013.
14   *South Australian Advertiser,* 31 January 1887.
15   *Evening News,* 22 March 1910.
16   *Riverina Grazier,* 6 December 1887; *The Age,* 21 April 1937.
17   *Daily Northern Argus,* 21 March 1888.
18   *Murray Pioneer and Australian River Record,* 11 June 1926.
19   *Mildura Cultivator,* 3 June 1908.
20   Hamilton-McKenzie, 2013; Kershner, 1953.
21   *Sydney Mail,* 23 January 1929.
22   *News* (Adelaide), 26 May 1954.
23   Kelly, 1954.
24   Hamilton-McKenzie, 2013.
25   *News* (Adelaide), 26 May 1954.

26 *News* (Adelaide), 26 May 1954.

27 *Express and Telegraph*, 7 January 1887.

28 *Bunyip*, 11 March 1932.

29 Lozano, 2015.

30 Kelly, 1954.

31 Cited in Hamilton-McKenzie, p. 67.

32 Frederick, 2019.

33 *Mt Alexander Mail*, 16 February 1885.

34 *Weekly Times*, 30 October 1886.

35 *South Australian Advertiser*, 31 January 1887.

36 *Brisbane Telegraph*, 13 February 1930.

37 *Argus*, 5 June 1926.

38 *Brisbane Telegraph*, 13 February 1930.

39 *Sydney Morning Herald*, 18 April 1934.

40 *Adelaide News*, 26 May 1954.

41 Cureton's evidence to the Mildura Royal Commission, reported verbatim in the *Argus*, 17 June 1896.

42 Cureton's evidence to the Mildura Royal Commission, reported verbatim in the *Argus*, 17 June 1896.

43 *Argus*, 5 June 1926.

44 Bellanta, 2002, digital version with no page number.

45 *Australian Star*, 17 April 1903.

46 Brett, 2017.

47 *Australasian*, 20 June 1885.

48 Guest, 2017.

49 Cureton's evidence to the Mildura Royal Commission, reported verbatim in the *Argus*, 17 June 1896.

50 *Chronicle*, 18 June 1896.

51 *Adelaide Observer*, 10 December 1898.

52 *Town and Country Journal*, 1 August 1896.

53 *Brisbane Telegraph*, 13 February 1930.

54 Mildura Royal Commission, 1896, p. VIII.

55 *Kerang Times and Swan Hill Gazette*, 26 October 1886

56 Mildura Royal Commission, 1896, p. XIViii.

57 *Kerang Times and Swan Hill Gazette*, 3 December 1886.

58 *Weekly Times*, 28 May 1887.

59 *Leader*, 14 August 1889.

60 Webster, 2017.

61 Cited in Webster, 2017, p. 33.

62 Ibid.

63 *Weekly Times*, 14 September 1889.

64 Cited in *Adelaide News*, 26 May 1954.

65 Webster, 2017.

66 *South Australian Weekly Chronicle*, 5 February 1887.

67 *The Age*, 11 December 1886.

68 Kershner, 1953, p. 119.

69 *Pictorial Australian*, 1 February 1887.

70   Mildura Royal Commission, 1896.
71   *Adelaide Observer*, 10 December 1898.
72   *Mildura Cultivator*, 17 July 1890.
73   Cureton's evidence to the Mildura Royal Commission, reported verbatim in the *Argus*, 17 June 1896
74   *South Australian Weekly Chronicle*, 8 January 1887.
75   Mildura Royal Commission, synopsis of evidence, p. XIVii.
76   *Sydney Morning Herald*, 18 April 1934.
77   Kelly, 1954.
78   *The Age*, 21 April 1887.
79   *Border Morning Mail and Riverina Times*, 13 March 1920.
80   Cited in Reeve, 1988, p. 25.
81   Mildura Royal Commission, synopsis of evidence, p. Xii.
82   *Sydney Mail*, 23 January 1929.
83   *Argus*, 4 May 1896.
84   For coverage of Deakin's appearance, see the *Bendigo Independent*, 25 July 1896, and the *Chronicle*, 1 August 1896.
85   *The Age*, 16 October 1954.
86   *Australian Star*, 17 April 1903.
87   *Daily Mail*, 20 March 1920.

7   A national calamity: The Federation Drought, 1895–1903

1   *Queanbeyan Age*, 26 January 1878.
2   *Riverina Grazier*, 23 February 1884.
3   *South Australian Register*, 24 February 1891; *Argus*, 25 January 1910; *Protestant Standard*, 26 April 1890.
4   *Coolgardie Miner*, 8 February 1898.
5   *Sunday Times*, 6 February 1898.
6   *Northern Star*, 24 April 1897.
7   *Adelaide Observer*, 5 June 1897.
8   *Evening News*, 3 February 1898.
9   *Yea Chronicle*, 5 June 1902.
10   This was the view of some newspapers – see the *Bendigo Independent*, 22 October 1902.
11   *Kilmore Free Press*, 30 October 1902.
12   *Evening Telegraph*, 25 March 1903.
13   *Euroa Advertiser*, 13 June 1902.
14   *Western Grazier*, 17 April 1901.
15   *Chronicle*, 24 February 1900.
16   *Sydney Morning Herald*, 17 August 1948.
17   *Queenslander*, 23 June 1900.
18   *Adelaide Observer*, 10 December 1904.
19   *Yea Chronicle*, 5 June 1902.
20   See, for example, the *Albury Banner and Wodonga Express*, 24 March 1905.
21   *Examiner*, 22 May 1902.
22   *Sydney Stock and Station Journal*, 2 October 1896.
23   *Albury Banner and Wodonga Express*, 28 January 1898.

24 *South Australian Chronicle*, 13 May 1876; *Colac Herald*, 20 March 1883.

25 *Wylong Star and Temora and Barmedman Advertiser*, 12 November 1901.

26 *Sydney Stock and Station Journal*, 12 February 1904.

27 *Australian Star*, 3 October 1902.

28 *Yea Chronicle*, 5 June 1902.

29 *Cobargo Chronicle*, 5 May 1899.

30 Holmes and Mirmohamadi, 2015, p. 193.

31 Vanclay and Lawrence, 1995.

32 *Kilmore Free Press*, 20 November 1902.

33 *Daily Telegraph*, 28 June 1903.

34 *Daily Telegraph*, 28 June 1903.

35 *Wagga Wagga Express*, 10 October 1899.

36 *Euroa Advocate*, 13 June 1902.

37 *Gympie Times and Mary River Mining Gazette*, 22 November 1900.

38 *Bulletin*, 30 August 1902.

39 *Brisbane Courier*, 17 August 1901.

40 *Dubbo Liberal and Macquarie Advocate*, 11 June 1902.

41 *Evening Standard*, 7 August 1902.

42 *Brighton Southern Cross*, 8 November 1902.

43 *Independent*, 12 June 1903.

44 *Bendigo Independent*, 13 October 1902; *Yass Evening Tribune*, 19 February 1903.

45 *Ovens and Murray Advertiser*, 25 October 1902.

46 *Evening News*, 21 February 1903.

47 *Dubbo Dispatch*, 18 August 1900.

48 *Narromine News and Trangie Advocate*, 1 April 1932.

49 *Braidwood Dispatch and Mining Journal*, 16 September 1938.

50 *Goulburn Evening Penny Post*, 21 January 1896.

51 *Manning River Times*, 18 January 1938.

52 ABC News, 21 December 2019.

53 *Sydney Morning Herald*, 14 January 1896.

54 *Wellington Times*, 25 January 1896.

55 *Advertiser*, 17 August 1903.

56 Australian Institute for Disaster Resilience, 'Environment – Federation Drought', <knowledge.aidr.org.au/resources/environment-federation-drought>.

57 *Ovens and Murray Advertiser*, 24 August 1901.

58 *Ovens and Murray Advertiser*, 11 May 1901.

59 *Ovens and Murray Advertiser*, 24 August 1901.

60 Garden, 2010.

61 *Brighton Southern Cross*, 8 November 1902.

62 Semmler, 1988.

63 Garden, 2010.

64 *Clarence and Richmond Examiner*, 1 May 1897.

65 *Western Champion and General Advertiser*, 10 August 1902.

66 *Leader*, 31 January 1903.

67 *Launceston Examiner*, 15 January 1898.

68 *Ovens and Murray Advertiser*, 21 March 1903.

69 Godfree et al., 2019, p. 15584.

70 *Australian Star*, 27 November 1902.

71 *Argus*, 1 January 1901.

72 *Sun*, 11 April 1912.

73 *Darling Downs Gazette*, 14 March 1903.

74 *Inverell Argus*, 1 August 1902.

75 *Advertiser*, 2 May 1900.

76 *Daily Telegraph*, 28 February 1903.

77 State Library of New South Wales, 'Dorothea Mackellar's My Country'.

78 *Australian Woman's Weekly*, 22 July 1939.

79 *Telegraph*, 26 January 1924.

80 Garden, 2011, p. 280.

81 *Sun*, 1 April 1922.

8   Populate or perish: Chasing the agrarian dream

1   *Herald*, 17 June 1905.

2   Dorsey, 2013.

3   Roosevelt, 1885, p. 14.

4   *Herald*, 13 May 1908.

5   *Herald,* 13 May 1908.

6   *Wellington Times,* 27 August 1939.

7   *Sydney Stock and Station Journal*, 2 June 1908.

8   *Yass Evening News*, 26 November 1900; *Wellington Times*, 22 November 1900.

9   *Freeman's Journal*, 27 August 1908; *Dubbo Liberal and Macquarie Advocate*, 26 August 1908.

10 *Wagga Wagga Advertiser*, 11 March 1902.

11 *Snowy River Mail*, 25 May 1902.

12 *Sydney Morning Herald*, 28 January 1920.

13 *Horsham Times*, 22 January 1915.

14 *Wagga Wagga Advertiser*, 29 March 1902.

15 Guest, 2017.

16 Guest, 2017.

17 *Sydney Morning Herald*, 6 February 1906.

18 *Register*, 4 October 1902.

19 *Bacchus Marsh Express,* 18 February 1911.

20 *Ovens and Murray Advertiser,* 18 January 1908.

21 Conkin, 1960.

22 *Bacchus Marsh Express,* 18 February 1911.

23 *Sydney Mail and New South Wales Advertiser,* 7 September 1904.

24 Conkin, 1960, p. 89.

25 Conkin, 1960, p. 89.

26 *Chronicle*, 15 March 1913.

27 *Maitland Weekly Mercury*, 16 December 1905.

28 *Weekly Times*, 22 January 1910

29 *Sydney Stock and Station Journal*, 2 June 1908.

30 *Daily News*, 27 October 1921.

31 *Leader*, 1 June 1906.

32 Beresford and Omaji, 1998.

33   Elliot, 2012.
34   *Australian Worker,* 13 November 1912; *Port Macquarie News*, 9 July 1921.
35   *Australian Worker,* 13 November 1921.
36   *Brisbane Courier,* 24 August 1926.
37   *Daily Telegraph,* 2 July 1923.
38   *Newcastle Sun,* 4 March 1924.
39   *Brisbane Courier,* 24 August 1926.
40   *Farmer and Settler,* 12 June 1925.
41   *Border Chronicle,* 6 January 1922.
42   *Independent,* 19 June 1903.
43   *Riverina Herald,* 2 October 1912.
44   Frost, 2004.
45   *Methodist,* 2 October 1926.
46   *Newcastle Morning Herald,* 8 June 1935.
47   Tulloch, 2015.
48   *Inverell Times,* 23 April 1912.
49   Cameron, 2005.
50   *The Age,* 12 June 1912.
51   *Inverell Times,* 8 July 1914.
52   *Western Mail,* 4 February 1943.
53   Royal Commission on Closer Settlement 1916, Final Report, p. 13.
54   *Sunday Times,* 1 January 1911; *The Age,* 10 June 1916.
55   Royal Commission on Closer Settlement 1916, Progress Report, p. 25.
56   *Benalla Standard,* 17 August 1915.
57   *Leader,* 21 February 1914.
58   *Mount Barker Courier,* 11 December 1908.
59   *Advertiser,* 15 March 1910.
60   *Sydney Morning Herald,* 5 April 1912.
61   Guest, 2017.
62   *Rochester Express,* 8 December 1914.
63   Fry, 1985.
64   McKernan, 2005.
65   Roche, 2011.
66   Fry, 1985.
67   Harrison, 2004.
68   *Daily Examiner,* 13 August 1929.
69   Jennings, 2011.
70   New South Wales State Archives, 'A Land Fit for Heroes? A History of Soldier
     Settlement in New South Wales'<soldiersettlement.records.nsw.gov.au/case-studies/
     abbott-albert-jarvis>.
71   *Daily Telegraph,* 26 March 1932.
72   *Observer,* 13 June 1925.
73   Roche, 2011.
74   ABC News, 24 April 2014.
75   *Bulletin,* 14 April 1927.
76   *Daily Mail,* 6 September 1921.
77   *Daily Mail,* 29 August 1921.

78   *Sydney Morning Herald*, 8 November 1921.

79   *Lithgow Mercury*, 29 July 1921.

80   Bridge, 2011.

81   *Evening News,* 21 February 1921.

82   *Western Champion,* 11 April 1929.

83   *Albury Banner and Wodonga Express,* 6 January 1922.

84   *Ballarat Star,* 8 October 1923; *Kalgoorlie Miner,* 19 June 1922.

85   *Goulburn and Evening Penny Post,* 22 November 1936.

86   Frost, 2014.

87   Powell, 1990.

88   Powell, 1990.

89   *Sydney Morning Herald*, 27 August 1921.

90   *Sydney Morning Herald,* 1 August 1928.

91   Cited in Strange, 2010, p. 136.

92   *Sydney Morning Herald,* 17 August 1927.

93   Strange, 2010.

94   Powell, 1990.

95   *Sydney Morning Herald*, 27 August 1921.

96   Strange, 2010, p. 137.

97   Harrison, 2004.

98   *Brisbane Courier*, 20 June 1917.

99   *Daily News*, 10 February 1939.

100   *Daily News*, 10 February 1939.

101   *News* (Adelaide), 22 May 1944.

102   See, for example, reports of the Wilcannia Reserve, *Western Grazier*, 2 July 1948; and Brungle Reserve at Gundagai, *Sun* (Sydney), 8 May 1949.

103   *Sydney Mail*, 16 September 1931.

104   *Sydney Mail*, 16 September 1931.

105   Human Rights Commission, 1997.

106   *Wellington Times*, 1 July 1937.

107   *Lone Hand*, 2 November 1908.

108   *Sydney Morning Herald*, 15 February 1947.

109   *Argus,* 29 September 1925.

110   *Corowa Free Press,* 21 August 1936.

111   *Argus,* 31 May 1930.

112   *Australasian,* 1 September 1928.

113   *Smith's Weekly,* 25 June 1925.

114   See ES Sorenson, 'Some Murrumbidgee Whalers', *Australasian,* 1 September 1928.

115   *Argus,* 31 May 1930.

116   *Australian Worker,* 29 August 1925.

117   *Freeman's Journal,* 25 January 1923.

118   *Mail Adelaide,* 25 September 1926.

9   Nature's vengeance: Australia's dust bowl

1   *Farmer and Settler,* 2 June 1944.

2   Egan, 2006.

3   *Pix,* 4 May 1940.

4   *Burra Record,* 19 December 1934.

5   Erosion and the impact of sand drifts and dust storms were only briefly discussed in the first wave of environmental histories of Australia that emerged during the 1980s, for example Bolton, 1981, and Reeve, 1988. Several recent academic journal articles have explored Australia's dust bowl, but they have not focused on examining its human toll. See Cattle, 2006, and Sauter, 2015.
6   Egan, 2006; Brinkley, 2012.
7   *Mirror*, 27 April 1935.
8   Cattle, 2016.
9   Egan, 2006, pp. 125–26.
10 Lampos, 2016.
11 *Macleay Chronicle*, 3 February 1937.
12 *Great Southern Herald*, 28 August 1935.
13 *Albury Banner and Wodonga Express*, 5 July 1935.
14 Follador, 2016.
15 Cited in Follador, 2016.
16 *Daily Mercury*, 29 May 1939.
17 *Sea Lake Times and Berriwirlock Advertiser*, 9 May 1915.
18 *Telegraph* (Brisbane), 30 December 1935.
19 *Sydney Morning Herald*, 31 August 1933.
20 *Sydney Morning Herald*, 17 January 1936.
21 *Sun*, 26 April 1936.
22 *Daily Telegraph*, 13 July 1937.
23 *Queenslander*, 28 September 1937.
24 *Sydney Morning Herald*, 26 December 1940.
25 *Canberra Times*, 16 May 1938
26 *Land*, 24 September 1937.
27 *Daily Telegraph*, 18 April 1938.
28 This account of the impact of dust storms was compiled from reports in the following newspapers: *Australian Worker*, 12 April 1939; *Sun*, 13 February 1939; *Land*, 9 January 1942; *Nambucca and Bellinger News*, 9 February 1940; *Herald*, 8 February 1945.
29 McDermott, 2020.
30 Cited in Gordon, 2009, p. 165. Gordon also traces the difficult life of Florence Thompson before and after the iconic photograph was taken.
31 *Australian Women's Weekly*, 9 December 1944.
32 *Argus*, 5 October 1946.
33 Cited in Whitford and Boadle, 2009, p. 66.
34 See, for example, the *Weekly Times*, 30 November 1935.
35 *Horsham Times*, 26 September 1939.
36 *Lachlander and Condobolin and Western Districts Recorder*, 24 June 1940.
37 *Bunyip*, 17 January 1936.
38 *Truth*, 15 August 1943.
39 *Braidwood Review and District Advocate*, 7 September 1943.
40 *Farmer and Settler*, 8 October 1936.
41 *Australian Woman's Weekly*, 13 February 1952.
42 Moore, 1972.
43 *Land*, 15 April 1932.

44 *Courier Mail*, 5 October 1940.
45 *Argus*, 15 April 1941.
46 *Argus*, 15 April 1941.
47 Sparrow, 2018.
48 Sparrow, 2018.
49 *Lachlander and Condobolin and Western Districts Recorder*, 29 July 1940.
50 *Daily Advertiser*, 26 June 1937.
51 *Warwick Daily News*, 14 November 1944.
52 *Northern Miner*, 7 November 1942.
53 *Ouyen Mail*, 13 March 1940.
54 Jacks and Whyte, 1939, p. 92.
55 *Murrumburrah Signal and County of Horden Advocate*, 17 August 1939.
56 *Truth*, 15 August 1943.
57 *Argus*, 5 January 1938.
58 Cited in Marchant, 1998, p. 26. See Marchant generally for a depiction of Lyons and the UAP.
59 Whitford and Boadle, 2008.
60 Whitford and Broadle, 2008 and 2009.
61 *Western Grazier*, 30 March 1945.
62 *Chronicle*, 28 December 1944.
63 Cited in Whitford and Boadle, 2009, p. 61.
64 Whitford and Boadle, 2008.
65 *Truth*, 15 August 1943.
66 *Smith's Weekly*, 28 October 1944.
67 *Argus*, 14 November 1944.
68 *The Age*, 15 November 1944.
69 *Barrier Miner*, 17 October 1944.
70 For reports of the storm see: *Sun* 20 November 1944; *Mercury*, 20 November 1944; *Daily Telegraph*, 20 November 1944.
71 *Sydney Morning Herald*, 16 December 1944 and 19 December 1944.
72 *Telegraph Brisbane*, 4 July 1938.
73 *Truth*, 3 December 1944.
74 *Western Mail*, 30 November 1944.
75 *Tribune*, 12 October 1944.
76 *Mail*, 16 December 1944.
77 *Western Mail*, 30 November 1944.
78 *Scone Advocate*, 25 February 1947.
79 *Western Grazier*, 19 January 1945.
80 *Advertiser*, 9 December 1944.
81 *Murray Pioneer*, 28 December 1944.
82 *Western Grazier*, 19 January 1945.
83 *Daily News*, 18 November 1948.
84 *Weekly Times*, 17 October 1951.
85 *Farmer and Settler*, 17 October 1952.
86 *Argus*, 3 August 1949.
87 Reeve et al., 2002.
88 Barr and Cary, 1994, p. 45.

89 Sauter, 2015.
90 *Advertiser,* 9 December 1944.
91 Bonyhady, 1997.
92 *Daily Telegraph,* 21 November 1945.
93 *Sun,* 4 September 1947.
94 *Horsham Times,* 26 September 1939.
95 *Land,* 14 September 1951.
96 Cathcart, 2009.
97 Gillanders, 2009.
98 *Murray Pioneer,* 20 October 1949; *Gippsland Times,* 8 July 1954.

10 Prosperity and its problems
1   *The War Illustrated,* 9 June 1945.
2   *News* (Adelaide), 13 November 1950.
3   *Farmer and Settler,* 4 January 1952.
4   *Bulletin,* 16 December 1959.
5   For a history of the work of the New South Wales Soil Conservation Service,
    see *Journal of Soil Conservation Service of New South Wales,* Vol 44, No 1, 1988.
6   Reeve et al., 2002.
7   Reeve et al., 2002.
8   Section 75 (1) (b) of the Commonwealth *Taxation Act,* cited in Australian
    Greenhouse Office, 2000, p. 7.
9   Australian Greenhouse Office, 2000, p. 7.
10 Barr and Cary, 1992, p. 223.
11 Farwell, 1947.
12 For an analysis of Cato's novel, see Sheridan, 2011.
13 *Lockhart Review and Oaklands Advertiser,* 9 February 1954.
14 Cited in Hughes, 2013.
15 Australian Greenhouse Office, 2000.
16 *Macleay Argus,* 30 June 1944.
17 *Macleay Argus,* 12 September 1944.
18 *Bulletin,* 1 August 1964.
19 *News* (Adelaide), 1 September 1948.
20 *Muswellbrook Chronicle,* 24 January 1947.
21 *Advertiser,* 3 May 1952
22 Stevens, 1963.
23 Hrdina and Gordon, 2004.
24 *Labor Daily,* 16 January 1937; *Evening News,* 24 November 1936.
25 Stevens, 1963; Hausheer, 2019.
26 Stevens, 1963.
27 *Walkabout,* 1 October 1965.
28 *Sun,* 10 June 1934.
29 Chisholm, 1954.
30 Chisholm, 1954.
31 *Canberra Times,* 14 November 1964.
32 Marshall, 1966.
33 Hoad, 1974, p. 31.

34 *Bulletin,* 9 December 1981.
35 Hoad, 1974, p. 31.
36 *Bulletin,* 20 November 1979.
37 *Advertiser,* 13 July 1935
38 *Pix,* 6 December 1947.
39 *Pix,* 6 December 1947.
40 Boon, 2020.
41 See *Sydney Morning Herald,* 16 January 1906; *Riverina Recorder,* 24 December 1932; and the *West Australian,* 24 December 1949.
42 Denholm, 1999.
43 *Murray Pioneer and Australian River Record,* 27 April 1923.
44 *Recorder,* 6 December 1938.
45 *News* (Adelaide), 621 November 1933; *The Age,* 6 June 1936.
46 *Cobram Times,* 30 June 1943.
47 *Weekly Times,* 22 March 1944.
48 Harris, 2006.
49 *Advertiser,* 19 October 1944.
50 *Weekly Times,* 6 September 1944.
51 *Cobram Courier,* 30 June 1943.
52 *Bulletin,* 7 August 1971.
53 Blackmore, 1986.
54 *Pix,* 6 December 1947.
55 Kingsford, 2003.
56 Cronin, 1951.
57 *South-Eastern News,* 24 June 1943.
58 *Riverine Gazette,* 22 July 1952.
59 Taylor and Schultz, 2010.
60 *Herald,* 13 June 1951.
61 *Lockhart Review and Oaklands Advertiser*, 9 February 1954.
62 *Walkabout,* 1 December 1959.
63 *Canberra Times,* 23 January 1993.
64 Goodall, 2002.
65 Vanclay and Lawrence, 1995.
66 McHugh, 1996.
67 Goodall, 2002, p. 32.
68 Mussared, 1993a.
69 Top Wire Traveller, 2020.
70 Murray–Darling Basin Commission, nd.
71 Mussared, 1993b.
72 Australian Productivity Commission, 2017.
73 McCaughan, 1947.
74 *Sydney Morning Herald,* 25 January 1936.
75 *Sydney Morning Herald,* 25 January 1936.
76 *Independent,* 21 February 1946.
77 *Sydney Morning Herald,* 11 November 1950.
78 *Sydney Morning Herald,* 11 November 1950.
79 *Riverina Herald,* 18 January 1947.

80 *Herald,* 3 June 1937.
81 *Argus,* 4 February 1956.
82 *Bulletin,* 23 December 1976.
83 Carson, 1962.
84 *Canberra Times,* 29 September 1965.
85 *Land,* 29 December 1950.
86 *Times,* 25 August 1989.
87 *Advertiser,* 13 June 1935.
88 Harvey, 1942, p. 37.
89 Kingsford and Thomas, 1995.
90 *Wellington Times,* 6 January 1944.
91 Kingsford, 2000.
92 Hogendyk, 2007.
93 Smiles, 2006.
94 Birdlife International, 'Lowbidgee Floodplain', <datazone.birdlife.org/site/factsheet/lowbidgee-floodplain-iba-australia>; see also Kingsford and Thomas, 2004; Kingsford, 2000.
95 Kingsford, 2000.
96 *Weekly Times,* 5 April 1941.
97 Macaulay, 1961.
98 *Canberra Times,* 8 March 1969.
99 *Advertiser,* 21 March 1953.
100 *Weekly Times,* 4 April 1941.
101 *Shepparton Advertiser,* 1 May 1953.
102 Leslie, 2001, p. 33.
103 *Bulletin,* 7 August 1971.
104 *Bulletin,* 17 April 1971.
105 *Australian Women's Weekly,* 29 April 1981.
106 Farwell and Serventy, 1982.
107 Larkins and Parish, 1982.
108 *Weekend Australian,* 10 February 2007.
109 Interview, Tony Windsor, October 2020.
110 Statement from Professor Peter Cullen, head of the Cooperative Research Centre for Freshwater Ecology, *Canberra Times,* 29 October 1994.
111 Cummins and Watson, 2012.
112 *Bulletin,* 26 June 1984.
113 Wentworth Group of Concerned Scientists, 2017.
114 Pittock, 2019.
115 *Advertiser,* 2 January 2014.
116 Mussared, 1989.
117 Eckersley, 1989.
118 *Sydney Morning Herald,* 15 September 1989.
119 *Canberra Times,* 15 December 1990.
120 Wentworth Group of Concerned Scientists, 2017.
121 *Canberra Times,* 9 January 1993.
122 Sorenson, 1991.
123 *Canberra Times,* 31 March 1994; Muir, 2014.

124 Smiles, 2019.
125 *Canberra Times,* 9 December 1991.
126 Wentworth Group of Concerned Scientists, 2017.
127 Mussared, 1995.
128 Senate Standing Committee on Environment, Recreation and the Arts, 1993.
129 See comments made by Mark Etheridge, President of the Australian Floodplain Association, News.com.au, 1 October 2009.

11 The struggle for reform

1   *Australian Financial Review,* 2 December 1992; *The Age,* 23 December 1992.
2   Rees, 1993.
3   Bramston, 2016.
4   Keating, 1992.
5   *Canberra Times,* 23 December 1992.
6   Muir, 2014.
7   Vauclay and Lawrence, 1995.
8   *Sydney Morning Herald,* 14 September 1994.
9   Vauclay and Lawrence, 1995.
10 Skinner, 1992.
11 Skinner, 1990.
12 *The Age,* 7 August 1993.
13 *The Age,* 7 August 1993.
14 *Sydney Morning Herald,* 10 May 1993.
15 *Sydney Morning Herald,* 8 August 1995.
16 *Canberra Times,* 30 March 1994.
17 Wahlquist, 1995.
18 *Sydney Morning Herald,* 13 September 1995.
19 ABC Background Briefing, 2018.
20 *The Age,* 7 June 1998.
21 *Greenwire,* 16 April 1996.
22 *Sydney Morning Herald,* 29 August 1993.
23 *Canberra Times,* 22 December 1992.
24 Mussared, 1993c.
25 *Reuters News,* 24 January 1996.
26 Douglas, 2011.
27 *Canberra Times,* 1 July 1995.
28 Bramston, 2016.
29 Gittins, 2000.
30 Toensing, 2009.
31 South Australian Murray–Darling Royal Commission, *Transcript of Evidence,* 23 August 2018, p. 2087.
32 *Canberra Times,* 20 October 1998.
33 *Sydney Morning Herald,* 11 March 1995.
34 Manne, 2004.
35 Cited in the Wentworth Groups of Concerned Scientists, 2017.
36 *Sydney Morning Herald,* 1 February 1996.
37 Davisson, 1998.

38 Dickie, 2002.
39 Keane, 2008.
40 Beresford, 2015, and Beresford, 2018.
41 *Daily Telegraph,* 14 March 2019.
42 *Crikey,* 21 August 2008.
43 Dickie, 2002.
44 Dickie, 2002.
45 Dickie, 2001.
46 Dickie, 2000.
47 Cited in Keane, 2008.
48 Keane, 2008.
49 Hansard, 2013.
50 Brewster, 2020.
51 *Sydney Morning Herald,* 11 May 2013.
52 Dales, 2011.
53 Friends of the Earth, 2004, <www.reasoninrevolt.net.au/objects/pdf/d1039.pdf>.
54 ABC News, 7 September 2018.
55 *Canberra Times,* 11 July 2002.
56 Coorey, 2000.
57 Coorey, 2000.
58 *Australian,* 18 March 2000.
59 *Australian,* 15 November 2000.
60 Coorey, 2000.
61 *Australian,* 1 June 2000.
62 Benson, 2001.
63 Coorey, 2000.
64 *Sydney Morning Herald,* 17 May 2000.
65 *Sunday Mail,* 15 October 2000.
66 House of Representatives Standing Committee on Science and Innovation, 2004.
67 House of Representatives Standing Committee on Science and Innovation, 2004, p. 46.
68 Cited in Howes, 2007, p. 29.
69 Benson, 2001.
70 Wahlquist, 2008.
71 *The Age,* 19 April 2003.
72 *Courier Mail,* 4 December 2002.
73 *Sydney Morning Herald,* 6 December 2002.
74 *Australian,* 8 March 2002.
75 *Australian,* 8 March 2002.
76 *Independent Daily,* 30 January 2019.
77 Sheehan, 2005.
78 *Daily Telegraph,* 19 July 2002.
79 ABC, AM, 25 June 2004.
80 *Courier-Mail,* 16 July 2002.
81 *Courier-Mail,* 20 July 2002.
82 *Sunday Herald-Sun,* 11 April 2004.
83 Senate Rural and Regional Affairs Committee, 2002.

84   *Sunday Herald-Sun,* 11 April 2004.
85   Marshall, 2017, p. 14.
86   *Barrier Daily Truth,* 6 April 2004.
87   Lewis, 2003.
88   Cited in Lewis, 2000.
89   Beck, 2007.
90   AAP, 13 March 2006.
91   Beck, 2007.
92   Sheenan, 2005.
93   Sheehan, 2005.
94   Interview, Dr Tim Flannery, October 2020.
95   SBS News, 24 February 2015.
96   Interview, Tony Windsor, October 2020.
97   *Sunday Herald-Sun,* 28 January 2007.
98   *The Age,* 25 January 2007.
99   *Sydney Morning Herald,* 3 October 2006.
100   *Australian,* 8 February 2021.
101   House of Representatives Standing Committee on Regional Australia, 2011, p. x.
102   Federal Register of Legislation, *Water Act 2007,* <www.legislation.gov.au/Details/ C2017C00151>.
103   *Herald Sun,* 26 January 2007.
104   Crase, 2017.
105   Interview, Tony Windsor, October 2020.
106   Kotsios, 2017.
107   Toohey, 2007,
108   Cited in Beck, 2007, p. 7.
109   *The Age,* 14 November 2007.
110   *Sydney Morning Herald,* 10 February 2007.
111   Haigh, 2007.
112   *Canberra Times,* 17 October 2006.
113   *Canberra Times,* 17 October 2006.
114   Beck, 2007.
115   Taibbi, 2010.
116   *Telegraph* (UK), 5 June 2008.
117   Cited in Aarons, 2010.

12   Smoke and mirrors: The making and unmaking of the Murray–Darling Basin Plan

1   News.com.au, 15 October 2009.
2   Wahlquist, 2009.
3   News.com.au, 17 August 2009.
4   Kemp, 2009.
5   ABC News, 16 December 2019.
6   Kingsford, 2019b.
7   House of Representatives Standing Committee on Regional Australia Inquiry into the impact of the Murray Darling Basin Plan in Regional Australia Submission by the National Irrigators' Council, 2010.

8   *Sydney Morning Herald,* 26 October 2010.
9   Inland Rivers Network, Submission to South Australian Murray Darling Basin Royal Commission.
10   ABC News, 8 October 2010.
11   ABC, *PM,* 12 October 2010.
12   Chan, 2017, pp. 236–37.
13   ABC News, 12 October 2010.
14   ABC News, 13 October 2010.
15   *The Age,* 15 October 2010.
16   ABC News, 14 October 2010.
17   ABC News, 17 October 2010.
18   ABC News, 17 October 2010.
19   Cited in House of Representatives Standing Committee on Regional Australia, 2011, p. 79.
20   Interview, Tony Windsor, October 2020.
21   *Canberra Times,* 18 May 2011.
22   ABC, *PM,* 7 December 2007.
23   ABC News, 7 December 2010.
24   ABC, *World Today,* 7 December 2007; *Sydney Morning Herald,* 20 October 2010.
25   Toohey, 2010.
26   ABC News, 28 January 2011.
27   ABC News, 17 October 2010.
28   Interview, Tony Windsor, October 2010.
29   House of Representatives Standing Committee on Regional Australia, 2011, p. 164.
30   ABC News, 15 September 2017.
31   South Australian Murray–Darling Basin Royal Commission, Transcript of Evidence, 23 August 2018, p. 2063.
32   South Australian Murray–Darling Basin Royal Commission Report, 2019, p. 23.
33   South Australian Murray–Darling Basin Royal Commission, Transcript of Evidence, 18 July 2019, p. 58.
34   South Australian Murray–Darling Basin Royal Commission Report, 2019, p. 76.
35   News.com.au, 14 June 2017.
36   ABC, *7.30 Report,* 23 May 2011; Wentworth Group, 2012.
37   South Australian Murray–Darling Basin Royal Commission Report, 2019, p. 65.
38   South Australian Murray–Darling Basin Royal Commission Report, 2019, p. 24.
39   South Australian Murray–Darling Basin Royal Commission Report, 2019, p 16.
40   South Australian Murray–Darling Basin Royal Commission Report, 2019, p. 23.
41   South Australian Murray–Darling Basin Royal Commission Report, 2019, p. 55.
42   Interview, Tony Windsor, October 2020.
43   Simons, 2020, p. 61.
44   Matthews, 2017, pp. 29–31.
45   Seccombe, 2017.
46   *Daily Telegraph,* 9 August 2017.
47   Farmonline, 13 December 2016.
48   Interview, Tony Windsor, October 2020.
49   Senate Rural and Regional Affairs and Transport Committee, 2018, p. 19.
50   *Guardian,* 19 July 2018.

51   Barbour, 2016; Robson, 2016.
52   Cited in Boyer, 2017.
53   *Canberra Times,* 29 October 1994.
54   *Daily Telegraph, 18 December 2016*
55   Wilderness Society, 2018.
56   Michael West Media, 22 October 2019.
57   ABC News, 27 July 2017.
58   The Australia Institute, 2019.
59   Interview, Professor Quentin Grafton, October 2020.
60   ABC TV, *Four Corners,* 2019.
61   *Sydney Morning Herald,* 25 February 2008.
62   *Courier Mail,* 7 September 2006.
63   Gray, 2019.
64   *Sydney Morning Herald*, 17 December 2019.
65   *Sydney Morning Herald*, 17 December 2019.
66   *Guardian*, 17 February 2020.
67   *Sydney Morning Herald*, 22 May 2020.
68   *Courier*, 5 October 2020.
69   *Guardian,* 8 December 2020.
70   The Knitting Nannas, 2021.
71   Environmental Defenders Office, 2020.
72   *Land,* 10 August 2020.
73   ABC News, 13 December 2018.
74   *Sydney Morning Herald,* 3 February 2019.
75   AAP, 7 April 2019.
76   ABC News, 14 February 2019.
77   Uren, 2007.
78   Uren, 2007.
79   Cited in *Four Corners,* 2019.
80   Grafton, 2019, p. 134.
81   Verrenda, 1998.
82   *Land,* 27 February 2017.
83   Rubinsztein-Dunlop, et al., 2019.
84   ABC, *Media Watch,* 15 July 2019.
85   Commonwealth Agriculture Department 2019.
86   ABC Regional News, 27 June 2017.
87   Hughes, Galeano and Hatfield, 2020.
88   Environmental Defenders Office Australia, Submission to the Murray–Darling Basin
      Royal Commission, 2018, p. 5.
89   Interview, Tim Flannery, October 2020.
90   Young, 2018.
91   Connell, 2015.
92   Interview, Tony Windsor, October 2020.
93   Interview, Tony Windsor, October 2020.
94   Triskele, 2019.
95   ABC Regional News, 21 June 2017.
96   *Sydney Morning Herald*, 24 February 2018.

97 *Guardian,* 6 June 2019.
98 Brewster, 2020; West, 2019.
99 West, 2019.
100 *Guardian,* 31 October 2019.
101 *Sydney Morning Herald,* 16 July 2020.
102 Price, 2019.
103 *Sydney Morning Herald,* 16 July 2020.
104 Independent Commission Against Corruption (nd), 'What Is Corrupt Conduct?'
105 ICAC, 2020, p. 9.
106 See Beresford, 2015; 2018.
107 *Australian,* 7 October 2019.
108 *Green Left,* 2 March 2020.
109 Grafton and Horne, 2014.
110 Professor Mike Young, Murray–Darling Basin Royal Commission, Transcript of Evidence, 25 September 2018, p. 3231.
111 Interview, Tim Flannery, October 2020.
112 Australian Competition and Consumer Commission, 2020.
113 Garcia, 2019a and b.
114 Connell, 2015.
115 Grafton, Landry, Libecap and O'Brien, 2009.
116 ABC Rural, 13 July 2019.
117 Australian Competition and Consumer Commission, 2000, p. 159.
118 Wright, 2019.
119 ABC, *Background Briefing,* 2018.
120 Bell, D, Submission to the Murray–Darling Royal Commission, p. 2, and transcript of evidence, 18 July 2019, p. 80.
121 Slattery, 2019a.
122 Interview, Professor Quentin Grafton, October 2020.
123 Wentworth Group of Concerned Scientists, 2020, p. i.
124 ABC News, 17 November 2020.
125 Environmental Defenders Office of Australia, 2018.
126 Webb et al., 2018.
127 *Land,* 2 April 2020
128 Kinbacher and Calver, 2019.
129 *Land,* 17 October 2019.
130 *Queensland Country Life,* 6 May 2019.
131 ABC Radio National, *Background Briefing,* 2018.
132 News.com.au, 20 April 2015.
133 Davies, 2019b.
134 Interview, Quentin Grafton, October 2020.
135 Farmonline National, 9 March 2020.
136 *Stock Journal,* 31 October 2019.
137 Environmental Defenders Office, Submission, 2018.

13 Marginalising the Indigenous voice

1 Bates, Submission to the Murray–Darling Royal Commission, 2018.
2 Marshall, 2017, p. 4.
3 Marshall, 2017, p. 5.
4 South Australian Murray–Darling Royal Commission, transcript of evidence, 23 August 2018, p. 2060.
5 Taylor, 2009.
6 *Guardian,* 13 September 2019; 7 March 2018. Eighty-four per cent of Australians support action by state governments to stop excessive land clearing; see World Wildlife Fund-Australia, *Australian Attitudes to Nature,* 2017.
7 Seccombe, 2019.
8 William Brian Bates submission to the South Australian Murray–Darling Royal Commission.
9 William Brian Bates submission to the South Australian Murray–Darling Royal Commission.
10 Weir, 2011, p. 187.
11 Glacken, 1992, p. 106.
12 'Australia's Murray Darling Basin Is Going Downhill', <www.ramblingsdc.net/Australia/MurrayDarling.html>.
13 *Guardian,* 18 December 2019.
14 Quackenbush, 2019
15 Wheeler, 2019.
16 Morgan, 2012, p. 454.
17 Marshall, 2017.
18 Langford, 2003.
19 Langford, 2003.
20 Hartwig, Jackson and Osborne, 2018.
21 Hartwig, Jackson and Osborne, 2018.
22 Australian Competition and Consumer Commission, 2020, p. 168.
23 Murray Lower Darling Rivers Indigenous Nations, Submission to the Murray–Darling Royal Commission, 2018.
24 Weir, 2009.
25 O'Brien, 2012.
26 *Daily Telegraph,* 8 May 2006.
27 Interview, Paul Lane, Lingiari Foundation, November 2020.
28 Interview, Paul Lane, Lingiari Foundation, November 2020.
29 *New Matilda,* 22 March 2010.
30 Weir, 2009, p. 250.
31 Hartwig, Jackson and Osborne, 2018.
32 Murray Lower Darling Rivers Indigenous Nations, Submission to the Murray–Darling Royal Commission, 2018.
33 Bates, Submission to the Murray–Darling Royal Commission, 2018.
34 Murray Lower Darling Rivers Indigenous Nations submission to the South Australian Murray Darling Royal Commission, 2018.
35 ABC News, 20 November 2020.
36 Australian Productivity Commission, 2020.

Conclusion: A path forward
1   Ngarrindjeri Regional Authority Inc., Submission to the Murray–Darling Royal Commission, 2018, p. 2.
2   Massy, 2020.

Postscript
1   *Guardian,* 21 February 2021.
2   Yahoo News, 15 February 2021.

BIBLIOGRAPHY

Books and articles

A

Aarons, P (2010) 'Water Policy', *Monthly*, June.

Alexander, JA (1928) *The Life of George Chaffey*, Macmillan.

Allen, M (2012) 'Exploiting the land laws – it wasn't only the squatters', in B Stubbs et al. (ed.), Australia's Ever Changing Forests, Proceedings of the Eighth National Conference on Australian Forest History.

Arnold, S (2019) 'Government Needs to Act on Menindee and Darling Disasters', *Independent Australia*, 12 January.

Atkinson, A (2003) 'Historians and Moral Disgust', in B Attwood and SG Foster, *Frontier Conflict and the Australian Experience,* National Museum of Australia.

Atkinson, W (2000) 'Chronology of the Yorta Yorta Struggle for Land Justice 1860–2000', <waynera.files.wordpress.com/2020/04/chronology-of-the-yorta-yorta-struggle-for-land-justice-1860.pdf>.

Attwood, B and Foster SG eds (2003) 'Introduction', *Frontier Conflict: The Australian Experience*, National Museum of Australia, Canberra.

Australian Explorer, 'Menindee', <www.australianexplorer.com/menindee.htm>.

B

Baker, D (1995) 'Wanderers in Eden: Thomas Mitchell Compared to Lewis and Clark', *Aboriginal History*, Vol 19, No 1.

Baldwin, D et al. (2016) 'Restoring Dissolved Organic Carbon Subsidies from Flood Plains to Low Land River Webs: A Role for Environmental Flows', *Marine and Freshwater Research*, Vol 69, No 9.

Barbour, L (2016) 'Barnaby Joyce: The Rise of the New National Leader and Deputy Prime Minister', ABC News, 11 February.

Barr, N and Cary, J (1992) *Greening a Brown Land: The Australian Search for Sustainable Land Use,* Macmillan.

Beck, J (2007) 'The Real Story Behind Howard's Murray Darling Water Laws', *New Citizen,* Vol 6 No 4 <cec.cecaust.com.au/pubs/pdfs/NC19–08.pdf>.

Beinart, W and Hughes, L (2007) *Environment and Empire,* Oxford University Press.

Bellanta, M (2002) 'Irrigation Millennium: Science, Religion and the New Garden of Eden', *Eras Journal,* June.

Benson, S (2001) 'Howard Says the 'B' Word then Bows Out', *Daily Telegraph,* 4 August.

Beresford, Q (2015) *The Rise and Fall of Gunns Ltd,* NewSouth Publishing.

Beresford, Q (2018) *Adani and the War Over Coal,* NewSouth Publishing.

Beresford, Q and Omaji, P (1998) *Our State of Mind Racial Planning and the Stolen Generations,* Fremantle Arts Centre Press.

Bishop, C and White, R (2015) 'Explorer Memory and Aboriginal Celebrity', in S Konishi, M Nugent, and T Shellam, *Indigenous Intermediaries: New Perspectives on Exploration Archives*, ANU Press.

Blackmore, DJ (1986) 'The River Murray Options for Salinity Reduction', Hydrology and Water Resources Symposium, Griffith University, Brisbane.

Bolton, G (1981) *Spoils and Spoilers: Australians Make their Environment, 1788–1980*, Allen & Unwin.

Bonyhady, T (1997) 'The Cross of Erosion', *Australian Humanities Review*, Vol 6.

Boon, P (2020) 'The Environmental History of Australian Rivers: A Neglected Field of Opportunity?', *Marine and Freshwater Research*, Vol 71.

Botterill, LC 'Soap Operas, Cenotaphs and Sacred Cows: Countrymindedness and Rural Policy Debate in Australia', *Policy Journal*, Vol 1, No 1.

Bottoms, T (2013) *Conspiracy of Silence: Queensland's Frontier Killing Times*, Allen & Unwin.

Boyer, P (2017) 'Barnaby Shows Coalition's Apathy to Murray–Darling Water Theft', *South Wind*, 2 August.

Bramston, GT (2016) *Paul Keating: The Big-Picture Leader*, Scribe.

Brett, J (2017) *The Enigmatic Mr Deakin*, Text Publishing.

Brewster, K (2020) 'Floodplain Harvesting in NSW', *Saturday Paper*, 18–24 July.

Bridge, C (2011) *William Hughes*, Haus Publishing.

Brinkley, H (2012) *The Dirty Thirties: A History of the Dust Bowl*, Book Caps.

Broome, R (2005) *Victorian Aboriginal History Since 1800*, Allen & Unwin.

C

Cahir, D (2014) 'Why Did Squatters in Colonial Victoria Use Indigenous Placenames for their Sheep Stations', in I Clark, L Hughes and L Kostanski (eds), *Indigenous and Minority Placenames: Australian and International Perspectives*, ANU Press.

Cameron, D (2005) 'Closer Settlement in Queensland: The Rise and Decline of the Agrarian Dream', in G Davidson and M Brodie (eds) *Struggle Country: The Rural Ideal in Twentieth Century Australia*, Monash University Press.

Campbell, J (2002) *Invisible Invaders: Smallpox and Other Diseases in Aboriginal Australia*, Melbourne University Press.

Carr, B (1982) 'Economics Dual Aim: Growth and Efficiency', *Bulletin*, 2 February.

Carson, R (1962) *Silent Spring*, Houghton Mifflin.

Casben, L (2019) 'Platypus Struggle to Survive, with Huge National Decline Over Last 200 Years, Research Finds', ABC News, <www.abc.net.au/news/2019–08–08/platypus-research-indicates-huge-national-population-decline/11394502>.

Cathcart, M (2010) *The Water Dreamers: The Remarkable History of Our Dry Continent*, Text Publishing.

Cattle, S (2006) 'The Case for a South-eastern Australian Dust Bowl, 1895–1945', *Aeolian Research*, Vol 21.

Chan, G (2017) 'NSW Minister Gives Himself Power to Approve Illegal Water Works in the Murray Darling Basin', *Guardian*, 3 August.

Chishlom, A (1954) 'A Noble Bird Is Vanishing', *Bulletin*, 30 June.

Clark, I (1995) *Scars in the Landscape*, Australian Institute of Aboriginal and Torres Islander Affairs, Canberra.

Cockburn, P (2019) 'Menindee Fish Kill Leaves Devastated Town Wondering if its Future Is Gone Too', ABC News, 20 January.

Cohrs, J (2012) *Ideological Bases for Violent Conflict: The Oxford Handbook of Intergroup Conflict,* Online book, <www.oxfordhandbooks.com/view/10.1093/oxfordhb/9780199747672.001.0001/oxfordhb-9780199747672>.

Collingwood-Whittick, S (2008) 'Ways of Seeing "Country": Colonial, Post-colonial, and Indigenous Perceptions of the Australian Landscape', *Literature in North Queensland,* Vol 35.

Conkin, P (1960) 'The Vision of Elwood Mead', *Agricultural History,* Vol 34, No 2.

Connell, D (2015) 'Irrigation, Water Markets and Sustainability in Australia's Murray Darling Basin, *Agriculture and Agricultural Science Procedia,* Vol 4.

Coorey, P (2000) 'Sold Up the River', *Advertiser,* 24 July.

Crase, L (2017) 'Murray–Darling Basin: Is it Time to Ditch the Plan?', ABC News, 25 July.

Cronin, B (1951) 'Murrumbidgee Irrigation Area', *Walkabout,* 1 April.

Cummins, T and Watson, A (2012) 'A Hundred-year Policy Experiment: The Murray–Darling Basin in Australia', in Quiggin, J, Chambers, S and Mallawaarachchi, T (eds) *Water Policy Reform: Lessons in Sustainability from the Murray–Darling Basin,* Elgar online, <www.elgaronline.com/view/edcoll/9781781000311/9781781000311.00012.xml>.

Cumpston, JHL (1951) *Charles Sturt: His Life and Journeys as an Explorer,* The Gutenberg Project, <www.gutenberg.net.au/ebooks07/0700391h.html>.

Cumpston, JHL (1954) Thomas Mitchell Surveyor and General Explorer, The Gutenberg Project, <www.gutenberg.net.au/ebooks07/0700531h.html>.

D

Dales, J (2011) 'Death by a Thousand Cuts: Incorporating Cumulative Effects in Australia's Environment Protection and Biodiversity Act', *Pacific Rim Law & Policy Journal,* Vol 149.

Davies, A (2019a) '"River is Sick": NSW Urged to Halt Floodplain Harvesting in Murray Darling', *Guardian,* 7 March.

Davies, A (2019b) 'Water Wars: Will Politics Destroy the Murray–Darling Basin – and the River Itself', *Guardian,* 14 December.

Davis, T (1908) 'Reflections of Thomas Davies', <trove.nla.gov.au/work/38043695>.

Dawson, B (2014) *In the Eye of the Beholder: What Six Nineteenth Century Women Tell Us About Indigenous Authority and Identity,* ANU Press, Canberra.

Day, D (1996) *Claiming a Continent A New History of Australia,* Angus & Robertson.

de Garis, SA (2013) 'The Cotton Industry in Australia; An Analysis', 19th Annual Pacific-Rim Real Estate Conference, Melbourne, 13–16 January, <www.prres.net/papers/DeGaris_THE_COTTON_INDUSTR_%20IN_AUSTRALIA%202013.pdf>.

Dickie, P (2000) 'The Rise and Fall of Cubbie Station', Melaleuca Media, <www.melaleucamedia.com.au/01_cms/details.asp?ID=35>.

Dickie, P (2001) 'Queensland Water Management Sold Down the Drain', *On Line Opinion,* 15 May, <www.onlineopinion.com.au/view.asp?article=1217&page=0>.

Dickie, P (2002) 'Rural Stakeholders Fear Being Sold Down the River', *Courier Mail,* 15 July.

Dorsey, LF (2013) *We Are All Americans, Pure and Simple: Theodore Roosevelt and the Myth of Americanism,* University of Alabama Press, ebook edition.

Draper, R (2009) 'Australia's Dry Run', *National Geographic,* April.

E

Easton, S (2019) 'MDBA Chief Denies Maladministration, Says Whistle Blowers Are Entitled to their Opinion', *Mandarin*, 25 February.

Egan, T (2006) *The Worst Hard Time: The Untold Story of Those Who Survived the Great American Dust Bowl*, Houghton, Mifflin and Harcourt.

Ehrenkranz, N and Sampson, D (2008) 'Origin of the Old Testament Plagues: Explications and Implications', *Yale Journal of Biological Medicine*, Vol 81, No 1.

Elliot, R (2012) 'Populate or Perish', *New Geography*, <www.newgeography.com/content/002858-populate-or-perish>.

Evans, R and Thorpe B (2001) 'Indigenocide and the Massacre of Aboriginal History', *Overland*, No 163.

Evans, R, Saunders, K and Cronin, K (1993) *Race Relations in Queensland: A History of Exclusion, Exploitation and Extermination*, Queensland University Press.

F

Farwell, G (1947) 'Westward The River Rolls', *Walkabout*, 1 September.

Farwell, N and Serventy, V (1981) 'The Murray – Australia Gets Varicose Veins', *Bulletin*, 28 July.

Fleming, F (2007) 'European Discovery of the River Murray System: The Overlanders', State Library of South Australia.

Foley, M (2017) 'Murray Darling Basin Authority Orders Water Releases from Menindee Lakes for Murray River', *Farm Online*, 6 October.

Follador, B (2016) 'Soil, Culture, and Human Responsibility', *In Context*, No 36.

Forbes, V (2019) 'Cubbie Station Is a Scapegoat', *Spectator Australia*, 13 February.

Foster, WC (1985) *Sir Thomas Livingston and His World 1792–1855*, The Institute of Surveyors NSW, Sydney.

Frederick, HH (2019) 'Australia's Spiritualist and Water Entrepreneur…and the Prime Minister', <www.entreversity.com/australias-spiritualist-water-entrepreneur-and-later-prime-minister-alfred-deakin>.

French, M (1990) 'The "Great Darkey Flat Massacre": Mystery, Oral Tradition, Popular History and Empirical Evidence', *Journal of the Royal Historical Society of Queensland*, Vol 14, No 5.

Frost, G, Malam, K and Williams, L (2014) *The Evolution of Australian Towns*, Department of Infrastructure and Regional Development, Canberra.

Frost, W (2004) 'Australia Unlimited? Environmental Debate in the Age of Catastrophe, 1910–1939', *Environment and History*, Vol 10, No 3.

Fry, K, (1985) 'Soldier Settlement and the Australian Agrarian Myth after the First World War', *Labour History*, No 48.

G

Gammage, B (2011) *The Biggest Estate on Earth: How Aborigines Made Australia*, Allen & Unwin.

Garcia, E (2019a) 'Corruption Is Killing Our Rivers', *Green Left*, 15 March.

Garcia, E (2019b) 'Rivers in Crisis: Water Theft and Corruption in the Darling River System', *Green Left*, 31 January.

Garden, D (2010) 'The Federation Drought of 1985–1903: El Nino and Society in Australia, in G Mussard-Guilbaud and S Mosley (eds), *Common Ground: Integrating the Social and Environmental in History*, Cambridge Scholars Publishing.

Garden, D (2014) 'Phases of Ecological Impact of the European Occupation of Victoria', *Nature Conservation Review*, <vnpa.org.au/wp-content/uploads/2014/02/Appendix-1-Phases-of-Ecological-Impact.pdf>.

Geisinger, A (1999) 'Sustainable Development and the Domination of Nature: Spreading the Seed of the Western Ideology of Nature', *Boston College Environmental Affairs Law Journal*, Vol 27, No 1.

Genoni, P (nd) 'The Mythology of Exploration: Australian Explorers' Journals', <espace.curtin.edu.au/bitstream/handle/20.500.11937/18593/127959_127959StreamGate.pdf?sequence=2&isAllowed=y>.

Gillanders, A (2009) 'Mirage of the Inland Sea: The Bradfield Scheme', *Journal Royal Australian Historical Society*, Vol 95, Part 1.

Gittins, R (2000) 'The Environment Minister Makes a Comeback', *The Age*, 12 July.

Glacken, C (1992) 'Reflections on the History of Western Attitudes to Nature', *GeoJournal*, Vol 26, No 2.

Glen, A and Short, S (2000) 'The Control of Dingoes in New South Wales in the Period 1883–1930 and its Likely Impact on their Distribution and Abundance', *Australian Zoologist*, Vol 31, No 3.

Godfree, R et al. (2019) 'Historical Reconstruction Unveils the Risk of Mass Mortality and Ecosystem Collapse During the Pancontinental Mega Drought', *Proceedings of the National Academy of Sciences of the United States of America*.

Goodall, H (2002) 'When the River Runs Backwards', in T Bonyhandy and T Griffiths (eds), *Words for Country: Landscape and Language in Australia*, UNSW Press.

Gordon, L (2009) *Doreatha Lange: A Life Beyond Limits*, WW Norton & Co.

Grafton, Q (2019) 'Policy Review of Water Reform in the Murray–Darling Basin, Australia: The "Do's" and "Do'nots"', *Agricultural and Resource Economics*, Vol 63.

Grafton, Q and Horne, J (2014) *Global Water: Issues and Insights*, ANU Press.

Grafton, Q, Landry, C, Libecap, G and O'Brien, R (2009) 'Water Markets: Australia's Murray–Darling Basin and the US South West', *National Bureau of Economic Research*, Working Paper 15797, <www.nber.org/system/files/working_papers/w15797/w15797.pdf>.

Gray, M (2019) 'Floodplain Harvesting an 'Unmeasured Threat to Water Security', *Earth First*, 8 March.

Guest, C (2017) *Sharing the Water: One Hundred Years of River Murray Water*, Murray–Darling Basin Authority.

H

Haigh, B (2007) 'Howard is Failing the Nation on Water Policy', *On Line Opinion*, 8 January, <www.onlineopinion.com.au/view.asp?article=5337>.

Hamilton-McKenzie, J (2013) 'UTOPOS?: A Consideration of the Life of Irrigationists, George Chaffey', *Australasian Journal of American Studies*, Vol 32, No 2.

Hardy, B (1976) *Lament for the Barkindji: The Vanishing Tribes of the Darling River*, Rigby.

Harris, E (2006) 'Development and Damage: Water and Landscape Evolution in Victoria, Australia', *Landscape Research*, Vol 31, No 2.

Harrison, R (2004) *Shared Landscapes Archaeologies of Attachment and the Pastoral Industry of New South Wales*, UNSW Press.

Hartwig, L, Jackson, S and Osborne, N (2018) 'Recognition of Barkandji's Water Rights in Australian Settler-Colonial Water Regimes', *Resources*, Vol 7, No 18.

Hausheer, J (2019) 'How President Herbert Hoover Helped Save the Koala', *Cool Green Science*, <blog.nature.org/science/2019/03/18/how-president-herbert-hoover-helped-save-the-koala>.

Henzell, T (2007) *Australian Agriculture: Its History and Challenges*, CSIRO Publishing.

Hickman, L (1975) 'It's a Woman's Country Too', *Australian Woman's Weekly,* 7 May.

Hirst, J (2010) *Looking for Australia*, Black Inc.

Hogendyk, G (2007) 'The Macquarie Marshes: An Ecological History', Institute of Public Affairs Occasional paper.

Holmes, K and Mirmohamadi, K (2015) 'Howling Wilderness and Promised Land: Imagining the Victorian Mallee, 1840–1914', *Australian Historical Studies,* Vol 46, No 2.

Hrinda, F (1997) 'Marsupial Destruction in Queensland 1877–1930', *Australian Zoologist*, Vol 30, No 3.

Hrinda, F and Gordon, G (2004) 'The Koala and Possum Trade in Queensland 1906–1936', *Australian Zoologist*, Vol 32, No 4.

Hughes, K (2013) 'Challenging the Moral Issues of His Time: Proud Ngarrindjeri Man of the Coorong, Thomas Edwin Trevorrow (1954–2013)', *Aboriginal History,* Vol 37.

Hughes, N, Galeano, S and Hatfield, S (2020) 'Recovering Water for the Environment in the Murray–Darling: Farm Upgrades Increase Water Prices More Than Buybacks', *Conversation,* 1 September.

Haines, AB (1935) 'Station Days', *Walkabout,* 1 April.

Harvey, D (1942) 'Birds of the Swamps', *Walkabout,* 1 June.

J

Jacks, GV and Whyte, BO (1939) *Vanishing Lands: A World Survey of Soil Erosion*, Doubleday, Doran and Co.

Jalata, A (2013) 'The Impacts of English Colonial Terrorism and Genocide on Indigenous/Black Australians', *Sage Open,* July–September.

James, T and Bain, S (2016) 'Genocide and Frontier Violence in Australia', *Journal of Genocide Research,* Vol 18, No 1.

Jenkins, G (1979) *Conquest of the Ngarrindjeri*, Rigby.

Jennings, K (2011) 'Water Under the Bridge', *The Monthly,* October.

Jervis, J (1955) 'How the Squatters Open Up Our Grazing Country', *The Farmer and Settler Weekend Magazine,* 4 November.

Jones, R (2012) 'Fire Stick Farming', *Fire Ecology,* Vol 8.

K

Karskens, G (2015) 'Appin Massacre', *Dictionary of Sydney*, <dictionaryofsydney.org/entry/appin_massacre>.

Keane, B (2008) 'How Cubbie (and Labor) Consumed the Murray Darling', *Crikey,* 21 August.

Kelly, L (1954) 'The Story of the Chaffeys', *Sydney Sun*, 26 February.

Kemp, M (2009) 'Fly & Dry Part 1: How the Water's Being Stolen, *Advertiser,* 26 June.

Kerkhove, R (2014) 'Tribal Alliances with Broader Agendas? Aboriginal Resistance in Southern Queensland's Black War', *Cosmopolitan Civil Societies Journal,* Vol 6, No 3.

Kershner, F (1953) 'George Chaffey and the Irrigation Frontier', *Agricultural History*, Vol 27, No. 4.

Kinbacher, L and Calver, O (2019) 'The Human Toll of Murray Darling Basin water reform', Farm Online, 6 May.

Kingsford, R (2003) 'Social, Institutional and Economic Drivers for Water Resource Development: A Case Study of the Murrumbidgee River, Australia', *Aquatic Ecosystem Health Management,* Vol 6.

Kingsford, R (2017) 'The Tragedy of the Murray–Darling River System Is Man-made', *Sydney Morning Herald,* 25 July.

Kingsford, R (2019a) 'The Catastrophic Fish Kill on the Darling River – Decades in the Making', *John Menadue – Pearls and Irritations,* 16 January, <johnmenadue.com/ richard-kingsford-the-catastrophic-fish-kill-on-the-darling-river-decades-in-the-making>.

Kingsford, R (2019b) 'The Successive Government Failures Behind the Fish Kills', *Sydney Morning Herald,* 31 January.

Kingsford, RT (2000) 'Ecological Impacts of Dams, Water Diversions and River Management on Floodplain Wetlands in Australia', *Austral Ecology,* Vol 25.

Kingsford, RT and Thomas, RF (1995) 'The Macquarie Marshes in Arid Australia and their Waterbirds: A 50-year History of Decline', *Environmental Management,* Vol 19, No 6.

Kingsford, RT and Thomas, RF (2004) 'Destruction of Wetlands and Waterbird Populations by Dams and Irrigation on the Murrumbidgee River in Arid Australia', *Environmental Management,* Vol 34, No 3.

Knitting Nannas, The (2021) 'Water for Rivers Oppose Flood Plan Harvesting Plan', 14 February, <knitting-nannas.com/water-for-rivers-oppose-floodplain-harvesting-plan>.

Kotsios, N (2017) 'The Murray–Darling Basin Plan: John Howard's Vision Still Controversial', *Weekly Times,* 25 January.

L

Lampos, C (2016) 'Hugh Hammond Bennett – the Dust Bowl Advocate', <cleolampos. com/hugh-hammond-bennett-the-dust-bowls-advocate>.

Lang, JD (1875) *An Historical and Statistical Account of New South Wales,* Sampson Low, Marston, Low & Searle.

Langford, B (2003) 'The Tide of History or a Trace of Racism? The Yorta Yorta Native Title Tragedy', *The Journal of Indigenous Policy,* Issue 4.

Larkins, J and Parish, S (1982) 'The Mighty Murray Could Turn to Salt', *Bulletin,* 30 November.

Laurie, A (1958) 'The Black War in Queensland', *Historical Society of Queensland,* 23 October.

Leslie, D (2001) 'Effect of River Management on Colonially-Nesting Waterbirds in the Barmah-Millewa Forest, South-Eastern Australia', *Regulated Rivers Research Management,* Vol 17.

Lewis, D (2003) 'Rivers of Gold', *Sydney Morning Herald,* 25 August.

Lindsay, G (2007) 'Aborigines, Colonists and the Law, 1838', The Francis Forbes Society for Australian Legal History, <www.forbessociety.org.au/wordpress/wp-content/ uploads/2013/03/Aborigines-Colonists-and-the-Law-1838>.

Littman, R and Paluck, E (2015) 'The Cycle of Violence: Understanding Individual Participation in Collective Violence', *Political Psychology,* Vol 36 No 1.

Lozano, H (2015) 'Water in Paradise', California, Florida, and Environmental Rivalry in the Gilded Age', *Environmental History,* Vol 20.

Lydon, J (2017) 'Anti-slavery in Australia: Picturing the 1838 Myall Creek Massacre', *History Compass* Vol 15, No 5.

Lyon, E (1952), 'Why Do We Kill Trees?', *Advertiser*, 3 May.

M

Macaulay, J (1961) 'What Future for Barmah Forest?', *Walkabout*, 1 August.

Macgregor, K (nd) 'T.P. Bellchambers Reserve', Discover Murray River, <www.murrayriver. com.au/stories/t-p-bellchambers-reserve-apamurra-sa-46/>.

Macklin, R (2017) *Hume Our Greatest Explorer*, Hachette.

Mahood, K (2019) 'Australia's Burning, Flooding, Disastrous New Normal', *New York Times*, 5 February.

Manne, R (2004) 'Left Out of Set as Howard's Grip Tightens', *Sydney Morning Herald*, 1 November.

Marchant, S (1998) Things Fall Apart: The End of the United Australia Party 1939 to 1943, Master of Letters thesis, Australian National University.

Margetts, D (2012) A Critique of Australia's National Competition Policy: Assessing its outcomes in a range of major assets, PhD thesis, University of Western Australia, <www.pc.gov.au/national-competition-policy.pdf>.

Marshall, AJ (1966) *The Great Extermination*, Heinemann.

Marshall, V (2017) *Overturning Aqua Nullius: Securing Aboriginal Water Rights*, Aboriginal Studies Press.

Martin, R and Handasyde, K (1999) *The Koala Natural History: Conservation and Management*, UNSW Press.

Massy, C (2020) *Call of the Reed Warbler: A New Agriculture A New Earth*, University of Queensland Press.

McCaughan, K (1947) 'The Fishermen of the Murray River, *Walkabout*, 1 August.

McCulloch, S (1966) 'Gipps, Sir George (1791–1847)', *Australian Dictionary of Biography*, Vol 1, Melbourne University Press.

McDermott, A (2020) 'How Photography Defined the Great Depression', *History*, <www. history.com/news/how-photography-defined-the-great-depression>.

McHugh, S (1996) *Cotton On Stories of Australian Cotton Growing*, Hale & Iremonger.

McKernan, M (2005) *Drought: The Red Marauder*, Allen & Unwin.

Mear, C (2008) 'The Origin of the Smallpox Outbreak in Sydney in 1789', *Journal of the Royal Historical Society*, June.

Mitchell, T (1838) *Three Expeditions into the Interior of Eastern Australia*, The Gutenberg Project, <www.gutenberg.org/files/13033/13033-h/13033-h.htm>.

Moore, E (1972) 'A Backward Look at the Vanishing Swaggies', *Walkabout*, 1 April.

Moran, A (2019) 'NSW Election: The Triumph of the Irrigators', *Catallaxy Files*, 24 March, <catallaxyfiles.com/2019/03/24/nsw-election-the-triumph-of-the-irrigators/comment-page-1>.

Morgan, M (2012) 'Cultural Flows: Asserting Indigenous Rights and Interests in the Waters of the Murray–Darling River System, Australia', in BR Johnston et al., *Water, Cultural Diversity, and Global Environmental Change: Emerging Trends, Sustainable Futures?*, Springer.

Morris, B (1992) 'Frontier Colonialism as a Culture of Terror', *Journal of Australian Studies*, Vol 16, No 35.

Morrisey, S (1972) 'The Pastoral Economy, 1821–1850' in J Griffith (ed.), *Essays in the Economic History of Australia*, Jacaranda.

Morrison, E (2014) *David Syme: Man of The Age*, Monash University Publishing.

Muir, C (2014) 'No Triple Bypass, No Miracle Cure, Just a Long Haul Back', Inside Story, <insidestory.org.au>, 9 October.

Muller, N (2011) '*Carved Trees of First Peoples from Western New South Wales*', *Australian Geographic*, 6 June.

Murray, A (1953) *Walk About*, Melbourne University Press.

Murray, DC (1889) 'A Trip on the Murray', *The Age*, 7 December.

Murray, K (2010) John Howard: A Study in Policy Consistency, PhD thesis, University Adelaide.

Mussared, D (1989) 'Murray's Ecology Left High and Dry', *Canberra Times*, 17 July.

Mussared, D (1993a) 'Upstream, Downstream', *Canberra Times*, 23 January.

Mussared, D (1993b) 'Jack Gets His Teeth Stuck into Water Quality Issue', *Canberra Times*, 16 January.

Mussared, D (1993c) 'Despite Cynicism, Greening Is Under Way', *Canberra Times*, 9 January.

Mussared, D (1995) 'States Agree to Cap Water Use', *Canberra Times*, 1 July.

O

O'Brien, K (2012) 'The National Water Initiative and Victoria's Legislative Implementation of Indigenous Water Rights', *Indigenous Law Bulletin*, Vol 7, No 29.

O'Gorman, E (2012) *Flood Country: An Environmental History of the Murray–Darling Basin*, CSIRO Publishing.

P

Pascoe, B (2018) *Dark Emu: Aboriginal Australia and the Birth of Agriculture*, Magabala Books.

Pike, R (2019) 'The Darling River Fish Kills', *The Saltbush Club*, 25 January

Pittock, J (2019) 'Fish Kills and Undrinkable Water' *The Conversation* 27 November.

Poulter, J (2014) 'The Smallpox Holocaust that Swept Aboriginal Australia', (We) can do better blog, <candobetter.net/node/3720>.

Powell, JM (1990) 'Taylor, Thomas Griffith (1880–1963)', *Australian Dictionary of Biography*, <adb.anu.edu.au/biography/taylor-thomas-griffith-8765>.

Price, J (2019) 'Patricia Karvelas Had Joyce on the Air and on the Ropes', *Sydney Morning Herald*, 23 April.

Pybus, C (2020) *Truganini: Journey Through the Apocalypse*, Allen & Unwin.

Q

Quackenbush, C (2019) '"A Harbinger of Things to Come": Farmers in Australia Struggle with its Hottest Drought Ever', *Time Magazine*, 21 February.

Quick, J (1883) *The History of Land Tenure in the Colony of Victoria*, JG Edwards Bendigo Independent Office, <www.austlii.edu.au/au/journals/AUColLawMon/1883/2.pdf>.

R

Rankin, B (2013) 'Alfred Deakin and Water Resources Politics in Australia', *History Australia*, Vol 10, No 2.

Read, P (1988) *A Hundred Years War: The Wiradjuri People and the State*, ANU Press.

Reece, B (2006) 'Our Killing Fields', *Eureka Street*, 24 June.

Rees, J (1993) 'Green for Danger: Environmentalists Anger May Rebound on Keating', *Far Eastern Economic Review,* 14 January.

Reeve I, Frost, L, Musgrave, W and Stayer, R (2002) *Agricultural and Natural Resource Management in the Murray–Darling Basin: A Policy and History Analysis,* Institute for Rural Futures, University of New England.

Reeve, IJ (1988) *A Squandered Land: 200 Years of Land Degradation in Australia,* The Rural Development Centre, University of New England.

Reisner, M (1993) *Cadillac Desert: The American West and its Disappearing Water,* Penguin.

Reynolds, H (1974) 'Settlers and Aborigines on the Pastoral Frontier', in BJ Dalton, *Lectures on North Queensland History,* James Cook University, <Settlers-and-Aborigines-on-the-Pastoral-Frontier>.

Reynolds, H (1980) 'The Land, the Explorers and the Aborigines', *Historical Studies,* Vol 19, No 75.

Reynolds, H (1982) *The Other Side of the Frontier Aboriginal Resistance to the European Invasion,* Penguin.

Richards, J (2008) *Secret War: A True History of Queensland's Native Police,* University of Queensland Press.

Riches, L (2019) 'What's Killing The River', *Overland,* 16 April.

Roberts, R (1937) 'Fighting the Dingo Menace', *Queenslander,* 22 April.

Roberts, S (1968) *History of Land Settlement in Australia,* Routledge.

Robson, K (2016) 'Barnaby Joyce: Cross Country', *Sydney Morning Herald,* 19 May.

Roche, M (2011) 'World War One British Empire Discharged Soldier Settlement in Comparative Focus', *History Compass,* Vol 9, No 1.

Roosevelt, T (1885) *The Winning of the West,* GP Putnam's Sons.

Rubinsztein-Dunlop, S et al. (2019) 'How Taxpayers Are Funding a Huge Corporate Expansion in the Murray–Darling Basin', ABC News, 8 July.

Russell, P (2010) *Savage or Civilised? Manners in Colonial Australia,* NewSouth Publishing.

Russell, R (2009) 'Colonial NSW in the 1920s to 1840s and Annabella Boswell', A talk given at the Colonial Weekend at the Coolangatta Estate.

Ryan L (2018) 'The Myall Creek Massacre: Was it Typical of the Time?' in L Ryan and J Lyndon (eds), *Remembering the Myall Creek Massacre,* NewSouth Publishing.

Ryan, S (1996) *The Cartographic Eye: How Explorers Saw Australia,* Cambridge University Press.

S

Sauter, S (2015) 'Australia's Dust Bowl: Transnational Influences in Soil Conservation and the Spread of Ecological Thought', *Australian Journal of Politics and History,* Vol 61, No 3.

Scott, B (2001) *The Squatters: The Story of Australia's Pastoral Pioneers,* Allen & Unwin.

Seccombe, M (2017) 'Proving Political Collusion in Water Buybacks', *Saturday Paper,* 23 September.

Seccombe, M (2019) 'Are the Nationals Still the Party of the Bush?', *Saturday Paper,* 5 November.

Semmler, C.(1988) 'Ogilvie, William Henry, 1869–1963', *Australian Dictionary of Biography,* Vol 11.

Sheehan, P (2005) 'A National Party that Is Anything But', *Sydney Morning Herald'*, 29 August.

Sheridan, S (2011) 'Reading All the Rivers Run, Nancy Cato's Eco-Historical Epic', *Australian Humanities Review,* Vol 55, November.

Simons, M (2020) 'Cry Me A River: The Tragedy of the Murray–Darling Basin', *Quarterly Essay,* No 77.

Simpson, M (2016) 'Industrial Revolution in Australia: Impact on the Wool Industry', Museum of Applied Arts and Sciences.

Skinner, S (1990) 'Fears for Native Fish', *Sydney Morning Herald,* 25 November.

Skinner, S (1992) 'Last Battle to Save the Land', *Sydney Morning Herald,* 19 January.

Slattery, M (2019) 'Problems with the Murray–Darling Basin Can't Be Skimmed Over', *Canberra Times*, 13 July.

Slattery, M and Campbell, R (2019) 'A Fish Kill Q and A Questions, Answers and Dead Fish in the Menindee Lakes', Australia Institute.

Smiles, B (2006) 'Macquarie Marshes: An Icon Issue for Wetland Survival in Australia', *National Parks Journal,* June–July.

Smiles, B (2019) 'Tackling NSW's River Crisis', *Green Left Weekly,* 8 November.

Smith, D Livingstone (2011) *Less Than Human: Why We Demean, Enslave and Exterminate Others*, Macmillan.

Smith, J (2018) 'Australia's Heaven Now Unrecognisable', News.com.au, 8 August.

Smith, J (2019) 'These Weren't Mistakes': Dodgy Policies to Blame for Murray Darling's Downfall', News.com.au, 14 March.

Smyth, J (2019) 'Mass "fish kill" in Australia Sparks Fight over Water Management', *Financial Times,* 19 January.

Sorenson, ES (1938) 'Waltzing Matilda on the Wallaby Track', *The Land,* 12 August.

Sorenson, T (1991) 'Disaster on the Darling', *Green Left Weekly,* 4 December.

Sparrow, P (2018) 'FDR and the Dust Bowl', Franklin D Roosevelt Presidential Museum and Library, <fdr.blogs.archives.gov/2018/06/20/fdr-and-the-dust-bowl>.

Stevens, D (1963) 'The Koala Is Being Rescued', *Walkabout,* 1 May.

Stone, B (2019) *The Squatters: The Story of Australia's Pastoral Pioneers,* Allen & Unwin.

Strange, C (2010) 'The Personality of Environmental Prediction: Griffith Taylor as 'Latter-day Prophet', *Historical Records of Australian Science,* Vol 21.

Sturma, M (1985) 'Myall Creek Massacre and the Psychology of Mass Murder', *Journal of Australian Studies,* Vol 9, No 16.

Sturt, C *Two Expeditions into the Interior of Southern Australia*, Vols 1 & 2, The Gutenberg Project, Vols 1 & 2,<www.gutenberg.org/files/4330/4330-h/4330-h.htm>.

T

Taibbi, M (2010) 'The Great American Bubble Machine', *Rolling Stone,* 5 April.

Taylor R and Schultz M (2010) 'Waterbird Use of Rice Fields in Australia', *Waterbirds: The International Journal of Waterbird Ecology,* Vol 33.

Taylor, T (2009) 'Linking Land Clearing to Drought and Climate Change', ECOS Magazine, <www.ecosmagazine.com/?paper=EC150p16>.

Thomas, K (1984) *Man and the Natural World,* Penguin.

Thorpe, N (2019) 'It's Profit Before People', *NITV,* 21 January.

Toensing, A (2009) 'Australia's Dry Run', *National Geographic,* April

Toohey, B (2007) 'John Howard' s Concentration of Power', *The Monthly*, April.

Toohey, B (2010) 'Re-thinking the Murray–Darling Buybacks', *Inside Story,* 3 November.

Top Wire Traveller (2020) 'What's Really Going on in the Murray–Darling Basin, <topwiretraveller.com/murray-darling-basin>.

Triskele (2019) 'Watergate: An ecosystem cultivated for sharks won't support goldfish', *Michael West Media*, 9 May.

Tulloch, L (2015) 'Is Emile in the Garden of Eden? Western Ideologies of Nature', *Policy Futures in Education*, Vol 13, No 1.

U

Uren, D (2007) 'In the Market for Water', *Weekend Australian*, 10 February.

V

Vanclay, F and Lawrence, G (1995) *The Environmental Imperative: Eco-social Concerns for Australian Agriculture*, Central Queensland University Press.

Verrenda, I (1998) 'Corrigan Puts His Reputation on the Line', *Sydney Morning Herald*, 7 February.

Volkofsky, A (2019) 'Fears for Future of Menindee's Birds as Drought Continues', ABC News, 26 June.

W

Wahlquist, A (1995) 'The River that Runs through Us', *Sydney Morning Herald*, 11 March.

Wahlquist, A (2008) 'Scientist's Contribution to Water Reform Unparalleled', *Weekend Australian*, 15 March.

Wahlquist, A (2009) 'Soft as Butter Tactics in the Murray–Darling Rescue Plan', News. com.au.

Walsh, M (1982) 'How Paul Keating is Taking on the left', *The Bulletin*, 2 February.

Waterson, D B (1968) *Squatter, Selector, and Storekeeper: A History of the Darling Downs*, Sydney University Press.

Weaver, J (1996) 'Beyond the Fatal Shore: Pastoral Squatting and the Occupation of Australia, 1826–1852', *American Historical Review*, October.

Webb, A et al. (2018) 'It Will Take Decades, But the Murray Darling Basin Plan Is Delivering Environmental Improvements', The Conversation, <theconversation.com/ it-will-take-decades-but-the-murray-darling-basin-plan-is-delivering-environmental-improvements-93568>.

Webster, A (2017) 'A Colonial History of the River Murray Dispute', *Adelaide Law Review*, Vol 38.

Weir, J (2009) *Murray River Country: An Ecological Dialogue with Traditional Owners*, Aboriginal Studies Press.

Weir, J (2011) 'Water Planning and Dispossession', in *Basin Futures: Water Reform in the Murray–Darling Basin*, ANU Express.

Weller, J (2012) *Wellington in the Peninsula 1808–1814*, Frontline Books.

West, M (2019) 'Barnaby Joyce, Angus Taylor, Australia and the Caribbean', Michael West Media, 21 April 2019.

Wheeler, S (2019) 'Don't Blame the Murray–Darling Basin Plan: It's Climate and Economic Change Driving Farmers Out', The Conversation, 11 December.

White, J (2011) 'Histories of Indigenous-settler Relationships: Reflections on Internal Colonialism and the Hybrid Australian Economy', *Australian Indigenous Studies*, Vol 1.

Whitford, T and Boadle, D (2008) 'Australia's Rural Reconstruction Commission, 1943–46: A Reassessment', *Australian Journal of Politics and History*, Vol 54, No 4.

Whitford, T and Boadle, D (2009) 'Remaking the Country: Australia's Rural Reconstruction Commission, 1943–46, *Journal Royal Australian Historical Society*, Vol 95, Part 1.

Willetts, J 'Sir Thomas Livingston Mitchell 1831 Expedition', <www.freesettlerorfelon.com/sir_thomas_mitchell_expedition.htm>.

Wilson, R (1992) 'Mitchell's Massacre on the Murray River', *Canberra Times Magazine*, 30 May.

Wright, C (2011) *Wellington's Men in Australia Peninsula War Veterans and the Making of Empire c 1820–40*, Palgrave Macmillan.

Wright, J (2004) *The Cry for the Dead*, API Network, Perth.

Wright, T (2019) 'Sold Down the River', *Sydney Morning Herald*, 28 April.

Z
Zuboff, S (2019) *The Age of Surveillance Capitalism*, Profile Books.

Reports, submissions and speeches
Australian Competition and Consumer Commission (2020) *Murray–Darling Water Markets Inquiry*, <www.accc.gov.au>.

Australian Greenhouse Office, (2000) *Land Clearing A Social History*, Technical Report No 4.

Australian Law Reform Commission (2010) 'The Settled Colony Debate', *Recognition of Aboriginal Customary Laws*, ALC Report 31, <www.alrc.gov.au/publication/recognition-of-aboriginal-customary-laws-alrc-report-31/5-recognition-of-aboriginal-customary-laws-at-common-law-the-settled-colony-debate/>.

Australian Productivity Commission (2017) *National Water Reform Draft Report*, <National Water Reform – Inquiry Report (pc.gov.au)>.

Australian Productivity Commission (2020) *Securing Aboriginal and Torres Strait Islander People's Interests in Water*, National Water Reform Draft Report.

Bates, W, Submission to the Murray–Darling Basin Royal Commission (2018), <William Bdger Bates submission>.

Bell, D (2018) Submission to the Murray–Darling Basin Royal Commission, <David Bell submission>.

Commonwealth Department of Agriculture, 'Water and the Environment (2019) Response to Four Corners Cash Splash, <www.awe.gov.au/news/on-the-record/response-to-4-corners-cash-splash>.

Eckersley, R (1989) *Regreening Australia: The Environmental, Economic and Social Benefits of Reforestation*, CSIRO.

Environmental Defenders Office Australia (2018) Submission to the Murray–Darling Basin Royal Commission. <David Morris EDOs submission>.

Environmental Defenders Office Australia (2020) 'Floodplain Harvesting: Without the Necessary Protection Legal Action Is a Risk', 9 December.

House of Representatives Standing Committee on Regional Australia (2011) '"Of drought and flooding rains": Inquiry into the impact of the Guide to the Murray–Darling Basin Plan', Commonwealth of Australia, <www.aph.gov.au/parliamentary_business/committees/house_of_representatives_committees?url=ra/murraydarling/report.htm>.

House of Representatives Standing Committee on Science and Innovation (2004) *Science Overcoming Salinity,* Parliament of the Commonwealth of Australia, <Science Overcoming Salinity>.

Human Rights Commission (1997) *Bringing Them Home: Report of the National Inquiry into the Separation of Aboriginal and Torres strait Islander Children from their Families.*

Independent Commission Against Corruption (ICAC) (2020) Investigation into Complaints of Corruption in the Management of Water in New South Wales and Systemic Non-Compliance with the *Water Management Act 2000,* <www.icac.nsw. gov.au>.

Intergovernmental Agreement on a National Water Initiative (2004) Between the Commonwealth of Australia and the Governments of New South Wales, Victoria, Queensland, South Australia, the Australian Capital Territory and the Northern Territory, <Intergovernmental Agreement on a National Water Initiative>.

Keating, P (1992) 'Redfern Speech: Year for the World's Indigenous People – Delivered in Redfern Park by Prime Minister Paul Keating, 10 December 1992', <antar.org.au/ sites/default/files/paul_keating_speech_transcript.pdf>.

Matthews, K (2017) *Independent Investigation into New South Wales Water Management and Compliance, Interim Report,* New South Wales Government, <apo.org.au/sites/ default/files/resource-files/2017-09/apo-nid106331.pdf>.

Mildura Royal Commission (1896) *Mildura Settlement,* Victorian Government Printer.

Murray-Darling Ministerial Council (2002) *The Living Murray,* Murray–Darling Basin Commission.

Murray–Darling Basin Commission (nd) Menindee Lakes, The Lower Darling River and Darling Anabranch, Information Paper No 1, <www.mdba.gov.au/sites/default/files/ archived/mdbc-tlm-reports/525_menindeelakesdarling.pdf>.

Murray Lower Darling Rivers Indigenous Nations (2018) Submission to the Murray– Darling Basin Royal Commission, <MurrayLowerDarlingRiversIndigenousNations. pdf>.

National Irrigators' Council (2010) Submission to the Standing Committee on Regional Australia Inquiry into the Impact of the Murray–Darling Basin Plan in Regional Australia, <www.irrigators.org.au/wp-content/uploads/2018/03/ NICSubmissiontotheRegionalAustraliaCommitteeInquiry.pdf>.

Natural Resources Commission (2009) *Riverina Bioregion Regional Forest Assessment River Red Gums and Woodland Forests Final Assessment Report,* <Forest Assessment River Red Gums>.

New South Wales Legislative Council (1845) *Report of the Select Committee on Aborigines* together with Proceedings of Committee, Minutes of Evidence, and Appendices, Government Printer, <1845 Condition of the Aborigines>.

New South Wales Legislative Council (1858) Select Committee on the Murders by Aborigines on the Dawson River, Government Printer, Sydney, <Report on murders by the Aborigines on the Dawson River>.

Ngarrindjeri Regional Authority Inc (2018), Submission to the South Australian Murray– Darling Royal Commission, <Ngarrindjeri Regional Authority Submission.pdf>.

Northern Basin Aboriginal Nations (2018) Submission to the Murray–Darling Basin Royal Commission, <Northern Basin Aboriginal Nations Submission.pdf>.

Queensland Legislative Assembly (1861) *Report of Select Committee on Native Police Force and the Condition of Aborigines,* <Report on the Native Police Force and the Condition of the Aborigines Generally>.

Royal Commission on Closer Settlement (1916) *Final Report Working of the Closer Settlement Acts in the Irrigable Districts*, Government Printer.

Senate Rural and Regional Affairs and Transport Committee (2018) *Integrity of the Water Market in the Murray–Darling Basin*, Commonwealth of Australia, <Second Interim Report – Parliament of Australia (aph.gov.au)>.

Senate Rural and Regional Affairs Committee (2002) *Water Policy in Australia*, <www.aph.gov.au/Parliamentary_Business/Committees/Senate/Rural_and_Regional_Affairs_and_Transport/Completed_inquiries/2002–04/water/report/c02>.

Senate Standing Committee on Environment, Recreation and the Arts (1993) *Water Resources: Toxic Algae*, Parliament of the Commonwealth of Australia.

South Australian Legislative Council (1860) *Report upon the Aborigines*, <aiatsis.gov.au/sites/default/files/docs/digitised_collections/remove/92284.pdf>.

South Australian Murray–Darling Basin Royal Commission (2019) Report, <Murray–Darling Basin Royal Commission Report>.

Victorian Legislative Council (1858–59) *Report of the Select Committee of the Legislative Council on the Aborigines*, Government Printer, <Report of the Select Committee on the Aborigines>.

Wentworth Group of Concerned Scientists (2017) *Review of Water Reform in the Murray Darling Basin*, <Wentworth-Group-Review-of-water-reform-in-MDB-Nov-2017.pdf>.

Wentworth Group of Concerned Scientists (2020) 'Assessment of River Flows in the Murray–Darling Basin: Observed Versus Expected Flows under the Basin Plan 2012–2019', <MDB-Assessment of flows.pdf>.

Wilderness Society, The (2018) Submission to the Murray–Darling Basin Royal Commission, <www.environment.sa.gov.au-suzanne-milthorp>.

Young, M (2018) Submission to the Murray–Darling Basin Royal Commission, <Mike Young Submission.pdf>.

Theses

Cahir, D (2001) The Wathawurrung People's Encounters with Outside Forces 1797–1849: A History of Conciliation and Conflict, Master of Arts thesis, University of Ballarat.

Beckett, J (1958) A Study of a Mixed-Blood Aboriginal Minority in the Pastoral Industry of New South Wales, Master of Arts thesis, Australian National University.

Dowling, P (1997) 'A Great Deal of Sickness': Introduced Diseases Among the Aboriginal People of Colonial South-East Australia, 1788–1900, PhD thesis, Australian National University.

Howes, H (2007) From Commission to Community: A History of Salinity Management in the Goulburn Valley 1886–2007, Master of Arts thesis, University of Melbourne, <Hilary Howes MA thesis final>.

Kelly, L (1980) Explorers and Aborigines: A Survey of Contact between Australian Aborigines and Six Land Explorers, 1828–1862, Honours thesis, University of Melbourne.

Sadeghian, D (2016) The 19th Century Squattocracy and Contemporary Inequality, Bachelor of Economics, Honours thesis, University of New South Wales.

Withycombe, P (2015) The Twelfth Man: John Fleming and the Myall Creek Massacre, Honours Thesis, University of Newcastle.

Media

ABC *Australian Story* (2019) 'The Darling of Menindee', 7 May.

ABC *Four Corners* (2017) 'Pumped', 24 July.

ABC *Four Corners* (2019) 'Cash Splash', 8 July.

ABC Radio National (2018), *Background Briefing*, 'Best Laid Plans: The Murray–Darling Basin in crisis (Part 2), 6 May.

The Australia Institute (2019) 'How to Make a Whistle Blower', podcast.

INDEX

www.ingramcontent.com/pod-product-compliance
Lightning Source LLC
Chambersburg PA
CBHW020450270326
41926CB00008B/558